CLOAK AND DOLLAR

Cloak and Dollar

A HISTORY OF AMERICAN SECRET INTELLIGENCE

Rhodri Jeffreys-Jones

Yale University Press   New Haven & London

Set in New Caledonia Roman type by Keystone Typesetting, Inc.

Printed in the United States of America

Library of Congress Cataloging-in-Publication Data

Jeffreys-Jones, Rhodri.
Cloak and dollar : a history of American secret intelligence / Rhodri Jeffreys-Jones.
    p.   cm.
Includes bibliographical references and index.
ISBN 0-300-07474-3 (C : alk. paper)

1. Intelligence service—United States—History. 2. Secret service—United States—History.
I. Title.
JK468.16 J4543 2002
327.1273—dc21   2001005845

A catalogue record for this book is available from the British Library.

The paper in this book meets the guidelines for permanence and durability of the Committee on
Production Guidelines for Book Longevity of the Council on Library Resources.

10 9 8 7 6 5 4 3 2 1

Contents

Preface

There is a family myth about Tom Watkins. He was my Grandad, or, in Welsh, Tadcu. In the 1930s he was blacklisted for having led a coal miners' strike. He walked all over Wales, England, and Scotland looking for a job. But the list followed him, and in that depressed decade he could find no paid employment. That was why he became a professional snooker player.

Snooker in those days had the same kind of shady reputation as its American cousin, pool. Tadcu would arrive in a new town, play a couple of games with conspicuous incompetence, lose a bit of money. Then came the Sting. Someone would bet too much against him and lose. Tadcu would scoop up his gains and move on rapidly to the next town.

The thirties snooker emporia shared the dim lighting of the coal levels, but not the comradely trust and support. One day, having accumulated a princely sum through his hustling activities, Tadcu met a member of the equine doping fraternity who convinced him that a certain mare would win against long odds. Tadcu placed his all on the four-legged promise. The action ruined Tom Watkins's character. The horse lost, Tadcu "took the Pledge" (promised God he would never touch another drop of alcohol), and he became a staunch member of "The Chapel" to the end of his days.

I did say "family myth." The whole story is unreliable. For example, I now know that Tadcu was a pillar of The Chapel *before* he took up snooker. Did this imbue him with a semblance of rectitude, making him an even more formidable exponent of the Sting? Or was the whole Sting-and-horse story made up or exaggerated by disapproving family members to discredit Tadcu in the eyes of a younger generation? It had, of course, the reverse effect.

All this suggests that the Confidence Man is rather a pervasive character, not one to be found only in America. But my argument in this book is that, in the United States, he has had an impact in an area desperately in need of honest analysis yet endemically prone to conspiracy and dissimulation—namely, secret intelligence.

In the twenty-first century, it is becoming all too evident that America and the rest of the world face great nuclear, terrorist, and other dangers. Only the naïve would assert that secret intelligence should play no role in combating those dangers, and no doubt it will continue to do so in the future as it has in the past. However, I suggest that there has been a long-standing conspiracy of spies, a great confidence trick designed to boost the fortunes of the spy rather than protect the security of the American people.

This idea is used to determine the focus of a book that not only covers a variety of recent events, but also reviews the entire history of U.S. secret intelligence. The selection of detail for omission is always a problem in such a text, but the task is made easier by the pursuit of a pervasive theme that still permits a review of every significant phase in American espionage history.

Some of the information, and much of the freshness of evidence and interpretation, stem from my great good fortune in having taught the subject to succeeding generations of able and enthusiastic students. Some of those students' dissertations and publications are listed in the endnotes and bibliography; it would be invidious to single out individuals here, as so many of my students have been an inspiration to me over the years.

I would like to thank not only my students but also professional colleagues who have offered me an enormous amount of advice. That help streamed in over a period of three decades, much of it in relation to my earlier publications in the field. But here, I might mention those who specifically advised me on the concepts and new research behind the current work: James V. Compton, A. Walter Dorn, Owen Dudley Edwards, Ralph Erskine, Meredith Hindley, Frederick P. Hitz, Gwenda L. Jeffreys-Jones, Loch K. Johnson, Frederick M. Kaiser, Marc Karson, W. Scott Lucas, Gary Marx, Robert Mason, Ernest R. May, Robert J. McMahon, Kevin O'Brien, David Painter, Eileen Scully, David Stafford, Nancy Tucker, Wesley Wark, Robin W. Winks, and Marilyn B. Young. My gratitude also extends collectively to those, several in number, who have so generously organized and contributed to the Internet discussion forums H-DIPLO and Intel-Forum. At Yale University Press, Lara Heimert was a supportive editor, Nancy Moore Brochin an eagle-eyed manuscript editor, and the anonymous reader an acute reader of the draft book. I am thankful to these individuals and to four further readers who from the perspective of their special expertise supplied comments on portions of the draft. These were Frank Cogliano, Jane Adler, Douglas M. Charles, and Tom Wales.

While this book aims to synthesize the scholarship of others and some of my earlier work, it draws also on additional research, which means that the list of librarians to whom I am indebted has grown. The following librarians and archivists were unstinting in the expert support they gave me in my research for the present book, and I thank each one of them: Marty Barringer and Nicholas Scheetz, Georgetown University Library; John Earl Haynes, Manuscript Division, Library of Congress; Alan Kucia and Jenny Mountain, Churchill Archives Centre, Churchill College, Cambridge; Kristine Marconi, Seeley G. Mudd Library, Princeton University; and Jennie Rathbun, Houghton Library, Harvard University.

As ever, research and writing need financial support, and, in the case of the current project, I was fortunate. My acknowledgments and gratitude are due the Canadian Bureau for International Education for the award of a Commonwealth Visiting Fellowship in pursuit of intelligence history, to the University of Edinburgh for grants from the Moray Fund and the Arts-Divinity-Music Faculty Group Fund, and to the Arts and Humanities Research Board of the British Academy for a Research Leave Award.

Although my culinary and dishwashing activities continued un-abated in the course of writing this book, my family gradually noticed that I was distracted by a rival activity. To say that they welcomed my inattentiveness would be to overstate the case. But my wife, Mary, was an inspiring pillar of support, while Rowena, Gwenda, and Effie were as tolerant as one has a right to expect. To all of them, my love.

CHAPTER 1

The American Spy Considered as a Confidence Man

How big should the American secret intelligence budget be? That may seem a simple, even a crudely simple question, yet it opens a window to a more complex and vital debate.

Those who think that U.S. intelligence spending is about right or too low offer a variety of justifications. There is the pragmatic argument that a big country with big responsibilities needs a big intelligence budget. Then there is the justification by historical precedent. Former CIA official George A. Carver, Jr., claimed the 1990 intelligence budget was only about 8 percent of the total military expenditure of around $300 billion. Stating that President Washington had in 1792 spent 12 percent of the entire federal budget on intelligence, he described the sum as "an enormous bargain." Certain non-American observers have made a similar point about the modest overall cost of U.S. national defense. The sums may seem enormous, they argue, but they need to be put in perspective. The cost of America's military activities in the late 1990s was less than 4 percent of the gross national product. American hegemony, according to British journalist Martin Walker, can "no longer be described as burdensome." So, the argument runs: if you can afford military and intelligence dominance, you might as well pay for it.[1]

A variety of arguments also emerges on the dissent side. Some critics have offered international instead of historical comparisons: according to the *Washington Post*, the 2000 intelligence budget of $30 billion was not merely larger than that of Russian intelligence, but larger than all Russian military expenditures combined. Other comparisons seem to confirm the exceptional size of the American intelligence budget. In 1993, the Western European Union decided to enter the most expensive area of intelligence activity, satellite surveillance, and planned a system costing $10 billion. But by the early twenty-first century, it had trimmed this amount to less than $1.5 billion, and the project was still not off the drawing board. The European Union was the only entity in the world that could compete with America in terms of wealth, yet its intelligence expenditure did not begin to compare with that of the superpower across the Atlantic.[2]

Critics of the size of the U.S. intelligence community have not confined their complaints to its cost. They have blamed it for the indiscriminate gathering of too much information and the neglect of analysis. Thinking is hard work, and with money at hand it has been too tempting to gather more information instead. According to this line of dissent, emphasis on information gathering has resulted in mediocrity. Critics have also found problematic the subordination of national security to bureaucratic ambition as a consideration affecting the collection and analysis of evidence. Another criticism has been that an overamplitude of intelligence resources has led to adventurism. With money no object after 1945, reckless covert operators across the globe made America's name mud, played into the hands of the nation's enemies, and even prolonged the Cold War they were meant to bring to a successful conclusion. Finally, some critics hold that American insistence on an intelligence monopoly has created the impression that the U.S. government is concealing the truth by withholding from others the means of independent investigation. The concealment of the truth from its allies has undermined efforts at international intelligence cooperation—contrary to the spirit of the republic that played such a key role in creating the United Nations. The U.S. intelligence monopoly has furthermore resulted in the American people being kept in the dark about alternative viewpoints—giving rise to both just and unfounded suspicions concerning the intelligence community's propensity to distort and exaggerate threats to national security.

The reasons for these perceptions of intelligence profligacy and its consequences invite explanation. One explanation stems from the biases of the critics. These range from the personal ambitions of reforming crusaders to the dewy-eyed idealism of some internationalists.

Such biases have, from time to time, produced exaggerated attacks on exaggeration.

Other explanations stem, however, from the nature and causes of the perceived phenomenon, bloated intelligence. One such cause is the well-known tendency of all bureaucracies to grow in a self-perpetuating and self-propagating manner. Federal government in general has expanded inexorably throughout U.S. history, and at an increasing rate since the 1930s—the growth of the intelligence community may be seen within that context. The obsession with secrecy in American government has assisted the process, by creating a fertile climate for those bent on empire-building by stealth. The process has been aided and abetted by the populist tradition in American politics, which has yielded a breed of politician to whom dry facts are no stumbling block, and for whom an unchallenged intelligence community is a potentially useful ally.

But, while the foregoing arguments must carry some weight, this book argues that there is a further, special reason why secret intelligence has tended to run amok with taxpayers' money. That reason is the emergence, within intelligence circles, of the confidence man.

The confidence man and the tools of his trade—smooth talk, hyperbole, deception—have been in evidence in most cultures, most of the time. In the first half-century of its existence, the United States was no exception. Even so straightforward an exercise as the exploration of the West could lend itself to charges of deception—in the 1856 campaign, for example, Republican presidential candidate John Charles Frémont was damaged by charges that he had exaggerated his prowess as an explorer and soldier at the time of the acquisition of California.[3]

However, in America's first half-century the practice of secret intelligence was relatively restrained. George Washington deceived mainly the enemy, not the American people. Likewise, while Frémont's search for California gold could be likened to an intelligence operation and while he did resort to hyperbole, he did not directly apply intelligence resources to the deception of the electorate. Furthermore, the scale of President Washington's intelligence expenditures was not to be matched for a century and more, and there was no significant intelligence bureaucracy in the pre–Civil War era. It is only since the middle of the nineteenth century that the character of American espionage has taken on a hyperbolic-expansionist hue.

American espionage has since the 1850s become progressively more commercial, more bureaucratic, and more populist. The wiles of the intelligence confidence man have been directed not just at foreign foes but at American citizens as well. The American public has been importuned to believe in a variety of menaces and crises that were by no means always what they seemed to be. They have ranged from Confederate assassination plots to Western land fraud, from white slavery to communism, from German sabotage to Chinese espionage, from crack cocaine scares to digital encryption. Although the American spy is not solely responsible for raising these alarms, he has played a leading part in their creation.

Repeated attacks on the intelligence confidence man only confirm the increasing prominence of his role. Since the outbreak of the Civil War, there have been consistent efforts to deflate his claims. In 1862, with the war at its height, Allan Pinkerton was dismissed from Abraham Lincoln's intelligence service for exaggerating enemy strength. In an attempt to reingratiate himself with the president, Pinkerton warned of an assassination plot. General George B. McClellan dismissed the warning as mere "conspiracy nonsense."[4] Half a century later, FBI chief Stanley W. Finch insisted that no daughter, wife, or mother was safe from "white slavery" gangs seeking to kidnap victims and force them into prostitution. There were immediate complaints that he was just trying to drum up anti-vice trade for the bureau: as the FBI critic Fred Cook noted, "Chief Finch was a master at painting the Menace." In a similar vein, historian David Kahn took to task the 1920s codebreaker H. O. Yardley. No slouch in touting his own talents, Yardley once claimed of the card game that ruined him financially, "I have constantly won at poker all my life." Kahn dryly noted the codebreaker's "potent salesmanship."[5]

World War II and the Cold War presented new opportunities to the intelligence confidence man—and to his critics. In 1941, the British director of naval intelligence, Rear Admiral John Godfrey, noted that in all branches of U.S. intelligence there was a "predilection for sensationalism"; for example, the War Department's estimate of German reserve air strength was 250 percent higher than that of the British.

Cold War intelligence leaders were as interested in propagandizing the American people as the communist opposition, and they regarded themselves as having developed appropriate skills. CIA director William Colby explained that intelligence had "become a modern enterprise with many of the attributes of journalism." Fifteen years later the Cold War was over, and European communism had collapsed. The CIA took a generous slice of the credit: Colby's successor Robert Gates referred to the outcome as "the greatest of American triumphs." Potentially, the end of the Cold War meant that the CIA had shed a menace. But the confidence man once again set to work. He deftly detached the CIA from the history of the Cold War, and suggested the agency was ideally suited to take on a proliferating array of new, noncommunist menaces.[6]

The increasingly brash and expansionist nature of espionage since the 1850s reflected broader changes in society—the rise of capitalist boosterism, the expansion of the federal government with commensurate opportunities for clandestine employment, and the emergence of the mass-appeal imperative in an ever more democratic society. The post-1850 culture of the confidence man was both reflected in, and promoted by, literature. In 1857, Herman Melville popularized the concept in his novel *The Confidence-Man,* a satire on social mores during the era in which Allan Pinkerton put espionage on a professional basis. Some of Melville's observations could have served as a primer for the 1950s CIA. For example, the CIA's Big Lie technique relied on the principle behind the novelist's fictional "World's Charity" scam—if you are going to tell a lie, tell the truth most of the time, and then make it a big one.[7]

The phenomenon of the "confidence man," or "con man," has continued to attract considerable attention, meandering Mississippi-like through American culture via Mark Twain's *Huckleberry Finn* (1884) and David Maurer's *The Big Con* (1940) to more recent works like George Roy Hill's *The Sting* (1973). It draws sustenance from an even broader cultural stream, the cult of the salesman. For while it may be true that not every salesman is a confidence man, every confidence man is in some way selling something, and the selling culture and its critics have been part of the milieu of American intelligence history.

The image of the salesman has often been negative. The carpetbaggers who arrived in the stricken South after the Civil War seemed to many local white people to be the epitome of soulless exploitation. The South was not alone in this opinion—Mark Twain wrote devastatingly of the selling culture in *The Gilded Age* (1873). The subject reappeared in the darkest of hues in 1947, the year of the CIA's creation, with the publication of Arthur Miller's play *Death of a Salesman*. Yet, critical though these writers may have been, they implicitly recognized that they were attacking a big target—the broad-grinned salesman, pitchman for the American way. The best-known American intelligence leaders have been salesmen, and they have found ready customers in a land where selling is accepted as a vital component of the free market economy.

Size is not the only characteristic of American espionage that draws on the U.S. cultural context. Another is a sense of continuity. This may seem surprising, as some prominent intelligence advocates have deplored the *absence* of continuity, a deficiency that has led, in their view, to amnesia about lessons learned in the past. It became part of the propaganda of the intelligence expansionists to say that this had been dangerous, and to argue that lack of intelligence preparedness led to America being caught unawares at Pearl Harbor. But such intelligence advocates have been preoccupied with *institutional* continuity and blind to *tradition*. To illustrate the tradition by means of just one case, that master of fictional deceit and sleight of hand Edgar Allan Poe had a certain appeal: both the codebreaker H. O. Yardley and the covert operator Edward Lansdale admired Poe's *The Purloined Letter*.[8] Memory does not depend on institutions alone.

Traditions affecting intelligence do not need to inhere in the craft itself. To take a notable example, American nationalism has played into the hands of intelligence promoters. Consciousness of nationhood and espousal of self-determination are powerful threads in U.S. foreign policy. Ever since America's own war of independence, U.S. citizens have been keen to help other societies to throw off the yoke of imperialism. The presence in America of immigrants from so many different lands has not only bolstered that aspiration but given the United States the potential means to arrive at informed analysis and offer clandestine support. As one senior CIA veteran noted in May 2000, America had a "competitive advantage" in being "a nation of nations."[9]

Support of nationalism worldwide meant more business for American intelligence. The boosters of intelligence exploited this potential in developing a Cold War philosophy of anti-communist nation-building. However, as the phrase implies, the nationalisms supported were not always spontaneous and indigenous. Too often, they stemmed from American clandestine support for not very democratic rulers. America's Cold War refusal to accept unwelcome election results further undermined international sympathy for the idea that the United States stood for self-determination. Finally, America had to face the music when, after the Cold War, micro-nationalism ran riot, destabilizing the Balkans and other parts of the world. America's clandestine operators were unabashed. Having contributed to the problem, they now claimed they were needed to solve it. Nationalism has been a traditional tool in the hands of the intelligence confidence man, and a dangerous one.

There has been another dark side to American nationalism. At its best, it has been liberal and tolerant. But it can also be introverted, and a cause of nativism. In intelligence history, this has manifested itself in the mistreatment of minorities. Ironically, the real American natives were among the early targets of white nativism. Fighting the French as a British officer in 1758, George Washington greatly admired the reconnaissance skills of the native American but never trusted him enough to give him autonomy: "I always send out some white people with the Indians."[10] In more recent times, examples have been numerous, not the least notorious being the persecution of black American leaders by FBI chief J. Edgar Hoover.

It is true that such racism did not always mar American intelligence operations. For example, Allan Pinkerton hired both blacks and women to spy for the Union during the Civil War.[11] However, there was a long-running tendency for WORM, white old rich men drawn from the Ivy League colleges, to monopolize leadership positions. This held true for the State Department intelligence organization U-1 (1915–1927), World War II's Office of Strategic Services (OSS), as well as the CIA. Only in the last decade of the twentieth century did the intelligence community start lowering the barriers against women and gays, and even then the prejudice against Chinese Americans remained.

The confidence man thrives in the world of those half-truths upon which chauvinism feeds. Once the Cold War was over, there seemed to be an opportunity for international intelligence cooperation, especially through the United Nations (U.N.). Potentially, that meant fewer jobs and less money for the Good Ole Boys in charge of U.S. intelligence. So patriotism proved, as in Samuel Johnson's day, to be the scoundrel's "last refuge." Superpatriots fanned French, Japanese, and Chinese intelligence efforts against the United States into a new menace. They attacked the United Nations and the notion of U.N. intelligence.

The tradition of the intelligence confidence man is aligned not only with the cult of the salesman and with chauvinism, but also with the ethos of the private detective. Allan Pinkerton served Lincoln as a public official but is even more famous for his development of the *private* detective agency bearing his name. By the end of the nineteenth century, private detection was in vogue all over America—for example, historians of the West have remarked on the presence in that region of the "cult of the American private detective." An essential feature of the private detective was his commercialism. By the early twentieth century, most money was to be made from industrial relations work, and private detectives were often represented as tools of the capitalists. For the detectives, however, profit came before class. It paid them not to eliminate labor radicalism. A Pennsylvania Steel executive put it succinctly: "Their expenses run up enormously and they only give you enough to lead you on." Pinkerton, William J. Burns, and other private detectives throve on anti-communist rhetoric—and to such a degree that they could not afford to let the menace fade away.[12]

There was a transmission of styles from the private detective agencies to the great state espionage organizations. To be sure, government bureaucracy develops its own momentum, and this affected the FBI, CIA, and other federal agencies. But public intelligence leaders were clearly not ignorant of the practices and reputation of their nineteenth-century private forbears. Indeed, there was a direct transference of professional expertise and style, and this is a further element of continuity in American intelligence history. Pinkerton-trained agents worked for the Secret Service in 1898. The fledgling FBI then borrowed Secret Service agents and expertise and also recruited directly from the private detective sphere, employing, for example, William J. Burns of the eponymous agency. Not surprisingly, the boosterite tradition was handed down. The taxpayer picked up the bill the private client had once paid, and was wooed accordingly.

The strength of materialist inheritance can even be illustrated in mirror image, for America's most significant traitors have been motivated by money. Whereas British agents betrayed for sex and ideology,

Americans like H. O. Yardley and Aldrich Ames committed treason for material gain. It is easy to succumb to dollar temptation when your agency thrives on hype and blustery self-promotion.

Once the torch had been passed from the private to the public sphere, a process took place that might be described as a "laying on of hands," a process that undermines still further the notion that American intelligence has lacked continuity. The upper-class, Ivy League clique that dominated American intelligence throughout World War I left its imprint on World War II. It bequeathed Allen Dulles to the second war, to work with William J. Donovan at OSS and then lead the CIA, from 1953 to 1961. Donovan became an iconographic figure for his successors, not least OSS veteran William Casey, who boosted secret intelligence to new heights when at the helm of the CIA, from 1981 to 1987. Meantime, over at the FBI no laying on of hands was necessary, as Hoover continued as director from his appointment in 1924 to his death in 1972. What all these individuals shared was a taste and a talent for intelligence hype. Hyperbole inhered in the processes of the laying on of hands and of continuity of service.

Intelligence expansion has taken place with the help of compliant and supportive government, and against a background of piously optimistic or sometimes opportunistic responses. For example, when the Department of Justice first established an investigative force in 1870–1871, the objective was not just to counter the Ku Klux Klan's intimidation of civil rights supporters, but to avoid duplication and waste.[13] Ever since then, the economy argument has been deployed—both the CIA and the Defense Intelligence Agency were supposed to have been economical solutions, but in fact, added layers of bureaucracy costing more money, as well as adding to the undigested information mountain. Another bizarre and oft-repeated practice has been the reward of failure. A disaster happens; the government sets up a preemptive inquiry to deliberate until the fuss dies down; the confidence men now say the disaster happened because they had too little money to spend on intelligence; the president and Congress authorize more intelligence funds. Thus, for example, Pearl Harbor spawned the OSS and CIA, and the National Security Agency's shortcomings in the 1990s inspired not punitive cuts but larger appropriations.

All of this suggests that the arts of salesmanship and spin are essential to survival in America. In order to make one's mark, one has to compete. For the intelligence advocate, to refrain from exaggeration would spell failure and bankruptcy. Yet, as Vance Packard observed in *The Hidden Persuaders* (1957), "We can choose not to be persuaded."[14] Moreover, some of the most successful intelligence ventures in American history have operated without fanfare, and perhaps more effectively for that. U-1 was so little publicized that hardly anyone knew about it at the time or since. Yet, it was a success. Similarly, during the Cold War the least-publicized people in the CIA, the analysts, were the most useful. Indeed, the paradox of CIA history is that its leaders have generated hyperbole, while its analysts have deflated it.

So, while this book may be about a chronic disease, it is not about a fatal condition. The excesses of the confidence men have always been balanced by the common sense of gifted critics, ranging from Melville in the nineteenth century to Senator Daniel P. Moynihan at the dawn of the twenty-first. Chronic though it may be, the inflationary disease in American intelligence need not become an acute problem in the twenty-first century. After all, as suggested above and shown in the rest of the book, U.S. intelligence also has a record of achievement that can serve as a more solid base for the future. Moreover, it began to swell and exaggerate only in the mid-nineteenth century. There is an older tradition and yardstick to which students of intelligence can turn—in George Washington's Revolutionary days, as the following chapter shows, the espionage system was lean and effective.

CHAPTER 2

The Washington Style

General George Washington was a master of military espionage. That is not an unusual claim to make, yet, for two reasons it is appropriate to confirm Washington's secret-intelligence prowess at the outset of this study. First, such confirmation illustrates just how effective American espionage can be at its best—a salutary exercise, given some of the mistakes made later on. Second, the sobriety of Washington's style serves as a foil to the overcolorful espionage accounts that developed later in the history of the republic.

George Washington made frequent and effective use of secret intelligence in the second half of the eighteenth century. This circumstance has inspired prolific writing—much of it speculative—based on flimsy or imaginary evidence, in stark contrast to Washington's own conservative style and discriminating judgments. A more balanced appraisal must take into account the fact that Washington did have a special advantage over most of his successors—he was, in addition to being a spymaster, a consumer of intelligence. Thus, it made no sense for him to distort the information he himself had commissioned. The method here is to illustrate his discriminating approach, relying on some recently disinterred if still fragmentary documentary evidence. The aim is to offer a glimpse of Washington's clandestine practices in the perilous course of the American Revolutionary War—beginning when the general and his Continental Army were holed up for the winter of 1776–1777 in the region of Morristown, New Jersey.

The year 1777 had begun on a promising note. On Christmas Day

1776, Washington crossed the half-frozen Delaware River with 2,400 men and eighteen cannon. In Trenton the next morning, he surprised and routed a force of German mercenaries fighting for the British. Then, on 3 January 1777, after a night march to conjure again the element of surprise, Washington fell upon the force of British regulars in Princeton, defeating them and driving them off toward New Brunswick. Both of these victories were reputedly, though here the evidence is vague, effected with the assistance of secret agents in place—for example, it is speculated that a dubious character called John Honeyman alerted Washington to the fact that the Germans in Trenton would be drinking heavily on Christmas Day and would be in bad shape the following morning, giving the Americans their opportunity to drive home an attack. Speculative though this may be, there is more certainty about the impact of the victories at Trenton and Princeton: they boosted the morale of the Revolutionaries, stimulated the interest of potential European allies, and made the ultimate defeat of the world's greatest imperial power seem a little less improbable.[1]

After Princeton, Washington took his men to the wooded hills in the vicinity of Morristown, where they would encamp as winter hardened. But he had problems. Notably, Gen. Sir William Howe was massing his British troops in and around New York City. Sir William had the Royal Navy at his disposal, which meant he could transport his numerically superior forces quickly—indeed, later in the year he would move an army into the early capital and congressional seat of the aspiring republic, Philadelphia, putting a southern squeeze on General Washington. While in retrospect British overall strategic incompetence is plain, Howe's force represented an evident threat to the Revolutionary army, even in the immediate aftermath of Princeton. Soon, Washington's force would consist of fewer than four thousand soldiers, the period of enlistment of many of his men having expired at the end of 1776, and desertion having taken its toll. He wanted an enlarged, more professional army, but he did not have the money to pay for it—Congress wanted victory without taxation. So the beleaguered leader did the best he could. He looked after the men who remained, taking several weeks to inoculate them against smallpox; he harassed and blockaded the British troops in New York and Staten Island to deprive them of supplies and drive down their morale; and he tried to out-bluff Howe in order to preserve his men from attack when his army was in a vulnerable condition.[2]

Accounts of Washington's deception operations have been handed down from one speculative writer to the next. Their story runs as follows. Wishing to lead Howe into thinking that his force was larger than it was, the American general spread his men thinly through the tree-covered hills, giving it the appearance of amplitude. Not content with this, and knowing that British secret agents were in his midst, he arranged for the manufacture of misinformation that would be allowed to fall into the "wrong" hands, for example, an apocryphal document putting the strength of the troops under his command at twelve thousand was insinuated into the hands of a British agent. In the wake of the American victories at Trenton and Princeton, the British were perhaps in a frame of mind to respect the Revolutionary army and its size. But Washington needed to know whether Howe had really been taken in by his deception tactics and what moves the British commander was contemplating. So he used the winter months of 1777 to put his intelligence service, as well as his army, on a sounder footing. Here, the evidence is less speculative. Washington's biographer Douglas Southall Freeman has unearthed reports by American intelligence agents on British military strength, on British strategic intentions, and on British estimates of American strength. It appears that Washington was forewarned of Howe's move on Philadelphia and seriously doubted that the British had been taken in by his own deceptions.[3]

Washington's own letters give an indication of his methods and skills as a spymaster in that critical year, 1777. It is evident that he expected his officers to be diligent in their use of spies and alert to any possibility of an attack on his forces. He told one officer in late March that "certain information" on the movements of the British general Lord Cornwallis indicated that "they intend an attack upon this army" before Washington could gain reinforcements: "I therefore depend upon your keeping a very good look out upon their line, and gaining any intelligence from people coming out of Town [New York], that I may have the earliest notice of their movements or intentions."[4]

Wariness, diligence, and a defensive realism bred of being in charge of a David versus Goliath operation—these were the qualities that appeared in Washington's intelligence missives in 1777, some of them

obtained by Philip Strong, who ran special operations for the Office of
Strategic Services in World War II and then amassed an archive on U.S.
intelligence history for a book that never appeared. Because the survival of Washington's Revolutionary army depended upon concealment,
secrecy was of the utmost importance. Late in July, Washington told
Col. Elias Dayton that British soldiers were on the move and asked him
to find out more—in particular, the number of boats at the command of
British officers. "The necessity of good intelligence," he added, "is
apparent and need not be further urged—all that remains to add is, that
you keep the whole matter as secret as possible. For upon secrecy,
success depends in most enterprises of the kind, and for want of it, they
are generally defeated, however well planned and promising a favorable outcome."[5]

In another letter, Washington indicated his flexibility in the matter
of payment. This was a thorny problem. In one way, the best spy was he
or she who served from patriotic motive, and who spurned pay. But in
the course of his retreat from Long Island and the surrounds of New
York, Washington had not recruited a sufficient force of stay-behind
agents who would send intelligence across the lines to appraise the
Revolutionary army of the British order of battle and likely movements.
The difficulty was that a person sufficiently patriotic to serve without
pay was likely to have made his or her Revolutionary sympathies evident in the course of prewar political debate. Thus, he or she would be
unable to pass as a Tory and gain the confidence of British officers. So
Washington, possibly contrary to his inclinations, decided on payment.
Congress had on 27 November 1776 promised $20,000 for intelligence
operations. But such operations soaked up funds—according to one
estimate as much as 11 percent of the total military budget. Much of the
time, Washington lacked the funds to properly compensate spies who
would face the hangman's noose if caught. On 29 September 1777, he
penned the following letter, probably sent to John Clark, one of his
main case officers dealing with spies:

> I rec^d yours of the 25th from Elizabethtown by John Meeker. I inclose you
> a passport for his and for John Hendreiks and Baker Hendreiks both of
> whom Col. Dayton informs me can be usefull to us. The Col. also informs
> me that these people and some others who have done us services in this
> way have never been paid for their . . . trouble. I therefore desire you will
> make them such compensation, out of the public money in your hands, as

you shall deem adequate. I beg you will give me the earliest intelligence of any thing material from New York or that quarter. . . . P.S. The persons who go over are to be allowed to carry over a small [illegible word] of market truck, and to bring back a few goods to give a colour of going upon Business of that kind only.[6]

So, in an exemption to the strict embargo rules barring trade with the enemy, spies crossing the lines were to be allowed to carry goods for sale. This would give them "cover," the illegality of the act would suggest to the British that they were disloyal to the Revolutionary cause, and they would be able to profit without drawing on an overstretched U.S. budget. No doubt, this would open the door to the employment of some dubious characters, but the potential gains would outweigh the dangers of unreliability.

Washington's espionage in 1777 was defensive. He was unable to prevent Howe's military initiative—the Royal Navy transported the British army to Chesapeake Bay, where they landed at Head of Elk, Maryland, on 24 August. Howe's force now marched on Philadelphia. Washington decided to harass rather than confront the 13,000-strong army, but even in this objective he suffered a reverse at Brandywine Creek. On 26 September, the British troops occupied Philadelphia—and still, as the letter quoted above illustrates, Washington feared attack from New York.

Yet, America was beginning to win the war. Events that were attributable neither to Washington nor to his regionally confined intelligence tactics strengthened his hand. Crucially, 17,000 Americans serving in upper New York stopped the southward thrust of German mercenaries operating out of British-held Canada. Revolutionary troops under the command of Gen. Horatio Gates twice defeated forces under the command of Gen. John Burgoyne, and then, on 17 October 1777, accepted Burgoyne's surrender of the entire British force at Saratoga—a name that would send an ominous shudder through royalist Europe.

With promises of bonuses and land grants, Washington's own soldiers were induced to serve for longer periods. As the Continental Army endured the winter of 1777–1778 having moved farther west to Valley Forge, professional European military help began to arrive—famously, the inspirational Marquis de Lafayette from France, and the engineer Thaddeus Kosciusko from Poland. The French had secretly supplied the Revolutionaries for some time, but, seeing signs of encouragement in the survival and expansion of the Continental Army as well as in the victories preceding Saratoga, in February 1778 they recognized U.S. independence and made formal alliance with the republic against France's old foe, England. Washington's good intelligence had contributed to survival, and survival had won a crucial ally.

A later example of Washington's espionage correspondence shows how he changed his instructions to spies to suit different circumstances. This letter is undated but contains a reference to the blockade of Long Island Sound "by some vessels belonging to his most Christian Majesty," the King of France. That dates the letter after July 1778, when a French fleet arrived off New York harbor, thus breaking the British naval monopoly. French naval operations meant better-protected oceanic supply routes for the Revolutionaries, and a weakening in the Royal Navy's grip on North American military operations—London withdrew some ships to protect the waters around the British Isles, fearing invasion of the Mother Country. In the letter, Washington noted that he had responded to Col. Alexander Hamilton's requests for espionage operations in New York and Staten Island (because of the urgent need for reassessment following France's intercession, Washington detailed his officer Benjamin Tallmadge to set up the Culper spy ring in New York). The secret agent sent to Staten Island had now reported that "The English have only four ships which mount more than forty guns, viz. The Eagle, Somerset and Ardent, each of sixty four and the Ises of fifty." The British were trying to remedy the position: "They are also fitting out a large ship, which they have for some time past made use of as a prison ship to carry (as is said) seventy guns." But their plight bordered on the desperate: "There are on Staten Island about two thousand soldiers who are much distressed for want of provisions, bread in particular."[7]

What is clear from Washington's intelligence synopsis is that he was prepared to absorb and thus encourage offensive, as distinct from defensive, intelligence. Not surprisingly, in this regard he grew in confidence as the war proceeded. In September 1780, he issued instructions to spies bound for New York, asking for all kinds of military and economic intelligence, and for information on the likelihood of British abandonment of the city. His written commentary on the reports sent to him, now deposited in the Houghton Library, Harvard University, indicates his keenness to probe for weaknesses. Dated November 1780, his notes are still cautious—for example, he is anxious to verify the reports he received by comparing them with one another. But, at the same time, he is willing to accept intimations of a collapse in British morale, of British naval weakness, and of the dwindling number of troops available to the imperial cause: "Opinion of the best judges is that the whole force does not exceed 9000—some say no more than 8000 men."[8]

Washington was a spymaster and general who was capable of a switch to attack mode, when circumstances favored that change. Much fighting lay ahead, but in 1781 Cornwallis launched, from Charleston, South Carolina, an attack that first brought British victories in Charlottesville and Richmond, Virginia, and then, through the combined might of the French navy and the Continental Army, the decisive American triumph at Yorktown on 19 October. The role of intelligence in events leading up to that final victorious campaign must be kept in perspective, yet Washington's skills in this regard are not open to doubt.

General Washington's record and prowess in the secret intelligence field is a yardstick against which certain claims can be measured. His actual prowess in clandestine matters may be compared with his overtly expressed claims to distinction as a spymaster—a simple matter, for he made no such claims. Second, his record may be compared with the claims made on his behalf by historians, and here there has been a readiness to gild the lily. Third, his record may be compared with that of future American spymasters. Finally, Washington's reticence concerning espionage may be contrasted with the hyperbolic tendencies of some of his successors.

Washington's reticence about secret service is remarkable. The clandestine story of the Revolution began, it is true, with a flourish. It is the stuff of legend that Nathan Hale volunteered to serve as a Revolutionary spy on Long Island, was captured, and was summarily executed not far from the intersection of today's Third Avenue and Sixty-sixth Street, New York City, on the morning of 22 September 1776. But Hale's naïveté in the matter of tradecraft no doubt encouraged Washington to place his intelligence on a more professional basis, to recruit agents in place in preference to penetrators—and to insist on a blanket of secrecy that would conceal his own intelligence achievements from future generations. This secrecy contributed to the illusion that Hale's mission was the last clandestine venture of its kind in the Revolutionary War. Not until Morton Pennypacker's diligent historical research culminated in his 1930 book *The Two Spies: Nathan Hale and Robert Townsend* did the extent of Washington's intelligence activities in and after 1777 become evident. Seldom can a spymaster have imposed such a successful ban on information about the activities of his secret agents.[9]

Washington's reluctance to blow his own trumpet stands in contrast with the inclination, on the part of some historians, to perfect the general's reputation. The juxtapositioning of two texts illustrates the point. The first is from the meticulous University Press of Virginia edition of the Washington papers. Washington is addressing a fellow British officer at the time of the French and Indian War:

> I always send out some white people with the Indians, and will to day or to morrow send an Officer and some alert white men with another party of Cherokees, as you desire it; tho' I must confess that I think these Scalping Partys of Indians we send out will more effectively harass the Enemy (by keeping them under continual alarams) than any Partys of white people can do: as small Partys of ours are not equal to the undertaking, and large ones must be discover'd by their Scalping Partys early enough to give the Enemy time to repel them by a Superior Force. . . .[10]

From this, it is evident that Washington was an early devotee of scouting and recognized its importance in New World warfare, that he did not allow scruple to get in the way of scalping, and that his trust in Native Americans was so low that he insisted that their warriors be accompanied by white men. Indeed, he added, "The Malbehaviour of our Indians gives me great concern, if they were hearty in our Interest their Services would be infinitely valuable; as I cannot conceive the best white men to be equal to them in the Woods: but I fear they are too sensible of their high Importance to us, to render us any very acceptable Service." Compare this with the text as rendered in 1943 by George S. Bryan, a historian who held up Washington as a model progenitor of the modern spymaster:

> I must confess it is my opinion that small parties of Indians will more effectively harass the enemy, by keeping them under continual alarms, than any white men can do. For small parties of the latter are not equal to the task, not being so dexterous at skulking as Indians; and large parties will be discovered by their spies (that is, the enemy's Indian spies) early enough to have a superior force opposed to them.[11]

Possibly Bryan used a later transcription of the Washington letter and the sanitization was therefore not his own, but it is clear that a good polishing is here being given to a national intelligence icon. To be sure, the word "skulking" is used, but almost in a humorous manner. The brutal phrase "Scalping Partys" has given way to "small parties" and "spies," with both Washington and his Indian allies presented in a "politically correct" light. With the free French and Britain allied to the United States in World War II at the time Bryan's book appeared, there is no suggestion that the French claimants to North America were being mutilated in 1758, and no hint that Washington, the future first president of the United States, was capable of mistrusting his allies.[12]

The historian Marcus Cunliffe observed that although Washington never regarded himself as a "Man of Destiny," his reputation became bloated in the hands of generations of overreverent writers who converted him into a dehumanized "Washington Monument." Although the details of his intelligence operations did not emerge for a long time, Washington's reputation as a spymaster did gradually solidify to become a part of that monument. Yet the evidence is not always straightforward. Mason Weems's *Life of Washington* (1809) famously told the tale of the little boy and his encounter first with the cherry tree, then with the irate father: "I can't tell a lie, Pa; you know I can't tell a lie. I did cut it with my hatchet." At first sight, the tale makes it seem unlikely that such an honest little boy would have grown into a devious spymaster. One refuge from this view is the theory that the story was apocryphal. But that is not necessarily so. In any case, it is very possible that its readers over the years saw the story's undercurrents: a rebellious youthful disposition (Augustine Washington had been droning on to his son about respecting his fruit trees) and a shrewd judge of human nature (the father insisted on honesty at all times, and the calculating little boy's anticipation that he would just love a confession is borne out in Weems's version of the tale: "'Run to my arms, you dearest boy,' cried his father in transports"). His honesty once established, what "Big Lie" might not the young Washington get away with in the future? He may have had a gentlemanly distaste for publicity, but there is no reason to believe he was averse to selective deception.[13]

Washington's spies, as well as the general himself, acquired over time a mythical standing. Nathan Hale stands firmly in the pantheon of American heroes, and not least for the story of his gallant death. Hannah Adams, one of the earliest professional woman writers in America, appears to have been the first to relate the tale. Her *History of New*

England appeared twenty-three years after Hale swung on the gallows, but in her account the Massachusetts historian spared neither detail nor sentiment:

> [Howe's] order was accordingly executed, in a most unfeeling manner, and by as great a savage as ever disgraced humanity. A clergyman, whose attendance was desired, was refused him; a bible for a few moments devotion was not procured, although he requested it. Letters, which, on the morning of his execution, he wrote to his mother and other friends, were destroyed. . . .
>
> Unknown to all around him, without a single friend to offer him the least consolation, thus fell as amiable and as worthy a young man as America could boast, with this as his dying observation, "that he only lamented, that he had but one life to lose for his country."[14]

By this account, Hale does seem to have died a brave death. The Yale graduate may have been familiar with the line from Joseph Addison's play *Cato* (1713), "What a pity it is / That we can die but once to serve our country." On the other hand, this may well have been Adams's literary gloss. Certainly, it seems unlikely that Hale should have written a letter to his mother, for she was dead. Thus, Adams's account cannot remain free of a suspicion of hyperbole.[15]

Secrecy is an invitation to myth, and the Revolutionary spy found, in 1821, the best possible literary exponent. James Fenimore Cooper's novel *The Spy* was published in that year. Pennypacker described it as "America's first great novel." Certainly, it is arresting for its American theme, and notable for its popularity—it sold 6,000 copies in the first year, and a play based on the book enjoyed a long run in New York City. The novel is about Harvey Birch, based, according to Pennypacker, on one of Washington's real-life agents, Enoch Crosby. In the novel, Birch is an apparent British spy who was in fact a double agent in the service of George Washington. Birch is unpaid, does not prosper after the war yet still seeks no monetary reward, and carries the secret of his clandestine services to the end of his days. How representative does that make him? In reality, Washington found it useful both to use dubious characters and to pay them, although it is known that he also worried about the lack of recognition for those secret agents who were brave and true to his cause. Perhaps Cooper was not wide of the mark when he relates Birch's reply and his commander's delight with it when Washington says some agents were worried that Birch might not forever remain silent: "Tell them I would not take the gold!"[16]

Birch was emblematic if not entirely representative, but another question remains: To what extent was America ready to accept Cooper's version of events? The success of Cooper's novel and of its author's subsequent literary activities answers the last question, but here it is appropriate to note a qualification offered by the American novelist in the twilight of his career. In the novel, Birch is the last survivor of a ruined, déclassé family. But in the introduction to the 1849 edition, Birch becomes "an agent whose services differed but little from those of the common spy. This man, as will readily be understood, belonged to a condition of life which rendered him the least reluctant to appear in so equivocal a character. He was poor, ignorant, so far as the usual instruction was concerned; but cool, shrewd, and fearless by nature "[17] Here there is on the one hand evidence of the snobbery that lost Cooper his popularity among his fellow citizens in his later years. On the other hand, there is an indication of a distinct cooling off toward the second oldest profession.

Viewing the Washington years with the wisdom of hindsight and from the present-day perspective, it would in fact not be too difficult to find fault with early U.S. espionage on two broad fronts, efficacy and Constitutional balance. In terms of efficacy, there were some notable failings in counterintelligence. Benjamin Franklin's undercover diplomacy in Paris on behalf of the Revolution was no secret to the British, in whose service Dr. Edward Bancroft was an effective spy. On the North American continent, Washington was rightly in constant agitation about enemy spies: infamously, for example, Benedict Arnold in 1779–1780 betrayed valuable intelligence to Gen. Sir Henry Clinton, before escaping to the safety of the British lines and ultimately to England.

Washington's intelligence system was also ineffective in another sense: he refrained from establishing a permanent bureaucracy that would perpetuate an institutional memory of tradecraft and allied practices. The American attitude toward espionage and an overweening state remained forever ambivalent, and in particular militated throughout the nineteenth century against a permanent, coordinated intelligence organization. One could argue that the formation of the Army Corps of Topographical Engineers in 1838 was a step in that direction, in that the corps dispatched explorers like John C. Frémont to gather intelligence in the West; President Abraham Lincoln established the U.S. Secret Service in his last cabinet meeting in 1865; the Office of Naval Intelligence was established in 1882, and the Military Intelligence Division three years later. Yet while both espionage and propaganda about it mushroomed in mid-century, it is not until the War of 1898, at the very earliest, that one can detect the beginnings of a bureaucratically organized government intelligence system.[18]

Washington sowed the seeds of Constitutional controversy. In 1790 Washington, by then president of the United States, obtained from Congress a law establishing the "contingent fund of foreign intercourse," more commonly known as the "secret fund." The initial sum provided was $40,000. Within three years this had grown to $1 million, or 12 percent of the federal budget. At this time, the fledgling republic seemed threatened by England to the east and north, and by the "Indian Confederacy" to the west. Trusted to deal with these dangers, the president had to declare to Congress the amounts he had spent from the secret fund, but not what he had spent them on. His successors availed themselves regularly of this provision of unvouched funds, and executive agents operating in secret were to play a significant role in American expansion: for example, in the acquisition of East Florida and Mexico. But, lacking oversight of such operations, Congress over the years grew restive. In 1893, after President Grover Cleveland had sent a secret commissioner to Hawaii with the apparent objective of surreptitious annexation, Senator George F. Hoar of Massachusetts secured passage of the Hoar amendment: the president could employ secret agents to obtain information, but such persons "could be in no sense an officer of the United States," and could not enter into agreements that would be "binding" on the United States.[19]

That kind of controversy flared up with particular intensity in the intelligence debate that occurred in the last quarter of the twentieth century, in the wake of revelations about the CIA. An inquiry chaired by Senator Frank Church of Idaho assumed that Washington and the other Founding Fathers had no intention of sanctioning a major, peacetime, executive-led intelligence community with immunity from congressional scrutiny and a wide remit including a panoply of "dirty tricks." In a rebuttal, the historian Stephen Knott argued that, on the contrary, Washington and his senior colleagues had every intention of giving

America a long-term intelligence capability—and Congress willingly gave them free scope. These two schools of thought are both "presentist," allowing contemporary concerns to overshadow the different agendas of Washington and his successors. They are also "originalist," in that they give the Founding Fathers an iconic status and imply that George Washington, slave owner, could do no wrong. But the enduring vigor of the debate is nevertheless testimony to an ambivalent and thought-provoking legacy.[20]

George Washington's emphasis on secrecy was a significant part of that ambivalent legacy. It contributed powerfully to a trend that culminated in the "national security state," in which government treated secrecy as an end in itself irrespective of need, and in which the cover-up became a widespread malpractice. Secrecy would become not a self-denying ordinance but a tyranny of silence imposed on others.

Just as serious, however, was the *breakdown* in secrecy and discretion that led future spymasters to engage in self-publicity of a type contrary to the Washingtonian style. Here, Washington is a worthy foil to his successors. For, just at the point where it could be best justified, discretion collapsed in a manner that proved destructive to the best interests of America. The responsibility for the initial breakdown rests very largely in the subject of the next chapter, Allan Pinkerton.

CHAPTER 3

Allan Pinkerton's Legacy

In 1861 the United States faced its second great crisis, and again military intelligence had a role to play. It was generally recognized that good intelligence could help decide the outcome of battles, campaigns, and even the Civil War itself. Intelligence would also be a determinant of the speed with which one side or the other might win the war, putting an end to the immense misery and sacrifice both North and South endured.

But Abraham Lincoln lacked George Washington's military and intelligence experience, and had to rely on the judgment of others. In July 1861, the president turned to Gen. George B. McClellan, a railroad executive who had served in the Mexican War, and who had more recently observed at first hand the horrors of modern war in the Crimea. Upon McClellan fell the duty of defending the national capital, building up the Army of the Potomac, and destroying Confederate forces in Virginia with the object of bringing the war to a victorious close. To these ends, the general sought help in his goal of acquiring a picture of enemy strength and dispositions. In his railroad career, McClellan had worked with Allan Pinkerton, and he now summoned the private detective to Washington to organize a military secret service.

It is acknowledged on all sides that the result was a disaster. Although the forces under McClellan's command were numerically superior to those under enemy command in Virginia, the Union general abetted by Pinkerton exaggerated Confederate strength, sometimes by as much as threefold.[1] Against this background, McClellan ordered no bold initiative to nip the rebellion in the bud. Instead, it was the Confederates' Gen. Robert E. Lee who attacked the too cautiously advancing Union army. The newly installed leader of the Army of Northern Virginia won the second Battle of Bull Run and other morale-boosting victories, and then in September 1862 fought the Northerners' superior force to a standstill before retreating in good if battered order from the bloodiest battle of the war, Antietam.

Historians have differed on the question of responsibility for the overestimation of Lee's strength. On one hand, it is argued that McClellan was a man of deep insecurities, ever afraid of failure, and a general who was less interested in risky, decisive action than in exaggerating enemy strength in order to justify demands for ever-larger aggregations of troops under his command. Pinkerton, according to this view, simply played the better-safe-than-sorry game, erring on the upward side in order to ensure that the Union would not be caught by surprise by undetected reserves of Confederate troops. Pinkerton, it is pointed out by his defenders and by McClellan's detractors, consistently estimated enemy strength at levels lower than those McClellan used in negotiations with Lincoln and Secretary of War Edwin M. Stanton.[2]

On the other hand, Pinkerton does seem to have delivered intelligence to please, and to have willfully twisted the evidence in order to give substance to McClellan's fears. The contrast with George Washington's appetite for intelligence on enemy weak points is stark. Pinkerton's estimate of enemy strength on 4 October 1861 was 98,400 men—fewer than McClellan's bargaining-chip estimate of 170,000 but still more than double Lee's actual strength of between 40,000 and 45,000 men (at the time, McClellan had about 76,000 under his own command). Commenting to McClellan a few weeks later in his 4 October report, Pinkerton wrote that the "estimate was founded upon all information then in my possession . . . and was made large, as intimated to you at the time, so as to be sure and cover the entire number of the Enemy that our army was to meet." In his interpretation of the phrase "made large," the intelligence specialist Edwin Fishel suggests that Pinkerton was not incompetent as some historians have assumed, but engaged in a conspiracy to distort the truth in collusion with General McClellan.[3]

Other writers have seen Pinkerton's distortions more as character traits. One Civil War historian described him as "imaginative," and another thought him "an overgrown Tom Sawyer."[4] Was Pinkerton a conspirator or was he overimaginative? The question is not an idle one, for he was to set a new and enduring style in American intelligence leadership. Some clues to the answer are to be found in the story of his early years, others in his role in Lincoln assassination plots, in his activities as a publicist, and in the mid-nineteenth-century American culture within which he operated. These clues help explain not just the man but the nature of his legacy.

Here is the story of Allan Pinkerton's youth as related by him in letters to his wife, son, and family friends long after he had made a success of his life in America. To rely on these letters may be risky—because his memory was sometimes faulty, because as a controlling father he may have been determined to create an image of family history that would shape the destiny of his descendants, and because, like many prominent figures in their declining years, he wanted to justify himself and his actions. But the letters were written at precisely the time when Pinkerton was inventing an image of secret service that was to endure to the present day. True or false, the man's image of himself as conveyed in his letters is inextricably linked to the vein of public hyperbole he bestowed on posterity.

Allan Pinkerton was born in the Gorbals on 21 July 1819. In this district of Glasgow, wealthy suburban development vied for supremacy with industrial construction. Pinkerton's father held a good job as a turnkey in the city jail, then died when Allan was a young boy. His widow had to work in a spinning mill in the struggle to bring up her family. Allan Pinkerton learned cooperage, a good trade. But by the latter part of the nineteenth century, when Pinkerton reminisced, the Gorbals had degenerated into Scotland's most notorious slum, and this seems to have colored his recollections of boyhood. "Ah!" he wrote in 1872, "the misery I think of since I have left Scotland, I cannot tell, I can scarcely survive it, the misery and wretchedness of the Gorbals."[5]

To the nineteenth-century mind, there were three escapes from poverty: death, self-improvement, and collective action. By the 1870s, Pinkerton was one of America's greatest exemplars and tribunes of self-improvement. But the private letters he wrote emphasized the collective action taken by British workers in their struggle to widen the franchise and to improve the plight of the poor. In Scotland, the agitators were known as Radicals. The more general term applied to them throughout Britain was Chartists. Many Chartists pursued peaceful tactics, collecting signatures on petitions—a "People's Charter" demanding a widening in the privileges of citizenship. Other Chartists could see little point in pursuing legitimate tactics when they did not have the vote, and resorted instead to direct action. In one conspicuous case, the Chartists attempted to take over the town of Newport in South Wales. But the authorities acted on the basis of good intelligence, and troops hidden in the Westgate Hotel suddenly opened fire on the demonstrators, killing several of them. Three leaders of the Newport Rising were arrested and condemned to death, a sentence later commuted to exile for life.[6]

Although the Newport fiasco marked the end of Chartism in Wales, Pinkerton was keen to stress his participation in such events. In 1873, he wrote to an English friend: "When we were Chartists. Moral force Chartists. I was a physical force man, but we liked each other although we were widely different. I went with some others such as my friend John Taylor of Glasgow to attend a meeting in Bermingham. you [sic] will probably know the rest the Yeomanry went down and scattered us with drawn swords. I went back to Scotland and was then married, and started for the wilds of America."[7] There is a certain authenticity to Pinkerton's spelling of Birmingham, as his phonetic version reflects the local accent, but he is nevertheless more usually associated with the Newport Rising. Apparently in a letter to his son Robert, Allan Pinkerton recalled the details of the King's 42nd Foot hidden behind the shutters of the Westgate Hotel, the advance of the Chartists armed with primitive muskets and farm implements, and the bloody rout that followed: "It was a bad day. We returned to Glasgow by the back streets and the lanes, more like thieves than honest working men."[8]

Pinkerton explained the termination of his radical youth in Scotland in terms of the discovery, unsurprising in the context of the story he told, that there was "a price on my head." He went into hiding, whereupon his fifteen-year-old girlfriend Joan Carfrae agreed to marry him, and to flee to a new life "making American barrels." In 1842, the newlyweds left for America, the departure a traumatic watershed in their lives. In 1878, he reminded his wife of the occasion in a letter celebrating their thirty-six years together: "As we sailed down the Clyde sights were many and varied of that land and those friends we were leaving."[9]

In America, Pinkerton was to invent both the anti-communist tradition and the clandestine American response to it. The evolution of his views on the working class are, therefore, of more than passing interest. A rare glimpse of his changing private views is afforded in a letter to Alex McDonald of Holytown, Scotland, of 29 January 1869, a letter published in the *Glasgow Sentinel* later that year. In the letter, Pinkerton observed that "Capital has invariably preyed upon the labouring classes," and that "The labouring classes have a right to organize." However, "Nothing tends more to injure the working classes standing properly before the public, and especially before that class of the public who stand between the working class and the public, viz., the middle class, than the evil effects which 'strikes' produce by resort to force." So, while retaining his stated sympathy with the laboring classes, Pinkerton now presented himself not as a "physical force" man, but as a law and order advocate. This marked a departure not only from his youth in Scotland but also from his stated associations in the 1850s with the direct-action wing of the abolitionist movement—he claimed to have been one of John Brown's supporters. And soon, Pinkerton would also abandon the principle of collective working-class rights in all but private correspondence, becoming instead a prominent standard-bearer for American capitalistic individualism.[10]

Did Pinkerton really wave good-bye to those friends on the banks of the Clyde? Did he leave his ideals in Scotland to make money and exploit workers in America? It is conceivable that Pinkerton was never a Chartist at heart, and so did not require a conscience-jerking effort to turn against the laboring class. In fact, certain threads of continuity may be discerned that bind Pinkerton the Scot with Pinkerton the American. One is clandestinity. Radicalism/Chartism in 1830s Britain was dangerous and had to be conducted in secret. When Pinkerton crossed the ocean and the class divide, he clung to the habit.

Another thread of continuity was Pinkerton's fascination with violence—he became a sanguine and at times sanguinary advocate of law and order in America, continuing in the behavioral vein established with the Chartists and, as seems probable, the abolitionists. Yet, the reputation that Pinkerton and Company and other private detective agencies acquired for extreme violence is not wholly deserved. The armed guards they supplied were certainly violent, but the investigators rarely carried guns and were expected to keep out of trouble. Moreover, the detectives did not always serve the capitalist class with the slavish obedience sometimes supposed, especially if loyalty stood in the way of a quick buck. But the detectives' violent conservatism was a potent myth, and owed much to the attitude and practices of Allan Pinkerton. Thus, Pinkerton may have been a radical more by temperament than conviction. In Illinois as in Scotland, he may simply have been swept into radical circles only by a fascination with violence.[11]

It could also be argued that it was the geographic context that changed, and not the man. Pinkerton's compatriot Andrew Carnegie advocated the overthrow of the monarchy in Britain but broke strikes in America. Similarly, Pinkerton could remain a radical in Scotland while pursuing a more conservative course in America simply because the two countries were different: working class violence was indefensible in America because there, in contrast to Scotland, the laboring man had the vote and could pursue legal and legislative remedies to his ills.

Continuity is evident in another respect, too: espionage and informing were rife in the Chartist movement. Just as England had its Cato Street conspiracy, so Scotland had its Richmond plot. On 8 September 1820, Andrew Hardie and John Baird had been executed at Stirling for allegedly subversive reform activities. In the next decade, sensational revelations came to light about the role in their conviction of Alexander Richmond, now alleged to have been an agent provocateur acting on behalf of the authorities. The question of police penetration of the Radical movement must have influenced Pinkerton in his formative, teenage years. Informers appear to have undermined the Chartist movement in Wales, too, at the time of the Newport Rising. Pinkerton had police connections through his father and his half-brother, William, who served in the Glasgow police force. Perhaps this helps explain why he escaped arrest for so long and was then allowed to escape. Aware of the significant interval, Pinkerton told his son William A. Pinkerton that he had been away from Scotland during this period, making a trip to Africa as a ship's cooper.[12]

Pinkerton may have been a police informer in Scotland, an activity that would supply an alternative explanation for his immunity from arrest as well as for his sudden emigration and for his later choice of profession. There is no proof of this, and it is just as likely that he was too obscure to be arrested and that he chose to emigrate because it was easier to obtain work as a cooper in North America. However, it can be said that from an impressionable age he had been soaked in an atmosphere of provocation, conspiracy, and betrayal—an apt preparation for his career in America.

While all these continuities may be acknowledged and are important, there was in Pinkerton's case, as in so many others, an inconsistency between the precepts of the young man and those of the older, successful person. If the extremism remained constant, it was an extremism of opposite poles. In part, the lurch to conservatism stemmed from the galloping effects of old age. In part, it resulted from self-interest. And in part, Pinkerton found it easier to exploit American working men than Scots, because they were not the comrades of his youth. Whatever the cause, Pinkerton did change, from being a secret rabble rouser in a collective cause to being a public booster of private espionage.

Pinkerton and Company in 1855 signed a contract to supply security services to a consortium of railroads, including the Illinois Central. The contract marked the takeoff point for the economic fortunes of Pinkerton and his agency. His proclaimed abolitionist sentiments may have marked him as a radical in one way, but they would do him no harm in the period of postwar Reconstruction, 1865–1877, a time when Republican businessmen were influential in the governance of America. However, his public prominence and success in the lucrative business of labor espionage stemmed from his activities during the Civil War itself. To be sure, his military espionage was an acknowledged fiasco. However, his story of the frustration of the 1861 Baltimore Plot on the life of Lincoln, especially when thrown into relief by the murder of the president four years later, guaranteed him fame and fortune.

On 5 August 1866, Pinkerton wrote to William H. Herndon, who had been a law partner of the now-deceased President Lincoln, requesting confidentiality regarding certain portions of the records of the Philadelphia, Wilmington and Baltimore Railroad (PWBRR), in which appeared some information on the Baltimore Plot. Pinkerton's stated reason was that, with the war over and Lincolnian magnanimity in mind, he wished to protect the identity of a former rebel now working as a broker for the railroad.[13]

His actual reason may have been that he wanted his version of events to prevail. He related this version to Herndon in a letter written later in the same month. The PWBRR had retained Pinkerton at the start of the war, to see if any acts of sabotage were being planned to cripple its operations. Timothy Webster played a key role in Pinkerton's story. (Webster would be one of Pinkerton's key secret agents, and was later executed in Richmond as a Union spy.) While working on the PWBRR commission, Webster penetrated a rebel ring and discovered that they planned to assassinate Lincoln as he traveled to Washington for his inauguration.

The president-elect's route from Springfield, Illinois, would take him through Maryland, whose citizens were largely sympathetic to the Southern cause. In Baltimore, he would have to change trains. The rebel plotters would start a pretend fight at Calvert Street station, and that would be the cover for the assassination of the traveling politician. To foil this plot as he claimed, Pinkerton laid plans to smuggle Lincoln through Baltimore thirty-six hours earlier than expected. Lincoln left Springfield on 11 February and started on an announced itinerary that would take him to Philadelphia, and then to Baltimore on the 23rd. But he canceled his meetings in Philadelphia, and his train, guarded by Pinkerton men deployed at regular intervals along its route, pulled into Baltimore's PWBRR station on the 22nd, at the stealthy hour of 3.30 a.m. and with its distinguished passenger disguised in an ordinary sack overcoat and "Kossuth" hat. Horses now pulled the president-elect's sleeping car through the streets of the city to the Washington station. After a nail-biting two hours' delay caused by the late arrival of a train from the West, Lincoln proceeded safely on his way to the capital.[14]

This plot-prevention story has been greeted with some skepticism. Lincoln knew Pinkerton from the days when he had been an attorney for the Illinois Central Railroad, and perhaps only too well. According to Pinkerton's own account, Lincoln was "cool, calm and collected" when told of the plot, and was reluctant to change his travel plans. After the event, the president said he did not really believe there would be an assassination, but "thought it wise to run no risk where no risk was necessary." Ward H. Lamon, Lincoln's friend, erstwhile law partner, and traveling companion through Baltimore on the not-so-fateful evening, wrote two books, one expressing belief in the plot, another stating, "It is perfectly manifest there was no conspiracy." John A. Kennedy, a detective from the New York City police department, went down to Baltimore, conducted an investigation on 28 February, and reported to the Baltimore Marshal of Police George P. Kane that there had been no plot. Yet, this may have been intelligence to please, as Kane (according to Pinkerton) was a Confederate sympathizer. Kennedy later claimed some credit on behalf of the New York police for having helped prevent the assassination.[15]

The existence or otherwise of the plot was never proved. Nor can it be ascertained whether Pinkerton's own agents provoked the plot or at least rumors of it—according to his own published account, they used his trademark technique: in order to gain the confidence of Confederate militants, they posed as "fire-eaters" exuding "blatant expressions of the most rebellious nature." But, real, apocryphal, or provoked, the plot was most useful to Pinkerton. In the short run, it cemented his tie to Lincoln and, just as important, the perception in status-conscious Washington that he was high in the pecking order within the presidential circle. At a time when business prospects must have seemed uncertain, it gave Pinkerton the opportunity to shore up his income. While the composite figure for his own relatively brief period of service is unavailable, it is known that John Potts, chief clerk of the War Department, made unvouchered disbursements of $426,869 in the period 1862–1865, and that Pinkerton's successor, Lafayette C. Baker, who died in 1868, left $458,299—discovered in cash, in a strongbox. In the longer term, Pinkerton's perceived intimacy with Lincoln gave him a reputation that helped him in the private business sphere.[16]

In the meantime, Pinkerton apparently continued to believe in the effectiveness of assassination fears in promoting his interests. Almost two years after his dismissal from the Union service in November 1862, he wrote to McClellan warning that a group of the general's friends were planning to kill Lincoln. McClellan dismissed this as "conspiracy nonsense," and there is no evidence that such a plot existed. But the assassination of Lincoln in 1865 played into Pinkerton's hands—it seemed that a martyred president had died for want of protection from the one man who could provide it. In spite of Lincoln's evident dissatisfaction with his military intelligence services, Pinkerton, partly through hero-worship and partly out of a healthy regard for future profits, continued to stress his exalted Civil War connections. "During the years of the war," he told Herndon, "I was pretty well acquainted with [Lincoln].

When he came to the Army of the Potomac to review the Troops I invariably met him. In fact my tent was more of a place of resort for him than even that of General McClellan."[17]

In his accounts of the Civil War, Pinkerton not only glossed over his own shortcomings but failed to credit the clandestine efforts of others. Understandably, he did not credit the work of Lafayette Baker, who usurped Pinkerton's role as Secret Service chief but not his promotional skills. Nor did Pinkerton place his own agents' work in the context of that of others on the Union side, and of their equally gallant and no less effective opponents who spied for the Confederacy. Confederate and Union spies vied for supremacy in Washington, Canada, and, crucially, Europe. European trade policies and diplomatic/military stances were potentially decisive factors, as they had been in the Revolutionary War. The chief of the U.S. secret service in Europe, Lincoln's ambassador to Belgium Henry Shelton Sanford, was a linguist with a law doctorate from the University of Heidelberg who enjoyed the advantages of diplomatic experience and cover. In the course of the war, he set up counterintelligence against the Confederate Secret Service, preemptively bought guns and saltpeter to keep them out the hands of Confederate agents, bribed sections of the press to take a pro-Union stance, and successfully conducted a whole range of other nefarious schemes that make Pinkerton's achievements seem nebulous and insignificant by comparison.[18]

On 14 April 1865, the Confederate sympathizer John Wilkes Booth fired the bullet that killed Abraham Lincoln. The president's death the next day gave Pinkerton's story of the Baltimore Plot a plausibility and significance it might not otherwise have attained, and at the same time inflicted the conspiracy industry upon posterity. The assassination was used to mediate the problems of succeeding generations, and it had lost none of its appeal by the era of the Cold War. For example, Vaughan Shelton's 1965 study of the Lincoln murder trial concluded that Lafayette Baker arranged the deed because he could see that Lincoln longed for North-South reconciliation, whereas the prolongation of Baker's own power depended on the perpetuation of crisis. Even if one of his critics dismissed his book as "four hundred pages of a deranged analysis of sources," Shelton's interpretation perhaps showed subliminal acuity on the self-perpetuating role of the intelligence services during the Cold War.[19]

The Baker conjecture is just one among several spawned by Lincoln's murder, for Lincoln conspiracy theories were all too readily adaptable to political ends. Secretary of War Stanton labeled the assassination a Confederate plot. The style of his response would appeal over a century later to those who made a living out of stories of Soviet machinations. In 1988, an officer of the CIA collaborated with an officer of the Defense Intelligence Agency and a Lincoln conspiracy theorist to produce a work that once again pinned the assassination on the KGB of its day, the Confederate Secret Service. Their book feasted on circumstantial evidence and was replete with spook-speak phrases like "department of dirty tricks" and "psychological warfare." The history of American espionage is in significant ways a history of the overheated imagination, and the combined effects of the Baltimore "plot" and Lincoln's actual assassination stoked a fire that would inflame the American mind for a century and more.[20]

After the Civil War, Allan Pinkerton built up a coda of sound practice for private detectives, established his own business as a major force, and pursued a further career as a publicist in the cause of private detection in general and of the Pinkerton agency in particular. The practices of the Pinkerton men were at variance with the high tone conveyed in the founder's improving maxims. Nevertheless, Pinkerton's activities as a publicist had an enduring effect in that they established the style of the American clandestine agency leader.

In proclaiming rules of good conduct for his detectives, Pinkerton was in part a mid-nineteenth-century moralist, in part a businessman who by emphasizing the purity of his own men meant to imply that the competition was rotten. His attitude toward the consumption of alcohol is a case in point. Pinkerton was not averse to taking a drink himself, and one of his agents, James McParlan, was legendary for being a "cold soak," a man who could drink most others under the table. But the Temperance crusade was all-powerful in nineteenth-century America, and Pinkerton was determined to protect his agency's reputation. In 1872, he fired off a rebuke to his general manager George H. Bangs because of his drink habit, but his worry was over reputation, not incompetence: "When is it going to end?" he asked, after one of his spies reported that Bangs had emerged, intoxicated, from a New York saloon.

"Think of the railroad officials in Philadelphia, 'drunk as a lord.' Oh! my God. I cannot stand it. Think of the General Superintendent of this Agency so miserably drunk as you were at 9 a.m. Yes 9 a.m. I thought it might have been 9 p.m., but no it was 9 a.m."[21]

Pinkerton worried about his agency's reputation because integrity was a good selling point. It was so useful for any detective to be able to stand on the moral high ground and point to the shortcomings of rivals. For example, in his *History of the United States Secret Service* (1867), Lafayette Baker claimed that detectives hired by the military were, with the exception of his own men, "selected . . . from the most worthless and disreputable characters." This practice of denouncing other spies was to contribute to the continuing American unease over clandestine practices, especially in times of peace. Pinkerton, of course, disagreed with Baker's contention that espionage was "contrary to the spirit of our republican institutions in time of peace," yet he was, like his former rival, conscious of the need to persuade people that spying was respectable, but only if entrusted to the right detectives.[22]

Pinkerton set forth his maxims in concise format—no doubt for the edification of customers as well as his operatives—in an 1873 pamphlet, *General Principles of Pinkerton's National Detective Agency*. Pinkerton men would not drink except when authorized to do so for operational reasons; they would meticulously record their expenses; the Pinkerton detective's defeat of crime would be a triumph of "THE PURE AND HONEST MIND OBTAINING A CONTROLLING POWER OVER THAT OF THE CRIMINAL." In the same pamphlet, Pinkerton emphasized that his agency was "an individual and private enterprise, and is not in any way connected with, or controlled by, any Municipal Corporation or Governmental authority." The detective profession was new, "a high and honorable calling," and a product of the "enlightened intelligence of modern times." But a sharp distinction had to be drawn between his own operatives and the scoundrels employed by others, such as the "Police of America" and other countries, notably England (where the police virtually licensed thieves in their quest for "stool pigeons") and France (in whose capital city, Paris, the detective force could be divided into those who had been convicted of crimes, and those who had committed crimes but had not yet been convicted).[23]

This powerful case for a private detective force was consistent with the spirit of the age, a time when fiercely competitive capitalism came of age in America. Pinkerton stuck to his case until the end, proclaiming, in a memoir published in the year of his death, 1884, that the detective profession was "honorable," the detective being an "officer" (as distinct from the more proletarian "operative") who should be "pure and above reproach."[24] By this time, Pinkerton had established a business worth many millions of dollars. After the Civil War, his organization became not just Pinkerton's agency, but the Pinkerton National Detective Agency (PNDA). The PNDA adopted its logo, an unblinking eye, and its marketing slogan, "The Eye That Never Sleeps." Its offices and its business proliferated. With the expansion of American industry, the agency prospered by supplying to employers detectives who would act as armed guards and labor spies. On the criminal front, PNDA detectives engaged in some spectacular activities, such as its unsuccessful pursuit of the homicidal bank robber Jesse James. More significantly for the history of both policing and counterespionage, the PNDA compiled a national data bank with files identifying criminals and suspects all over America. In a nation chronically distrustful of the state, a private agency had supplied an important need.

The PNDA, furthermore, was a step in the direction of the institutionalization of American espionage. In Lincoln's last cabinet meeting, the United States Secret Service had been reconstituted and put on a permanent footing, but it was not to be a major force in American life until the 1890s. By this time, the Office of Naval Intelligence (1882) and the Military Information Division (1885) had also been formed. However, in the years when America was emerging as an industrial giant and world power, the PNDA was unchallenged as the nation's prime investigative organization.

But the PNDA was vulnerable to American business fluctuations. Even before the Crash of 1873 and the severe depression that followed, the agency was running into lean times: Bangs warned Pinkerton that "Money is very tight, and bringing a high per cent on the street." By this time, Pinkerton had developed a spending habit. There is no evidence that Kate Warne, his chief female operative and probably his mistress, constituted a drain on his assets and, in any case, she died in 1868. However, Pinkerton did father nine children by his wife, Joan, three of whom survived into adulthood. These and The Larches, his country estate near Onarga, Illinois, which had "no equal in the West" and where Pinkerton entertained in lavish style, cost substantial sums to maintain. Working for America's new breed of employers at a time when labor unions were attempting to challenge managerial hegemony would be one way of boosting income, but Allan Pinkerton decided that a massive publicity campaign would also be necessary. The urgency of this need must have seemed greater because other detective agencies were beginning to establish themselves, making it imperative to assert the superiority of the service provided by the Pinkertons.[25]

Pinkerton was no ebullient self-projectionist. Even the clarion call of the dollar might not have galvanized him, but for the operation of certain additional factors. In the first place, if Pinkerton fondly remembered his association with the clandestine wing of Chartism, he had no doubt absorbed also the importance of the open propaganda campaigns conducted by these British reformers, campaigns that perhaps influenced his decision to embark on the literary trail.

However, it is just as important to take note of the culture in which Pinkerton found himself, in his adopted land of America. The nation was experiencing a boom in the cult of the Confidence Man. True, the con man was neither exclusively American nor exclusively mid-nineteenth century: Cotton Mather complained about opportunist preachers taking advantage of Bostonians in the seventeenth century, while David Maurer's classic study *The Big Con* appeared in 1940 and was about twentieth-century grifters (Maurer identified Pinkerton's haunts, Chicago and New York, as having been the "big-con" centers in the 1890s). But the con man did reach an apogee of both fame and infamy just before and during the Gilded Age.[26]

So many people were getting rich quick, and often by dubious means; the Ulysses S. Grant administration (1869–1877) staggered from one financial scandal to the next, with the president himself taken in by con men; the sorry course of Reconstruction in the South gave the word "carpetbagger" its place in the American vocabulary. The inventor of the American detective story, Edgar Allan Poe, was fascinated by "diddling." Mark Twain and Herman Melville wrote critically of the confidence man, yet in doing so perhaps unwittingly made him more mesmeric. In *Democratic Vistas* (1871), Walt Whitman portrayed the best people of the day as "but a mob of fashionably dress'd speculators." Twain's *The Gilded Age* (1873) condemned the new rich, yet his novel gave the era its glittering name, the very people he condemned glorifying in its image. Pinkerton lacked the charm and what Poe called the "grin" of the confidence man, but he must have been influenced by the spirit of his age, and in his grim and plodding way he subjected his adopted countrymen to a stream of propaganda about his own and the PNDA's achievements.[27]

In 1873, Pinkerton published *The Bankers, Their Vaults and the Burglars,* partly based on his reminiscences, and partly instructive. Published in Chicago, the book was not a best-seller, but it was fairly well received and this encouraged its author to continue. *The Expressman and the Detective,* also published in Chicago, came out the following year and sold 15,000 copies within the first sixty days. The New York publisher G. W. Dillingham now pursued Pinkerton, and his literary career gathered pace, with seventeen further volumes appearing in print. Pinkerton was determined to publicize his books, and showed initiative in doing so. Exploiting his connections with the railroad industry, he would have fliers advertising his books left on the seats of passenger train cars. One such flier publicized *The Detective and the Somnambulist* (1875), on sale for $1.50. It described Pinkerton's detective stories as "the most surprising books since *Uncle Tom's Cabin.*" Pinkerton was not in the habit of advertising his agency directly. That was for his undesirable competitors. But by promoting himself, he hoped to gain the same end: "The News Agent accompanying the train will pass through this car in a few minutes, and will take pleasure in showing you the three great books of the century." Pinkerton was the author of the other two as well. A further flier gave the *Boston Post*'s reaction to *The Detective and the Somnambulist:* "A book which the millions will want."[28]

In the preface to *The Detective and the Somnambulist,* Pinkerton called attention to the fact that it and the other two volumes "are LITERALLY TRUE." The opening remark in his 1884 memoir was: "This work is what it purports to be." These remarks were, in part, a typical nineteenth-century literary sales pitch. If you are clever enough to buy this book, the advertisements were saying, you will read an account so sensational that you will be tempted to question its veracity. If you buy, you will be getting double value for your money, for it is not only entertaining but true. But these claims may also be read as defensive, for the authenticity of Pinkerton's writings is questionable. One relevant factor is a severe stroke that Pinkerton endured in January 1869, at the age of fifty. He made a slow and courageous recovery, but illness and intimations of mortality may have played tricks with his memory. Another factor is the great fire that reduced much of wooden-structured Chicago to rubble in October 1871, and in which four hundred volumes of Pinkerton records perished. This was unfortunate for Pinkerton in that it became difficult to verify some of the things he was saying. On the other hand, it meant he could make extravagant claims without fear of contradiction. Finally, by 1876 Pinkerton had, as he told his son Robert, a team of ghostwriters working on his stories.[29]

All this means that Pinkerton and his shadow writers made some extravagant and mythical claims, invented dialogue, and were shaky on points of detail. It did not mean, however, that Pinkerton was untrue to his message. That message was egotistic, hyperbolic, and commercial. It was also anti-labor and anti-communist. The Molly Maguires affair would give Pinkerton the perfect opportunity to develop that message.

In the fall of 1875, the anthracite coal-mining region of eastern Pennsylvania was in the last throes of a deadly struggle between the Molly Maguires, a secret labor organization composed of Irish Americans, and their Protestant managers and employers. Secretive, whispering men purporting to represent the "Mollies" were issuing death threats in the time-honored manner of the freedom fighters in Ireland. But so were their opponents, who organized themselves vigilante-style and issued a blacklist of 374 persons allegedly involved in Molly crimes.[30]

Still, when the O'Donnell family went to bed in their home in Wiggins Patch on the evening of Thursday, 9 December, they could have had no inkling of the tragedy that was about to befall them. It happened as a result of the unproven transgressions of Charles O'Donnell, who had remained loyal to the workingmen's cause. As the winter sunshine began to pierce the industrial gloom the next morning, it revealed a scene of heartrending carnage. Several members of the family lay beaten and wounded. The masked gang responsible had pumped fifteen bullets into Charles O'Donnell's head, and had also shot dead his pregnant sister, Ellen, as she descended the stairs.

Who shot Charles O'Donnell and why? It suited the coal barons to maintain that this was a typical Mollies execution, and they won the day when the Mollies' leaders were arrested, convicted of a variety of crimes, and hung. Yet suspicion remained that episodes like this were the work of James McParlan, a Pinkerton detective who had been hired by the mine owners to infiltrate the Mollies. McParlan extracted secrets from the Mollies by drinking them into a state of indiscretion. But he may also have been acting as an agent provocateur, or even as a plotter of assassinations.[31]

This is a murky and uncertain story, but what is beyond doubt is that the Pinkerton Agency entered the fray against the Mollies not with a view to fighting crime but in order to make money. According to Allan Pinkerton, the mine owners approached him in desperation and pleaded with him to help save their industry from "a noxious weed which has been transplanted from its native soil—that of Ireland—to the United States." However, in retrospect it is clear that Pinkerton made the first approach, in the hope that the new work would extricate his agency from its financial problems.[32]

But there is more to the story than this. It would appear that Pinkerton had, by this time, become an ideologue. In the wake of the Paris Commune of 1871 and of its bloody repression, the time was ripe for America's first Red Scare. Charles Loring Brace capitalized on the events in France, claiming in his book *Dangerous Classes of New York* (1872) that the "prolétaires" of that city had created some of the most violent districts in the world—a flight of hyperbole that set the tone for decades of scaremongering about the allegedly violent Left.[33] The 1870s witnessed not only the Mollies episode but the railroad strikes of 1877, bloodily repressed by federal troops. Pinkerton's book *Strikers, Communists, Tramps and Detectives* (1878) therefore sowed a seed in fertile ground when its author declared: "Every trades-union has for its vital principle, whatever is professed, the concentration of brute force to gain certain ends. Then the deadly spirit of Communism steals in and further embitters the working man against that from which his very livelihood is secured; and gradually makes him an enemy of all law, order and good society." Anticipating America's future missionary role, Pinkerton observed that the problem would be found "the world over." Composed of "a class of human hyenas," the Karl Marx–inspired Communist International would introduce violent, sex-crazed, drunken debauchery to America. He painted a stark picture of "a swift and far-reaching peril" within the United States. The danger was unprecedented in American history, and in being sudden and unanticipated it would be worse than the Civil War. The invisibility of the threat only made it more dangerous: "It was everywhere; it was nowhere."[34]

This method of portraying Menace as a justification for counter-intelligence expenditure established a formula for future scares. Yet, Pinkerton's propaganda never did sweep all before it. For example, his feud with the James brothers was in one sense a public relations disaster. Jesse and Frank were pathological murderers who would shoot at anyone who got in their way: on 26 September 1872, to cite an infamous example, they and a confederate robbed the Kansas City fair on horseback, getting away with less than a thousand dollars but not before shooting wildly and maiming a little girl. But the James brothers were venerated, if not as proto-revolutionaries, then at least as social bandits. An adoring section of the press had shrouded them in a Robin Hood–style myth (at least one half of the comparison is valid—they did rob the rich, even if they did not give to the poor). The *Kansas City Times* called the raid on the fair "so diabolically daring and so utterly in contempt of fear that we are bound to admire it and revere its perpetrators," perpetrators who seemed to have "come to us from stories Odenwald, with the halo of medieval chivalry upon their garments."[35]

Allan Pinkerton may have pursued the James brothers, but he could not compete with the James myth. He encouraged, and his son William possibly organized, the January 1875 vigilante-style attack on the James home, a small log cabin in Clay County, Kansas. The raiders threw a flare-bomb through the cabin window. The preparatory intelligence work had been poor, and the outlaws were not there. However, inside were Frank and Jesse's mother, Zerelda, and two small children. The explosion killed eight-year-old Archie, half-brother to Frank and Jesse, and took off Zerelda's arm. Although the PNDA chief's sons Robert and William denied they had been physically present at the time of the attack, Jesse now swore he would assassinate Allan Pinkerton. As things turned out, the bounty hunter Robert Ford got to Jesse first, shooting him in the back as he hung a picture in 1882. But in the meantime, numerous editorial writers had done Jesse's work for him, assassinating what Allan Pinkerton by now valued most of all—his reputation.[36]

The James affair tarnished the Pinkerton image but was not necessarily bad for business. Allan Pinkerton's law and order stance made him friends in an era when Americans were unable to overcome their anti-statism and set up a federal detective force—while Congress had in 1871 appropriated money to enable the Justice Department to hire detectives, the formation of the FBI lay decades in the future. Considerable sentiment, therefore, still favored private detection. Availing itself of that sentiment, in 1882 and 1885 the PNDA successfully fought enactment of "spy" laws by the New York State legislature that would have restricted the operations of its detectives—the young state legislator Theodore Roosevelt was one of those who helped kill the bills.[37]

However, opinion changed in the wake of the Homestead lockout and gunfight of 1892. In that year, Andrew Carnegie decided to put an end to unionism in his steel mills, and the conflict centered on his state-of-the-art steelworks at Homestead, just down the Ohio River from Pittsburgh. Carnegie (like Allan Pinkerton) was on record as approving of labor unions, so, to avoid opprobrium and accusations of hypocrisy, he went fishing in Scotland, leaving his deputy H. C. Frick in charge. The workers now occupied the plant from which they had been excluded, and Frick engaged the PNDA. The sheriff of Allegheny County cautiously refrained from deputizing the Pinkertons, but three hundred of them, armed with rifles, approached the steelworks by river barge. The workers were waiting for them, beating the Pinkerton men off after a battle that resulted in several deaths. Ultimately, the corporation won the labor dispute with the aid of the state militia, and steel remained unorganized until the formation of the United Steelworkers in the 1930s. But the Pinkerton men lost the propaganda war. Several congressional investigations ensued into what was one of the greatest political scandals in American history. The PNDA, founded by a man who considered himself to be a folk hero, went down in folk infamy. As summed up in the words of a popular song:

> God help them tonight in the hour of their affliction
> Pray for him who they'll ne'er meet again
> Hear the poor orphans tell their sad story
> Father was killed by the Pinkerton men.[38]

The Pinkerton men at Homestead were really armed guards rather than detectives, but public opinion was not impressed by such semantic distinctions. The mud stuck, and the agency founded by Allan Pinkerton may be said to have contributed to an anti-mystique of secret intelligence. The PNDA intensified American fears concerning abuse of power, excessive secrecy, sociopolitical partisanship by the powers that be, attempts to deceive and manipulate the general public, and, especially, any secret malpractices directed at U.S. citizens.

Allan Pinkerton's agency never recovered from Homestead. Yet, Pinkerton and his definition of the role and character of the undercover operator lived on, having a formative influence on the history of American espionage. Adulatory biographies appeared at regular intervals. For example, in 1999 a CIA in-house journal presented him as a politically correct secret service chief who had hired black spies during the Civil War.[39] That was true enough, and Pinkerton hired women, too. There were, then, just enough verifiable and admirable facts behind the Allan Pinkerton story to enshrine the memory of the man who lit the everlasting flame of American secret service.

CHAPTER 4

Did Wilkie Crush the Montreal Spy Ring?

When two American officers testified to Congress that Spain had conspired to blow up the U.S. battleship *Maine,* the Spanish naval attaché Ramon de Carranza challenged each of them to a duel. An aristocrat and a patriotic firebrand, Carranza despised the profession to which the outbreak of war consigned him shortly thereafter. The young lieutenant longed for a ship to command and was unhappy when the War of 1898 placed upon him the duty of espionage against the United States. Yet, in spite of his loathing for this task, he did perform it diligently and, it could be argued, quite effectively.[1]

Carranza's spy ring thus gave the U.S. Secret Service an opportunity to expand into the field of counterespionage. Although some historians have questioned the seriousness of the Spanish spy menace, the Secret Service's expansion in response to it was real enough, and from 1898 on America has had a constantly proliferating civilian intelligence bureaucracy. The struggle between Spanish spy and American counterspy ushered in some other identifiably modern intelligence practices, too: ethnic/religious bias in the identification of surveillance targets, disinformation about enemy activities, American-British-Canadian clandestine cooperation, and not a little hyperbole and panic in the face of an alleged foreign menace. The war was short, and the scale of intelligence operations and associated propaganda relatively limited, but, by the time peace arrived, the transition from the era of private Pinkertonism to the era of public espionage was under way.

◆ ◆ ◆ ◆

The ultimate fate of Carranza's spy network is open to debate, but its initial potency must have seemed considerable. Spain in 1898 hoped for help from Catholic and monarchist Europe. This expectation of Catholic sympathy and aid may have accounted for its choice of Montreal, in French Canada, as Carranza's center for intrigue. As a neutral British dominion, Canada seemed a safe haven. Montreal had the additional advantages of housing a Spanish consulate general led by Eusebio Bonilla Martel, of being the hub of Canada's railroad system, of being the headquarters of several major corporations, and of having proximity to the strategic sea route from the Atlantic Ocean to the Great Lakes—along which U.S. naval units steamed.[2]

Some of the reports on Spanish espionage were exaggerated. Improbable rumors that Spanish agents were about to raise the holy banner among the Catholic masses of North America jostled for position with unsubstantiated stories about Iberian plans to sabotage installations and poison troops in the United States. But there was firmer proof of other undercover operations. Pro-Spanish elements operated in cities like New Orleans, Mobile, Key West, and Tampa. A member of the Cuban revolutionary junta reported at length to the Secret Service about the extent of Spanish activity in New Orleans. The report, sent via a U.S. customs official on 8 June 1898, intimated that Franco-Iberian sentiment and activity existed in New Orleans; that money had been collected before the outbreak of hostilities to furnish Spain with a gunboat; that the reactionary Spanish Society included several former army officers; and that resources were being sent to Spanish forces through the coastal towns of Mexico.[3]

The Secret Service obtained proof of another danger to U.S. national security when it began to intercept letters bearing suspicious addresses. One of these, from Agnes Harrison of Santa Cruz, was posted to Spanish premier Praxedes Sagastes the day after Congress authorized war and described the coastal defenses of San Francisco and how they could be circumvented. Fears of a Spanish naval bombardment took hold. As one Secret Service agent put it, "The strength of the Spanish fleet was so magnified in the popular imagination that timid folk, living in seaboard cities, trembled for their safety. . . . The air was rife with rumors of plots and spies." Such fears were allayed fully only on 10 May, when Admiral William T. Sampson's fleet blockaded Santiago de Cuba, immobilizing the Spanish fleet as a prelude to its destruction. In April,

Spain's fleet of armored cruisers posed a potential threat to Eastern Seaboard towns. The idea that Spanish shells might rain on American civilians and their property was not entirely speculative, for Segismundo Bermejo, minister of the Spanish Admiralty, had ordered the destruction of naval bases along the American coast.[4]

Luis Polo y Bernabé, the Spanish ambassador in Washington, left for Canada four days before the declaration of war on 25 April. It is not surprising that the Secret Service saw through Bernabé's advertised intention of traveling directly on to Spain. Secret Service operatives, two of them in an open manner and another pair unknown to Bernabé, supervised the ex-minister's removal to Canada.[5]

Exactly a month passed between the arrival of the leading figures in the Spanish party in Canada and their departure for home. The Iberian officials, with the assistance of a Canadian detective agency, used the intervening time to establish an information bureau initially located in Toronto. Carranza, who had accompanied Bernabé to Canada in April, justly complained that his job in running the bureau had been made unnecessarily difficult by the indiscretions of his superiors. When Bernabé moved his entourage and the information bureau from Toronto to the Windsor Hotel in Montreal, the overconspicuous nature of his operations was shown in the identity of other guests at that establishment. Representatives of various Spanish political factions, secret service agents, and journalists who mercilessly pursued and identified everyone else jostled shoulders with Spanish spies on the back stairs.[6]

When Bernabé and his party finally sailed for Liverpool on 21 May, Carranza and his aides pretended to accompany them. At various ports along the St. Lawrence, the spies discreetly left the ship and traveled back to Montreal, where Carranza had rented a house on Tupper Street. This attempt at subterfuge was fully described in the Canadian press, from whose columns it also appears that a secret service agent—operating under deepest cover with the nom de plume Tracer—was a witness to the proceedings.[7]

As these circumstances indicate, Carranza was up against not just clumsiness on his own side but also a substantial if sometimes equally ponderous U.S. counterintelligence effort. The U.S. Secret Service had experienced mixed fortunes since its establishment in Lincoln's last cabinet meeting. In recent years, it had been criticized for hiring agents on the patronage system. Leaders of the service had the task of combating counterfeiting, and had been trying to revive the agency's role in guarding the president from attack. But the latter attempt came in for criticism because it involved the use of unvouchered funds in a practice that extended the powers of the Secret Service without legislative approval. Congress was touchy on this point, and had only recently reprimanded the White House for using secret agents in the conspiracy to acquire Hawaii at the behest of U.S. business interests. Then, just before the Spanish War, the competence of the Secret Service came under scrutiny when a counterfeiting operation on a huge scale forced, for the first time, the recall of an entire issue of U.S. currency. Blamed for all this, Secret Service Chief William P. Hazen was reduced to the rank of operative.[8]

Thus, when John E. Wilkie took over, America was ready for a new broom. The climate was conducive to the continuation of old practices—Wilkie blithely proceeded with the use of unvouchered funds—as well as for reform, and the introduction of new initiatives. Though Wilkie had worked as a special crime reporter in Chicago, he did not have extensive experience in espionage or detective work. What commended him to his superiors in a business-oriented administration was his essential soundness. He had worked as a city editor on the *Chicago Tribune* and had gained foreign experience by engaging in banking and steamship business in London. This made him the natural consort and choice of his friend Frank A. Vanderlip, assistant secretary at the United States Treasury Department, which had oversight of the Secret Service. When the sinking of the *Maine* in February 1898 made war seem certain, Wilkie appealed to the secretary of the treasury, Chicago banker Lyman J. Gage, for funds to set up a special counterespionage force within the Secret Service. Gage sent him in company with Vanderlip to see President McKinley, who approved special funds and then a few weeks later increased them tenfold. With this financial backing, Wilkie introduced reforms reminiscent of the strictures of Allan Pinkerton, demanding probity and meticulous reporting procedures from his agents. His "auxiliary" or counterespionage force was, he insisted, composed of the cream of available talent—described by his son Don as "shadow men, linguists, banker types, business types." He bragged of having fifty applicants for every available post. Don later revealed that 90 percent had been disqualified because they could not speak Spanish, so the pool of available talent was not really immense. Yet, patronage had been dealt a blow, and the Secret Service could now be represented as being run in a business-like manner.[9]

Impeded though he was by "the most extraordinary vigilance" exercised by Wilkie's men, Carranza tried to obtain information that would be of use to Spanish naval officers and generals. One of his gambits was to dispatch secret agents to gain information about coastal defense and naval strategy. The first of Carranza's spies to be caught was a naturalized English immigrant, George Downing. Downing had been a petty officer on the *Brooklyn,* the navy cruiser that was later instrumental in the destruction of the Spanish fleet at Santiago. He undertook to obtain information of a strategic nature from the Navy Department and from government navy yards, but Carranza made the mistake of briefing Downing in a hotel room of typical nineteenth-century design. It formed part of a set of connecting rooms that could be rented individually or as a suite. On this occasion Carranza occupied just one of the rooms, with the door leading to the other chamber locked but not soundproof. On the other side of the door, an American agent was making notes, a summary of which soon reached Wilkie. On 7 May, Downing was arrested in Washington in the act of mailing a letter about navy movements. Two days later, he was found hanging from the bars of his cell window. Wilkie maintained that the remorseful traitor had committed suicide. Carranza conceded that Downing, one of his "two best spies," might have hanged himself, adding, "or else they did it for him."[10]

Carranza was a naval lieutenant, but his brief included army intelligence. In pursuit of information that would assist Spanish commanders in the field, he employed further secret agents with special functions. He tried to engage men who would enlist in Tampa and San Francisco with the object of joining American land forces in Cuba and the Philippines, learning about U.S. military dispositions, crossing the lines to the Spanish side, and telling all. Needing men with military experience, Carranza appealed to a Canadian detective agency, which in turn referred him to one Frank Arthur Mellor.

A native of Kingston, Ontario, Mellor was a former artilleryman who knew which soldiers would be open to offers. A bigamist and a reckless pugilist (one of his wives said he would have taken on heavyweight champion Robert Fitzsimmons), he knew how to exploit other men's weaknesses. He soon got two members of the Kingston battery drunk and bribed them to spy for Spain. One of them "whose name," said Wilkie, "might have been Atkins," was to go to San Francisco and enlist for the Philippines. But Atkins sobered up and decided "he'd be blowed if he'd fight against White men for any . . . foreigner." Pausing only to get drunk again, Atkins staggered into the consul's office in Kingston on 11 May, where he made a full statement. Learning that he had been double-crossed, Mellor took prompt action. He beat up Atkins and frightened him into leaving for Liverpool. But Mellor's brutal action came too late. When details of Atkins's confession reached Wilkie via the Department of State, they compromised Mellor.[11]

In addition to recruiting others for spy work, Mellor himself had attempted to enlist at Tampa in the American forces destined for Cuba. He used the identity of a Montreal barman who had promised silence and cooperation in exchange for a woman provided by Mellor. The army refused to accept Mellor, so he tried to justify his pay by sending strategic information to Carranza. Wilkie's suspicions had already been aroused by Atkins's story, and Secret Service men were watching Mellor in Florida, waiting only for proof before arresting the suspect. At this point, help arrived from what an American consular official called the "Secret Service of the Dominion of Canada," no doubt a euphemism for British intelligence, as Canada had no service of its own. This organism provided Wilkie's men, via diplomatic channels, with the current alibis and letter box numbers of Mellor's superiors in Canada. Armed with this information, the U.S. postal authorities intercepted a telegram Mellor sent to Carranza on 24 May, and although the coded and pseudonymous message could not have been used in court without revealing details of Canadian cooperation, Mellor was at last placed in custody.[12]

Proof of the case against Mellor was now sought with further Canadian help, this time unofficial. An estate agent enabled American spies to enter Carranza's house at 42 Tupper Street, Montreal, on 27 May while the Iberian master spy was at breakfast. The spies seized a letter allegedly written by Carranza to his cousin, Adm. J. B. Ymay. According to Wilkie and Ralph D. Redfern, a U.S. Secret Service agent who claimed the credit for having stolen the document, the U.S. version of the "Carranza letter" was genuine and compromised Mellor by referring to the date of his arrest. Ultimately, however, Mellor was neither convicted nor released. On 12 August 1898, ten days after the protocol of peace, he became another victim of the prison system, dying of typhoid at Fort McPherson.[13]

When the British government received a copy of Carranza's letter, it found itself confronted with an evidential and diplomatic problem. According to Wilkie, an American agent stole the Carranza letter, having entered the spy's Tupper Street house on the pretext of wishing to rent it. The letter, seals unbroken, was entrusted to an American railroad engineer, who took it as far as Vermont, then mailed it to Wilkie in Washington. On receiving the letter, Wilkie ordered his Montreal agent to disappear, "to make it absolutely certain that his identity should not be discovered," waited a week (no explanation given), then made public a translation of the text (a full version appeared in the *New York Herald* on 5 June) and gave the State Department a photographic reproduction to show to the British ambassador in Washington. But Carranza claimed that parts of the letter had been forged and other sections badly translated—perhaps Wilkie had sought to hasten the end of Carranza's spy ring by committing the crime of secret forgery, as well as that of publicly admitted theft.[14]

Since the matter had been made public, the British government was obliged to respond. The British ambassador in Washington, the increasingly popular and successful Sir Julian Pauncefote, communicated the contents of the letter as published to Joseph Chamberlain, Britain's secretary of state for the colonies and the cabinet member responsible for Canada. Chamberlain had married the only daughter of W. C. Endicott, secretary of war in Cleveland's first administration (the engagement was kept secret during the controversial campaign of 1888), and the historian A. E. Campbell has remarked that Anglo-American cooperation was, at the end of the nineteenth century, "an axiom of British policy."[15] Nevertheless, American truculence in recent disputes over British interests meant that London was by no means certain to follow the wishes of Washington.

Chamberlain telegraphed the governor general of Canada, Lord Aberdeen, with a decision that favored the United States in principle: "The Law Officers of the Crown advise that Carranza should be requested to leave British territory, if the facts are as stated." Britain and

America were about to close ranks in favor of Anglo-Saxon (as opposed to Latin) imperialism. Sir Wilfrid Laurier, the Canadian premier, was obliged to explain to Chamberlain, using Aberdeen as an intermediary, exactly how legal proceedings constituted an obstacle to the immediate departure of Carranza. Joseph Kellert, chief of the Metropolitan Detective Agency, Montreal, whom the Spaniard had accused of stealing the letter, sued Carranza and his colleague Juan Du Bosc for damages stemming from false arrest and obtained against them a writ that, under the laws of the province of Quebec, prevented potential debtors from absconding; Du Bosc, in turn, threatened to sue the British government; later, several parties concerned with the Tupper Street theft, including Kellert himself, agreed that the Canadian private detective, and not a Secret Service agent, had organized the break-in.[16]

Chamberlain, though forceful in his request for Carranza's deportation, asked that the facts be verified. In a successful attempt to allay Britain's doubts, Secretary of State William R. Day intervened. He arranged for Pauncefote to call on Wilkie to inspect the original Carranza letter. Pauncefote stated that the purpose of this visit was "to establish the fact whether any interpolation had been made." The British ambassador took with him not a forgery expert but Calderon Carlisle, legal adviser to the British embassy and a Spanish scholar. Carlisle confirmed that the Spanish text put before him had been correctly translated by the Americans. To Pauncefote it was "manifest" that "there was no erasure or interpolation whatever in the letter."[17]

In the absence of any alien act in force in Canada, and in light of the seeming inapplicability of either common law or imperial legislation, Aberdeen turned for advice to the Foreign Office in London. Legal experts pointed out that the royal prerogative could be invoked. Thus armed, the British prime minister and foreign secretary, Lord Salisbury, authorized his ambassador in Madrid to inform the Duke of Tetuan, the Spanish minister for foreign affairs, that Carranza's withdrawal was to be requested. The British ambassador, Sir Henry Drummond Wolff, was instructed to say that Her Majesty's government looked "for the cooperation of the Spanish government . . . feeling that Carranza's proceedings were unknown to his superior officers in Madrid," thus plainly inviting the Spanish government to make the usual disavowal of a spy caught in the act. But Tetuan refused to take the bait. He said he believed Carranza's claim that the letter as published was a counterfeit.

Stubbornly, the Duke raised a further question. If the British believed the letter to be genuine, why did they demand the recall not just of Carranza but of Captain Juan Du Bosc as well? Du Bosc, formerly chief attaché at the Spanish embassy in Washington, had stayed on with Carranza in Montreal but was not compromised by the published version of the stolen letter.[18]

Du Bosc assured Tetuan that Carranza was as innocent of espionage as he, but Chamberlain betrayed the leanings of the British government when he told Aberdeen that the lieutenant's expulsion was the only alternative to the "adoption of most painful measures." The pro-Washington partisanship of Salisbury's Foreign Office stood out so starkly against the background of recent Anglo-American discord that it attracted adverse comment. Spanish newspapers complained about the Canadian expulsions. They averred that Englishmen were sending news to the United States from all parts of Spain. The Spanish press also pointed out that the former U.S. consul in Cadiz was now in Gibraltar, the British rock that gave so fine a view of Spanish fleet movements in the straits below, and was making regular telegraphic reports to his superiors at home. According to Spanish journalists, it was unjust to expel Carranza from Montreal while leaving the American consul in Gibraltar free to pursue these activities. In Westminster itself, the expulsion request was regarded as legally anomalous. The attorney general had to deny, in answer to a parliamentary question, that expelled Spanish officials would be entitled to sue for damages. When Laurier succumbed to pressure and demanded the departure of Du Bosc as well as of Carranza, the chief attaché agreed to leave, but he retained the right to take legal action against the British government.[19]

A year passed without any new revelation about the Carranza letter. Then, in the columns of the *Montreal Star*, George F. Bell made a confession. A twenty-three-year-old English immigrant to Canada, Bell claimed that it was he who had broken into 42 Tupper Street and delivered the Carranza letter to Wilkie. Using stolen Spanish stationery, Wilkie had employed an expert to forge a new letter. Bell had kept quiet for a year for fear of prosecution for theft, but now he was speaking out because Wilkie had paid him only $50 instead of a promised $1,000 plus expenses. The *Star* of 8 July 1899 published the full text of both "Carranza letters," one called "George F. Bell's version" and the other "the Washington version." In a full discussion of the Tupper Street theft, the

Star tended to give credence to Bell, in spite of the Englishman's status as an alleged if unconvicted counterfeiter, and of his admission that he had offered his services to Spain as a double agent. The *Star* was inclined to accept Bell's version of the Carranza letter because it seemed to be confirmed in a textually exact manner by Carranza's original allegations concerning interpolation. The *Star* story was reprinted by the *Boston Evening Transcript,* which two days later carried a refutation by Ralph Redfern, who was still working for the Secret Service in Boston. Redfern insisted that it was he who had stolen the Carranza letter, and that the original and genuine document was still on file in the Secret Service office in Washington. The *Transcript* of 8 and 10 July 1899 preferred the Redfern story and "the Washington version," but, whether by accident or design, the original letter disappeared from the files of the Secret Service, so neither side of the story can be verified.[20]

Soon after the event, Wilkie described the affair of the Carranza letter as "one of the sensations of the war." He concluded his account of the role of the Secret Service by observing of Carranza: "With his removal from the field of activity, the Spanish spy system received its death-blow."[21] The case can be made, then, that Wilkie shared not just Allan Pinkerton's Scottish descent but also his taste for intelligence hyperbole. For the Secret Service's role in 1898 was a little less glorious than Wilkie claimed. Spanish spy operations in Montreal did not cease after the "death-blow" of Carranza's departure. Indeed, it is not beyond the bounds of possibility that the demise of the Montreal spy ring was an Iberian deception operation, and the Carranza letter a plant, all designed to create the impression that the culprits had been caught when, in fact, the real espionage was gathering momentum.

Certainly, on 5 and 13 July 1898, a certain "Bonilla," presumed to be Bonilla Martel, the Spanish consul general in Montreal, sent coded messages to Victoria, British Columbia. War Department cryptographers failed to crack the code, which was a new one, but they and Secret Service officials reasoned that the messages probably contained information, forwarded by spies south of the Canadian border and destined for Manila, about U.S. military intentions in the Philippines. Research by historian Graeme Mount into the records of the Spanish foreign affairs ministry in Madrid indicates that Martel, in fact, simply took over the running of the Montreal spy ring. Or had he been in charge all along? From the beginning, Martel had been the conduit for intelligence on American military secrets. Madrid continued throughout the summer of 1898 to send him money for *vigilancias* (spies), and, utilizing Spain's consulates, he operated an active intelligence network throughout Canada, as well as in the West Indies. As late as 5 February 1899, the day before the Senate approved the peace treaty with Spain, the Secret Service was trailing Spanish agents traveling between New York and Montreal. This final commission of the war was undertaken by Secret Service agent Owen Owens, who suffered the indignity of being approached at a critical moment by a *New York Sun* reporter and asked whether he was the Secret Service man who was checking on the Spanish agents.[22]

Whatever the verdict on the crushing or otherwise of the Montreal spy ring, the operations of the Secret Service need to be placed in context. For one thing, they represented only a part of the overall U.S. intelligence effort. Though the Secret Service may have brought about a significant change on the organizational side of civilian U.S. intelligence, it was just one cog in the wartime espionage machine.

On the other hand, though, in spite of its shortcomings the Secret Service was relatively successful compared with other U.S. agencies. American intelligence operations were quite extensive in 1898. U.S. consulates in far-flung locations such as Gibraltar, the Philippines, and Hong Kong reported on Spanish naval movements and other matters. Sometimes these reports went through the Secret Service, but the Office of Naval Intelligence (ONI) also played an important and independent role. Before the outbreak of hostilities, the ONI had devised a war plan. This plan appears to have been implemented: on the instigation of Assistant Secretary of the Navy Theodore Roosevelt, an American fleet attacked and defeated the Spanish squadron in Manila. The objective was to make it possible to use the Philippines as a bargaining chip in an effort to pry Cuba from the grip of Spain. But this ploy needs to be put into perspective in two ways. First, the American military and naval victories worldwide were so comprehensive that no Filipino bargaining chip was necessary. Second, although the ONI claimed credit for the outcome, and although intelligence may inform military strategists, a war plan is not synonymous with secret intelligence.

America had spies in Spain, for example in the main navy town,

Cadiz, and further agents in the naval staging post, the Cape Verde Islands. But their operations were amateurish. For example, one navy secret agent, Edward Breck, traveled around Spain equipped with tell-tale accouterments such as secret pistols and false mustaches. He enjoyed the role, not the function, obtaining no useful information. If he escaped arrest, perhaps it was because the Spanish authorities regarded him as a harmless eccentric. Admiral Pascual Cervera y Topete's well-armored and ordinanced fleet of five cruisers and four destroyers sailed west from the Cape Verde Islands, an evident threat to U.S. shipping in the Straits of Florida and to the Eastern Seaboard, but U.S. naval intelligence promptly lost the fleet. When U.S. intelligence reported its eventual arrival in the Cuban port of Santiago, it was deemed a triumph of detection. But the arrival of a full battle fleet is surely hard to miss, and navy intelligence failed to notice that the Spanish ships were in a poor state of repair, lacked coal, and were no match for the U.S. Navy. If an informed estimate had been made of the relative strengths of the U.S. and Spanish fleets, an earlier attack might have been launched, and the war might have ended even sooner than it did.

The Military Intelligence Division also had its claim to fame in the Spanish War—indeed, the exploits of one of its agents, Lieut. Andrew S. Rowan, inspired that get-through-at-all-costs addition to the English language, "Message to Garcia." Rowan's mission was actually to obtain intelligence *from* Garcia, not take a message *to* him. He landed in Cuba in an open boat on 24 April, two days after the war started. He made his way inland, meeting the revolutionary general Calixto Garcia Iñiguez, who gave him maps and other information to take back to Washington. According to historian G. J. A. O'Toole, American journalists had routinely made this journey: "Contrary to legend, Rowan incurred little personal risk in his famous mission to Garcia."[23]

It is evident that the exploits of the Secret Service were by no means the only intelligence operations in the War of 1898. Equally evident, however, is the fact that no branch of U.S. intelligence outshone Wilkie's agents. Yet, other perspectives must also be introduced. How real was the threat posed by Cervera's fleet and, therefore, by the spy ring that informed its movements? At the outset of the war, Cervera had warned the Spanish minister of the marine that the U.S. Navy had twice the tonnage of its Spanish equivalent, as well as more than double the number of guns. Perhaps thinking of the modern component of his fleet,

Cervera nevertheless said that Spain could conceivably defeat America in a naval battle. But damage would be sustained, and, because of its industrial strength, America would be able to repair its ships more rapidly. The position, then, was grim but not entirely bleak—and it is conceivable that Cervera, fearing he might lose the war and be blamed for it, was exaggerating the superiority of the Americans. Still, the Spanish squadron that berthed in Santiago was in poor shape, with some ships in need of repair and (partly owing to American preemptive buying) all of them short on coal. On 3 July six Spanish ships steamed out of Santiago to confront the blockading U.S. fleet. In a two-hour battle, they were all destroyed. So, the wisdom of hindsight would make it appear that Spain's navy was a phantom threat to U.S. national security. But just because the British were defeated in the Revolution, or the Confederacy in 1865, nobody argues that they never posed a threat in the first place. In spring 1898 the Spanish naval threat was real, and so was the Secret Service's contribution to the disabling of the spy ring that serviced it.[24]

Looking at the Secret Service from yet another perspective: Did this counterintelligence agency achieve its effectiveness at a price? There can be little doubt that its history in the Spanish war is a chapter in the longer story of American nativism, and of infractions against civil liberties. Many Americans in the 1890s were suspicious of Catholics of southern European origin, and the Secret Service wasted time and manpower on wild-goose chases after blameless Spanish or Italian immigrants. One such chase that led to the detention of an innocent man was the pursuit of Edward G. Montesi, who had emigrated to the United States from Italy at the age of fourteen, in 1870. In 1898, he intended to sail on the English steamer *Tartar Prince* to revisit his native land. He was by now an American citizen, with the Stars and Stripes tattooed on his right arm and a box of handkerchiefs embroidered with the Cuban flag in his luggage. Montesi's wife, her maid, and their two daughters were to accompany him as saloon passengers. At midday on 11 June, a crowd of friends gathered on a Brooklyn pier to see the family off.[25]

Shortly before the *Tartar Prince* sailed, Secret Service agent Martin Kastle arrived on board with customs officials and three soldiers. An informant with a grudge against Montesi had alleged that the Italian was a Spanish courier, and Wilkie had sent Kastle on the midnight train from Washington. In order to avoid demonstrations by Montesi's friends or any unfavorable press publicity, Kastle waited for the steamer to sail before acting. He then arrested Montesi without preferring a charge, searched his luggage, read his private correspondence, and eavesdropped on private conversations between the Italian and his wife. Kastle found nothing of an incriminating nature. Nevertheless, he ordered the *Tartar Prince* to drop anchor off Governor's Island and took the entire Montesi family and their luggage ashore. There Kastle met the inevitable reporter from the *New York Sun,* who suggested that the Montesis be put straight back on the steamer and given a warm send-off. Kastle refused. The innocent Montesis missed their boat, only to be released the next day without being charged with any crime.[26]

Considered alongside other episodes of contemporary nativism, this event and other similar actions by the Secret Service were minor. Yet, they were symptomatic of an intolerance that was to characterize U.S. counterintelligence for many years to come.

The hint of hyperbole in Wilkie's claims also helped set a pattern for the future. In publicizing the Secret Service's achievements, its chief was a child of his day as well as an heir to the Pinkertonian tradition. After all, he lived in an era of sensationalism. The yellow press was rampant in the late 1890s, when the great proprietors W. R. Hearst and Joseph Pulitzer fought a circulation war. Lurid headlines distorted the news as a matter of routine. As Lincoln Steffens noted, a murder was a murder, but in the hands of an opportunist reporter two murders could be a crime wave.[27] Press treatment of the sinking of the *Maine* was so extreme in its excoriation of the Spanish authorities (who probably had nothing to do with the disaster) that it can be considered one of the causes of American entry into the war. This was also the era of the muckraker, when investigative journalists sensationally exposed city corruption, business malpractices, and other evils.

Wilkie's public profile did not compare with that of Pinkerton before him or with those of his twentieth-century successors. But he was a recognized figure, a circumstance that set him apart from the spymasters of Europe. Not unusual for an American espionage leader, he privately reveled in cloak and dagger mystique. Don Wilkie recalled the contents of one room in his childhood home on Morgan Avenue,

Washington, D.C., not long after his father became chief of the Secret Service. John Wilkie's second-storey study contained a "collection of criminal relics that would have stirred the envy of Madame Tussaud. . . . Counterfeiting paraphernalia, bogus money, pistols and sinister knives and what not—these souvenirs which fascinated me had all been taken from dangerous criminals by Secret Service men in the performance of their duty."[28] Thus, Wilkie was a credible link in a paradoxical American chain—intelligence practitioners who were afficionadoes of secrecy, yet, at the same time, public leaders.

John Wilkie ensured that the Secret Service would continue, in peacetime, as a significant agency. He received an apparent setback on 6 September 1901, the day that Leon F. Czolgosz shot President McKinley at the trade fair in Buffalo, New York. This assassination took place in spite of a guard of three Secret Service agents backed up by a hundred on-site security officers. But circumstances played into the hands of the durable Wilkie. For one thing, Czolgosz made a perfect villain. Though he was born in America, his foreign-sounding name made him a target for nativist paranoia. As if this were not enough, the feebleminded gunman confessed under interrogation to "anarchism," a creed that—after a wave of terrorist attacks—had for the time being joined "communism" in the lexicon of American revulsion. Czolgosz, then, attracted venom that might otherwise have been directed at the inefficiency of the Secret Service. Moreover, this was the third presidential assassination in thirty-six years—first Lincoln, then Garfield at the hand of Charles Guiteau, and finally McKinley.

Although all thirteen efforts to kill U.S. presidents have been by gunmen, the reflexive reaction in nineteenth- and twentieth-century America was not to legislate against pistols but to support and pay for greater presidential protection. Don Wilkie, in an appeal described by one scholar as "hyperbole," excoriated Congress for not appropriating funds to protect the president. But, in fact, the Secret Service received increasing support during the presidency of Theodore Roosevelt.[29] Not for the last time, success had rewarded failure.

Yet, Congress was aware of the expansionist tendencies of the Secret Service. Some of its members wanted the service to concentrate on its anti-counterfeiting work, and regarded its presidential work and budgetary practices with suspicion. Each month, Wilkie paid the presidential guard without congressional authorization, and House appropriations subcommittee clerk James C. Courts recalled that Wilkie "was compelled each month to make a false certificate." There were strong fears concerning the potential development of a federal spy service and police state. Some of the Secret Service's activities continued to have implications for civil liberties—it compiled lists of "anarchists" in cities the president proposed to visit and, with the Post Office, set up a mail surveillance operation. Some congressmen feared that Wilkie was building up an intelligence empire. In 1904, the *Chicago Inter-Ocean* anticipated later worries about an American police state, reporting that Wilkie had authorized investigations of cabinet members and members of Congress: he appeared to be "not particular about drawing the line between law makers and law breakers."[30]

As these suspicions confirm, John Wilkie conformed to the stereotype of the secret service booster. He established espionage bureaucracy within the federal domain, and he was a bridge between the private and public intelligence traditions. On the other hand, his counterespionage achievements were real as well as rhetorical. Furthermore, the brevity of the war with Spain limited his opportunities for expansionist hyperbole. If Wilkie could claim paternity of some of the sensationalist agencies of the twentieth century, he was also father to their quieter sibling, U-1. This virtually unheard-of agency is the subject of the next chapter.

CHAPTER 5

U-1
The Agency Nobody Knew

Two emblematic secret intelligence agencies emerged in the opening decades of the twentieth century. The first of these was the Bureau of Information. Formed in 1908, it was later dubbed and is now commonly known as the FBI. The second was an agency without a name. Formed in 1915, it flourished briefly and dominated the intelligence scene before the FBI finally made its mark. Insiders referred to it simply as U-1.

U-1 was so obscure and so secretive that it did not even have to try to suppress the news of its existence. Nobody knew about it, so nobody asked questions. It was elitist and snobbish, intellectual and quiet. It was also in some ways effective, and an emblem of how American secret intelligence might be organized in the future. Yet, ominously for the quieter mode of espionage, U-1 was dissolved in 1927.

The appellation U-1 stems from the terminology introduced following World War I, when the government in Washington attempted to rationalize the ad hoc intelligence arrangements that had sprung up during the fighting. According to the then prevailing system, American intelligence arose from many sources, as if by capillary action, to one central pool in the Department of State, known from 1919 as U-1. In their own methods of organization, the Office of Naval Intelligence (ONI, founded in 1882) and the Military Intelligence Division (MID, 1885) by now reflected the regional subdivisions of the Department of State. For its part, the Department of State made the functional intelligence subdivisions of the office of the undersecretary of state conform to military enumeration. "U" derived from the first letter of the word "undersecretary." According to the arrangement, U-3 corresponded to M.I.3. "M.I." was the acronym for Military Intelligence, and U-3 dealt with counterintelligence, just like M.I.3. Information from all intelligence services flowed into U-2, U-3, U-4, and so on. There were usually about six subdivisions; the numbers kept changing according to the administrative vagaries and security requirements of the day. These branches then conveyed information or distillations of it to U-1. This central intelligence organism evaluated and disseminated information and transmitted it to the secretary of state.

The origin of the agency without a name may be traced to the year 1915, the year when the administration of President Woodrow Wilson decided that the State Department would take a more active role in intelligence matters. Intelligence interacted with delicate diplomatic problems both in the period of American neutrality and after the entry of the United States into World War I in 1917. This invited a more proactive policy by the State Department, but it also created problems. Notably, the U.S. government had to tread the fragile line between America's anti-imperialist principles and its support for imperialist European partners, notably Great Britain.

This problem helps explain the delay in setting up the organism later known, if only to the privileged few, as U-1. Elected on a minority vote in 1912, Wilson had placated the radical wing in the Democratic Party by appointing William Jennings Bryan secretary of state. Bryan was a fierce critic of British imperialism—indeed, he had written a booklet, *British Rule in India*, that denounced it as "arbitrary and despotic."[1] He was, furthermore, an opponent of any drift away from the policy of neutrality proclaimed by the Wilson administration upon the outbreak of war in 1914. Bryan was a democratic, Prairie pacifist who was congenitally distrustful of what he deemed elitist, Eastern conspiracy. He opposed war preparations, and it was not even remotely possible that he would have approved the formation, within his own department, of a secret intelligence bureau.

But Bryan's days as secretary of state were numbered. On 7 May 1915, a German U-boat sank the British passenger ship *Lusitania*, killing 128 Americans aboard. President Wilson protested this act. Upset by the belligerency of Wilson's language in addressing the Germans and perhaps foreseeing America's entry into the European bloodbath, Bryan resigned as secretary of state. The way was now open for war preparations, and for the development of secret intelligence resources.

The new secretary was Robert Lansing. He had previously occupied the number two post in the department, that of counselor. Both Lansing and the president took an interest in intelligence matters, but, possibly because they saw the wisdom of not being too closely involved, they entrusted the development of the new intelligence system to a person at one remove. This was the new counselor in the Department of State, Frank L. Polk. A remote kinsman of President James K. Polk, who had saturated Mexico with spies in 1845 as a prelude to war, Frank Polk had attended the exclusive private school Groton before graduating from Yale and studying law at Columbia. In the Spanish-American War, he served as a captain with the New York National Guard and then, back in civilian life, alternated between building up his law practice and fighting the corrupt Tammany Hall political machine in New York City. Appointed to the position that put him second in command at the State Department, he handled a wide variety of issues, ranging from salt taxes to discrimination against Asians.[2]

As counselor, Polk had a senior legal status and advised the government on issues arising from America's neutral status in the war. But as America became more deeply involved and seemed likely to join in hostilities, this man of wide-ranging talents took on an important new responsibility—he coordinated the activities of those agencies that gathered intelligence data abroad. He also established liaison with the British and French embassies in matters of counterintelligence, and he oversaw the work of domestic intelligence services. Polk's diary shows that this work was under way prior to America's entry into the war. On 16 June 1916 he wrote, "Saw [Secretary of the Treasury William Gibbs] McAdoo re Secret Service." Just as revealing of his desire to establish a proper financial footing for counterintelligence was his 3 March 1917 entry, just a month before the U.S. declaration of war: "Went to Congress re money for Secret Service." These entries are a clear indication of State Department coordination at work.[3]

Polk's dedication to intelligence is reflected in the way in which he continued his efforts after the war's end. Peace had already blossomed by the time he set up the "American Black Chamber," a unit charged with the responsibility for breaking the codes of foreign powers and reading their secret messages. Polk also established the "foreign-intelligence section" within the State Department, which would continue in peacetime the clandestine activities his office had conducted during the war. By this time, Congress had agreed to create for him (in 1919) the special post of undersecretary of state, the initiative that gave rise to the designation "U-1."

◆ ◆ ◆ ◆

Once America had entered the war in April 1917, the intelligence effort intensified. In May, Gordon Auchincloss was appointed assistant counselor to help Polk coordinate secret activities. Like Polk, Auchincloss had attended Groton and Yale. He even belonged to the same New York clubs, the Links and Piping Rock. The intimate and elitist nature of the World War I intelligence group may be illustrated further. Auchincloss had the additional link of being married to the daughter of Colonel Edward M. House, close personal adviser to President Wilson (Princeton '79). Secretary of the Treasury McAdoo's department contained the Secret Service. McAdoo, a graduate of the University of Tennessee, married Eleanor Randolph Wilson, the president's daughter. Secretary of State Lansing (Amherst '86) was not quite Ivy League, but in 1890 he had made a similarly advantageous marriage, to the daughter of John W. Foster, who subsequently served as secretary of state. Meantime, Allen W. Dulles (Princeton '14) embarked in World War I on a diplomatic career in Vienna and Berne, where he used his official status as cover for secret operations. Allen Dulles was Foster's grandson, his mother being Mrs. Lansing's sister. He became director of the CIA in the 1950s, when his brother John Foster Dulles also served as secretary of state.

The elitist composition of this close-knit group was in significant ways a liability to the U.S. intelligence effort. Although Ivy League schools provided a good education, they represented only a limited segment of the talent available to the government. Their dominance imposed a stranglehold not just on opportunity but also on excellence. U-1 was not a mirror held up to the face of American society. It was arguably ill equipped to represent fully the international goals of a country that was becoming more cosmopolitan as an influx of immigrants contributed increasing ethnic, racial, and religious diversity. There was a certain arrogance about the group that precluded any thoughts of congressional oversight. Article II, Section 2, Clause 2 of the U.S. Constitution gave the Senate the right to confirm or not to confirm the presidential selection for secretary of state, and Polk did go cap in hand to Congress when he needed appropriations for the Secret Service, but there is little evidence of systematic consultation with the legislative branch of government.

Anglophilia was a close cousin to the blue-blooded snobbery of the day, and the personnel of U-1 were affected by it. A significant example is their relationship with Sir William Wiseman. After an indifferent career in business, Wiseman was put in charge of British intelligence in the United States in December 1915. Wiseman's deputy in Washington was Norman Thwaites, who like Wiseman had been wounded in France, and had the advantages of connections in American newspapers and high society, and of being friendly with Frank Polk. Wiseman soon acquired friends among those Americans who were ready to be impressed by a Cambridge University boxing blue who was heir to a baronetcy stretching back to 1628. The English spy encouraged members of the House to regard him as an avuncular figure, and allowed Auchincloss to use his London tailor.[4]

The human frailties of the people in U-1 cost America in a number of ways. Not least, the unrepresentative clique showed a sympathy with imperialism that was not only at variance with U.S. ideals but also unwise in that it provoked deep and lasting bitterness in India, Germany, and elsewhere. The Wilson administration in public proclaimed its sympathy with the principles of self-determination and open diplomacy. In secret, however, it plotted with the British to prop up the empires of Allied powers while working for the demise of the German, Austrian, and Turkish empires. The assumption that such double-dealing would remain undetected was unwise, a miscalculation that left America vulnerable to the charge of hypocrisy.

At a meeting in San Francisco on 1 November 1913, a group of Indian revolutionaries formed the Ghadr (sometimes spelled Gadar) Party. Its aim was to topple the British Raj and replace it with Indian home rule. The outbreak of war created an opportunity for the Ghadr. It was able to secure German support for its revolutionary activities. Notably, it organized arms shipments to insurrectionary groups in India. The Indian branch of the British secret service sent a top agent to North America to deal with this: Robert Nathan established his base in

Vancouver in May 1916. Of course, the activities of the Ghadr in the United States could be regarded as infractions of American neutrality. But then, so could the activities of Poles, Czechs, and others who worked for the overthrow of the Austrian Empire in Central Europe.

The U.S. intelligence establishment simply chose sides. Possibly there was a racial motive—Indians were colored, Poles were not, and prejudice is known to have infected the Wilson administration right up to the person of the president himself. Whether or not racism was a factor, U-1 and its agents certainly felt comfortable cooperating with the British. American agents operated hand in glove with Wiseman, Nathan, and other British agents in tracking the Ghadr and other Indian nationalists. Once America was engaged in the war and public opinion was suitably inflamed, the Ghadr leaders were arrested and given a show trial in San Francisco. That was only to be expected. But what showed American neutrality to have been a sham was what emerged so clearly before and during the trial: the American secret services had uncritically accepted British guidance, even before the United States had entered into the war. The people of India did not forget this, nor did those in America who were just waiting for the opportunity to prick the bubble of self-righteousness in which the Wilson administration was so precariously floating.[5]

America bobbed along in England's wake in another respect, too. Ireland, like India, was struggling for its independence. Like the leaders of the Ghadr Party, some Irish nationalists living in America saw an opportunity when the war started, and accepted German help. Well before America's entry into the war, they attracted the hostile attention of the Secret Service, at the back of which lay the State Department and a president who continued to be an advocate of self-determination while holding ethnic prejudices, especially toward the Irish.[6]

In the period of American neutrality, U.S. agents—mostly Secret Service at first, but later FBI as well—conducted a number of raids on the espionage network established in America by the German government. Certainly, the German secret agents were a threat to law and order—for example, in their plots to sabotage the production and transport of war materials produced in the United States and destined for Britain. Any doubts on that score were soon dispelled by the explosion on Black Tom Island in New York harbor on 30 July 1916: the German operatives' detonation of two million tons of dynamite killed three men and a child, and destroyed a loading facility for munitions destined for Britain.[7]

But the Secret Service's harassment of German agents was doubly convenient for the British, as it also impeded Central Power collaboration with Indian and Irish nationalists. One of its raids took place on the morning of 18 April 1916, on the Wall Street intelligence center secretly run by Wolf Von Igel. In a safe in Von Igel's office lay documents detailing the workings of Germany's extensive spy organization. But that morning, Von Igel had the documents laid out on a table ready for packaging. Fearing a raid, the Germans planned to move the items to their embassy in Washington, where they would be protected by diplomatic immunity. No doubt as the result of sharp intelligence by the Americans and their British mentors, FBI agents arrived at just the right moment. Von Igel tried to shovel the documents back into the safe but was blocked by a flying tackle.[8]

The U.S. government now had extensive details, right down to telephone numbers, of Germany's secret operations in North America. The raid on Von Igel's office confirmed the existence of Irish as well as Indian collaboration with the Germans. In fact, the Easter Rising took place in Dublin just after the New York raid—apparently, the State Department did not process the information quickly enough to warn London, but British intelligence already had advance knowledge from its own resources of the rising and of the associated, German-sponsored, ill-fated landing by Sir Roger Casement on the west coast of Ireland. One consequence of the Von Igel raid was that the Wilson administration could claim to have learned of Irish-German plotting not from the British, but from their own resources. The American authorities nevertheless did not release news of the captured Irish documents for some time, for fear that the administration would be accused of non-neutral behavior in raiding Von Igel's office on behalf of British imperialism. However, the news was leaked on the eve of the Indian trial, in a move calculated to convict by association Irish-American nationalists who by now operated in a country fired by anti-German zeal. The Wilson administration, although acquiring espionage tradecraft and learning how to run psychological operations against its own citizens, left itself vulnerable to charges that it was not representing the will or principles of the American people.[9]

British intelligence handled the affair of the Zimmermann telegram in a way that ultimately awoke even the most Anglophile American officials to the dangers of manipulation. This was no light matter, as the Zimmermann episode was the most important of the immediate factors that precipitated U.S. entry into World War I. The background is that the British Admiralty had a cryptographic unit, known as Room 40, which had broken some vital German codes. The British had kept this secret from Washington. But, early in 1917, they decided that the publication of the notorious telegram would help draw the United States into the war on the side of the Allies.

The Germans had been trying for some time to involve Mexico in a potential anti-American conspiracy. This policy was ill-advised—the Mexicans were not interested and, after years of civil war, were too weak to be of assistance anyway—yet it was pursued with stubborn resolve. On 17 January 1917, British naval intelligence intercepted a coded telegram from German Foreign Secretary Arthur Zimmermann to his ambassador in Mexico, Heinrich von Eckhard. Room 40 was able to decipher its contents:

> We intend to begin on the first of February unrestricted submarine warfare. We shall endeavor in spite of this to keep the United States neutral. In the event of this not succeeding, we make Mexico a proposal of alliance on the following basis:
> Make war together, make peace together, generous financial support, and an understanding on our part that Mexico is to reconquer the lost territory in Texas, New Mexico and Arizona.[10]

The British could not at once reveal the contents of this message to the Americans. To do so would have betrayed to the Germans the fact that Britain was reading some of their most secret codes, while indicating to the American public that in the cherished Anglo-American relationship, the English were wearing the pants. The British also needed a trusted intermediary and decided to take into their confidence the U.S. diplomat Edward Bell, who already liaised with British intelligence in London. Bell had been a Harvard classmate of assistant secretary of the navy Franklin D. Roosevelt and was trusted by the U.S. diplomatic/ intelligence coterie—his family had helped keep the *arriviste* Astors off the New York Social Register. Although he was an Anglophile and had divorced his lesbian wife to marry an Englishwoman, he suspected the British Foreign Office of manipulating America and demanded to see the original of the Zimmermann letter. He decoded a part of it himself in order to verify the authenticity of the version that would be sent to Washington.[11]

Having convinced Bell, the British authorities still waited until 24 February, by which time a story had been concocted that the telegram had been "bought in Mexico."[12] It now fell to Frank Polk, on duty as acting secretary of state because Lansing was on a three-day vacation, to deliver the telegram to Woodrow Wilson. Perhaps, as he approached the president's office, Polk reflected on his kinsman's acquisition by conquest of the "lost territory" in 1846. But Wilson had a more pressing problem. For him, the Zimmermann telegram was a heaven-sent opportunity to discredit the anti-interventionists in Congress, who were mounting a filibuster against the administration's bill to arm merchant ships. The president, who was in any case shocked by what he regarded as German treachery, exploited the situation to the full. Thus, manipulative though they may have been, the British were pushing on an open door in exploiting the Zimmermann telegram to draw the Americans into the war. This was precisely why America's internationalists and advocates of foreign espionage came under such heavy suspicion in future years.

The weaknesses of U-1 were not confined to elitism and ethnic bias. There is also a question mark over its ability to control America's sprawling and ever-expanding intelligence community. To be sure, its authority derived directly from the president and his closest advisers. It is also true that it represented a new type of expansion in federal bureaucracy. But although "agency" may be a convenient term to apply to the organism, it could not be compared, in size or resources, with the great agencies of the future, such as the Works Progress Administration of the New Deal years, or the Central Intelligence Agency in more recent times. Polk and Auchincloss did have some able assistants, notably Leland Harrison (Harvard '07), and they did have clerical support, but the evidence nevertheless suggests that U-1 simply did not possess the resources to keep an eye on certain important developments.

One of these took place following the Armistice, when the American Expeditionary Force (AEF) established its headquarters in Trier, Germany. With the approval and support of the military hierarchy, the chief of the intelligence section in the AEF, Col. Arthur L. Conger, undertook a secret mission—so secret, in fact, that the details did not begin to emerge until 1955. Threading his way through the social chaos of a defeated nation, Conger dealt with Walter Loeb, an intelligence operative speaking for the workers' and soldiers' council in Frankfurt, and the German foreign minister, Count Ulrich von Brockdorff-Rantzau. They promised that a reconstructed Germany would be republican and democratic, moving toward a constitution on the American model. Conger, in turn, promised that America would insist on a peace based on Wilson's Fourteen Points address, a magnanimous statement of principles that, if put into effect, might encourage Germany to cleave to democratic ways. But President Wilson was in no position to insist on a magnanimous peace: at the negotiating table, he had to heed the views of the leaders of France and Britain, whose armies had borne the brunt of the fighting.[13]

What was particularly unfortunate about Conger's activities was that he acted without presidential authority. Even if he had been an authorized executive agent, he could not have concluded binding agreements without the approval of the U.S. Senate—the point made by the Hoar Amendment in 1893.[14] What made things worse was that the president was not fully informed of Conger's actions. Secretary of State Lansing knew more about them but, in deference to the generals who protected Conger's hegemony, decided to do nothing.

In a final meeting with Conger in June 1919, Loeb complained that the imposition of a punitive peace would cause another war. It cannot reasonably be argued that Conger significantly contributed to raising German expectations to the point where, when dashed, they would change to bitterness and a willingness in due course to embrace Hitler and another war. After all, his operations were so secretive that only a handful of Germans knew about them. But the Conger episode does show how U-1 lacked the means, and possibly the will, to control military intelligence even in a case with significant diplomatic dimensions.

A compendium of U-1's operational limitations must, finally, include the point that it was only one of several sources of information flowing into the White House. Whatever the prejudices of America's politicians, they were at least erudite. In formulating policy, the Democratic administration had to match the informed criticism of such Republican leaders as former president Theodore Roosevelt, a cosmopolitan man of letters, and the chairman (from 1919) of the Senate Foreign Relations Committee, historian-turned-statesman Henry Cabot Lodge. If these, too, were patricians (both were Harvard men), at least they were

learned ones who would make sure that the administration was informed at all times of pertinent facts, especially ones inconvenient to
it. The president was a match for such critics. A former president of
Princeton University and an accomplished political scientist, Wilson
had from the outset of his presidency imported experts to advise his
administration. The Research Division of the Commission on Industrial
Relations (appointed by Wilson's predecessor but active during his administration) formulated a blueprint for an American welfare state. In
fall 1917, Wilson set up The Inquiry, a collection of experts and scholars who would advise the administration on the complexities of international affairs in anticipation of negotiating a just and lasting peace at
the war's end. This open intelligence source was not infallible but, on
balance, helped make the American president better informed about
European affairs than Europeans themselves. Commenting on the impact of The Inquiry on the 1919 peace negotiations, Wiseman wrote:
"Wilson often surprised his colleagues in Paris by his deep knowledge
of the affairs of the Balkans, the bitter political struggle in Poland,
or the delicate question of the Adriatic. If Wilson's theories seemed
strange and impractical to the realists of Europe, at least they could find
no fault with the accuracy of his facts."[15] Thus, the Wilson administration had a good intelligence apparatus, but secret intelligence was just
one part of it—U-1 was merely one cog, if the central one, within that
secret part.

Yet, despite all this, U-1 can be compared favorably with its rivals then, since, and in different countries. While the U-1 milieu may
have been undemocratic and even incestuous, it did prove to be a har-
monious and watertight arrangement. The organization was not too
large, so it was less likely that vital details would be lost in a morass of
bureaucracy. U-1 did not present the opportunities for buck-passing
and evasion of responsibility that tend to exist in larger organizations.
Though manipulated by the "friendly" British, at least American intelligence of the U-1 era resisted enemy penetration. Morale was high,
and already there was talk of U.S. intelligence being more discreet than
its British counterpart. British secret intelligence, Polk privately noted
in 1920, "had been carried on with a brass band."[16] This was one of the
very few moments in the history of Anglo-American intelligence relations when such a comparison might have been entertained.

U-1's achievements in counterintelligence were impressive. Early in the war, German secret intelligence chief Col. Walter Nicolai set up an espionage ring in the United States. The U-1/Secret Service response was effective but, in being so discreet, not appreciated. In 1940, for example, with the prospect of another war, an army intelligence spokesman claimed that the War Department had had to take over counterespionage activities during World War I "due to the inability of the civil authorities to meet the situation at that time."[17] But the MID and ONI really only protected military installations. U-1 in conjunction with the Secret Service demolished the operational capabilities of German secret intelligence.

As soon as Bryan resigned, Secret Service Chief William J. Flynn began to transmit details of German activities to the Treasury Department, where Leland Harrison placed them in a file labeled "Human Espionage Activities." The Secret Service kept a close watch on German ambassador Johann von Bernstorff, sending to Harrison at U-1 details of matters ranging from his clandestine arms purchases to his extramarital arrangements. In September 1915, for example, Harrison received a 200-page transcript of the ambassador's most revealing phone calls. "When a receiver was taken down in the embassy," Flynn recalled, "a light flashed in the Secret Service apartment" rented for surveillance purposes. "When a phone bell rang in the embassy one rang in our apartment. Four stenographers worked in relays."[18]

When other types of action were required, they were boldly undertaken. The Von Igel raid is one example, but it was not the first. One hot afternoon in July 1915, Dr. Heinrich F. Albert, ostensibly a commercial attaché but in fact the most senior of Nicolai's spies in America, nodded off on an elevated train as it passed through Harlem. When he woke up, he noticed that his briefcase, containing details of German undercover activities in America, was gone. In the vain hope of recovery, the Germans offered a reward for the return of the article. In fact, they assumed the British secret service had snatched it. The opportunist thief, as it turned out, was a U.S. secret agent—Frank Burke. A veteran of Secret Service work in the Spanish War, Burke had been following Albert. Seeing his chance and moving silently, he seized his prize and made off at speed. The contents of Albert's case did not prove espionage and failed (like the Von Igel raid) to yield information that would have interdicted the Black Tom bombers. However, they indicated that the Germans planned to disseminate propaganda (spreading rumors of a split between Wilson and Lansing), and to foment industrial unrest in American factories supplying the Allies. The administration gave selected papers from the briefcase to the *New York World,* which began a sensational serialization greatly to the advantage of British propaganda.[19]

Polk had an attribute that was invaluable in the world of deception—skepticism. He was healthily impatient with hysteria and false information. For example, when Gulf Oil demanded action, claiming that its interests in Mexico were under threat, Polk sent them packing with the observation that they too often cried wolf. When others saw Reds under every bed following the Bolshevik takeover in Russia, Polk refused to panic. No, he told military intelligence in 1918: *Nation* editor Oswald G. Villard should not be denied a passport just because he had an open mind toward Bolshevik Russia.[20]

It was Polk who unavailingly pressed on Wilson and former newspaper editor George Creel the view, ultimately proved correct, that the Sisson papers were forgeries. Edgar Sisson was a journalist who gave up the editorship of *Cosmopolitan* magazine to serve as the Russian representative on the Committee on Public Information (CPI), Wilson's propaganda agency headed by Creel. Serving in this capacity, he acquired some documents indicating that there had been German-Bolshevik collaboration in securing a German-assisted leftward shift in Russia in exchange for Russia's withdrawal from the war. Publication of the papers was an attractive scheme from the American government's point of view in that it would at one stroke highlight German unscrupulousness and throw into doubt the spontaneity of the Bolshevik Revolution. Because the British had questioned the authenticity of the documents, the Americans sought expert advice. Experts who should have known that revolutions do not stem from foreign conspiracies pronounced the documents authentic. The official publication of the Sisson papers followed in October 1918, having the effect of increasing Russian suspicions of U.S. diplomacy and, no doubt, contributing to Bolshevik truculence in the future. It is therefore to the credit of Polk and his colleagues that they fought against majority opinion in an attempt to prevent publication of the papers.[21]

The case of the Voska war guilt papers provides another example of independent intelligence assessment within the State Department. Emanuel Voska had been forced to leave his native Bohemia when still a young man for holding nationalist and socialist views unacceptable to the authorities of the Austrian Empire. He arrived in the United States, where he made a fortune in the marble-cutting industry. During this period, he became an advocate of the creation of a Czechoslovak state based on his native Bohemia. At the outbreak of World War I, he created, with the assistance of Wiseman's colleague and rival Guy Gaunt, a network of hyphenate-American counterspies. In 1915 Voska was partly responsible for the penetration of the New York spy ring organized on behalf of Austria-Hungary. Then, when the United States entered the war, Voska became involved in foreign intelligence. He operated in East Central Europe on behalf of the office of the counselor and the MID. The experience hardened Voska's attitude toward Bohemia's ancient oppressor Austria, and, when victory came, he needed no second invitation to join in war-guilt investigations.

At the conclusion of hostilities, Secretary Lansing became chairman of a commission to determine responsibility for the outbreak of the war. In the long term, the concept of war guilt was to have some dire consequences. Held responsible for the aggression, Germany was forced to pay reparations for war damage. British economist J. M. Keynes and his widening circle of supporters believed this burden to be fatal to the chances of democracy under the Weimar Republic of the 1920s. Germans were understandably bitter on the subject of reparations, since (encouraged by the MID's Conger, among others) they erroneously believed that Wilson had induced them to capitulate in 1918 with a promise of no indemnities.[22]

At the end of the war, the services of the American operational espionage network were placed at the disposal of the war-guilt investigators, coordinated by Creel. Voska was entrusted with the job of discovering some proof for the view that the assassination of Austria's crown prince at Sarajevo in 1914 had been a German-Austrian plot to trigger world war. At one point, he told American peace commissioner Gen. Tasker H. Bliss that he was examining documentary evidence that might confirm that hypothesis.[23]

A transcript of the Bliss-Voska conversation reached Leland Harrison. At this point, Allen Dulles recommended that Voska not be allowed to continue his work in the Bohemian capital, Prague. Dulles's objection was based not on the belief that Voska's claims concerning captured documents would turn out to be spurious but on the conviction that the consequences of gratuitously antagonizing Austria would be unfavorable. He suggested that "it would be inadvisable for Captain Voska to return to Bohemia if there is any other possible way of closing up his work in that country." But Voska was able to finish the war-guilt project to his own satisfaction. On 19 March 1919, he wrote to Leland Harrison: "To-day I received a report from Prague that, finally, the documents which we were after were located in a secret section of the military division in Hofbibliothek, Vienna."[24]

Voska told Harrison that he had obtained access to "letters and documents which will give information as to who is responsible for the war." One of the letters was from Ritter von Bilinski, a Polish conservative the Austro-Hungarians had entrusted with the administration of Bosnia-Hertzegovina until just before Ferdinand's assassination. The author of another letter was Stephen Tisza, the Hungarian premier. Voska already had photocopies of both the Bilinski and Tisza letters. Some letters had been removed from the Hofbibliothek to Prague for duplication; others were being inspected and copied in Vienna. Voska was about to return to the United States and had made arrangements for the original materials to be returned and kept in the office of Edward Benes, the Czechoslovak foreign minister, "where men assigned by the State Department can inspect the documents."[25]

Voska and his sympathizers suspected that an Austrian faction had conspired with Poles, Hungarians, and the German government to provoke war by murdering the crown prince. State Department officials discounted the theory. Harrison later told Richard Crane (Harvard '04), who had been Lansing's private secretary until 1919 when he became America's first ambassador to Czechoslovakia, for his "ear alone that all the information submitted by Voska was carefully gone over by Dr. [James B.] Scott, who, as you may remember, was with Mr. Lansing, our representative in the Commission set up by the Peace Conference, to examine into the question of the responsibility for the war. As a matter of fact, Dr. Scott did not find anything in the way of valuable evidence in the papers."[26]

Harrison was anxious to cover up the affair of the Voska papers because its ventilation would have been discomfiting for his colleagues. Lansing and Scott had endorsed the finding of their commission to the effect that the Central Powers were guilty in general terms of plotting war. It would have been disagreeable to have to publish evidence showing that there had been no plot behind the Sarajevo assassination but that American spies had tried to find one. U-1 had established that there had been no such plot, or at least that no proof was forthcoming. Its skepticism was a tribute to U.S. intelligence, even if it did not publicly dispel the Sarajevo conspiracy theory.

In any assessment of the strengths and weaknesses of U-1, it should be noted that American intelligence was stronger in the East than the West. In Western Europe, America had in Britain and France powerful allies fully competent, or at least experienced, in the business of espionage. Furthermore, in that theater of war, intelligence problems were mainly military in character, whereas the particular forte of the Americans was political intelligence, both by virtue of their libertarian tradition and as reflected by the domination of the State Department over the MID and ONI, however grudgingly accepted.

A second reason for the oriental inclination of American espionage was that the United States is a natural bridge between West and East, both in human terms, because of its myriad immigrant groups, and in geographic terms. Normally, the best way for French Prime Minister Georges Clemenceau to meet a Polish leader like Jan Paderewski would have been to take the train through Germany. War with the Central Powers meant that the principal statesmen of Europe could best communicate not via Metz and Berlin, but via Brest and Vladivostock, through the United States. Paderewski became the friend of Woodrow Wilson, and Americans the brokers of international politics.

Although there is some evidence to show that Americans were elsewhere followers, even dupes, of British intelligence, a different reading may be made of affairs in the East. In East Central Europe and the Far East, the British tended to be dependent on the Americans. Voska had originally been recruited by the British, but he was controlled by the MID and the State Department. Indeed, there is reason to believe that Washington did not always keep London fully informed about America's undercover intentions; at one stage, for example, Wiseman plaintively demanded to know "whether [MID chief Ralph] Van Deman is playing with [the Poles] or the Bohemians."[27] Despite his fantasies about Austrian war guilt, Voska was perhaps the Allies' second most effective agent in East Central Europe.

The Allies' most effective secret agent in East Central Europe had already made his mark well before the outbreak of peace with all its problems. He was W. Somerset Maugham. Just how this English novelist came to work for the Americans is not entirely clear. Perhaps fearing blackmail or simply out of prejudice, the British authorities balked at taking sole responsibility for sending a gay spy into the heart of revolutionary Russia. Possibly Maugham took umbrage at the British establishment, "exalted personages" of whom well-bred men spoke "with acidulous tolerance," and who had harassed his American friend F. Gerald Haxton. Certainly, Maugham was fond of Americans. He described his colleague Voska as having "but one passion in life, if you omit an extreme desire for good cigars, and that was patriotism."[28]

Another factor was that the Americans were willing to pay for Maugham. Whatever their difficulties with him, the British retained considerable control over Maugham's activities and perhaps tolerated American involvement less because they detested gays than because they were broke. It was Wiseman who set up the American payments, and Maugham's reports went to the Foreign Office as well as to the State Department. Even as late as 20 November 1917, Auchincloss referred to him—in a manner that betrayed his ignorance of spelling, literature and possibly operational details—as "a man named Maume, who had just returned from Russia."[29]

It may seem surprising that Maugham was an able spy. He is best remembered for his literary achievements and his sometimes affectedly decadent tastes. Who can forget his reproach to the chief of British intelligence, "In my youth I was always taught that you should take a woman by the waist and a bottle by the neck." To the literary critic Robert Calder, Maugham was "a habitué of the Café Royal who had gone to war" and "who did not succeed, of course." Clearly, the notion of a brilliant writer being an effective spy can seem incongruous.[30]

But it is wrong to assume that artists cannot be pragmatists, and the American decision to finance Maugham was wise. He was an experienced secret agent, and was being sent to East Central Europe, an area of U.S. expertise where it was more sensible to act under the partial aegis of U-1 than under the exclusive direction of British intelligence. Nor can it be said that Maugham failed. The author's own lament that "all his careful schemes had come to nothing" can be dismissed as the literary flourish of a melancholy persona. Except for his failure to stop the Russian Revolution, a mission impossible if ever there was one, Maugham was rather successful.[31]

Sir Eric Drummond of the British Foreign Office thus described the author's mission: "Mr W. Somerset Maugham is in Russia on a confidential mission with a view to putting certain phases of the Russian situation before the public in the United States." But Wiseman later noted that Maugham had been given a brief that included not just intelligence and propaganda, but covert action, too: he was "to guide the storm." When the Anglo-American intelligence mission began in July 1917, the fragile democratic government of Aleksander Kerensky was nominally in charge of Russia. But the situation was chaotic. Russian armies were in a state of collapse on the Eastern front, leaving the Germans free to divert troops to the West. It seemed imperative to fill the Eastern power vacuum in a way that would help the war effort and at the same time destroy the effectiveness of the socialist revolutionaries. Operating in tandem with Voska and with the assistance of half a million dollars supplied from America, Maugham worked on a plan to encourage the Cossacks, Poles, and Czechs to mount military operations that would redivert German resources to the East and create a possible impediment to the spread of communism. But he stopped short of making sanguine promises to the effect that he could revive the Eastern front or prevent the Bolshevik takeover in Russia. The sobriety of his claims distinguished them from those made by others, including the oversanguine Wiseman. There was nothing any secret agent could have done to stop the October Revolution, and Maugham was lucky to escape from it alive. But by war's end, he had helped formulate an American policy on East Central Europe that would last into the Cold War and, arguably, pay dividends in the long run.[32]

From all this, it may be deduced that U-1's demise in the 1920s did not stem from its wartime inadequacies. An alternative hypothesis is that it was politically weak, in the sense that its backers lacked the gift for public relations and hyperbole that characterized more expansive institutions like the Pinkerton Agency and the FBI.

But the truth is that the Wilson administration was by no means hostile to public relations. Seen as cold and aloof, President Wilson wanted to be more of a "man of the people," and even before the outbreak of the war in Europe he established a publicity bureau with the function of guiding press coverage of his administration. Newspapers, he told Harvard president Charles W. Eliot in July 1914, should be supplied with the "real facts." Just after America entered the war, President

Wilson created by executive order the CPI. Its director, George Creel, described the CPI as "a vast enterprise in salesmanship, the world's greatest adventure in advertising." Until its abolition by Congress in 1919, the CPI engaged in extensive propaganda. It bombarded Europe with millions of propaganda leaflets. At home, the CPI whipped up patriotism through the publication of pamphlets such as Edgar Sisson's *The German-Bolshevik Conspiracy* (1918). In the words of one historian, the CPI was "enormously effective in mobilizing opinion" and "did not always resist the temptation" to deal in the "fabrications, combinations of hyperbole and nonsense" that lay behind allegations of German atrocities.[33]

With this armory at its disposal, the Wilson administration could have made a more public case for U-1. But it chose not to. It saw the need for discretion in foreign-intelligence matters, and its Republican successors in the 1920s did not change that approach. U-1 was not destroyed by its sponsors' incompetence or reticence in public relations. Rather, it was destroyed from within.

Even the most intimate cliques can fall apart. This is what happened to the Wilson entourage under the strain of war, postwar reconstruction and diplomacy, and, from fall 1919, the president's five-month illness. One major cause of disillusionment in 1919 was the apparent hypocrisy of a president who blamed the outbreak of the war on secret intrigue and advocated open diplomacy as an essential ingredient in the peace yet sanctioned disinformation about Germany and locked the press out of the peace negotiations in Paris. In times of national emergency, espionage could be tolerated, but in peacetime the concept was less attractive, at least in part because of the infamous nature of the activities conducted by self-promoting private detectives. In 1919, Secretary of State Lansing noted that "Muttered confidences, secret intrigues, and the tactics of the 'gum-shoer' are discredited." By this time, he was at odds with Wilson over the conduct of the peace negotiations, and, in February 1920, just three weeks before the start of the new Republican administration, the president secured his resignation. Liberated from the constraints of cabinet loyalty, Lansing now publicly condemned President Wilson for having conducted the Paris peace negotiations in secret and in violation of his professed faith in open diplomacy.[34]

So, just when Frank Polk was reshaping American intelligence with peacetime operations in mind, he found that his chief in the Department of State was beginning to oppose the whole principle of espionage. It is tempting to see in Lansing's opposition to undercover work the beginnings of a patriarchal opposition to espionage that strengthened in the "naïve" and "isolationist" 1920s. Certainly, the destructive hand ultimately came from within—it was that of Secretary of State Frank B. Kellogg, who in June 1927 ended centralization by abolishing the subunits of U-1. But his reform did not stem from moral considerations. The theory behind it may be summarized as follows. In the early years of the carbon copy and photoduplication, there had been an enormous accretion in the amount of information made available from various intelligence sources. It became impossible to handle the data. The State Department therefore established a central evaluation system. However, the inflow of information did not abate as the years passed, while back files increased arithmetically in bulk and geometrically in inferred complexity. The tasks of selection and evaluation proved to be beyond the capability of any one team of bureaucrats. U-1 had become inferior as a source of information to the MID or ONI taken individually, since each of these agencies profited from having less ground to cover. U-1 was an obstacle between the secretary of state and vital information.[35]

The foregoing theory no doubt underestimates the capabilities of central bureaucracy, but it is important historically because it underlay Kellogg's reform of 1927. The secretary of state decreed that "The office designated U-1 is hereby abolished. All correspondence hitherto sent to that office will now be routed to U [that is, the undersecretary of state himself]." He left the details of reorganization to the erstwhile chief of U-1, Alexander C. Kirk. Kirk wrote virtually identical letters to J. Edgar Hoover of the FBI, A. J. Hepburn of the ONI, and Stanley S. Ford of the MID, explaining the new arrangements and the reasons for them. Branches of U with "special functions" would surrender them to geographic state department divisions; high-priority MID reports hitherto routed via Kirk and U-1 would now go straight to Kellogg.[36]

Kellogg's desire to obtain a clearer picture of international problems like communism is evident from his correspondence, but it was not the only reason for the reform of intelligence in 1927. The secretary wanted to ensure that his own house was in good democratic order. He was particularly sensitive to criticism about class discrimination. In this connection, Kirk hinted at the controversy centered on the personality of Undersecretary of State Joseph C. Grew.[37] As undersecretary from 1924 to 1927, Grew had been responsible for coordinating intelligence work; Kirk, as assistant undersecretary, was his aide and confidant. Grew, however, came under fire from the Senate Committee on Foreign Relations and the press for allowing foreign service appointments to be managed by a "Harvard clique." A feature writer for the National Editorial Association complained that Grew was a member of "the inner circle of social diplomats which has set the well-to-do diplomats over the hard-working consuls . . . the teahounds of the service are getting all the breaks." Exposed to such criticism, Grew was too weak to withstand the enmity of Kellogg, who distrusted him. After accepting the post of ambassador to Turkey, Grew wrote apologetically to Kirk, his now vulnerable protégé: "I received distinct impressions that the Administration wanted me to go."[38] Grew had fallen prey to democratic feeling and jealousy over patronage.

Yet, while the Ivy League/undemocratic image problem was real enough, the conviction that U-1 was no longer an efficient mechanism was at the heart of the Kellogg reform. Kirk dutifully conveyed this view in his letters to the intelligence chiefs, writing: "The reason for this change is a desire to render certain information received from without immediately accessible to the officers in the Department directly interested in the subject matter thereof."[39]

For reasons that changed from one administration to the next, the State Department remained reluctant to resume its World War I role of centralizing secret intelligence. In 1940, Assistant Secretary of State Adolf A. Berle (Harvard '13) attended a meeting with Hoover and military intelligence leaders with a view to integrating foreign and domestic espionage to meet the new international crisis. He later recorded, "We had a pleasant time, coordinating, though I don't see what the State Department has got to do with it."[40] Mainly because of inertia and lack of enthusiasm at the center, rather than because of operational shortcomings or inept public relations, U-1 never revived—and exchanged obscurity for extinction.

CHAPTER 6

Burns, Hoover, and the Making of an FBI Tradition

Burns glanced behind him. His men, the apocryphal surveyors, tried to look busy. Still uncomfortable, he tugged at his own choice of disguise, a suit of hunting clothes. He once again adjusted his binoculars. Screwing his eyes against the glistening waters of the Puget Sound, he focused more carefully on the beach. Yes, they were naked.

The anarchists of Home Colony had chosen their location at Tacoma on the West Coast as the place to try out their own version of the American idyll. But by 1911, their community was splitting into two camps, known as the "Nudes" and the "Prudes." Bitter litigation would follow: the "Great Nude Bathing Cases" went all the way to the U.S. Supreme Court. Burns conveyed his own characterization of the difficulties: "They exist in a state of free love, are notoriously unfaithful to the mates thus chosen, and are so crooked that even in this class of rogues there does not seem to be any hint of honor."[1]

But the circumstances that took Burns to Tacoma on the Puget Sound had nothing to do with nude bathing. After twenty years with the Secret Service, he had quit in 1909 to form, with his son Raymond, the William J. Burns National Detective Agency. He had already been involved in a number of high-profile cases, some of them creditable and none more so than the notorious trial in Atlanta, Georgia, in which the detective helped to secure the acquittal of Leo Frank on the charge of murder, only to see him killed by an anti-Semitic lynch mob. Burns had a lucrative security contract with the American Bankers' Association, but he wanted to make even more money and was determined to keep himself in the public eye.[2]

The National Erectors' Association now retained him to track down the perpetrators of the National Dynamite Campaign, especially those who had blown up the *Los Angeles Times* Building on 10 October 1910. This explosion had killed twenty of the newspaper's employees, and circumstantial evidence led Burns to believe that the dynamiters had holed up among the anarchists in Tacoma—hence the binoculars and the prurient presence of heavily disguised private detectives. Eventually, Burns did help secure evidence that led to the conviction of the leading officials of the International Association of Bridge and Structural Ironworkers (IABSI). These officials had dynamited or conspired to dynamite dozens of skyscrapers, railroad bridges, and other steel structures being erected by nonunion labor. In a terrifying display of technical ingenuity, for example, the use of short-fused time bombs, they heralded the advent of modern gangsterism and terrorism—in fact, hoodlum chronicler Damon Runyon soaked up "ambiance" in IABSI enforcer Tom Slattery's Long Island bar. Burns's attempt to show that the IABSI was part of an anarchist-communist conspiracy to destroy America was plausible because of this sheer violence, and because it was a time when conservatives in any case worried about the increasing popularity of the Socialist Party of America and the revolutionary Industrial Workers of the World (IWW). It was all too easy to overlook the facts that IABSI was led by conservative Irish Americans and that the union had not, in fact, planned the *Times* explosion.[3]

Yet the successful businessman is no fool. In October 1910, a leading construction engineer complained, "No detective agency is to be relied upon; their expenses run up enormously and they only give you enough to lead you on." But Burns, like Allan Pinkerton before him, was ready to tackle the doubters. He could point to his training with the Secret Service and, like Pinkerton, stressed his probity, if in a manner that cast doubt on the integrity of his competitors and of undercover work in general: "I render reports," he noted in 1915, "and on those reports place the amount of money expended each day, which no other detective agency does." Burns knew how to play on American fears: in an age of rising divorce rates and of feminism, of industrial turbulence and rapid change, he played on sex, anarchism/communism, and violence—all these ingredients being conveniently present in Tacoma.

Though he could not hope to emulate Pinkerton's literary output, he did court publicity. Among his works were *The Masked War* (1913), his sensational account of how he saved America from the National Dynamite Campaign, and *The Crevice* (1915), a self-aggrandizing detective novel. He reached an even wider readership through the popular press.[4]

The William J. Burns National Detective Agency grew to become the Pinkertons' main competitor. But Burns's impact on intelligence practices and culture is also felt because he served as director of the FBI between 1921 and 1924. His return to public service imported private practices to the government sphere and helped blur still further the boundaries between one tradition and the other.

Burns was one of those who imported commercial values from the private to the public sphere. The FBI developed assets and expertise that benefited the United States enormously. But what came to be inseparable from the agency was the quest for the sensational, a quest that focused typically on Red Scares, on threats real or imagined to the public order, and on lascivious detail. At its worst, the distortion amounted to a political agenda.

All this invites interpretation. Burns and his successors may be regarded as participants in public hysteria over hot-button issues like anti-communism. On the other hand, their anti-communism may be seen in a more rational light sometimes because it was justified by circumstances, at other times because it served as a tool to advance or preserve the power of its practitioners.[5] To a certain extent, Burns and his successors were the gullible victims of their own irrational disregard for factual precision. In that regard, they were the product of societal values as well as shapers of opinion. But were they also sometimes calculators of the most cynical kind, who really neither believed in nor worried about revolutionary threats or attacks on public morals and order but exploited public fears in order to obtain more money and power?

An examination of the different phases in the history of the FBI and especially the career of Burns's successor, J. Edgar Hoover, suggests that calculation did to a startling degree underpin the persistent distortions emanating from the agency. There is a special reason why they were able to get away with such self-serving distortions. FBI officials were free to deceive in large part because, from the beginning, the bureau had the latitude to operate independently of congressional scrutiny. Open debate and scrutiny are antidotes to deception and conspiracy. But despite congressional suspicions concerning the formation of the FBI, that scrutiny did not come to pass. An opportunity for binding precedent was lost, with repercussions not just for the bureau but also for other federal intelligence agencies in the future.

On 26 July 1908, Attorney General Charles J. Bonaparte established an investigative unit within the Department of Justice. Previously, his department had hired agents, when they were needed, from the Secret Service—as long ago as 1871, Congress had appropriated $50,000 for this purpose. The argument then had been that efficiency would be achieved. With "efficiency" one of the key ideas of Progressive reform, Bonaparte once again justified expansion in its name. The Secret Service, he had told the House Appropriations Committee in January 1908, was inflating the cost of agents it loaned to other agencies by 33 percent. His argument that direct employment would be economical was music to the ears of some members of Congress, who accused the Secret Service's chief John Wilkie of empire-building (at the time, he had 144 agents on loan to various government departments) and charged that the lending-out system led to evasion of congressional scrutiny. Against this background, Bonaparte directly employed 35 agents, recruited mainly from the Secret Service but embryonically an independent force. In the following year, this became known as the Bureau of Investigation, and, in 1935, after some further name changes, it was dubbed the FBI. The new agency (referred to here as the FBI, regardless of period) gradually expanded into a major intelligence agency with mainly domestic responsibilities but with significant foreign assets in World War II and then in the post–Cold War era.[6]

But in 1908 the new arrangement did not please every legislator—indeed, it was anathema to some. Congress had in the past sniped at the president's use of secret funds and of individual agents, and there were already brooding suspicions of the Secret Service. But the debate in that year marked an abrupt awakening to the fact that large-scale clandestine bureaucracy loomed on the American horizon. While some supported the view that the creation of the FBI would be a brake on Wilkie's ambitions, critics accused President Theodore Roosevelt's administration of trying to set up the trappings of a police state by stealth, and without consulting Congress. They drew comparisons with the notorious police system that Joseph Fouché had operated on behalf of Napoleon, who happened to be Attorney General Bonaparte's grand-uncle.[7]

But President Roosevelt, both visionary and wily, turned the table on his critics. His reputation as a reforming president helped him at a time when Congress, the Senate in particular, was smarting from the attacks of critics who had accused it of being stuffed full of rich, corrupt men who were in the pockets of the nation's millionaire predators. One of his reforms—indeed, a reform that marks Roosevelt as a leader of prophetic quality—was conservation. He was particularly incensed at the exploitation of natural resources in the West by capitalists operating hand in glove with corrupt legislators. His "Square Deal" politics meant getting tough with capitalists who abused monopoly power, and his appointment of Bonaparte, an anti-trust campaigner, was a signal of intent. Though Roosevelt was a politician to his fingertips and in the end settled for little more than rhetorical trust-busting, he was able to market the FBI as a blow in the fight for probity and conservation.[8]

Land fraud was rife in the far west, where timber prospectors known as "cruisers" roamed the great forests on behalf of speculators. Corrupt developers would then put up dummy buyers, who would obtain the 160 acres due them under the terms of the Homestead Act, only to hand over the land to speculators in exchange for minor reward. In a further, "lieu-land" scam, territory assigned for homesteading was exchanged for valuable swaths of virgin forest. To facilitate and mask this "Great Barbecue" as it was called, the looters paid off public officials and legislators. The most prominent of these was Oregon's veteran Senator John H. Mitchell, a man who took his bribes in $1,000 notes. The Roosevelt administration's investigation was backed by the "muckrakers," led by the formidable journalist Lincoln Steffens. The Secret Service assigned Burns to the case, and, after a highly publicized trial, Mitchell was convicted in 1905. Thus, the future private detective and FBI director first made his name as a hunter not of labor radicals but of rogue capitalists—his game, like that of so many intelligence leaders, was fame and fortune first, anti-radicalism second.[9]

The Mitchell trial may have been spectacular, but it was just one of several land fraud cases and Burns continued to pursue suspects both in the West and on Capitol Hill. Roosevelt turned this circumstance to his

advantage. When Congress in December 1908 refused further appropriations to pay for the Justice Department's exclusive use of former
Secret Service agents, the chief executive stated that his opponents
were helping "the criminal classes." Now in the twilight year of his
presidency, he accused his congressional opponents of being motivated
by self-preservation and of not wishing to be "investigated by secret-
service men." The rumor circulated that Roosevelt's agents had acquired information on congressmen that "would prove interesting reading." Chief Wilkie's assertion that no Secret Service man had "ever
shadowed a Congressman or Senator" must have sounded like one of
those denials that affirms its opposite. Against this background, the government dropped most of its fraud investigations, but Roosevelt established the proto-FBI during a congressional adjournment by executive
fiat. Although he had some support on the Hill, he had created an apparent precedent for secret government acting in defiance of Congress.
In future years, Roosevelt's solution would become the problem.[10]

The incoming administration of President William H. Taft appointed a new attorney general, George Wickershaw, who in turn appointed Stanley W. Finch to be the first director of the FBI, effective
March 1909. Finch had been with the Department of Justice since 1893
and had obtained a law degree in 1908, the year of the FBI's formation.
The newly installed Finch retained seven land fraud investigators but
knew that, with the decline of the western scandals, his fledgling agency
would need other law-enforcement challenges in order to prove its
continuing worth. He at once engaged an additional eighty-two agents
to work on anti-trust cases (more numerous in the "conservative" Taft
administration than under Roosevelt), bankruptcy and banking violations, obscenity cases having an interstate dimension, and alleged infractions of the Chinese exclusion law.[11]

Then, an opportunity presented itself with the passage of the Mann
Act in 1910. In the wake of lurid press stories about innocent young
girls being abducted into brothels, this law aimed to eradicate "white
slavery." In Congress, it was generally accepted that, as one member
delicately put it, "Intercourse is commerce," so that, under the interstate commerce clause in the U.S. Constitution, a federal agency could
become involved. In 1911, the bureau established an extra office in

Baltimore to investigate white slavery cases. In April 1912, Wickershaw placed the FBI under the direction of A. Bruce Bielaski, a Secret Service veteran and graduate of George Washington University law school. This allowed Finch to be a special commissioner in charge of the high-profile investigation of white slavery. In 1912, anti-trust cases still took the lion's share of the FBI's investigative budget, $47,279, with white slavery second, at $31,449. But by the following year, the position was reversed: $28,700 on anti-trust and $59,639 on white slavery.[12]

Some members of Congress protested that enforcement should be left to local authorities, and once the FBI began to investigate and to expand into every state there were complaints that the "enormous expense" was a "burden on the people." Finch, however, met the challenge with some money-raising hyperbole:

> Unless a girl was actually confined in a room and guarded, there was no girl, regardless of her station in life, who was altogether safe. . . .
>
> There was need that every person be on his guard, because no one could tell when his daughter or his wife or his mother would be selected as a victim.

Finch was attempting to make the FBI a people's agency by making it the savior of America from a universal threat that was at least in part his own invention. As the FBI critic Fred Cook noted many years later, "Chief Finch was a master at painting the Menace."[13]

Like the Secret Service in 1898, the FBI inspired a legion of private informers. The bureau paid prostitutes and madams, and some informers were motivated by gripes and prejudices. As a result, the agency risked loss of popularity. There was, for example, mixed reaction to its investigation of John Arthur Johnson. "Jack" Johnson was the first black boxer to become heavyweight champion of the world. In 1910, he successfully defended his title by beating the "last white hope," James J. Jeffries, at Reno, Nevada. Johnson shocked contemporary opinion by openly consorting with white women. In 1912, he was charged with having abducted Lucille Cameron, a white girl age nineteen, from Minneapolis to his home in Chicago. She refused to implicate him. Then, in May 1913, following a further FBI swoop, he was sentenced to a year in prison for crossing a state border with a former prostitute who would become his third wife. Although the FBI had in this case appeared to move in harmony with contemporary racial prejudice and sexual worries, it had crossed a dangerous line. First, African Americans were beginning to fight back effectively against Jim Crow. Second, athletes command respect, however they choose to live their lives, and Johnson was a great fighter—indeed, some say he was the best heavyweight ever. Finally, the case seemed to threaten federal intrusion into ordinary people's lives in an unacceptable way.[14]

When World War I started, the FBI was, then, ready for what Cook called "its next Menace." There was at first no room for the FBI in the counterintelligence field, dominated as it was by the Secret Service with its powerful backers. But in 1916, Congress authorized the Department of State to use the FBI for investigations. Once the United States entered the war, the bureau found a way to expand. Bielaski boosted the agency by recruiting the ordinary people of America to its side. He encouraged the formation of a vigilante force, the American Protective League (APL), which would help the bureau in its work. The APL's mission was to track down and deal with "slackers," men who would not join the armed forces, or who resisted the war. APL volunteers received badges. These were to be concealed except in emergencies, and bore the inscription "American Protective League, Secret Service Division." This was just irresistible to the legions of men who lived dull lives and aspired to be patriots. As soon as the war broke out, the FBI increased the number of its agents from 300 to 400, but these numbers were dwarfed by the APL volunteers—100,000 had joined within three months, and the total rose to 250,000.[15]

The APL had scant respect for civil liberties, degenerated into a vehicle for the reactionary Right, and was difficult to control. Some of its members were vicious criminals. In the West, they seized the opportunity to persecute the IWW, the revolutionary organization that had challenged the power of the region's lumber and mining magnates. Reactionaries circulated the smear that the IWW was financed by "German gold."[16] On 1 August 1917 Frank H. Little of the IWW executive committee was dragged from his rooming house in Butte, Montana, and lynched. At the time, the public applauded this treatment of a radical who had so outrageously suggested that the capitalists be put in the front trenches. But on more mature reflection, a number of Americans began to ask questions about the APL.

In January 1918, appalled by the FBI-condoned APL excesses and perhaps feeling that his own agency was being both compromised and marginalized by the aggressive newcomer to the field, Secret Service Chief William J. Flynn resigned. Flynn had worked for the Secret Service more or less continuously since 1897 and had succeeded Wilkie as its chief in 1912.

Flynn was especially appalled by the use of the words "secret service" on APL badges, but his departure reflected a deeper power struggle. His boss, Secretary of the Treasury William McAdoo, had denounced the APL and now tried to restore the ascendancy of his own agency by proposing a central intelligence bureau to be run by Flynn. A power struggle ensued between the intelligence czars in the Treasury Department (fighting for the Secret Service), Justice Department (institutional home of the FBI), and armed services. On 6 March 1918, an interdepartmental meeting took place to consider McAdoo's complaints about the APL and to review two options: an intelligence clearinghouse along the lines of U-1 but confined to domestic matters, and, McAdoo's plan, a new agency headed by a director who would be directly responsible to the president.[17]

McAdoo was a formidable figure in the Wilson administration. He could list, among his achievements, the organization of the Liberty Bond scheme that helped finance the U.S. war effort: in a high-powered patriotic sales pitch utilizing the Boy Scouts, women's organizations, and movie stars like Charlie Chaplin, the government ultimately succeeded in selling five thirty-year bond issues between 1917 and 1920. So it was testimony to the gathering strength of the challenge to McAdoo's Secret Service that the March 1918 negotiations ended in bureaucratic deadlock. The FBI escaped the imposition of impediments to its expanding role. In November McAdoo, though still nursing ambitions for the Democratic presidential nomination, resigned in order to restore his finances in private business.[18]

The Secret Service would increasingly give way to the newer agency, concentrating more and more on the important but circumscribed function of protecting the president and his entourage. As the Secret Service slipped from its ascendant position, so did U-1, which, though retaining its function in foreign intelligence until 1927, faded from the counterintelligence scene once the war was over. An elitist arrangement had given way to a much more democratic one, not just in terms of the intelligence leadership but also in terms of public support. Already by 1918, the FBI had risen with the help not of a State Department clique but of a waxing popular tide. It had learned to exploit sensational issues like sex and threats to the public order. It had utilized public hysteria in pursuing political ends and disregarding civil liberties. It had achieved budgetary expansion. It was the latest embodiment of the tradition of the con man.

In fall 1918, the FBI made another of its inspired mistakes. For some time, the bureau and the APL had been rounding up real and alleged draft dodgers. Following a War Department estimate in August 1918 that more than 300,000 men had evaded the draft, Bielaski and his APL henchmen planned a nationwide swoop. This duly went into effect at the appointed hour, 7 a.m. on 3 September 1918. Tens of thousands of FBI/APL agents accosted men of fighting age all over America, demanding to see their draft cards. Hundreds of thousands of non-card-carrying "slackers" were arrested and placed into "bull pens" pending further action. The operation was a disaster. Many men simply did not bother to carry their cards—America, after all, was not a police state. The bull pens contained innocent people who had no objections at all to shooting Germans. The chief of New York's FBI office revealed that only a small minority of the 60,187 detained in his city were real "slackers." A clerk in the Justice Department let slip that 99.5 percent of the arrests nationwide had been made in error.[19] The September swoop was a fiasco that helped put the FBI in the forefront of American consciousness, because it was the dress rehearsal for the archetypal menace to America, the Red Scare.

At this point, it is appropriate to introduce to the narrative the person whose name is inseparable from both the Red Scare and the ensuing history of the FBI. J. Edgar Hoover came to personify some of the most pernicious myths associated with American intelligence, yet he is himself in need of demystification. There was nothing extraordinary about his background. He was born in a modest house on Seward Square, five minutes' walk from the U.S. Congress. He grew up in the culture described by biographer Richard Gid Powers as "Southern, white, Christian, small-town, turn-of-the-century Washington."[20] He lived in that house on Seward Square until the death of his mother in 1938, and he never married. Like other officials in the FBI and indeed Secret Service, he knew from an early age that the glittering prize of an

Ivy League education with its privileged access to positions of power was beyond his grasp. He took his law degree locally, like Bielaski, from George Washington University. Hoover was a talented hard grafter who made it to the top.

Hoover served as director of the FBI from 1924 until his death in 1972. He first rose to prominence in the wake of a bomb attack on the home of Attorney General A. Mitchell Palmer on 2 June 1919. The blast was never fully explained, but a leaflet retrieved from the remains of the bomber (who was killed in the explosion) indicated that he was an anarchist who wished to overthrow the capitalist system. The bomb attack came in the midst of several events, ranging from a general strike in Seattle to the formation of American communist parties. These events fomented in the United States a short-term fear of revolution that came to be known as the Red Scare—according to one chronicler of the event, "few occurrences in American history . . . have involved so much exaggeration and fear." Palmer's immediate response was to appoint a new team to combat radicalism. He put Flynn in charge of the FBI. Flynn's principled resignation over the use of the words "secret service" on APL badges made him an apparently appropriate choice, and he had kept himself in the public eye through his activities as a private detective. His war work seemed to give him the experience to run an intelligence operation against an internal foe with external connections— "Moscow Gold" now played the part formerly attributed to "German Gold." To Flynn's experience, Palmer now added the ingredient of youthful vigor. In July, Hoover, at the age of twenty-four, became special assistant to the attorney general; he soon found himself in charge of the Radical Division of the FBI.[21]

Hoover was a man of exceptional organizational skills. In future years, for example, he revitalized the attack on the white slave trade, responded to the 1919 Motor Vehicles (Dyer) Act by establishing an auto identification laboratory, and took up where the Pinkerton Agency had left off by keeping a national file on criminal records backed up by a fingerprint bank and other tools of the investigative trade. At last, America, inhibited hitherto by a chronic distrust of federal institutions, could take its place in the front rank of nations dedicated to law enforcement. In 1919–1920, Hoover dedicated himself to the pursuit of Left-wing radicals. His Radical Division fed the *New York Times* misinformation leading to stories that the IWW and "Bolsheviki" lay behind the Washington, D.C., race riot of 1919.[22] Hoover's operating assumption was that radicalism was alien and that aliens were behind radicalism. Establishing a degree of independence from Flynn and his civil liberties strictures, he used a newly formed veterans' organization, the American Legion, to achieve goals previously pursued by the APL. In an early display of his organizational skills, Hoover and his colleagues compiled by November 1919 a list of 60,000 suspects. Arrests, harassment, and about 500 deportations followed.

This policy of mass persecution was based on hyperbole about a revolution around the corner that never came. It was popular in the short run, and could be regarded as the making of the modern FBI. But like the "slacker" raids, it came unstuck. On the first day of 1920, a "Palmer raid" by FBI agents resulted in the arrests of 6,000 people in 33 cities, but this dragnet inquiry produced no evidence of a revolutionary plot, and critics began to ask why, in peacetime, people were being detained for weeks without being charged. The politically ambitious Palmer now predicted that widespread revolutionary activity would break out on the first of May. When it did not, the bubble was pricked. The majority of Americans remained strongly anti-communist but, for the time being, suspended their belief in scare stories.

Unlike Palmer, who left his job under a cloud of disapproval in 1921, Hoover survived this change in public mood. There has been considerable speculation about the nature of the man who became one of America's greatest bureaucratic survivors. By and large, historians have agreed on Hoover's character. He was publicly intolerant both of homosexuality and of any hint of heterosexual unorthodoxy. He was racist and ideologically conservative, especially on the subject of the Left. He was a power seeker, a guardian of the FBI's autonomy, and an empire builder.[23]

There has been less agreement about what made Hoover the man he was. Those who have stressed his family and background have no doubt identified a significant factor in his sexual, racist, and ideological makeup, but it is possible to be led astray by such considerations. Because he lived with a powerful mother and vacationed for many years after 1928 with FBI associate director Clyde Tolson, the idea circulated that he was gay. No doubt the relationship with his mother had an influence, and perhaps her overbearing presence made him seek independence by other means and explains his concern with FBI autonomy, but the evidence does not sustain the conclusion that Hoover was a practicing homosexual. His sexual puritanism and pursuit of "deviants" may have had less to do with his need to conceal his own proclivities than with a calculating approach to power and publicity.[24]

Family and local background do not entirely explain Hoover's anti-communism, either. It is true that Russian communism was atheistic and anti-property, and that this was odious to a man who prayed before eating and deferred to the rich. But Hoover did not allow dogma to affect his judgment. In spring 1920, a House Rules subcommittee held hearings on the FBI's deportation procedures, and in testimony bureau irregularities were exposed. At the same time, it became apparent that there was no significant communist threat to American democracy and institutions. Palmer had pinned his presidential ambitions too closely to the image of himself as savior of America from the Red Menace, so he took a fall.

If Hoover had been an ideologue, he, too, might have continued to plug the anti-radical issue, suffering defeat and disgrace. But he was too much of a pragmatist. He did not abandon his hostility toward communism. However, he did put the issue back on its shelf, ready to be taken down and dusted off next time the FBI needed a boost and the public was in a receptive mood. Cannily, Hoover took no part in the pursuit of Nicola Sacco and Bartomoleo Vanzetti. Arrested for murder in 1920 and executed seven years later, these two Italian anarchists were subjected to a trial whose increasingly conspicuous unfairness dragged down the reputations of those involved. For the time being, Hoover had distanced himself from anti-radicalism.[25]

Pragmatism limited, also, the impact of Hoover's racism. He is legendary for his persecution of black leaders, from Marcus Garvey in the 1920s to Martin Luther King, Jr., in the 1960s. His interest in Dr. King's sexual peccadilloes is especially notorious—the FBI file on King runs to one million pages. But Hoover also pursued that deadly foe of the African American, the Ku Klux Klan. The FBI moved against the Klan in the 1920s, and then in a particularly ruthless way in the 1960s, when its agents destroyed Klan morale by spreading false rumors about its leaders sleeping with one anothers' wives. None of this negates the fact that Hoover was a racist, yet the evidence suggests that he subordinated his prejudice to his ambition, and that he moved against targets only when he felt confident it was expedient and advantageous to do so.[26]

One of Hoover's most notable characteristics was his love of power, with its associated lust for empire. Hoover's exercise of power was legendary. If someone crossed him, the bureau would investigate that person. By adroitly mentioning to Senator Smith some compromising detail about Senator Jones's private life, he let it be known that he probably knew something about Smith, too, so he had better not cross the bureau. Although this kind of manipulation made him enemies, they were afraid to strike and, in any case, Hoover kept a majority of Americans on his side. A recent student of Hoover's style summarized "current scholarship" as indicating that Hoover was a genius at public relations.[27]

The love of power and empire-building are not locally inspired and are by no means uniquely American. Nevertheless, Hoover's hyperbolic, public relations–oriented style of achieving expansion may be seen in the context of American *national* tradition. Though wily, Hoover did not invent the idea that money was to be made by exaggerating menace. He did not even invent the American list of menaces: after all, Allan Pinkerton had dwelled on the communist menace, the menace of loose morals, and the menaces of vice and crime. Here, though, a significant difference exists. Pinkerton, Flynn, and Burns all served as federal officials, but all had experience also as private detectives and brought to the public sphere the approach of the risk-taking, profit-making confidence man. In contrast, Hoover spent his entire working life inside the federal bureaucracy.

In that sense, William J. Burns played a transitional role. In 1921, Burns was building up his detective agency into the Pinkertons' major rival, but was suddenly plucked from this relative obscurity. The new Republican president, Warren Harding, had promised reform of the Justice Department, saying "Too much has been said of Bolshevism in America."[28] His attorney general, Harry M. Daugherty, looked around for someone to replace Flynn. In the 1880s, Burns had been a police commissioner in Columbus, Ohio, and there had made Daugherty's acquaintance. Attorney General Daugherty now prevailed upon Burns to join the "Ohio gang," that government circle that was so different in social and geographic origins from the Wilson set and was so much more corrupt, yet shared with it the characteristic of being a clique. Burns became director of the FBI in March, and Hoover started as assistant director in August.

Under Burns, the FBI developed some of its hallmark practices. One of these, government by burglary, beat a well-trodden path to the Watergate scandal of the 1970s. For Daugherty asked Burns to investigate members of Congress and journalists who were beginning to criticize the corrupt practices of the Harding administration. Bureau agents broke into the office of Senator William Borah in 1921, and in 1922 they repeated the offense in the case of Congressman Oscar E. Kellar, who was trying to initiate impeachment proceedings against Daugherty. It should be added that in the process of converting his bureau of truth into an agency of mendacity, Burns revived the anti-socialist scaremongering his appointment had been meant to dispel. "Radicalism," he told the House Appropriations Committee in 1924, "is becoming stronger every day in this country." This must have been far from obvious in the ultra-capitalist 1920s, so he resorted to the usual explanation that invisibility can only spell greater danger: "They are going about it in a very subtle manner. For instance, they have schools all over the country where they are teaching children from 4 to 5 years old."[29]

Just like any detective agency anxious to prove its worth and its constant indispensability, the FBI made a show of presenting regular reports. These reports reflected an expanding foreign intelligence interest, in spite of the outbreak of peace and "isolationism." Hoover argued that the FBI's 1916 appropriations statute permitted the agency to investigate foreign threats to America, provided the State Department requested it. Under the Wilson-Palmer aegis, Hoover had already reported to U-1 on a regular basis regarding Mexico, and he occasionally reported also on the political situation in European countries such as Britain and Portugal. With Harding-Daugherty in office, he modified his remit to reflect the concerns of Republican foreign policy makers. For example, in the midst of the Washington Armament Conference of 1921–1922, he warned of a growing cordiality between Germany and Japan.[30]

In 1924, Burns found himself under pressure because of complaints about the FBI's disregard for civil liberties; by this time, Harding was dead, and Daugherty was in disgrace. In any case, Burns wished to concentrate anew on his lucrative private agency and perhaps felt that in Hoover a trustworthy successor was ready at hand. His resignation in a sense marks a parting of the ways between the private detective and American espionage: the shamus would from now on concentrate on divorce cases and labor espionage, leaving government work to government agents.

In another sense, though, the privately generated tradition of the confidence man lived on in the recesses of government bureaucracy. As a sketch of his career illustrates, Hoover generated an FBI tradition that had an enormous impact. Ever the opportunist, Hoover seized on the possibilities offered by Prohibition and the rise of professional gangsterism. The FBI's G-men became legendary sharpshooters and mob-busters. The advent to the White House in 1933 of the left-of-center Franklin D. Roosevelt did not upset the pragmatic Hoover. FDR declared a war on crime; Hoover became his general-in-chief. Congress gave the FBI new powers to combat interstate racketeering; thus armed, the FBI chief showed himself to be a master of the photo opportunity, contriving to be present whenever a master criminal was arrested. In his courtship of publicity, Hoover wrote or had ghosted a huge number of articles for popular periodicals, including *Reader's Digest, Parade, American Magazine, Rotarian*, and *Collier's*. The gangster movie emerged as one of Hollywood's most appealing genres. James Cagney, the star of *G-Men*, became the latest reincarnation of the American hero, as indispensable to the male psyche as Hoover had now become to FDR and to his successors in the White House.[31]

With so many hoodlums either dead or in jail, Hoover needed, by the end of the 1930s, a new menace. The fascists and the reemergence of German power and intelligence activities obliged. In 1938, the FBI won extensive press plaudits for its role in smashing a German spy ring, although in fact some of the main culprits had slipped through the net because of poor coordination between various American police forces and federal agencies. The scare was useful to FDR, who was trying to turn the nation away from its isolationist stance and prepare it to engage once more with issues of international security.[32]

The FBI now began to perform another potentially useful service, spying on the anti-interventionists who criticized the president's foreign policy. One of these was Charles A. Lindbergh, who on the outbreak of war in 1939 cautioned against American involvement. Lindbergh had been a famous and respected figure since 1927, the year of his pioneering flight across the Atlantic aboard the *Spirit of St Louis*. Recently, he had been active on behalf of the anti-interventionist America First Committee. The FBI tailed, probably wiretapped, and attempted to discredit Lindbergh, and meted out similar treatment to other critics ranging from Senator Gerald P. Nye of South Dakota to the *Chicago Tribune*. An unsubstantiated FBI report on Lindbergh in June 1941 indicated that he consorted with prostitutes and pimps, attempted to marry two laundry girls, and had a history of bootlegging whisky by airplane from Canada to Montana. Hoover knew how to increase and exploit the unpopularity of his targets in order to enhance the FBI's power and budget.[33]

Well before America's entry into the war, Hoover took advantage of the gathering storm to entrench his position in Latin America. In May and June 1940, he took advantage of his powerful, direct line to FDR to impress his authority on those who sought to revive intelligence central-ization and to counter German secret operations in Central and South America. On 24 June, the president confirmed the FBI's jurisdiction in the western hemisphere, saying that the State Department could also assign it to work in "the rest of the world," though that would normally be the domain of naval and military intelligence. A few days later, Hoover established the Secret Intelligence Service (SIS), which, under FBI direction, operated first in Cuba and Mexico and then throughout South and Central America and the Caribbean until its demise after the war. The director's long-standing interest in Mexico redoubled when, on 20 August 1940, a Soviet secret agent brutally murdered exiled Russian communist Leon Trotsky in his home in Coyoacan, Mexico.

Before the war started and before the Nazis had been dispatched, Hoover saw an opportunity to begin research on the next menace to U.S. security. In the meantime, his network efficiently garnered in-telligence about Germany's extensive operations. For example, the FBI overcame and negated one of the newer German technologies deployed in Mexico, the concentration of photo-reduced secret data onto microdots. There was little he could do to force the neutral gov-ernments of Mexico and Argentina to expel German secret agents, but at least he kept FDR informed and embarrassed the enemy.[34]

During the war, Hoover was able to defend his western hemispheric turf against all comers, including Gen. William Donovan's burgeoning new intelligence agency, the Office of Strategic Services. The bureau's personnel and expenditure figures attest to the success of Hoover's empire-building. When he took over as director, there were 401 FBI agents. By 1938, the number had grown to 658, with the FBI consuming

14.7 percent of the Justice Department budget. World War II brought renewed expansion—reaching 4,370 in 1945 and a budgetary share of 42.9 percent. After the war, a furious Hoover had to cede his Central and South American responsibilities to the CIA, but the new communist menace of the Cold War years fueled further FBI expansion. By 1955, the bureau had 6,269 agents and a budget of $81 million, now taking up 45.2 percent of the Justice Department budget.[35]

By this time, salvation was at hand in the shape of a new Red Menace. The FBI prospered in the counterintelligence field at home, and whenever the CIA faltered, the bureau expanded overseas until, by century's end, it had several overseas stations. Once again, Hoover exaggerated the menace. To be sure, there were spy networks in America, and U.S. communists wittingly or otherwise danced to Moscow's tune. But Hoover failed to perceive—or shrewdly concealed—the distinction between subversion, the attempt to change American society, and the very much rarer phenomenon of espionage, the attempt to betray it. Bluster began to displace competence. At the height of the Cold War, Hoover categorically denied the existence of a menace that had at least some substance, the Mafia. He failed to crack this hybrid organization whose distribution of narcotics threatened to weaken the very fabric of American society. So he simply pretended that the menace was a fiction, a stratagem that suggests he knew the trade of the confidence man inside out. Hoover's reputation depended on the selective inflation of only those menaces he could claim to defeat.[36]

Hoover epitomized and strengthened the hyperbolic aspects of the American espionage tradition. Historian David Garrow is right to argue that he was not a one-man show. He inherited from Burns and others the mantle of the nineteenth-century private eye and confidence man. Because of congressional disagreements at the time of creation, he inherited a bureau with no mechanism for legislative oversight, and with an underdeveloped sense of duty with regard to public accountability and candor. As Senator Daniel P. Moynihan observed many years later, such lack of openness encourages exaggeration.[37]

CHAPTER 7

H. O. Yardley
The Traitor as Hero

In 1957, there appeared a seductive little book by H. O. Yardley called *The Education of a Poker Player*. It sold 100,000 copies and ran through fourteen printings. Although Yardley was a habitual loser, *The Education* became a classic text on the game. This and the big sales were in part a result of its storytelling style and the frequency of its sexual anecdotes. The self-assurance of the author, too, inspired confidence in would-be practitioners of a game that in no small degree depends upon bluff: "I have constantly won at poker all my life."[1]

The Education contains another point of interest. It is introduced and commended by Ian Fleming, whose first spy thriller novel, *Casino Royale*, had appeared three years earlier. The creator of James Bond said he had "fathered" the publication of Yardley's book. Fleming was understandably drawn to Yardley. The two writers shared not just an interest in gaming and high living but also outrageous immodesty—for example, Fleming claimed to have drafted the memo that persuaded the Americans to set up a central intelligence system.[2]

Seeking celebrity himself, Fleming was further motivated by his desire to be associated with Yardley, a personality who had become an icon in U.S. intelligence history. The legendary CIA director Allen Dulles joined Fleming in this pursuit. In a testament to his trade, *The Craft of Intelligence*, Dulles praised what he and others regarded as Yardley's greatest achievement: the 1920s codebreaking unit, known as the American Black Chamber. Dulles recalled the Washington Disarmament Conference of 1921, when the Americans, British, and

Japanese were negotiating battleship tonnage ratios in the Pacific: "Decipherment of the Japanese diplomatic traffic between Washington and Tokyo by the Black Chamber revealed to our government that the Japanese were actually ready to back down to the desired ratio if we forced the issue. So we were able to force it without risking a breakup of the conference."[3]

Yardley lost his government position in 1929 when President Herbert Hoover's administration dispensed with the Black Chamber. After World War II, the incident came to symbolize the naïveté of an American isolationist policy that contributed to U.S. weakness in the face of the rise of fascism, lack of preparedness to fight Hitler's Germany, and unreadiness to meet the intelligence challenge posed by Japan's surprise attack on Pearl Harbor in 1941. Yardley's bad treatment, and the sense of mission that led him to attack America's unilateral intelligence defenselessness, became articles of faith among those who advocated peacetime intelligence expansion in the Cold War years. Yardley became the lost soul crying out courageously in the intelligence wilderness of the interwar decades.

However, more is now known about Yardley, his deeds, and his legacy, and scholars have for some years been hinting at different perspectives. Already by the 1930s, in fact, there were those who thought badly of Yardley not just in America, but also abroad. For example, the British codebreaking chief Alastair Denniston thought him untrustworthy. But it was still a shock when, in 1967, a book by Ladislas Farago claimed that Yardley was a traitor who had sold American cryptographic secrets to the Japanese. Farago based his case on Japanese Ministry of Foreign Affairs documents that had been available on microfilm at the National Archives since the late 1940s. But U.S. historians had ignored this evidence, and even now it took time for the truth to sink in—Yardley for the time being retained his place in the pantheon of American spy heroes. In 1982, British military historian Ronald Lewin cautiously suggested that Yardley was a "maverick" who did not understand the concept of loyalty to colleagues, and who was incapable of discretion. Finally, in 1988, the U.S. National Security Agency confirmed that the sale-of-secrets story was true. The unthinkable had become official.[4]

Yardley's now-proven treason only complicates the challenge of interpreting his actions and significance. Did his treason and moral weakness undermine his effectiveness as a tribune of intelligence prepared-ness? After a life in publishing that included a stint in charge of Oxford University Press, Denniston's son Robin (who listed Farago among his published authors) embarked on a dual new career—as a Church of England vicar, and as a postgraduate student at the University of Edin-burgh. In the course of his research, he traced Yardley's moral decline over the years. But while this descent helped discredit Yardley as an apostle of U.S. codebreaking and intelligence, Robin Denniston sug-gested a further reason for the mistrust surrounding Yardley's reputa-tion. Disinformation is so endemic in the world of secret intelligence that nobody believes you even when what you say is true. Governmen-tal secrecy only makes matters worse. In the absence of confidence-enhancing openness, the intelligence crusader emerges, in Robin Den-niston's words, "not as a hero but as an Ancient-Mariner-like figure telling his version of events to an audience of skeptics and doubters."[5]

However, Yardley—like Pinkerton, Burns, and Hoover before him—may be placed in a broader cultural context, the American tradition of intelligence hyperbole. He may have been a "maverick" and a traitor, but he was also an American type. Yardley was a persuasive storyteller not just through his prolific writings but also in conversation with his colleagues. David Kahn, a historian of American cryptanalysis, noted his "potent salesmanship."[6] The argument may therefore be made that Yardley failed to "save" U.S. intelligence in the 1930s not just because he was a traitor, but also because his message was an exaggeration. Intelligence did not need saving—it had already been saved.

With more ample evidence now available, it is possible to give a truer account of Yardley and his significance. The story of his life as he told it is quite instructive, for, like other plausible people, he based his stories mainly on the truth. But his history is told here with one eye on guard against embellishment, and with an occasional plunge into the icy stream of reality.

Herbert Osborn Yardley was born in 1889 in Worthington, a place he later described as a "little Indiana frontier town." Yardley's mother died when he was sixteen, and after that he ran wild in Worthington's saloons. Seven of these establishments had poker games. Only one of them was "clean"—it employed a man called "Runt" to frisk those entering for weapons. In this environment, Yardley learned to play soberly while drinking hard—or at least, so he convinced himself.[7]

At the beginning of the Wilson administration, Yardley became a clerk in the State Department code room. He was not entirely comfortable there, reacting with a mixture of "amused contempt" and jealousy to members of the State Department elite who would drop by to scan the telegraphic traffic. They drank wine, not whisky; boasted of amorous affairs but showed little wisdom; and were little more than "smartly dressed pigmies, strutting around with affected European mannerisms." However, Yardley's poker skills and enthusiasm found a new outlet. For he now developed an interest first in the security of U.S. codes and next in the breaking of those used by other nations. He began to show the first signs of what came to be known in cryptological circles as the "Yardley symptom"—an obsessive compulsion to gnaw away at a mathematical problem, day and night, until it is solved. His compulsive nature combined with his intelligence began to yield results, and Yardley, while not in the very highest rank of codebreakers, was undoubtedly able.[8]

Yardley was also a persuasive and opportunistic expansionist. When America entered the war in April 1917, he was slim, young (if balding), vigorous, and full of confidence. Observing that the army was rocketing in size, he asked the chief of the Military Intelligence Division to create a new codebreaking section. One of the arguments he used was that as a matter of urgency America would have to match the codebreaking efforts of the other "Great Powers." He had in mind not just those nations which were now at war with the United States, but also allies like Great Britain—the lesson of the Zimmermann telegram had imprinted itself on Yardley's mind.[9]

As chief of MI-8, the War Department Cipher Bureau, Yardley expanded operations until, at its height, his team numbered 160. He drew in particular on alumni of the University of Chicago. Newly formed, his unit could not hope to match the efforts of the British, but it did chalk up some successes. These included the development of a process to clarify letters written in secret ink, the breaking of codes used by Latin American countries, and the delivery of cryptologically derived information that led to the arrest and conviction of Lothar Witzke, the German secret agent responsible for the Black Tom explosion.[10]

Yardley visited London and Paris during the peace conference. He entertained his British and French counterparts at expensive hotels that included the Piccadilly, Strand, Savoy, Ritz, and Trocadero. He recalled that no serious work was done, and "the whole Peace Conference developed into one grand cocktail party." Yet, he added, "we were all dreaming now of a powerful peace-time Cipher Bureau," and in due course he returned to Washington to lay plans. U-1 chief Frank Polk approved them in May 1919. Yardley's Black Chamber, as it was labeled, was to receive an annual budget of $100,000. The State Department was to contribute $40,000 and military intelligence the rest. Pointers to future trouble lay in the facts that the navy was excluded from the deal because of interservice rivalry, and that Congress insisted the money could not be spent in the District of Columbia—so instead, Yardley set up shop just off New York City's Fifth Avenue.[11]

Yardley was now at the height of his intellectual and persuasive powers. At the request of the State Department, he and his team worked flat out on breaking the Japanese diplomatic codes. The effort induced in Yardley a state of psychological exhaustion, but he and his team succeeded. On the personal recommendation of America's most famous general, Army Chief of Staff J. Joseph Pershing, Yardley was awarded the Distinguished Service Medal in the fall of 1922.[12]

Yardley's accomplishments seemed particularly significant because of the series of international conferences taking place in Washington, D.C., in 1921–1922. These conferences followed in the wake of the Treaty of Versailles, which had brought World War I to a formal conclusion. They dealt in particular with the implementation of a new international order in the Pacific. The Wilsonian ideals of international cooperation and open diplomacy would be tested anew in a region of rising importance to the United States.

In the communications conference that opened in Washington in December 1920, America pressed for open access. This led to differences with Japan over the island of Yap, the point where the cable systems of the Pacific emerged from the ocean. The Germans, who had developed this rocky outcrop 1,700 miles south of Japan, were obliged to surrender it as part of the punitive measures imposed on them at war's end. Control of the island presented the possibility of message monitoring for diplomatic and military as well as business purposes. The Treaty of Versailles gave Japan that control, but the United States was not a signatory of the treaty and demanded access. The negotiations are recorded in *Japanese Diplomatic Secrets,* a well-documented book written by Yardley. (It was immediately suppressed but was declassified in 1978.) According to Yardley, the Black Chamber gave America a vital advantage in the Yap negotiations. The U.S. diplomats seated across the table from Japan's Ambassador Kijuro Shidehara had the advantage of being able to read Japanese diplomatic exchanges. From these, it was evident that Shidehara worried about the European practice, recently emulated by America, of using cable intercepts "to spy into political and especially military secrets."[13] However, it was also plain that Japanese public opinion was more interested in confirming Japan's territorial mandate than in the pursuit of commercial or intelligence goals.

Armed with this knowledge, Secretary of State Charles Evans Hughes pressed hard. By the end of 1921, he had acquired both cable and wireless rights in Yap together with commercial concessions, Shidehara clinging simply to the principle of mandate. Yardley may have been right in his guess that he had brought a smile to Secretary Hughes's face.[14] America could look again with renewed confidence at the strategic approaches to that great chimera, the China market. On Shidehara's side, not too much had been lost—so long as public opinion in Japan did not shift, and so long as nobody knew that the Americans had used undercover methods to fool their Japanese counterparts. The losers were those in America who really did believe in international trust and open diplomacy, but they were unaware of their loss because the State Department kept its secrets.

Because Yap remained secret, it could not make Yardley famous. However, another issue did. The Washington Conference on the Limitation of Armaments met in response to the notion that an arms race had contributed to the outbreak of World War I, and that weapons competition would need to be limited in the future. The naval powers undertook to play their part by reducing capital ship tonnage. In the Pacific, this was to be achieved by means of an agreed ratio. Hughes proposed 500,000 tons each for America and Britain, and 300,000 tons for Japan. Instead of this 10.10.6 ratio, Japan wanted 10.10.7 or better, but they finally settled on American terms. According to Yardley, Hughes once again achieved this goal by having the advantage, thanks to the Black Chamber's interceptions and decipherments, of knowing the Japanese hand—especially Tokyo's instruction to Shidehara on

28 November 1921 that he could, if all else failed, settle for 10.10.6. Summing up the impact of that decrypt, Yardley wrote: "Stud poker is not a very difficult game after you see your opponent's hole card."[15]

The naval ratios ploy did make Yardley famous, but in retrospect the achievement is questionable. The decryption and translation of messages took time, and Yardley did not convincingly demonstrate that the Black Chamber had kept pace with the rapid cut and thrust of the negotiating table. Nor was he the only person to claim he was reading Japanese messages—the British, too, claimed to have been at it. Furthermore, American HUMINT, or human intelligence, seems to have beaten the Black Chamber by more than a month in uncovering Japan's bottom negotiating line, for the U.S. naval attaché in Tokyo had reported on 17 October 1921 that Japan would settle for 10.10.6. Did Japan really want 10.10.7? Certainly, they did not need it, as the age of the great battleship was over. They may not have realized this any more than the Americans, but it was still evident that the costs of naval construction were crippling. Japan's strategic priorities lay elsewhere, in continental Asia. In the "Shidehara era" of diplomacy stretching through the 1920s, Japan showed a realistic appreciation of U.S. naval strength, and sought American friendship in order to neutralize a potentially dangerous foe. The 10.10.7 ratio was something to be fought for, but it was also a prize ripe for forfeit in calculations that lay beyond Yardley's comprehension.[16]

The naval ratios settlement reflected common sense on both sides of the Pacific. Shidehara was able to continue good relations with the United States, and, by now negotiating as Japan's foreign minister, he was able to conclude a similar agreement in a subsequent Washington naval conference in 1930. His resolution to remain friendly with the United States continued in the longer term. In the wake of World War II, he would serve as Japan's prime minister, working closely with American occupying forces. However, developments in the meantime undid his restrained and peaceful diplomacy. Yardley's contribution to these unfortunate events was more tangible than his claim that he had outsmarted Japan in 1921.

◆ ◆ ◆ ◆

In 1929, Yardley encountered the severe blow to his career that finally destabilized his childlike personality and gave him a reason to betray his country. Following the 1928 presidential election, the incoming administration remained Republican, but the faces were new. President Herbert Hoover installed Henry Stimson as secretary of state. Yardley decided to wait until May before telling Stimson of the existence of his secret codebreaking unit. His logic would become a fixture in the thinking of American intelligence leaders. Before revealing the dreadful secrets of state, it was best to wait for the onset of that mood of realism that would inevitably replace the high aspirations and ideals of a presidential campaign. However, Yardley's ploy failed. Stimson decided to abolish the Black Chamber. Its staff were given notice. In the first of several "Halloween massacres" affecting the intelligence community over the years, on 31 October 1929 the codebreakers found themselves out of work and with no pension benefits. That was just two days after Black Tuesday, the massive Wall Street crash that heralded a decade of depression and dismal employment opportunities.[17]

There are several reasons, some of them more speculative than others, for the closing of the American Black Chamber. The unit was already in a reduced condition, operating on only about a tenth of its 1920 budget with only six staff members. This was because the army had progressively withdrawn its support, leaving Yardley fatally vulnerable to a cessation in State Department funding. The army had, within its Signals Corps, a newly formed Signals Intelligence Service (SIS). Its mission was to train codebreakers for a future conflict rather than to build up a peacetime empire, which left no room for Yardley's unit.[18]

In any case, the Black Chamber had been suffering from a decrease in the volume and success of its work. Peacetime conditions partly explain this. Another factor was the continuing and perhaps strengthening American concern with open government. During the wartime emergency, the cable companies had ignored the 1912 Radio Communications Act, which forbade the divulgence of the contents of cables. But the advent of peace changed their attitude. In 1926 the Black Chamber had only seven intercepts to decode, and then the Radio Act of 1927 further curtailed its lifeblood when it forbade intercepts. Closure seemed in keeping with the principle of open government and also with prevailing attitudes, summed up in the *Christian Science Monitor*'s observation that "This fine gesture will commend itself to all who are trying to develop the same standards of decency between Governments as exist between individuals."[19] The Hoover administration was predisposed to cut back on federal spending, and an agency that did so little work did not recommend itself as an exception to the policy of austerity.

At this stage, the possibility of conspiracy must be introduced, even if it is speculative. It could simply be the case that the Americans gave nothing away when they closed the Black Chamber, because its secrets were already known. SIS chief William Friedman asserted that the Japanese knew all along about "the theft of some of their messages" during the 1921 naval reductions conference.[20]

By the mid-1920s, there was also a suspicion within the State Department that America's own diplomatic codes had been broken, depriving the United States of any intelligence advantage it had hitherto enjoyed. In May 1925, Secretary of State Frank B. Kellogg heard from Albert H. Washburn, his minister to Austria, that there had been a security leak. Several Austrian army officers, skilled in cryptography, had found themselves unemployed and out of funds because of the fall of the empire. Washburn's message intimated that one of them, referred to as "Stein," had succumbed to temptation in order to obtain employment and money. Washburn's message ran:

> German secret agent former Colonel secretly got in touch with former Austrian officer on the pay roll of the American Military Attaché here and upon being encouraged under instructions, offered at the second meeting one milliard [i.e., billion] Austrian crowns approximately $15,000 for "cipher tables of the American diplomatic B to P inclusive." Obvious reference is to A-l or B-l the existence of both codes being possibly known.

Kellogg took the possibility seriously. He issued an instruction to Vienna through a top security cablegram marked "No distribution," but still in the possibly vulnerable B-l code.[21]

Kellogg preserved a note of skeptical optimism, asking Washburn to "try to ascertain whether agent or agent's principals have copy of code books to which desired cipher tables refer." His next instruction, however, betrayed his real fears: "If not, how is it known that books range from symbols B to P inclusive?" It does appear that the American diplomatic codes had been partially cracked or captured. Stimson's dissolution of the Black Chamber stemmed from his belief that it would have relatively painless consequences, for by then rival powers may have been aware not only of American secrets but of which of their own secrets and codes the Americans knew. They may even have been operating a double code, one for the benefit of the Black Chamber, another for real business. As a codebreaking unit, the chamber was in any case virtually moribund. In practice, the State Department may have given away nothing in 1929.

If the State Department had nothing to lose, why did it wait four years before withdrawing support from the Black Chamber? One can speculate that Kellogg did not think of the move whereas Stimson did, or perhaps 1929 was a more propitious year for impressing foreigners. Another possibility is that the delay reflects the desire of the State Department to make German secret agents think the Americans were ignorant of their security leak. A sudden rejection of codebreaking would have been too easy to interpret. For fear of giving away his knowledge of the leak, Kellogg warned his minister in Vienna to exercise "discretion [over] the advisability of endeavoring to obtain answers" about the extent of German cryptographic knowledge. The Americans could afford a delay in closing down the Black Chamber because they had no immediate fears about any further consequences of the leak; if they pretended for a while to be unaware that their code had been broken, the leak might prove useful by allowing them to feed the Germans false information. For military security matters, Friedman was developing alternative codes.[22]

The theory offered by Yardley and his admirers to explain the demise of the Black Chamber is no less speculative than the foregoing surmise. According to Yardley, the closure was the work of "a naïve President."[23] This image fits in with the theory that the Republican administrations of 1921–1933 were overidealistic and too trustful in their conduct of American foreign policy. What seemed to epitomize the alleged naïveté was the Kellogg-Briand Pact. Negotiated in 1928 by Secretary of State Kellogg and his French counterpart, it was a promise of nonaggression and peaceful settlement of international disputes, but it carried no power of enforcement. Sixty-two nations signed up, including the United States, Germany, the Soviet Union, and Japan. President Hoover approved the pact in the summer of 1929, just when the Black Chamber was receiving its death sentence.

According to a popular version of events disseminated by Yardley and his followers, Secretary of State Stimson was shocked when he finally learned about the Black Chamber and its activities, uttering the now-famous words, "Gentlemen do not read each other's mail."[24] It is this statement, above all, that has become the epigraph at the start of a widely believed collective chapter about American diplomatic folly, a story about isolationism that led to lack of intelligence preparedness and to Pearl Harbor.

The demise of the Black Chamber needs to be put into proper perspective. If naïveté played a part in its closure, it was just a supporting role. After any great war, it is customary to wind down one's defense and intelligence provision, and not only for economy's sake. The arrangements for winning one war will not necessarily win the next. Just as battleships were out of date after World War I, so were the tired and possibly compromised operations of the Black Chamber. Codebreaking provision was being wound down in Britain as well as in America. General intelligence demobilization was widespread in the United States, and in this context codebreaking was not singled out for exceptionally brutal treatment. The field had not been consigned to terminal neglect, as Friedman's Signals Intelligence Service would show in coming years. It would appear from unpublished portions of Stimson's diaries that he was content with the War Department's arrangement "for the purpose of keeping together an expert body of code experts," and that he objected solely to the breaking of diplomatic codes. He made his famous/infamous "gentlemen" statement in the wake of World War II, when as secretary of war he had made extensive use of decrypt product; it may even have been an instance of self-parody. Like those Wilsonian open-government idealists who stooped to espionage, Stimson was a realist as well as a gentleman.[25]

In one sense, though, it is probable that Stimson was an innocent at the time of Yardley's dismissal. For, almost certainly unbeknownst to the secretary of state, the cryptanalyst was by this time a traitor. In 1928, Yardley had been short of money for the usual reasons—gambling debts and the costs of funding a Prohibition era drinking habit. He felt betrayed by an American establishment that had consistently pared down his codebreaking unit. But he was motivated by money, not by principles or ideology. That mercenary trait makes him closer to his American private detective antecedents than to those celebrated ideological traitors of 1930s England, the Cambridge spy ring.

Primarily in search of money, Yardley approached a Japanese journalist for an introduction to Tokyo's representatives in Washington. He was able to meet Setsuzo Sewada, the counselor at the Japanese embassy. Japan's top two cryptographers now traveled to America to interview Yardley. Sewada paid the Black Chamber man $7,000. For this, the American traitor supplied Japan with America's codebreaking secrets together with some compromising information on British intelligence, and he promised to sabotage any further U.S. work on Japanese codes.[26]

Japan responded to Yardley's revelations by changing and upgrading its encryption systems. The new and more intractable codes were in future known by colors, such as Purple. While it is sometimes argued that Japanese plotting against America and the unpredictability of the Pearl Harbor attack stem from the naïve closure of the Black Chamber, the truth is that the Black Chamber had become a threat to the national security of the United States. Yardley's betrayal, not his dismissal, contributed to the American codebreakers' inability to read the vital messages in 1941, the year of the Pearl Harbor attack.[27]

Yardley not only facilitated Japanese aggression but supplied Tokyo with a motive. Once again, his craving for money swept aside scruple. Even allowing for the lower price levels of 1929, $7,000 does not last long if you are a compulsive spender. So Yardley decided to venture into print—a decision that cast a shadow on U.S.-Japan relations.

The world was ready for the type of exposé that Yardley had in mind. Millions had died in the war in the name of a new era of trust and international cooperation. But as the years passed, disillusionment set in even before the demoralizing Crash of 1929. As part of this process, it was becoming fashionable both to acknowledge and to criticize spying by one's own side. In 1928, Somerset Maugham published *Ashenden,* a collection of short stories about World War I espionage that were fictional but not far removed from the unromantic reality. In the same year, the Belgian surrealist René Magritte painted "L'Espion," portraying a keyhole-peeper who was respectably dressed yet cut down to size by the disembodiment of the woman upon whom he pried. Dashiell Hammett's novel *The Red Harvest* in 1929 ripped into the Pinkerton agency for its anti-labor practices out west. In 1930, Morton Pennypacker published his book *The Two Spies: Nathan Hale and Robert Townsend,* showing the extent of George Washington's espionage activities. The book, according to its author, caused "a mild sensation."[28]

Perhaps encouraged by the developing mood, Yardley ventured into his own, peculiarly mercenary, brand of apostasy. He wrote a book about his work as government codebreaker called *The American Black Chamber*. The book extolled his achievements and exaggerated them. Notably, he claimed credit for what he portrayed as the advantageous outwitting of the Japanese at the 1921 naval conference. He wrote scathingly of the decision to close the Black Chamber. He discussed the top-secret work of the U.S. government, and he freely shared British official secrets. A serialized version appeared in the popular *Saturday Evening Post* in April and May 1931. When the book appeared on 1 June, it was an instant success, selling about 18,000 copies. Lucrative lecture invitations followed, and Yardley had for the time being achieved a satisfying income. In the meantime, the book came out in translation in Japan, where it sold almost twice the number of copies bought in the United States.[29]

Yardley did not write *The American Black Chamber* in the spirit of principled apostasy. His aim was not to expose abuses of power or to bring about reforms that might be beneficial to the American people. On the contrary, publication of the book was harmful to the United States. Japan's leaders, or at least its key foreign policy makers, already knew about American codebreaking. But now, as a result of sensational stories in the newspapers *Osaku Ikainichi* and *Tokyo Zichi*, the entire Japanese nation knew. No nation likes to feel that it has been deceived and outwitted. Yardley later suggested that the Japanese had planned to assassinate him. For once, he may not have been overdramatic. More immediately, the Japanese Foreign Ministry tried to discredit Yardley as a man of dishonor by claiming he had told Japanese embassy officials in 1921 that he was breaking their codes, and that he had tried to sell them the translations. Foreign Minister Shidehara and his policy of engaging in friendly conferences with the Americans came under attack in the House of Peers, and militaristic critics rounded on him for, as they claimed, so weakly surrendering Japanese interests to the untrustworthy Americans, and for failing to ensure that the Japanese codes were not more frequently changed in order to protect Tokyo's secrets. This reinvigoration of Japanese anti-Americanism created a climate in which the concessions over naval tonnage and Yap seemed suddenly unforgivable. Japan shrank from further dealings with the United States over arms limitation. Shidehara and his moderate colleagues found it increasingly difficult to control Japan's military expansionists. In September, Japan invaded Manchuria. In December, the Japanese cabinet fell, and with it Shidehara and the restraining hand of civilian governance. The era of international trust had been tenuous, and now it was over.[30]

◆ ◆ ◆ ◆

Yardley's disservice to his country did not end with the publication of *The American Black Chamber*. With lecture invitations declining and money once again running out, he took to writing thrillers, two of which were made into Hollywood movies. He also planned a further publication on the work of the Black Chamber. The resulting manuscript, "Japanese Diplomatic Secrets," consisted in large part of verbatim quotations from and transcripts of the messages decrypted by Yardley's team, especially at the time of the Yap cable negotiations. The book was ready for publication in 1933. The Macmillan Company was poised to publish *The Dark Invader,* the memoir of former German naval intelligence officer Franz von Rintelen, who had helped organize sabotage operations in the United States during the period of America's World War I neutrality. When that book did come out, its author found he could not return to Germany, where he would have been arrested for treason. Meantime, in Britain the novelist and former intelligence agent Compton Mackenzie was on trial for publishing a book, *Greek Memories,* that divulged some details about British espionage and, worse, exposed the farcical behavior of its higher practitioners. Fearing that the publication of "Japanese Diplomatic Secrets" would further impair relations with Japan, the American authorities stepped in with a legally dubious move. In February 1933, they impounded the typescript copies of Yardley's book.[31]

In the pre-digital era, the rewriting of a 970-page manuscript would have been a daunting task. But in any case Congress now passed the Act for the Preservation of Government Records. The bill, signed into law by President Franklin D. Roosevelt in June 1933, is known as the Yardley Act. It was by no means as draconian as the British Official Secrets Act of 1911, but it did make a serious crime of any future disclosures about U.S. codebreaking. This and the whole process by which "Japanese Diplomatic Secrets" was suppressed created the expectation that any author writing about the American espionage establishment would be summarily dealt with—even if, as was evident in some future cases, the author's objective was to expose genuine abuses. In this indirect way, Yardley had dealt a blow to open government.

Although Yardley's treason did not become known until later, his cavalier treatment of secrets bearing on national security effectively ended his career. In the late 1930s he worked for the nationalist government in China, where homesickness led to depression and his work suffered from his excessive drinking and insufficient acquaintance with the latest cryptanalytical techniques. In August 1940 he returned to Washington, perhaps hoping for work now that war had once again broken out in Europe. Friedman and the new cryptographic establishment gave him the cold shoulder. In December, America and Britain began tentative discussions on cryptanalytical cooperation, presenting another potential opportunity for employment. But the head of the British Code and Cypher School, Alistair Denniston, warned that "We are entitled to recall that the Americans sent over at the end of the last war the now notorious Colonel Yardley for purposes of cooperation. He went so far as to publish the story of his cooperation in book form." Unwilling to accept his pariah status, Yardley offered his services to the Canadians, who were thinking of setting up a codebreaking facility independent from the British. Denniston made a special trip to Ottawa, threatening the Canadian government that if they took on Yardley, the British would deny them cryptographic cooperation.[32]

Yardley was a colorful character, but the lessons of his life are grim. Where hyperbole rules in the intelligence world, truth and realism fly out the window, and, in the worst-case scenario, the first whispers of treason creep in to take their place. That was the Yardley story. He was no voice crying out in the wilderness, no maverick except in the sense that the scoundrel often hides behind the skirt of manufactured individualism.

Yardley's motivation, like that of private detectives before him and future generations of traitors, was mercenary. This is one of the points lost on some students of American treason, who assumed that Yardley's rough contemporaries, the ideologically driven Cambridge spy ring in Britain, provided the likely model for serious foreign penetration of U.S. intelligence.[33]

Despite all this, Yardley's reputation as a father of American cryptography lived on for many years. He was buried with military honors at

Arlington National Cemetery, becoming an icon and a martyr to the lost cause of interwar intelligence. The misrepresentation of Yardley was not only a prerequisite for devotees of a bloated intelligence community but also a useful preface to that badly written primer, the story of Pearl Harbor.

CHAPTER 8

Pearl Harbor in Intelligence History

At 7 a.m. on 7 December 1941, Japan's bomber attack force showed up as a mysterious blip on the oscilloscope of the U.S. Army's Mobile Radar Station on the northern tip of Oahu. Normally, the radar closed down at 7 because of military economy measures—measures that also explain why the radar's operators, privates Joseph L. Lockard and George E. Elliott, were poorly trained. But Elliott was intrigued by the blip, prevailing on his bleary eyed comrade to keep the radar operating. The two soldiers chatted idly over the next thirty-nine minutes until they lost contact due to radar distortion caused by a mountain range. They realized that large numbers of aircraft were approaching and even relayed that information to the skeleton staff that remained on duty at the island's radar headquarters. But through a collective leap of faith, everyone assumed the planes were friendly. At 7.49 a.m., precisely on time, Comdr. Mitsuo Fuchida gave the attack order, and everyone was disabused.[1]

The Japanese killed more than two thousand people, and the raid propelled America into World War II. One construction of the event is that it was not really predictable, and that, from the lowly Lockard right up to President Franklin D. Roosevelt, no single American could be held responsible. But that kind of conclusion is generally unacceptable after any event involving heavy and sudden loss of life. The bereaved and their families and political representatives reject the concept of history as muddle; they demand clear answers. They see collective death as a tragedy, an event that need not have happened, and they want to blame someone, or else the system. This outlook played into the hands of propagandists, for whom Pearl Harbor was a heaven-sent opportunity. On the intelligence front, Pearl Harbor became an important justification for the creation of the Central Intelligence Agency, and then for the expansion in the CIA's functions, budget, and personnel. Examined more closely, however, Pearl Harbor did not justify the CIA, or its expansion, or its questionable activities—or even its good practices. In intelligence terms, it was significant not in itself but as an irrelevance that metamorphosed into a justification.

The intensity of the debate over Pearl Harbor—one of the most controversial events in American history—reflects not just the casualties on that day but also the losses in the ensuing war, in which over a million Americans were killed or wounded. The debate is acrimonious for the further reason that it is linked to other controversies such as that over the merits and faults of the New Deal, and to controversial personalities ranging from the president to his senior admirals. Like other long-running historical debates, the discussion has changed its character in response to subsequent political issues, but with the complication that the slow release of the sensitive documentation has led to highly charged accusations of cover-up.

Because of the heat generated in any wide-ranging debate, it is all too easy to lose sight of intelligence issues and to confuse them with other matters. In the case of Pearl Harbor, there was some overlap, and it is sensible to consider the intelligence debate in the context of broader historical discussion. But at the same time, it is important to keep in mind that the intelligence debate is one determined by the agenda of expansionists and restrictionists. Expansionists have a detailed agenda. They mourn the loss of Yardley, deplore the lack of intelligence preparedness between the wars, paint a bleak picture of U.S. intelligence in 1941, credit the British for rescuing American intelligence and putting it on a sound footing, advocate a permanent arrangement for central intelligence, and applaud the creation and expansion of the CIA after the war. Restrictionists are suspicious of the CIA, convinced that the Founding Fathers did not sanction intelligence bureaucracies, skeptical of the role of intelligence in the Pearl Harbor catastrophe, and suspicious of the role played in it by U.S. politicians.

These themes are evident from a review of the Pearl Harbor debate and historiography. Although the debate does not fit neatly into categories, it may be followed in a roughly chronological manner. First, as in the case of other great debates, there is the official point of view. The administration of Franklin D. Roosevelt had to explain what had happened. In a series of official investigations between 1941 and 1946, the responsibility for Pearl Harbor was pinned on Adm. Husband E. Kimmel, commander of the Pacific Fleet, and on Gen. Walter C. Short, the army commander in Hawaii. These two officers were held to have been negligent in their defense of Pearl Harbor. The conclusion was welcome to the Democratic administration for both patriotic and more selfish reasons. The patriotic reasons were diverse. One centered on the need for high wartime morale: the identification of two guilty men was a way of providing a simple explanation of what had gone wrong, and of preserving national unity at a perilous time. Another consideration was that the focus on individuals—or scapegoats—distracted attention from U.S. codebreaking capabilities. This was desirable because it was, as ever, wise to keep the Japanese in the dark about those capabilities.[2]

But speculation about codebreaking might also have implicated the White House in culpability for the Pearl Harbor attack—if codebreaking product informed Roosevelt of the imminence of attack, why did he not alert Kimmel and Short? The more convenient identification of Kimmel and Short as prime culprits stifled any speculation about possible blemishes on the conduct of American foreign policy in the months leading up to what Roosevelt called the "day of infamy." This motive extended beyond the White House. Congress, too, was dominated by Democrats. The Democratic majority, seeing an advantage in blaming Kimmel and Short, did so in its 1946 report, although the Republican minority on the congressional investigating team disagreed. By 1947, congressional Democrats had in one respect shifted their ground. Legislators testifying in favor of the proposed CIA argued that intelligence had let America down in 1941, hence the need for a new superagency. The Democrats' motivation, however, remained constant—they had to show that Roosevelt and his Democratic administration could not be blamed for Pearl Harbor. The culprit had changed, but the whitewash remained in place.[3]

For reasons of patriotic secrecy but also with an eye on their own reputations, politicians writing memoirs about World War II were reticent on the subject of intelligence. A semi-official interpretation did, however, emerge from the writings of William L. Langer. During the war, this historian was in charge of the research and analysis branch of the Office of Strategic Services, the intelligence agency led by Gen. William Donovan. After the war, Langer took more time off from Harvard University to establish the Office of National Estimates within the CIA. Concerned with justifying intelligence policies to posterity, he advised on the establishment of the Office of the Historian in the CIA, leading to the production of several official secret histories, some of them subsequently declassified.[4]

Although Langer did not favor indiscriminate expansion, he was a firm advocate of peacetime intelligence provision, using Pearl Harbor to justify his appeals—a stratagem that influenced his interpretation of the 1941 attack. In a 1946 lecture in which he advocated the establishment of the CIA, he argued that Pearl Harbor stemmed from a lack of "integration" in the American intelligence community. Even during the war, he stated, attempts at improved coordination had been mere "expedients."[5]

In 1948, Langer accepted the job of writing an officially sanctioned history of U.S. entry into the war. Allen W. Dulles, president of the Council on Foreign Relations and a future director of the CIA, appealed for help in this project to Adm. Sidney W. Souers, America's first director of central intelligence after the war and now executive director of the newly established National Security Council. Souers smoothed the way for Langer to obtain privileged access to the relevant secret documents. In the early 1950s, Langer and his collaborator, S. Everett Gleason, produced a two-volume study that portrayed President Roosevelt as a reluctant belligerent struggling with public opinion. Langer and Gleason—"court historians," to their critics—ignored the uncomfortable intelligence issue.[6]

From the outset, there were those, the revisionists, who wished to revise or challenge the official version of events. Their motivation varied. Out of military loyalty, family honor, or just a sense of fair play, one category of debater fought early and often to clear the names of Kimmel and Short, the "scapegoats" of Pearl Harbor. Other commentators worried that President Roosevelt had not properly consulted Congress during the period before America entered into the war—in this respect, his omissions undermined constitutional government. Partisan Republicans resented Roosevelt's long spell in the White House (1933–1945) and looked for signs of presidential incompetence that could be used to discredit and end Democratic governance. Left-wing critics of the New Deal such as Charles Beard argued that it had failed to reduce unemployment and restore prosperity because it had not gone far enough, and that Roosevelt had manipulated Japan into starting a war in order to create a distraction that would extricate him from his political difficulties at home. On the Right, critics made a similar case for the opposite reason, that the New Deal had gone too far, substituting socialist for business values—by taking America into the war and contributing to the defeat of Germany, Roosevelt furthermore gave the Soviet Union a great opportunity to expand its communist empire.[7]

The disparate but influential school associated with 1930s anti-intervention and isolationist sentiment held that Roosevelt had been determined to take America into the war. Faced with a reluctant nation and opposition in Congress and unable to provoke Germany into initiating hostilities against America, he had tried to force Japan into launching an attack. At a congressional hearing in 1946, it was learned that on 25 November 1941, Roosevelt indicated it was likely the Japanese would mount a surprise attack soon. Secretary of War Stimson paraphrased the president's words: "The question was how we should maneuver them into the position of firing the first shot without allowing too much danger to ourselves." Critics like George Morgenstern and Charles Tansill fastened onto that remark. Tansill's thesis was summed up in the title of his 1952 book, *Back Door to War*. Admiral Kimmel himself could be said to have joined the revisionists. Administration critics had been furious about the withholding of evidence from Congress, and about its availability to Langer and Gleason but not to other historians. Kimmel argued in a 1955 memoir that the government also kept regional commanders in the dark about what they knew, from the output of codebreaking to the imminence of a Japanese attack on Pearl Harbor. So, whereas the "court historians" held that intelligence was weak and uncoordinated, the extreme version of the revisionist school held that it had been effective—indeed, inconveniently so for the White House conspirators.[8]

The Bancroft prize for the best history book published in 1962 went to Roberta Wohlstetter's *Pearl Harbor: Warning and Decision*, a work that faulted but did not blame U.S. intelligence. Like so many people, Wohlstetter worried about the possibility of another surprise attack, an attack that this time would have catastrophic consequences, as it would be made with thermonuclear weapons. At the time she wrote the book, America was going through the agonizing "missile gap" debate about whether the Soviet Union had stolen a march over the United States in terms of nuclear strike capability. In writing the book the way she did and in expressing admiration for Langer and Gleason, Wohlstetter additionally may have intended to defend the CIA, which was under attack at the time for having made a mess of the Bay of Pigs invasion, the attempt to end communism in Cuba. However, her book was by no means an unqualified endorsement of the merits of intelligence in general, let alone the CIA in particular.[9] Wohlstetter seemed persuaded that there is no fail-safe means of guarding against surprise attack. The best defense, in her view, is a well-equipped and flexible military that can respond effectively even when attacked without warning.

In her salutary analysis, Wohlstetter reproached those who with the wisdom of hindsight identified signals that should have warned Roosevelt and the military of the time, place, and nature of the Japanese attack. In a departure from the position of CIA boosters who dwelled on the attenuated state of U.S. intelligence in the 1930s, she argued that America's decision makers had an amplitude of intelligence. In fact, the intelligence bureaucracy was so large that its size was an impediment to efficient functioning. The real problem was that, at the time, it was impossible to single out the real and significant "signals" from all the background "noise." No one person had an overview of the significant information from which it would be possible to draw the right conclusions. In that sense, at least, the advocates of central analytical intelligence could draw comfort from Wohlstetter's book and continue to believe in that mechanistic solution to the challenge of eternal vigilance, the collective analytical supremo.[10]

Although Wohlstetter's book achieved the status of a classic, it did not impose closure on the Pearl Harbor debate. On the contrary, the use of Pearl Harbor for propaganda and CIA-boosting purposes underwent a revival under the ministrations of a disparate yet in some ways cohesive group that one might call the counterrevisionists. A number of counterrevisionists wanted to mount a kind of defense by proxy of the CIA at a time when it was coming under fire for incompetence, immorality, disregard for civil liberties, and transgressions against the U.S. Constitution. The Bay of Pigs, revelations in 1967 about CIA funding of private groups, and a spate of attacks in the mid-1970s all took their toll and stimulated the counterattack on the agency's critics. In the late 1970s, spice was added to the debate when new documentation began to become available, including some decrypted Japanese messages code-named "Magic." All this came at a time when "neoconservatives" and the presidential candidate Ronald Reagan sought to boost, or "unleash," the CIA after a period of congressionally imposed restraint.

In a variety of ways, the counterrevisionists argued anew that intelligence failures lay behind the Pearl Harbor tragedy. While some allowed that President Roosevelt had made mistakes—for example, by paying insufficient attention to decrypts—the general drift was in the direction of exculpation of the White House. In 1981, just when President Reagan was taking office, former CIA deputy director of intelligence Ray Cline claimed that a reading of Wohlstetter suggested that better intelligence coordination in 1941 might have yielded very different results, and made Pearl Harbor an "intelligence triumph." He saw President Roosevelt as wise, 1930s American intelligence as unprepared, and last-minute British intelligence tuition as the means by which America had saved itself in the nick of time from fatal naïveté in World War II.[11]

The lack of preparedness of American intelligence once again became an article of faith, among the "politically correct" as well as more conservative people. Historian David Kahn, for example, argued that U.S. racial prejudice against the Japanese was one factor that had blinded Americans to the seriousness of the threat from Tokyo; for example, some intelligence experts subscribed to the theory that "slant-eyed" Japanese pilots would be no good in dogfights. Kahn argued that American intelligence on Japan was quantitatively as well as qualitatively deficient. He bluntly dismissed Wohlstetter's depiction of an abundance of intelligence as "not true."[12]

With the product of codebreaking now more widely available, the counterrevisionists turned their attention to those decrypted messages that seemed to indicate when, where, and how the Japanese were going to strike. Did President Roosevelt know about the attack in advance, and did he keep his commanders in the dark to ensure that the Japanese planes and submarines scored a good hit, thus shocking U.S. public opinion into supporting a war declaration and an all-out effort to defeat the enemy? The counterrevisionists said no, for three main reasons. First, with the Japanese remembering Yardley and changing their codes with conscientious frequency, codebreaking remained of limited utility. Second, those codes that were broken were sometimes broken too late. Just because they had been broken by 1945 did not mean that Roosevelt and his advisers were reading them in October–November 1941. Third, the Japanese fleet had maintained radio silence as it approached its target in Pearl Harbor, making it impossible in this vital period either to read radio messages or to estimate where they were coming from.[13]

The end of the Cold War in 1989 stimulated Pearl Harbor debate in two very different ways. First, it meant that the advocates of Big Intelligence had to hunt for new rationales for expansion. The intelligence-failure-at-Pearl-Harbor metaphor was convenient to expansionists because it was not Soviet-specific and therefore not consigned to oblivion with the collapse of the communist enemy. But the end of the Cold War also liberated potential critics who hitherto might have deemed it unpatriotic to criticize national security policy. Though some of them were advanced in years, these critics can for the sake of convenience be labeled the neorevisionists. One such writer, Edward L. Beach, had served as a submarine officer in the Pacific war. There was nothing wrong with revisionism, he wrote in 1991. The senior protagonists at Pearl Harbor were all dead, national security no longer dictated that secrecy should be preserved concerning what happened fifty years ago, and it was time the truth came out.[14]

The neorevisionists launched a new wave of skepticism about Pearl Harbor. Sometimes their claims were just as sensational as those of the intelligence propagandists who sought any means to keep the CIA in business, but they also brought to light some disturbing new evidence. Beach was careful not to criticize Roosevelt in a politically partisan manner, but he argued that Washington had made scapegoats of Kimmel and Short. This finding did not at first carry great weight, as it met with a powerful counterblast from Henry Clausen, who had conducted an army investigation of Pearl Harbor in 1944–1945. In 1992, Clausen published a book based, he claimed, on privileged information, in which he emphasized anew the incompetence of Kimmel and Short. Then in 1995, Congress came down on Clausen's side. A debate on the future of the CIA was taking place at the time, and politicians could not afford to ignore an issue so freighted with significance. So the Senate and House committees on the armed services held hearings, and Undersecretary of Defense Edwin Dorn was asked to produce a report that would take into account new information, and to address the issue of whether Washington had withheld intelligence from Kimmel and Short that might have enabled them to defend Pearl Harbor more effectively. Dorn conceded that Kimmel and Short should have been provided with more intelligence but concluded that, on the basis of the intelligence that they did have, they should have ordered "a higher level of vigilance" than was maintained in Hawaii on 7 December 1941.[15]

However, the lid could not be forced down in this way, and conspiracy theorists began to revive even some of the most extreme suspicions of the 1940s. Details of who did what on the fateful day came under renewed scrutiny. The microscope was even trained on the dining arrangements of Prime Minister Winston Churchill and President Roosevelt on the evening of the attack. At 9 p.m. British time (11 a.m. in Hawaii), Churchill was just ending his meal at his country house when the news came through; a little while later, Eleanor Roosevelt served up supper for twenty-four guests—she made scrambled eggs, as it was the servants' night off at the White House. Meanwhile, the president worked on his "Day of Infamy" speech to Congress calling for a declaration of war. According to former British secret agent James Rusbridger in a 1991 book, the postprandial Churchill remained utterly calm when apprised of the attack. According to Rusbridger, Churchill was *so* unruffled he must have known in advance—but he had not warned Roosevelt because he longed for a shocking deed that would force the Americans into the war and save the desperately hard-pressed British. However, according to World War II U.S. Navy veteran Robert B. Stinnet in a 2000 book, Roosevelt may well have known for some time anyway, as *he* remained quite serene when discussing the attack with Eleanor's supper guests. Yet he had not warned Kimmel and Short, because he, like Churchill, had longed for that dramatic deed that would spur the American public to support the war.[16]

The point might be made that Churchill and Roosevelt were great leaders, and that great leaders do tend to exude icy indifference in moments of crisis. On the other hand, neorevisionism was significant in two ways. First, it did draw conclusions from a fuller range of evidence—previously available only to the privileged few who were predisposed to exonerate Roosevelt and blame Kimmel and Short and/or weak intelligence. Stinnett, for example, had established that the Japanese Fleet did not maintain full radio silence as it closed in on Pearl Harbor.

American direction-finding equipment could and did track its course. Second, there does seem to have been a conspiracy of silence on Pearl Harbor. Although the British protest that they are just as open as the Americans, their Pearl Harbor records remain sealed. On the American side, the conspiracy of silence may not be said to have emanated exclusively from the White House, but the effect has nevertheless been to cover up the evidence and hamper the work of the revisionists.[17]

By means of energetic propaganda, a version of the Pearl Harbor story convenient to the Roosevelt administration and to CIA expansionists has been woven into intelligence history. Yet, true or false, the story was paradoxically inappropriate to intelligence needs. Precautions against surprise attack have little to do with the CIA's more significant functions—to name just two examples, estimating Soviet military strength, and covert operations. For this reason, the myth of Pearl Harbor as the epitome of lack of preparedness in peacetime has distorted perceptions of America's post–World War II intelligence mission.

The Pearl Harbor myth also, of course, has distorted perceptions of interwar intelligence history. It was all too easy to tell the story of declining intelligence resources in the two decades after Versailles, a story that seemed to end so logically the day Japanese bombs and torpedoes shattered the tranquillity of American isolation. However, since the mid-1970s, historians have begun to question the depiction of interwar intelligence as uniformly inadequate. At the same time, a closer examination of the 1920s and 1930s reveals certain intelligence weaknesses that did not contribute to Pearl Harbor but perhaps constituted a stronger justification of the intelligence reforms that culminated in the CIA.

In terms of bureaucracy, resources, and personnel, most branches of American intelligence declined from the end of World War I to the mid-1930s. Successive Republican administrations abolished U-1 in 1927 and the Black Chamber in 1929. Also in 1929, the army released the director of its Military Intelligence Division (MID), Gen. Ralph Van Deman. The MID thus lost a leader who had skillfully advocated its cause during and after the war. At its peak in 1918, the MID had 1,441 personnel, but the number had already dropped to 90 by 1922. The MID simply had too little to do. Its weekly intelligence reports filled five volumes annually until 1921, but just one volume thereafter. The division ran into further trouble when it tried to expand into new areas like anti-radicalism, anti-feminism, and Broadway theater censorship. The *Army and Navy Journal* warned in 1923 that "the intelligence officer is not a policeman. He is not a diminutive edition of a Burns-Pinkerton detective." By 1937, the MID had only 69 personnel. The Office of Naval Intelligence (ONI), too, experienced reductions. It employed 306 reservists at the end of the war, but the number had dropped to 42 by 1920.[18]

If these figures do tell a story, it must be told from several perspectives. First, personnel figures for America in the 1920s indicate a greater commitment to intelligence than before the war. Second, even if overall budgetary cuts did result in a severe pruning, MID spending in the 1920s rose as a percentage of the War Department's budget. Third, America was not alone—most countries had reduced intelligence expenditure between the wars. Fourth, U.S. intelligence was not necessarily incompetent, compared with its foreign counterparts. For example, the much-vaunted British intelligence authorities wasted money bribing the French press, targeted Irish and other anti-colonialists above more dangerous enemies, and arrived at an adequate German order of battle estimate only just in time to help in World War II.[19]

Despite the criticism since directed at them, the Republican presidents of the 1920s did use secret intelligence. According to Philip G. Strong, chief intelligence officer for the U.S. Pacific Fleet in World War II, President Calvin Coolidge had a "$30,000 slush fund" he could spend through the ONI or army intelligence. Even more striking is the evidence that President Herbert Hoover used the ONI to perform an operation of doubtful legality. Hoover in 1930 received information that his Democratic opponents had a file of confidential information on him. The contents and even existence of the confidential file have never been confirmed, but Hoover feared that, if disclosed, the secrets would ruin him and his administration. He asked the ONI to neutralize the problem, and the task fell to New York District intelligence officer Glenn Howell. An ambitious man who dreamed of a "Central Intelligence" body that would coordinate the activities of all government clandestine agencies, Howell already had experience as a burglar—in 1929, he had broken into the safe of a Japanese official in New York, photographed information on military logistics, and returned the papers to the safe, all without detection. He now orchestrated a pre-dawn raid on the Democratic office thought to contain the embarrassing file. Instructions were given that no record of the raid should be provided to the National Archives or any other open repository. According to Howell's log the raided office contained not a stick of furniture, let alone sensational files. Yet the story, even with its unsolved mysteries and farcical end, underscores the willingness of the reputedly naïve but actually unscrupulous Hoover administration to use undercover methods.[20]

In the interwar years, it was intelligence business as usual, but on an expanded scale compared with pre-1914 days. Secret British-American countersubversion cooperation flourished throughout the period. Foreign intelligence, including the hiring of local spies, was one of the duties of military attachés, and here the picture might at first sight seem bleak. In October 1928, general staff officer Col. Stanley S. Ford stated in a lecture at the Army War College that the departments of State, Commerce, Labor, and the Navy "maintain agents throughout the world, and have furnished to the MID much valuable information." But (he added, circumspectly): "There are some writers who persist in the statement that the United States maintains spies in foreign countries to obtain military secrets. Of course there is no truth in this statement, and officers should deny it emphatically whenever occasion arises."[21]

Statistics seem to confirm this impression. At the end of World War I, the number of military attachés reporting to the MID was 111. The number for 1933–1937 had declined to just 32. However, the relative position should be kept in mind here. Only two countries (France and Britain) had more military attachés than the United States, and America had more attachés in this period than either Germany or the Soviet Union.[22]

In the Hoover administration, the United States may have denied that it engaged in spying, but, as in other countries, such denials were merely routine. Some clues to reality may be found in an ONI instructional document called "Duties of Naval Attaché." In 1930, the annual revision of this document was undertaken by ONI director Capt. A. W. Johnson, and was approved by Secretary of the Navy Charles Francis Adams. According to Johnson, the Navy Department did not in times of peace "countenance the frequently quoted assertion that a naval attaché is a spy under the protection of international law. At the same time this should not be interpreted to mean that an attaché must ignore the use of agents whose employment may be rendered necessary in the investigation of any questions that bear upon national defense or loyalty to his own country."

Captain Johnson gave attachés explicit advice on how to procure information without detection, advice showing that America did use spies in the 1930s. For example, to guard against exposure, Johnson advised attachés never to demand or issue receipts when dealing with their own agents. Agents sponsored by or seconded from the ONI were to be financed from specially opened bank accounts. Local control of ONI agents fell upon the attachés, thus avoiding the risks involved in the system when it was originally set up in 1919, whereby a single card index of spies was kept in the Navy Department in Washington. According to Johnson's report, spies might be of either sex, but they should be American, patriotic, and "of good social position." They should be approached through front organizations but would be easy to recruit, since in each European capital "there can always be found a class of typical Americans" who would be "only too glad to offer their services." If the ONI had scruples, then, they seemed to center on the insistence that Americans be used for espionage, in preference to nationals of the targeted country.

The instructions of 1930 warned that American intelligence operatives should be on guard against strangers. The attaché should bear in mind that "The use of immoral women as agents is regarded as being very precarious. A woman that will sell herself is usually willing to sell her employer. In addition, women of this type exert a very demoralizing effect upon the men under whom they are placed." The instructions further warned that the State Department would disown any attaché who was exposed in his use of dubious methods: "There have been several occasions when foreign attachés have been caught while indulging in questionable activities that were intended to bring in particularly desirable information. In each case the reputation and career of the officer concerned did not profit by their mistaken zeal." The message was clear: an attaché might employ spies, as long as he was not caught.[23]

Some naval intelligence officers appear to have been quite effective in the interwar years, and others gained experience during those peaceful decades. Captain Edward Howe Watson sipped tea and American martinis with senior Japanese naval officers in 1921, and learned that Tokyo was ready to soften its position on naval tonnage. His junior, Ellis Zacharias, went on to be deputy head of the ONI in World War II, when he ran psychological operations against Japan. Roscoe H. Hillenkoetter helped organize elections in 1928 in Nicaragua, where the navy was involved in counterinsurgency operations designed to keep Augusto Sandino from achieving power. "Hilly" then traveled all over Europe as a naval courier before becoming assistant naval attaché in Paris in 1933. He worked secretly with the French resistance in 1940–1941. Then, after being wounded on board the *West Virginia* during the Pearl Harbor attack, he organized naval intelligence in the Pacific. In 1947, this product of the interwar intelligence system became the first director of the CIA.[24]

From the mid-1930s, expenditure on the MID began to expand both in absolute terms and as a percentage of the total War Department budget. At the same time, the army's Signal Intelligence Service (SIS) also began to grow in both personnel and expenditure. In 1937–1938, its staff doubled from seven to fourteen. In the meantime, the Navy codebreaking unit known as OP-20-G, working from makeshift temporary buildings on Washington's Mall, had built up a staff of seven hundred worldwide. In 1940, the SIS and OP-20-G joined forces to build a working replica of the enciphering machine used by the Japanese to construct messages in the color code Purple. This work did not prevent the Pearl Harbor tragedy, but it did lay the foundations for good intelligence in the Pacific. The British, who, like the Americans, had underestimated Japanese military capability, could not compete with U.S. wartime intelligence expertise on Japan.[25]

In one way, this revival in American intelligence might seem to lend itself to the "flowers in the desert" theory. When the rain comes, the orchids emerge, only to wither with the return of more clement sunshine, and there is no point in trying to encourage cultivation in arid conditions. In any case, the seeds of today may not be suitable tomorrow. World War I intelligence practices, like the heavyweight battleship, would be outmoded in the next war. Best to start anew. Already, in the interwar years, fresh thinking was taking place. American intelligence made use of business travelers, developed new technology such as the microdot, initiated scientific espionage, and inquired into chemical warfare threats. Potentially, America could embark on a new phase of intelligence history with a blank sheet and some original flair.[26]

But as war approached, evidence of conservative thinking emerged. In 1937, a general staff officer remarked of the MID: "This organization is such that the necessary expansion to meet war requirements can be made by the expansion of present operating sections in, or by the addition of new sections to, the existing branches."[27] The desire to defend and if possible expand one's turf, so very evident in that remark, was to be a continuing source of conflict and weakness in the intelligence community. The rigidly expansionist mindset was as problematic a legacy as was the habit of peacetime contraction in intelligence facilities.

Another weakness of pre-war U.S. intelligence was its overestimation of the strength of Germany. David Kahn noted the racism involved: "America underrated the little yellow men of Japan, but overrated the blue-eyed blonds of Germany." In 1938, Assistant Secretary of War Louis Johnson in a memorandum to President Roosevelt endorsed the findings of his military attaché in Berlin. In a gross exaggeration reminiscent of the Pinkerton syndrome during the Civil War, his memorandum overestimated German warplane production by almost 1,000 percent. The inflated figure contributed to the fear, in the early stages of the war, that Germany would be able to allocate planes in sufficient numbers to fly offensive missions against Brazil—a distance of 1,800 miles from German bases in Africa, compared with 2,800 miles from the nearest American air base. To forestall Nazi-orchestrated revolts in America's backyard, Roosevelt embarked on his program of economic support for Brazil, dubbed the Pot of Gold, and gave J. Edgar Hoover's FBI the remit to counter fascist subversion.[28]

With American participation in the war becoming more imminent, military estimates of German strength improved. In May 1941, Army Chief of Staff Gen. George C. Marshall commissioned an estimate to inform the organization of war materials production. Major Albert C. Wedemeyer, who undertook the task, had recently been an exchange student at the Berlin War College. In his report, he fused his own appraisal of military intelligence on Germany with his knowledge of American resources. Wedemeyer still erred on the side of pessimism, but he concluded that, if America entered the war, Germany could be beaten.[29]

But the Wedemeyer estimate was not really a vindication of the interwar intelligence system and its reporting on Germany. For one thing, the dye was already cast. The grim realization was already dawning on most Americans that war with Germany was a serious possibility, and the willingness to entertain that development had nothing to do with more moderate intelligence estimates. If anything, intelligence followed in the wake of opinion. President Roosevelt was notoriously prone to disregard formal intelligence sources, tending to make up his mind on the basis of informal contacts and information. That may have been a weakness in the American system, but in this case it was a weakness with a fortunate outcome, as Roosevelt remained impervious to incompetent guesswork about enemy strength that could have distorted U.S. defense spending, diplomacy, and war strategy.[30]

Advocates of intelligence reform after 1945 did not really need Pearl Harbor. To be effective, intelligence reform would have to address problems unconnected with the debacle in Hawaii, especially that of how to assess the strengths, weaknesses, and intentions of America's most dangerous enemies. Preoccupation with Pearl Harbor may even have had a harmful effect. Not long after the CIA's formation, intelligence theorist and philosopher Wilmoore Kendall warned that the "shadow of Pearl Harbor" had brought about a "compulsive preoccupation with *prediction,* with the elimination of 'surprises' from foreign affairs."[31]

In July 1941 Roosevelt created a new intelligence post, that of coordinator of information (COI). After four months in operation, the COI failed to anticipate the bombing. But Pearl Harbor was not the true test of the efficacy of the COI and its successor, the Office of Strategic Services (OSS). The challenge for COI/OSS was to free itself from the hyperbole of Pearl Harbor, to divest itself of the tradition of the confidence man, and to set up an effective analytical intelligence structure that could influence and improve strategic decision-making.

CHAPTER 9

Hyping the Sideshow
Wild Bill Donovan
and the OSS

William E. Colby directed the CIA between 1973 and 1976. Twenty years later, he perused a letter that had been dropped into the mailbox of his office in Washington, D.C.:

> My name is Asbjørn Øye, I'm the district manager for the Norwegian State Railways in the Tronheim area and I'm the son of the stationmaster at Valøy station in 1945!
> Therefore, I have personal interests in the establishing of the memorial park at the Jørstad river bridge.
> I remember very well the "big bang" early in the morning the 15 of April 1945 when you, and your soldiers, "blowed up" the Tangen bridge and I remember the chaos this attack created among the German soldiers who had their camp in the waiting room at the station!
> I remember also very well the tough guys who came down from the mountains in May 1945![1]

Memories—who can resist them? Bill Colby certainly could not, and to mark the anniversary he typed a short memoir, "V-E Day in the Norwegian Mountains." He wrote of the days, fifty years ago, when he had been with the Norwegian Special Operations Group of the Office of Strategic Services (OSS). He recalled their objective in the winter of 1944. The Allied armies were closing in on the forces of the German High Command, but the Germans had at their disposal 400,000 additional troops, soldiers whom the Russians had pushed out of Finland and into Nazi-occupied Norway. Because the Allied navies controlled the seas, the only way of moving those troops to the defense of the beleaguered fatherland was to move them south along the one available rail line, the Nordland Railroad.[2]

Colby's group had the job of hitting that railroad. Thirty-two of them flew out of Scotland in black-painted B-24 Liberator bombers with the object of parachuting into the critical area. Only sixteen got there alive, but these sixteen were able to team up with six members of the Norwegian Resistance. After a frustrating delay, Colby received his marching orders and led his team down from the mountains and blew up the Tangen bridge. Colby left a tiny American flag on the spot, to indicate it was a U.S. operation and to minimize the chances of reprisals against the local population. Then he led his men back into the mountains. After thirty hours of cross-country skiing to and from the scene of the attack, they came at last to a steep ascent, nicknamed Benzedrine Hill in honor of the pill Colby had to take before attempting it. They made it to the top and back to base camp, only to be attacked without warning by a small German ski patrol, with one man shot on each side.[3]

Yes, those were days to remember. In his account, Colby did not entirely succumb to sentimentality. The war was really over, which was why there had been delays for fear of risking needless civilian casualties. Furthermore, Colby subsequently learned that "our blasts of the railway had been repaired by Yugoslav captives of the Germans in fairly short order." Nevertheless, it was possible, half a century later, to have the following rather gratifying conversation:

> Where were you on V-E Day, Grandad?
> In the North Norwegian mountains, feeling frustrated.
> Whatever were you doing there, Grandad?
> Trying to slow German troops moving to fight the Allies in Germany.
> How did you happen to be there?
> It's a long story. . . .

Memories of that story, the fabled history of the OSS in World War II, have played a powerful role in the subsequent history of U.S. intelligence. In particular, there has been a tendency to lionize the leader of the OSS, Gen. William J. Donovan. It is probably true that without the inspiration of Donovan, Colby would not have had his character-forming adventure in the Norwegian mountains. In 1981, Colby described Donovan as the greatest spy of all time. His reverence was typical of the feelings of many whose horizons and opportunities had been broadened as a result of their service with the OSS.[4]

However, the claims of Donovan and the OSS to greatness in World War II are questionable. Allowances should be made, it is true. Donovan's denigrators often had an axe to grind, and because of the obscure and collaborative nature of any intelligence agency's work, its successes are not always easy to chronicle. Nevertheless, the OSS's record of achievement is mainly unimpressive. Donovan and his men did not match the accomplishments of their British counterparts, and it is doubtful that they were the most effective branch of the U.S. intelligence services.

So why did Donovan acquire iconic status? In a nutshell, he was a charismatic and visionary leader credited by his admirers with having bequeathed on America the idea of a peacetime agency for central intelligence.[5] In the process of breathing life into that idea, he gave a major fillip to the tradition, within U.S. intelligence, of promotional hype.

William Joseph Donovan was born on New Year's Day 1883 in Buffalo, New York. He was a second-generation Irish American, and it is possible that his family had been involved in the clandestine struggle against British ascendancy in Ireland. Donovan made a "good" marriage into one of Buffalo's wealthy Protestant families and rose to become a member of the Wall Street establishment. By the 1920s, though, he had acquired another kind of reputation. There is some debate about the origin of his nickname, "Wild Bill." One theory holds that he acquired it in 1905, when playing quarterback for Columbia University. Demurring from this view, his brother, Father Vincent Donovan, thought the "Wild Bill" nickname was born in 1916, when Bill led a cavalry unit in southern Texas during the Pancho Villa raids: the superfit captain asked his men why they could not keep up with him, and a plaintive voice rose from the ranks: "We ain't as wild as you are, Bill." But Bill Donovan's wife, Ruth, traced the provenance of the epithet to her husband's service with the New York 69th Infantry in World War I. In offensives at the Meuse-Argonne and elsewhere, almost a fifth of the 69th's men were killed, with 81 percent wounded, Colonel Donovan included. Donovan emerged from the war as a heavily decorated American soldier, second in this regard only to Douglas MacArthur. A hero's welcome awaited Donovan on his return to the United States.[6]

Already a legendary figure, Wild Bill served as acting attorney general in the cabinet of President Calvin Coolidge, and he expected to become the incumbent to the office when Herbert Hoover entered the White House in 1929. But Donovan was now to experience the first of two disappointments: Hoover decided not to appoint him attorney general, in part because he thought Donovan was a poor administrator and too much given to intrigue, a reputation that was to dog Donovan for the rest of his public career.[7]

Donovan's second disappointment was his defeat in the 1932 New York gubernatorial election. The governorship of New York was a proven stepping-stone to the White House, and Donovan's star seemed to be ascending when he received the Republican nomination in the face of stiff competition. But because of the 1929 Wall Street crash and the subsequent Depression with its attendant suffering, 1932 was not to be a good year for Republicans. Organized labor attacked Donovan, charging that, as a lawyer, he represented the interests of capitalists against workers. Some Protestants regarded Donovan's Catholicism as objectionable, while some Catholics took exception to Donovan's marriage to a Protestant and to the infrequency with which he attended Mass.[8]

In the course of his campaign, Donovan summoned to his side a rising star in the area of public relations. Edward L. Bernays needed no second invitation to "meet this man who was already somewhat of a spectacular figure." He developed a critical perspective on the problematic nature of Donovan's character. Bernays traveled from New York City to Buffalo specially for a meeting with the candidate, but he could not talk to him because Donovan could not be prized away from the business of "shaking hands and smiling and being charmingly warm." He tried again a few days later in Donovan's New York apartment overlooking the East River, a place described by Bernays as designed to give the impression of "fine living." Again, Bernays and Donovan "never got down to cases," so the PR man left early. No doubt, Bernays was by this time suffering from a bruised ego, but his judgments may not have been entirely the product of his spleen: "Donovan was the man who was so busy being busy that he was too busy to do the things he might have been busy about." In light of his 1932 encounter with Donovan, Bernays later wondered "just how he made OSS function beyond handshaking." Donovan had never developed a campaign strategy in the gubernatorial race, and it was no surprise to Bernays when he went down to a heavy defeat.[9]

Donovan was a product of the Irish clandestine tradition, of sectarian Protestant-Catholic rifts, a man of split loyalties, a social and religious chameleon. He liked publicity and power, but was badly organized and a poor listener. A failed politician, he now hoped to attain power by means other than the democratic process. Such was the person behind the OSS and, in some important ways, the CIA.

By the end of the 1930s, Donovan was in his mid-fifties, but still in search of wider horizons. He spent time in August 1939 advising on the set of *The Fighting 69th,* a movie featuring Donovan's career, with James Cagney starring as one of his fictional privates. The prospect of a political career, however, looked distant. President Roosevelt knew Donovan slightly from their student days at Columbia, but they were, after all, political adversaries. To make matters worse, Donovan had been making isolationist speeches, while FDR was increasingly concerned that America should be in a position to help contain the expansionist ambitions of Adolf Hitler. But a major change was now to take place in Donovan's outlook and career.

The outbreak of World War II and the stunning triumphs of Hitler's armies jerked him out of his isolationism. A second factor that may have propelled him into public service was the tragic death of someone who had been especially close to him, his daughter Patricia. On 8 April 1940, the vivacious twenty-two-year-old George Washington University student lost control of her car on a treacherous stretch of road in Virginia and sustained fatal head injuries. It was not long after this event that Donovan decided to overlook his political differences with President Roosevelt and to serve his country.[10]

To put Donovan's contribution into its proper context, it is important to remember that America had a tradition of central intelligence stretching back to the World War I organism, the State Department's U-1. The demise of U-1 in 1927 had not obliterated from memory this particular method of coordinating intelligence. However, with war imminent in Europe, President Roosevelt turned not to the State Department, but to the FBI, MID, and ONI: on 26 June 1939, he ordered them to establish a coordinating committee. Though State was not officially represented on this Joint Intelligence Committee, by 1940 it was customary for an official from that department to sit in on its meetings as the representative of the president. This job fell to Assistant Secretary of State Adolf A. Berle. Like his predecessor Frank Polk in the previous war, Berle belonged to the charmed inner circle of the American ruling class; he had attended the right schools and was a longtime political associate of President Roosevelt's. But, in contrast to Polk, he was lukewarm about intelligence work. After a meeting with Hoover and other members of the committee on 31 May 1940, he noted that "We had a pleasant time, coordinating, though I don't see what the State Department has got to do with it." This may have been because of the committee's obsession with spy rings and sabotage. Early in June, it met again, and Berle now claimed to have converted the FBI and MID to a plan that would "transfer some of this paranoid work into positive and useful channels." The committee decided at the June meeting to set up a "secret intelligence service." Berle wrote in his diary that this was something "every great foreign office in the world has, but we have never touched." There is a hint, here, that Berle thought the State Department might resume its former role as the coordinator of foreign intelligence, and he did continue to have a hand in intelligence matters for some years. But he did not try to become the spymaster in charge of a central intelligence agency; rather, he bequeathed to Donovan and his successors the seeds of the notion that such a personage might materialize in the future.[11]

On 21 June 1940, the British liner *Britannic* arrived in New York and disgorged a passenger who was well equipped to take advantage of the American interest in intelligence coordination. His name was William S. Stephenson. Like Donovan, Stephenson had fought bravely in World War I: a flying ace, he had shot down six German planes, and won the Military Cross for gallantry. More recently, he had been a successful businessman in his native Canada. In New York, he now directed British Security Coordination, a passport control organization. Passport control was a routine form of cover for British secret agents. Stephenson's real job was the coordination of British intelligence activities in the western hemisphere. To this end, and with a view to quashing German secret operations in both South and North America, he had already established a relationship with J. Edgar Hoover and the FBI.[12]

Stephenson's most pressing mission was to help bring America into the war on the side of the beleaguered British Empire. Because he was an intelligence officer, his means of doing so was conspiratorial, and, in

1940, the circumstances did favor undercover tactics. While President Roosevelt desired a more expansive role for the United States, a powerful band of U.S. senators did not, and they watched his every move. Facing a presidential election in the fall, FDR could ill afford to make bold political moves in public. Stephenson therefore looked for a discreet agent of influence in Washington, and he fixed on Donovan. In reality, Donovan did not yet have a powerful voice in the White House. But by acting on the assumption that he did—rather in the manner of Sir William Wiseman in similar circumstances in 1917—Stephenson fostered a myth that begot its own reality.

Stephenson later claimed that it was he who had urged and arranged what was to be a seminal trip by Donovan to London in July 1940—his story holds that he was plotting with Donovan within an hour of checking in at the St. Regis Hotel on 21 June. True or false, such stories fanned the fears of conspiracy theorists who believed that the OSS and CIA were tools of British imperialism. However, Stephenson, as much a product of North American culture as Donovan himself, was given to chronic self-inflation. It is by no means evident that he initiated the London trip, though he may have been one of its facilitators, and it is simply untrue that he invented the idea of American central intelligence. More reliable and significant is the fact that he *subsequently* developed a working relationship with Donovan and helped to inflate Donovan's influence on both sides of the Atlantic.[13]

Donovan's briefing for the London trip came largely from his longtime friend and sponsor, Frank Knox. The proprietor of the *Chicago Daily News* and nominated secretary of the navy on 20 June, Knox campaigned to have Donovan made secretary of war or assistant secretary of the navy. Thwarted here, he prevailed on Roosevelt to sanction Donovan's fact-finding mission. Knox commissioned Donovan to investigate German Fifth Column activities on behalf of his newspaper, detailing a *News* correspondent, Edgar Mowrer, to assist him. Knox gave Donovan the additional brief of looking into Anglo-American naval intelligence collaboration. Finally, Roosevelt charged Donovan with the task of inquiring whether Britain, now standing alone in Europe, would be able to withstand the Nazi onslaught—Roosevelt wanted to help, but he could not afford to tie his nation to a sinking cause, and the American ambassador in London, Joe Kennedy, had been sending back pessimistic reports.[14]

Entrusted with these missions, Donovan was destined to become a significant figure in British-American intelligence relations and, to a smaller extent, diplomatic relations. His bandwagon had begun to roll, and many were those who wanted to be on it, or who would claim in retrospect to have been part of his enterprise. The British ambassador to Washington, Lord Lothian, urged the Foreign Office to roll out the red carpet. Stephenson claimed to have done likewise. According to another report, when Donovan boarded his Pan American Clipper flying boat bound for London via Lisbon on 14 July, he found himself sitting not so accidentally beside Wiseman.[15]

For the British propaganda machine was now in full swing. According to its script, Stephenson, the unstuffy Canadian, was installed in New York, while Lothian, a man who liked to put his feet on the desk, exuded an informal, noncondescending friendliness in the Washington embassy. London had turned toward America a beguiling, democratic countenance. Meanwhile, however, England afforded Donovan a seductively *non*egalitarian welcome. The king gave him an audience, Prime Minister Churchill received him, and Col. Stewart Menzies, the prototypical "C," or chief of M.I.6, briefed and befriended him. Chaperoned by high-ranking British officers, Donovan effected a whirlwind guided tour of British defense installations. Returning to America on 4 August, Donovan did not quite advocate an American monarchy, but he did deliver intelligence to please his masters. Britain would survive, but needed more destroyers. The first conclusion was improbable if fortuitously true (Germany simply decided not to attack across the English Channel); the second was true enough, helping to bring about the destroyers-bases deal that opened the floodgates bringing U.S. munitions to Britain.[16]

But Donovan took back with him also a well-developed set of views on German Fifth Column activities. The term "fifth column" had originated in the recent civil war in Spain, and had inspired the title of Ernest Hemingway's play of that name (1938). It sprang into renewed prominence in the wake of the success of the German forces' blitzkrieg triumphs in 1940, triumphs that swept aside French and British armies that should have been a match for them. The Fifth Column presumption was that Germany was not winning by fair means: it relied on a behind-the-lines gang of traitors, spies, and saboteurs who weakened the political will to resist, and the efforts of those armies thrown into the battle against Hitler. Perhaps there had been some truth to this idea in Austria, Czechoslovakia, and Poland, where the Nazis had been able to appeal for the support of ethnic Germans. But the French and the British, and soon the American interventionists, claimed that there was a Fifth Column menace in their countries, too. In these other countries, the Fifth Column menace had little basis in reality. Hitler, it is true, thought that America had been going downhill since the South lost the Civil War, and that the country was a "Jewish rubbish heap," but there was little prospect that he would be able to exploit social or racial divisions in American society, least of all the intensely loyal German American population.[17]

In later years, Donovan himself hinted that the Nazi Fifth Column threat should be put into perspective. In hearings on the European Recovery Program in 1948, he warned the Senate Foreign Relations Committee about the communists' "fifth columns throughout the world." These were more dangerous than the Nazi Fifth Column, which "had no real social base in our country." In 1940, however, Donovan found the myth of the Nazi Fifth Column to be highly convenient, and may even have persuaded himself to believe in it. On his return to America, he and Mowrer published a series of newspaper articles warning of the menace; Knox wrote an introduction, and three leading American news agencies distributed the resultant pamphlet worldwide.

Donovan's propaganda was effective because America was ready for it. Recent events had given fresh impetus to the long-standing American tendency to find scapegoats for social ills. In 1938, the FBI smashed a German spy ring, and in 1939 the inevitable film followed: *Confessions of a Nazi Spy*, starring Jewish actor Edward G. Robinson, pointed to the Fifth Column menace. Also in 1938, Congress had established the House Unamerican Activities Committee under the chairmanship of Representative Martin Dies to investigate American fascism. Meanwhile, popular lecturers and writers like Jan Valtin were warning, on the basis of firsthand experience, of the dangers of German subversion. Donovan and his American and British sponsors were pushing on an open door, and they found a receptive audience.[18]

The pamphlet *Fifth Column Lessons for America* rehearsed the Fifth Column argument: the "quasi-impossibility" of the German victories; the German minorities that betrayed their host countries; the lack of urgency in war preparations (Norway had been too supine to suspect the ulterior motives of German visitors before the invasion; France could not "be induced to quit the lunch table long enough to fight"); the susceptibility of democracies to penetration by foreign agents. Happily, "the British soul was never really tainted by Nazi propaganda," but Hitler was out to exploit racial and class tensions in the United States, "where our masses are strikingly susceptible." By raising these fears, the pamphlet laid the groundwork for Donovan's campaign for a central intelligence agency that would combat the postulated menace—and fight fire with fire.[19]

On 16 December 1940, Donovan once again departed for Britain. Once again, he received special treatment: on a flight to Gibraltar, his hosts surprised him with an inegalitarian birthday dinner. Served by a smart orderly, it consisted of hot turtle soup, followed by lobster, pheasant, and Stilton, washed down by three bottles of Moselle. On this trip, he visited places on the periphery of the main armed conflicts, traveling from Gibraltar to Belgrade, and thence to Cairo. The experience was to influence his strategic approach to the war. It also strengthened his resolve to press for an American secret service. On 18 March 1941 Donovan's BOAC amphibian at last arrived at the La Guardia flying boat dock; three weeks later, army intelligence chief Brig. Gen. Sherman Miles wrote to Chief of Staff Gen. George C. Marshall about a complaint he had received from the ONI: apparently, and to his great regret, Donovan was resolved "to establish a super agency controlling *all* intelligence."[20]

A bureaucratic battle now ensued. The military and the FBI objected to the proposed arrangement. Roosevelt was inclined to favor it but cast around for someone other than Donovan to put in charge. At this point, on 25 May, the British director of naval intelligence, Rear Adm. John Godfrey, arrived in America. One of Godfrey's missions was to assess the state of American intelligence. His mission report, dated 7 July 1941, indicated that American intelligence on Japan was good, but that in other respects there was cause for concern. The ONI did not process intelligence and was degenerating into a "graveyard for statistics." In all branches of U.S. intelligence there was a "predilection for sensationalism"; for example, the War Department's estimate of German reserve air strength was 250 percent higher than that of the British. Although Americans used the acronym SIS to refer to individual agents of various departments, these agents were "amateurs," and it was really incorrect to speak of a "U.S. Secret Intelligence Service." However, a Joint Intelligence Committee had been set up in London to handle the American side of things, and a corresponding "Junior JIC" had sprung into being in Washington to liaise with it. Godfrey had offered Donovan full backing and tuition from British intelligence. In the meantime, Colonel Donovan had prepared a memorandum for the president, urging the creation of "a very large scale" and "novel" intelligence organization. In a meeting with the president, Godfrey "advocated" Donovan's "qualifications as Coordinator of Intelligence." As in the period of professed American neutrality prior to World War I, Anglo-American intelligence cooperation was proceeding apace; indeed, Sir William Wiseman is credited with having arranged the meeting between Admiral Godfrey and President Roosevelt.[21]

Here, the matter of British intelligence and the origins of the OSS and CIA needs to be put into perspective. Was American central intelligence a British idea? For a variety of conflicting reasons, this idea has been attractive to some. It does seem plain that Godfrey was keen on the idea, possibly because he thought it would make the Americans more effective allies, and because he thought it would be as well to reinforce the position and opinions of Donovan, whom the British regarded as their friend. However, it is equally plain that central intelligence had an American pedigree. Furthermore, the notion of a major organization that would continue in peacetime was distinctively American, owing nothing to the British. Did the British teach the Americans the trade of intelligence? Yes, in due course they did. But here it should be remembered that the British had been in the war for a while. British intelligence on Germany in the 1930s had been distinctly shaky, but once the country was in mortal peril, minds were concentrated and some of the best brains flooded into the intelligence business. Naturally, by 1941 British intelligence was in the position to be of help to its American "cousins." This was a product of the chronology and contingencies of war, and not, as is sometimes implied, of British super-intelligence and constant preparedness in peacetime.[22]

Given British confidence in Donovan, it made sense for Roosevelt to put him in charge when he established the Office of the Coordinator of Information (COI) on 18 June 1941. But what was Donovan's definition of mission, and what was the raison d'être of the COI? The distinct lack of evidence on these subjects might suggest that the obfuscation was deliberate and covered up an exciting master plan. But there is another interpretation: The COI and, indeed, its successor, the much more grandiose OSS, were the product of foggy or even nonexistent reasoning allied to a large dose of bureaucratic opportunism boosted by effective hyperbole.

So far as is known, Donovan first recorded his thoughts on American intelligence in a memorandum for Knox dated 26 April 1941. In this, he described British intelligence and laid down the organizational principles that should, in his view, govern a U.S. central intelligence organization. In a further memorandum on 10 June, this time for the president, he again made organizational recommendations and noted a need for the central analysis of incoming information from a wide variety of sources. When Roosevelt issued an executive order establishing the COI on 18 June, the administrative provision thus mainly concerned the collection, coordination, analysis, and dissemination of information. But its reference to "such supplementary activities as may facilitate the securing of information important for national security not now available to the Government" afforded the opportunity to expansionists, then and since, to maintain that covert action was graced by original intent, the phrase "securing information" being used to open up infinite possibilities.[23]

America did need a central intelligence organization, but the reasoning behind the COI and OSS nevertheless invites scrutiny. Although the main justification for the COI, as for the OSS and CIA, was central analysis, Donovan was distinctly unenthusiastic about it. Nor did the COI, once established, prove to be an effective analytical tool against surprise attack. Operation Barbarossa, Germany's secretly planned onslaught on the Soviet Union, began just four days after the COI's inception, so it is understandable that the COI had not predicted it. But by 7 December, the date of Pearl Harbor, the office had been in operation for five months. Its nonprediction of the Japanese surprise attack led to the inauguration of the tradition whereby the government rewarded failure: Pearl Harbor, according to the involuted logic of bureaucratic hyperbole, occurred because the COI was too weak to wield authority— notably, the codebreakers did not entrust Donovan with the top-secret product of their work. The answer lay in the almighty dollar. Give Donovan more money, people will respect him, and he can centralize properly.

In reality, there is no reliable systemic antidote to surprise attack, as the planners of a surprise take into account the characteristics of the enemy intelligence system. Centralized intelligence for medium- and long-term predictions makes much more sense. But, while Donovan did have an interest in strategic intelligence, he instinctively appreciated that nonimmediate intelligence is boring and academic and may not attract funding. So longer-term intelligence analysis, the prime raison d'être of a central agency, played a small part in the calculations of this master of hyperbole.

Although dutifully recited for years to come as a justification for a central agency, analysis played second fiddle to other considerations as far as Donovan was concerned. Owing to its palpably chimerical nature, the Fifth Column menace was also in due course relegated to a distant tier in the orchestra. Donovan had another vision of the way in which he could play a role. He pinned his hopes on covert operations—as a means of projecting himself and his organization onto the world stage, a means of asserting his status in wartime Washington, and, not least, a means of performing the final rite of passage that would transport him from his near-Fenian origins to a position of respectability in the blue blood establishment.

Yet, judged in terms of covert operations and in other ways, too, the OSS was a sideshow. That is not to say that its history was dull. On the contrary, Donovan and his colleagues were true heirs of American intelligence's hyperbolic tradition, contributed to the process whereby the statist tendency of the New Deal developed into a full-blown national security state, and set in train the process of bureaucratic empire-building that culminated in the CIA. Furthermore, the OSS did enjoy some successes—for example, cultivating the resistance movement in Germany and building an espionage infrastructure that was to prove useful after the war. One should not take too seriously some of the extreme charges of venality and incompetence levied against the OSS by embittered German opponents or later ideological enemies.[24]

The problem remains, though, that the OSS, established by executive order on 11 July 1942 with more resources than the COI but no great clarification of mission, was a relative failure. In comparative terms, the OSS was overshadowed by its intelligence colleagues in Britain on the one hand, and in the U.S. military on the other. Both the codebreaking unit in Bletchley Park, England, and the American-led codebreaking efforts in the Pacific sphere contributed to shortening and winning the war in a manner that the OSS could not hope to match.[25]

Nevertheless, the time arrived when Donovan's thoughts turned to how to preserve his agency once peace had arrived. With an eye to future survival, Donovan put the order out to OSS branches: list your achievements for the sake of posterity. The resultant reports, returned mainly in November 1944, illustrate the priorities as well as the achievements of Donovan's organization. Those priorities reveal an institution concerned for its own integrity—like the Pinkerton agency in the nineteenth century, the Special Funds Branch had "kept a good accounting record" despite the "irregular" nature of OSS activities. It revealed an agency flexing its muscles—challenging the hegemony of the Department of State through its Foreign Nationalities Branch, and establishing a capability independent of the British vis-à-vis the forging of documents.[26]

But above all, the reports on OSS achievements reveal an agency obsessed with bureaucracy at the expense of contributions to the war effort. This obsession might have been based on any of several factors: the OSS had been frozen out by other branches of the war machine and could not find a useful role; the agency did not want to reveal what it had been up to or betray its operating methods; it had invested too much in hyperbole and expansion and too little in serving the nation, a factor consistent with much of U.S. intelligence history. Thus, the reports became a numbers game. The European Theater of Operations division boasted not of harassing German troops in France but of "outfitting" 120 OSS agents. William L. Langer said the "basic achievement" of the Research and Development branch had been the recruitment of "hundreds" of scholars whose worth could be measured in terms of their prodigious output of documents. But did anyone listen to Langer and his crew, and did they contribute to the winning of the war? On this point, the OSS was characteristically mute. A cynic might draw his own conclusion from both the title of the document "Outstanding Accomplishments of the Personnel Procurement Branch" and its opening statement that its "overall contribution may best be measured" by increases in OSS personnel. The rest of the report went into detail about how Personnel Recruitment had done well in combating what one might be forgiven for mistaking as the OSS's main enemies—its rivals in the U.S. armed forces.[27]

After the war, with the prospect of a permanent peacetime central intelligence agency, Adm. William D. Leahy commissioned a study of the OSS on behalf of the Joint Chiefs of Staff. He requested an official "war record of the operations." OSS veteran Kermit Roosevelt undertook this study and, once again, measured the agency's successes in bureaucratic terms. No mention here of how the OSS may have hastened victory. Instead, it is learned that "additional office space was leased at 630 Fifth Avenue, but rapid expansion soon made it necessary to establish branch offices in other locations." Donovan noticed the deficit and, in a foreword, observed preemptively that "limitations of time prevented a fuller recording of OSS operations and experience." Perhaps Roosevelt had steered the easier course of writing bureaucratic history from conveniently assembled documents—or did he simply reflect the empire-building, bureaucratic culture that was a feature of American espionage history and, from the 1930s, of the history of U.S. government as a whole? Little wonder that the report did not convert Leahy, who had always been critical of Donovan—in his 1950 memoir, the admiral made some acid remarks about Donovan's poor operational record in Africa and the Far East, and about his access nevertheless to ample funds.[28]

In assessing the OSS's achievements, it is appropriate to look beyond the narrow, officially admitted remit. The proclaimed aim of the agency was to hasten the defeat of Germany and its allies. But at the same time, the OSS, along with the White House and other branches of government dealing with foreign affairs, had the goal of restraining the ambitions of America's allies a goal that, in the interests of alliance harmony, had to remain unadmitted. British power, including its intelligence monopoly, had to be challenged partly to further American economic and strategic interests and partly to advance the anti-imperialist principle that had for so long been a staple of U.S. foreign policy. Similarly, the American opposition to totalitarian Communism dictated a resistance to the expansion of the Soviet empire. Finally, the OSS had self-perpetuation as one of its goals—an ambition rooted in thinly disguised self-interest, to be sure, but it was also grounded in the genuine belief that post-war America would be a great power in need of a major peacetime intelligence capability.

A synoptic overview of the OSS's performance does tend to confirm that it was, by and large, a sideshow as far as fighting the enemy was concerned. But, through hard political graft aided by propaganda and hyperbole, Donovan and his colleagues made at least some progress in other respects.

Although Donovan's first love was covert operations, it is as well to begin with Research and Analysis, the branch that was, after all, at the heart of what was meant to be an intelligence agency. In a lecture in 1946, Research and Analysis Chief Langer indicated that the State Department was the leader in intelligence matters. It is true that this diplomatic man was addressing a State Department audience, and at a time when the Central Intelligence Group (the CIA's precursor) was small and marginal, but his comment did reflect the peripheral status of the OSS in the recent war. Yet Langer went on to say that although America had started behind the British in intelligence terms, it had ended ahead. While it may be true that the analysts were consigned to the wilderness in policy terms, they did amass and generate expertise on different parts of the world, including the Soviet Union. Langer took some of that expertise and a few personnel with him to the CIA, and it could be argued that the dispersal of Research and Analysis professors to academia disseminated the techniques of area expertise and strengthened the pool of academic advisers available to future policy makers.[29]

The first of the covert operations later used to boost the OSS's reputation and thus to justify the need for permanent large-scale intelligence operations was launched in the early weeks of 1942, when the COI had not yet given way to the more ambitious agency. Detachment 101 of the COI (and later the OSS) was dispatched to Burma. Its mission was to revive the "Burma Road," the 700-mile trail from the Irrawady River in Burma to Kunming in China. This would enable the Allies to resupply the Nationalist forces in China, who were fighting the Japanese invaders and also functioned as the chief bulwark against the Chinese communists. Preemptive attacks by crack Japanese troops defeated this plan, as well as another to splice a new approach route into the Burma Road.

Determined to find a role, Detachment 101 now offered a rescue service to the crews of Allied aircraft shot down while flying over "The Hump," the Himalayan protrusion separating the Nationalists from their suppliers (the activities of the intrepid crewmen gave rise to the expression "over the hump"). The detachment also harassed Japanese military units and, to assist them in this purpose, recruited a local hill tribe, the Kachins. The story has some of the typical ingredients of an OSS venture. It featured rivalry with the British (101 chose to support the Kachins, as the British strategic operations executive had already engaged the services of the other hill people, the Karens. OSS officers left the British authorities in no doubt as to their distaste for empire). The OSS, and later the CIA, supported anti-communist elements (the Kachins as well as the Chinese Nationalists were to be used in this way). Detachment 101 alienated the American military (a particularly acute problem in the Pacific sphere). Finally, there was the subsequent glorification of an extremely marginal operation. For example, the OSS, only a minor component in the forces operating in Burma, claimed to have killed between 5,000 and 15,000 Japanese soldiers—yet the total Japanese loss along the "Irrawadi line" was fewer than 6,000 men. As late as 1989, a book derived from a TV series insisted that the OSS Kachin operations were "brilliantly successful." The OSS propaganda machine was more effective than its operations had been.[30]

Operation Torch, launched on 8 November 1942, was an American-dominated attack on the Vichy stronghold in French North Africa. British Prime Minister Winston Churchill, President Roosevelt, and Colonel Donovan supported the plan, but others were lukewarm. The operation would reinforce British efforts against Gen. Erwin Rommel. From Roosevelt's point of view, it was a way of demonstrating to the American public that America was at last fighting back, for, in the eleven months after Pearl Harbor, the United States had seemed to be on the defensive. Donovan welcomed the attack as a means of demonstrating the OSS's usefulness: he aligned himself with the positive strategic assessment of the operation's potential; he promised that the OSS would through clandestine maneuvers persuade the majority of the Vichy French not to resist the American landings; he predicted that OSS guerrilla and sabotage teams would smooth the way for the advancing regular soldiers, minimizing casualties and helping the Allies to establish a North African foothold with relative ease.

But Donovan's optimism and promotional instincts had run away with him. OSS sabotage operations were not sufficiently effective to offset certain shortcomings in the Allies' military planning. Far from passively accepting the American invasion, the Vichy French fought it, giving the Nazis time to mass their forces to the east in Tunisia. Within three days, 1,400 Americans and 700 Frenchmen lay dead. At this point, the Allies deemed it prudent to strike a deal with Adm. Jean Darlan, a Vichy officer hitherto noted for his collaboration with the Germans. This deal stopped the Vichy resistance, but the American presence in North Africa had been purchased at a cost to American lives and principles.

The full price paid may have been even greater than this. One of the stated aims of Operation Torch had been to relieve pressure on the Red Army, which was engaged in an immense struggle against Axis armies on the Eastern front. Perhaps not fully aware of the logistical problems involved in a seaborne invasion of Europe, the Soviets had complained that the Western Allies were not doing enough, and that they were allowing the Red Army and the Russian people to bear the brunt of the fighting (at the time of Torch, the Russians and Germans were fighting the Battle of Stalingrad, in which 1,300,000 men, women, and children died). Torch would indicate to Moscow the seriousness of American intent. However, it could be portrayed as a marginal and ill-advised operation. The 250,000 men committed to it were inexperienced, rendering them inadequate to strike a decisive blow against the German forces occupying strategic areas of North Africa. They nevertheless constituted a force large enough to divert strength from the army of invasion being prepared in England for what came to be known as D-Day. Regarded in this dark manner, Torch delayed the invasion of France that was the prerequisite for the hammer blow against Germany itself. Thus, according to its detractors, Torch prolonged the war and lengthened the roster of war dead.

Two countervailing considerations need to be mentioned here. First, Operation Torch could be said to have pinned down German forces in North Africa that might have been transferred to Europe to prolong Nazi resistance. Second, the operation may have kept the Soviets quiet within the anti-Axis alliance while forcing them to fight on alone in the main battle against the fascists. This weakened the communists, reducing their ability to seize even larger tracts of Europe as the war drew to a close. However, in relation to Torch itself, there is little evidence that this reasoning had been used. There were few winners in Torch, but the OSS, in spite of its detractors' reservations, emerged as a player of bureaucratic significance.[31]

K Project was an ambitious plan. Spreading from the summer of

1943 to the spring of the following year, it was the central feature of a plot to detach Romania, Bulgaria, and Hungary from the Axis powers. Bulgaria became its focal point because Angel Nissimov Kouyoumdjisky seemed to be such a promising agent. Kouyoumdjisky—K, for short—was born in 1887 in Samakoff, Bulgaria, and had become an international businessman. In 1919 he became a Spanish citizen, apparently for reasons of commercial convenience. In 1920, he set up his own Franco-Belgian bank specializing in the financing of Bulgarian exports to the United States. When King Boris III allowed German troops to march across his country in 1940, K disassociated himself from the Nazis and made friendly gestures to the Allies. For example, he gave two million cigarettes to the French army and to the British and French Red Cross, and he donated an ambulance to the American Ambulance Corps in France. In 1942, he applied for U.S. citizenship and offered his services to the Americans. Because K had remained on cordial terms with King Boris as well as with senior Bulgarian businessmen and church leaders, Donovan and his colleagues took seriously K's plan to extricate Bulgaria from its German ties and to persuade the nation to declare for the Allies.[32]

The plot offered the following potential advantages. The Nazis would be weakened by the necessity to confront the Allies on an additional front. Any German troop diversion would be potentially useful as the Allies prepared for the landings in France. At the same time, the Russians, who were informed of K Project, would be strung along with the idea that the Allies were trying to help them, while in reality the Red Army would continue to bleed, making it less effective in any attempt at communist domination. The exclusion of the Red Army from Bulgaria was an avowed aim of K Project, though that was of course not mentioned to the Russians. From K's point of view, the arrival of the Americans in Bulgaria to bolster King Boris once he changed sides would save his country from both fascist and communist totalitarianism, and would protect his business interests (he claimed to have assets within Bulgaria worth between $15 million and $20 million). From the American point of view, the two totalitarian forces would be checked, and the British would be given a bloody nose in an area they claimed as a sphere of influence. From the OSS's point of view, the adventure would be a further display of its effectiveness and of its indispensability in war and peace.[33]

But dictators also have their intelligence services and, perhaps, an advantage in the ability to be able to act decisively without the delaying effects of consultation. In March 1944, Germany sent five divisions into Hungary. In September the Red Army entered Bulgaria, and in November it took over Hungary as the Germans retreated. The same fate befell Romania. K Project appeared to achieve little more than some clandestine meetings in Istanbul, and to have been yet another OSS failure.

K Project might have succeeded if not for problems that were beyond Donovan's control and that prevented early, decisive action. These problems were British obstruction and K's self-serving ambitions. Donovan, however, brought British ire upon himself by planning the Bulgarian move behind their backs. Early in 1944, the British responded by tightening their control over secret operations in the eastern Mediterranean and Balkans, and John E. Toulmin, director of OSS—Middle East, reflected British anger when he complained, "I think that our cousins [British intelligence] are watching the 'K' Mission very carefully and might possibly stoop to attempt a sabotage operation on it."[34]

K was an operator who could not resist a business opportunity. At the outset of his relations with Donovan in August 1942, he had refused to become an agent of the OSS, giving as his reason the desire to remain above suspicion in the eyes of the Turkish government. But this made him a free agent, if not a loose cannon. In March 1944, K argued that German troop morale was on the point of collapse. Notably, each soldier was on a ration of only two cigarettes a day. Because of Russian advances, the sole supply line for such psychologically important goods was via Turkey, Hungary, Romania, Bulgaria, and Yugoslavia. Thus it was the "duty" of America and Britain to obstruct the supplies. Even at this late stage, with the British in high dudgeon and with K Project in a state of collapse, Donovan agreed to study K's plan for "preclusive buying," either blissfully unaware of, or rashly indifferent toward, K's personal interest in the cigarette business. On the principle of "set a thief to catch a thief," it might be thought that Donovan would have seen through Kouyoumdjisky more readily. Instead, one promotion man's admiration for another seems to have run away with him.[35]

If the Burma Road, Operation Torch, and K Project entered into OSS mythology, so did the exploits of Allen W. Dulles, culminating in Operation Sunrise. As OSS chief in Switzerland, Dulles cultivated the German resistance, encouraging plots to assassinate or overthrow Hitler. In Operation Sunrise, too, he conspired with German officers, trying to bring about a "secret surrender" in Italy and an earlier end to the war, an eventuality designed to have the additional benefit of stopping the Red Army at a point farther east, in this way saving areas of East Central Europe from the pall of communism.

Dulles's activities were admirable in more than one way. In the 1930s, despite the lucrative trade his law firm might have had through Berlin, he had shown an abhorrence for the Nazi regime. And, despite his later reputation as a ruthless Cold War spymaster, it is certain that he was motivated by high principle.[36] Second, he showed himself to be more open-minded toward the Germans than were the more nationalistic British, who wanted no truck with the German resistance. Third, the contacts he made with elements of the German secret service helped him lay the foundations for later operations against the Soviets.

However, the resistance movement failed, Germany surrendered before the Italian plot could mature, and Dulles's German contacts included individuals guilty of or implicated in crimes against humanity. Smuggled away from the War Crimes Tribunal via the "Rat Line," some of these individuals later emerged to trouble the conscience of the West. Dulles's activities helped establish a behavior pattern for postwar U.S. intelligence, especially the CIA. They also foreshadowed the ineffectiveness and problems of future covert operations. But at the same time, they contributed to the institutional momentum of the OSS/CIA, and constituted another criterion on the agenda for the mythologization of the OSS in World War II.[37]

In fall 1943, two things became apparent to the newly promoted General Donovan and other observers of the war. First, the Allies were going to win. Second, the Soviet Union would be a post-war rival of the United States. Bearing in mind the prospects of a victorious peace and superpower rivalry as well as, of course, his own bureaucratic ambitions, Donovan began in earnest his campaign for a peacetime central intelligence agency. With the Soviet Union still an ally, he could not spell out a "main peacetime enemy" doctrine, but at least he could articulate what he saw as the main principles involved: an agency that would operate independently of the British, would answer to the president, not the military, and would confine its activities to the foreign sphere.

Donovan's memorandum of 10 September 1943 set forth a propaganda line that would prove to be effective in postwar politics, and that had an influence on the way in which future historians conceptualized U.S. intelligence history. Before the war, he argued, Britain, Russia, Germany, and France had maintained permanent intelligence organizations separate from the military. The United States had lagged behind and had become dependent on foreign help. The OSS had shown the way forward by establishing a worldwide capability, and now there was a "need for a continuing independent intelligence organization functioning in peacetime as well as wartime." Just over a year later, Donovan repeated his prescription. Following accusations that the new agency would be a mere branch of British intelligence, President Roosevelt now sent Donovan a brief note asking, "Will you be thinking of this in connection with the post-war period?" It was a document of considerable rarity, as FDR was canny at the best of times and practically mute when it came to intelligence matters, making it difficult for Donovan and his followers to prove that he ever gave his approval for a large peacetime agency. In reply, Donovan sent Roosevelt yet another blueprint, referred to in a cover letter in which he suggested a legislative basis for peacetime intelligence and observed: "In accordance with your wish, this is set up as a permanent long-range plan."[38]

After the war, Donovan continued his campaign for a full-service peacetime intelligence agency that undertook covert operations as well as intelligence work pure and simple. He received personal setbacks: President Harry Truman disbanded the OSS, and Donovan's enemies, numerous because he had been so manipulative and forceful during the war, saw to it that he did not return to public life in his former role. However, when the CIA was established through legislative process in 1947, it reflected not only Donovan's blueprints but also his continuing influence.

Indeed, the man had become a legend and a symbol of the CIA's beneficial provenance. Intelligence people almost invariably paid homage to Donovan. Langer must have smarted from Donovan's neglect of Research and Analysis, yet in 1946 he endorsed the former OSS chief's plan for peacetime intelligence. In the aftermath of the creation of the CIA, the supportive literature continued to appear. In an influential 1948 book, *Sub Rosa*, OSS veterans Stewart Alsop and Tom Braden praised the OSS while admitting that Donovan had been uncertain "what it was supposed to do." As the years passed, the Donovan myth showed few signs of abating. William Casey, appointed by President

Ronald Reagan to serve as director of the CIA, was the last OSS veteran to serve in such a senior capacity. Well before he accepted the CIA post, he indicated his agreement with every important Donovan precept and referred to his wartime boss's "genius and greatness." Donovan's fame spread abroad, too. The Canadian Sir William Stephenson credited Donovan with the 1940 destroyers-bases deal (more usually seen as the achievement of Churchill, Roosevelt, and British ambassador Lord Lothian). The British economic warfare specialist Viscount Eccles told his wife that Donovan had spurred Roosevelt into action in North Africa, and that one of his speeches was "a furry towel to rub with." His view complemented that of OSS veteran and Donovan biographer Richard Dunlop, who stated that Detachment 101 "held the key to Allied victory in Southeast Asia."[39]

Just as Donovan had become the new Allan Pinkerton, so the OSS threatened to supplant the mythic role held previously by the Pinkerton Agency and then the FBI. To publicize the case for peacetime intelligence, Donovan set up a committee to help scriptwriters interested in the OSS. On the eve of the creation of the CIA, three Hollywood films appeared extolling the exploits of the now defunct agency. The film *OSS* contained an opening credit sequence bearing Donovan's accreditation of its authenticity. Featuring Alan Ladd and Geraldine Fitzgerald ("They never lived so dangerously"), it grossed a then-respectable $2.8 million. James Cagney and Gary Cooper starred in the other films. Arguably, Donovan ran a sideshow during World War II, while proving himself a master of a particularly contagious variety of hype.[40]

Donovan bequeathed on his successors the device of boosting central intelligence through peripheral activities—covert operations that inspired and excited but were of questionable efficacy. In the process, he kept alive the tradition of intelligence hyperbole. However, influential though he may have been, he was far from being the sole or even the main generator of the idea of central intelligence. As the next chapter shows, the CIA welled up from several sources.

CHAPTER 10

Allen Dulles and the CIA

On Sunday, 13 May 1945, SS commander Karl Wolff was celebrating his forty-fifth birthday. He stood sipping champagne with his guests on the lawn of the Bolzano royal palace in the Dolomites. It was as if V-E Day, five days earlier, had never occurred. Then, all of a sudden, a loud, rumbling noise intruded. It heralded the arrival of a convoy of heavy United States Army trucks. They ran over the ancient cobblestones, circling the palace. American soldiers jumped out. They herded Wolff and his assembled SS officers into the trucks and ferried them off to a prisoner-of-war cage. Commander Wolff had started his birthday in style, but now his war was over.

Wolff's arrest symbolized, also, the demise of an ambitious and controversial secret operation initiated by a leading American spy, Allen W. Dulles. In World War II, Dulles headed the OSS's operations in neutral, strategically placed Switzerland. Stepping in where the British had feared to tread and operating with Bill Donovan's tacit support but without proper White House consultation, he established contact with the German resistance and, in Italy, with Nazi officers like Wolff who could see the writing on the wall and were interested in a "secret surrender" that would have saved the lives of soldiers on both sides.

It would also have saved their own bacon, for behind these plans lay a sinister agenda. Part one of that agenda succeeded only too well: America, through its clandestine agencies, would protect useful German contacts from arrest for war crimes and crimes against humanity. Part two of the agenda encouraged an early surrender to the Allies in the West that would preempt the expansion of Soviet control in Central/East Central Europe. However, the rapid advances of Allied troops, especially the Red Army, made Dulles's plot redundant, so on 13 May Wolff had little to celebrate except his birthday.

This failure did not in the least deter Dulles from mythologizing his own achievements. He had always been a publicist. When put in charge of U.S. intelligence in Switzerland, he attached a plaque to his door indicating his name and position—unheard-of conduct where secrecy-obsessed Europeans were concerned, but a harbinger of his style as director of the CIA in the 1950s, when he reveled in being not just an American celebrity but world-famous. His World War II experience contributed to his expertise and, more important, to his mythmaking capacities.

Dulles's best-selling book, *Germany's Underground*, appeared just when the proposal for a Central Intelligence Agency (CIA) was coming to fruition in 1947. The Soviet menace had taken the place of the Nazi threat, and it was with this in mind that Dulles thought an account of secret operations against Germany could be instructive: "Here we have an unprecedented opportunity to study the totalitarian technique and to learn lessons for our own defense."[1]

In August of the same year, 1947, General Donovan had just returned from a visit to France when he happened to meet James Forrestal on the steps leading up to Columbia University's library. This was a stroke of luck, for the former OSS chief was still pressing hard for intelligence expansion, and the chance encounter was an ideal opportunity to press his views on the man who had been appointed to the newly created job of secretary of defense. Donovan warned Forrestal that the communists in France were on the march. Party membership was up to 900,000. Almost 30 percent of the electorate had voted communist in the November 1946 election. The Reds were engaging in dirty tricks. They were purchasing and destroying all literature that showed them in a bad light, and were buying up printing presses in an attempt to control the flow of information.

Donovan could not have talked to a more receptive listener. Forrestal used his position to urge that the soon-to-be-formed CIA should retaliate in kind. Authorized by President Truman and the newly formed National Security Council, the CIA did precisely that. Acting through front organizations such as the American Federation of Labor, the

CIA bought up all the newsprint in France, poured money into non-communist political parties, issued "black propaganda" (falsely attributed misinformation), and encouraged Corsican gangsters and former fascists to combat the communist-led Marseilles general strike. At the time, the Marseilles strike had seemed to threaten the very foundation of U.S. foreign policy, the plan to reconstruct Europe along nonsocialist lines with the help of the American funding program known as Marshall Aid. By the time the Marseilles strike collapsed on 9 December 1947, several of its leaders had been liquidated.

The French Left faltered in its march to power: it was not until 1981 that François Mitterand became the first socialist president of the Fifth Republic. The main reason for the communists' loss of momentum was the conservative outlook of the majority of French voters. But CIA boosters lost no opportunity to claim that it was they who had halted the tide of communism, not just in France but in Italy, too, and beyond. The era of "can-do" CIA hype had dawned. The agency's "cowboys," operators who conceived of themselves as being in the American individualist tradition, boasted of further successes in the course of the next decade, notably in Iran and Guatemala. Their failures in Albania, Indonesia, and Eastern Europe were conveniently concealed, on the pretext that secrecy was essential to national security.

Yet, this kind of adventurism could not have been further from the minds of those congressmen who supported the CIA provision in the National Security Act of 1947. The congressional debates and hearings of January–June show no hostility toward Moscow—indeed, they fail to mention either communism or the Soviet Union. Congressional intent—and this is significant, as the CIA was unique worldwide in being a democratically established agency—was to set up an analytical and predictive secret intelligence capability with a view to avoiding another Pearl Harbor. Congressmen explicitly denounced the idea of an "American Gestapo."

A review of the CIA's establishment and of Dulles's career as a spymaster reveals that the agency was set up in a way that made it prone to hyperbole, and that Allen Dulles had made the most of that opportunity. However, any balanced assessment of the years from the war's end to the 1960s also yields powerful redeeming evidence, especially in the vital area of threat assessment. Hype was a disease that impaired the performance of an intrinsically healthy beast.

In a manner unparalleled in other countries, America's prime secret intelligence agency materialized in a blaze of publicity. The OSS prepared the way, bequeathing its romantic aura to the CIA as Donovan promoted Hollywood movies about the "silent and significant deeds" of World War II. The press gave the proposed new agency nationwide and mainly favorable publicity. The *New York Times* claimed in July 1946 that Harry Truman had a better grasp of intelligence than any previous president. In December, the *New York Sun* demanded a permanent intelligence agency that would put an end to the failings of World War II. In the following year, the *Washington Post* and the *Washington Evening Star* insisted that more money would need to be spent on intelligence. The *St. Louis Post-Dispatch* praised the efforts of a native son, Sidney W. Souers, a refinance expert who took charge of the interim Central Intelligence Group (CIG), served as America's first Director of Central Intelligence (DCI), and created the embryonic CIA.[2]

The single-most important reason for the formation of the CIA was the determination of President Truman to achieve that objective. His concern stemmed from the threat posed to U.S. national security by a Soviet Union whose Red Army had so recently demonstrated its power on the Eastern Front. At various times, Truman has been seen as slow to awaken to his responsibilities, or as motivated to act against Moscow just because he feared the Republicans would capitalize on the issue. But in reality, he was a Cold Warrior from the beginning. In intelligence terms, this led to unbroken cooperation with the British in codebreaking, with Germany giving way to the Soviet Union as the prime target. Then when the CIG received its first "tasking" directive on 29 April 1946, it was given a single target: "There is an urgent need to develop the highest possible quality of intelligence on the USSR in the shortest possible time." This focus never changed in the formative years of the CIA, remaining constant throughout the Cold War.[3]

Yet it was Congress that passed the National Security Act of 1947 unifying the armed forces and centralizing intelligence in the CIA. If Truman was the prime mover, Congress was the essential facilitator, and the legislators' motives differed from those of the president. In hearings on the bill, the Soviet threat was not even mentioned. Other justifications were offered for the proposed CIA. Preponderant among these was Pearl Harbor. Apparently expert opinion could be adduced to support the view that Pearl Harbor dictated the need for central intelligence. George S. Pettee was one example of such an expert. Pettee had moved from Harvard at the start of the war to become the government's leading economic analyst of Europe. In 1946, he produced a pioneering work on intelligence theory called *The Future of American Secret Intelligence*—one of a cluster of contemporary publications that discussed, and by and large advocated, central intelligence. Here, Pettee berated the "state of recurring unpleasant surprise" that afflicted U.S. foreign policy makers and had been responsible for Pearl Harbor. In the CIA hearings, witness after witness and one legislator after another subscribed to that view. Alabama's Congressman Carter Manasco (Dem.) summed up a popular suspicion: "If we had had a strong intelligence organization, in all probability we would never have had the attack on Pearl Harbor; there would not have been a World War II." To his Republican colleague from Illinois, Ralph Edwin Church, as indeed to most participants in the hearings, Pearl Harbor was "proof" of the need for better intelligence machinery. As late as 1950, historian Michael Hogan shows, warnings of another Pearl Harbor were "commonplace in budget negotiations" despite opposition from those who feared a potential American "police state."[4]

The focus on intelligence failure at Pearl Harbor was an attempt at depoliticization for political motives. It meant a rejection of conspiracy theories about New Dealers seeking a Back Door to War. It meant that the president would be able to run spies with the justification or pretext of saving the nation from future surprises—and, as the 1893 Hoar amendment already allowed, this would be without significant congressional oversight or consent. The State Department held back from this kind of work—although it housed the Bureau of Intelligence and Research (INR), which comprised some former OSS analysts, it would play only a minor role in the post-war intelligence community. From the outset, others within that community intended to take full advantage of post–Pearl Harbor momentum. In the course of the 1947 deliberation, CIG legislative counsel Walter L. Pforzheimer withdrew from the relevant section of the National Security Act a clause that would have authorized "covert and unvouched funds" because that would have opened up a "can of worms," but he observed that "we could come up with the housekeeping provisions later on." This suited Gen. Hoyt S.

Vandenberg, who as director of CIG was already, in the words of historian David Rudgers, engaged in a "quest for empire." Vandenberg privately told senior government officials he would draft "a short section indicating the necessity for clandestine operations" that would "not be placed in the record."[5]

Though kept in the dark in this way, Congress was to a degree complicit in the multiplication of functions that followed. The National Security Act of 26 July 1947 authorized the CIA to correlate, evaluate, and disseminate intelligence, but also "to perform such other functions and duties related to intelligence affecting the national security as the National Security Council may from time to time direct." Congress made only a minimal attempt to oversee the result. In 1948 the House rejected a proposal for an eighteen-member joint oversight committee. The little supervision that took place fell to a subcommittee of the Armed Services Committee. It met irregularly and had a cozy relationship with CIA officials. But the agency was in for a shock, for Republican Senator Joseph P. McCarthy exploited the void in responsible supervision. The Wisconsin anti-communist crusader charged the agency with Leftist sympathies and tried to investigate it. The process of oversight thus became associated with an irresponsible brand of Right-wing politics. However, public opinion moved sharply against McCarthy in 1953–1954. This shift played into the hands of those CIA leaders who had a fortress mentality, for the principle of congressional oversight of intelligence for the time being fell into disrepute, along with the far Right.[6]

Unlike the FBI, the CIA was sanctioned by an act of Congress. But like the bureau if for different reasons, the CIA came into existence without being subjected to tight congressional scrutiny. This allowed expansionist elements in the CIA further license to proceed with their plans. In the long term, justifications for the CIA other than the Soviet menace were to prove useful. Pre–Cold War rationales like Pearl Harbor once again made sense to those who thought Big Intelligence should continue beyond the end of the Cold War. At the beginning of the Reagan administration William J. Casey, the OSS veteran who had just been appointed director of the CIA and would double its budget, anticipated the need to look beyond the Soviet Union even if that was still the "first priority." He noted the "many . . . problems of concern to intelligence" such as "nationalism, terrorism, and resource dependency." While he would have agreed with President Truman's tough stance on the Soviet Union, he also recalled the instrumental role played by Pearl Harbor in the creation of the CIA. The skillfully nurtured remembrance of Pearl Harbor was a long-term public relations triumph for intelligence expansionists.[7]

The propaganda climate of the post-war years helped Allen Dulles deploy his public relations skills. With his privileged background, one might think he would have had no inclination or need to promote himself and his agency. His role models were impeccably genteel. He boasted a grandfather and an uncle who had served as secretary of state, and looked back in the fondest way to the tranquil days he had spent with them as a boy, especially camping and fishing on the shore of Lake Ontario. In the manner of patrician gentlemen, he and his brother John Foster, who would be secretary of state, could anticipate high office as a natural progression—something that could be achieved with a minimum of fuss.[8]

However, as early as age seven, Allen Dulles showed a precocious taste for the limelight, writing a history of the Boer War that was duly published by his proud grandfather. Yet that was an isolated harbinger of things to come, and to portray Dulles purely as a publicity seeker throughout his life would be simplistic. Next to spelling errors, the most salient feature of the book was its anti-imperialist sentiment. That sentiment is evident, too, in the young man who worked under Frank Polk during and after World War I. Dulles grappled with the problems of dismantling the Austro-Hungarian empire, of ensuring that Britain did not frustrate nation-building efforts in the Balkans, and of blocking the expansionist ambitions of the newly formed Soviet Union. Dulles's work in Europe in 1917–1919 was on the borderline between diplomacy and secret operations. His uncle, Secretary of State Robert Lansing, explained to him the Zimmermann telegram affair, and even forty-five years later Dulles recalled the significance of that in the context of the need for U.S. secret intelligence.[9] But all this was very private. In keeping with the style of U-1, there was no trumpet-blowing.

Between the wars, Dulles worked fairly obscurely as a lawyer. In 1938, his willingness to embrace the limelight showed when he unsuccessfully bid, as an ardent internationalist and opponent of Hitler, for the nomination to be Republican candidate for the East Manhattan congressional seat. Then, as head of OSS Switzerland in World War II, he had to observe operational silence. All the while, however, he appears to have longed for a more expressive role. He admired General Donovan's buccaneering style. Though he and Donovan were later rivals for the leadership of the CIA, Dulles ultimately paid generous tribute to the former OSS chief and declared himself convinced of the "soundness of his approach." If Dulles was heir to a family tradition of quiet gentleman-diplomats, the American confidence man had also touched his brow.[10]

As director of the CIA in the years 1953–1961, Dulles was a consummate publicist. A renowned raconteur, he would regale congressmen and other spellbound leaders with secret service stories. This was partly in order to distract his listeners from what he was really up to, and partly because he was fascinated by the clandestine world and enjoyed talking and writing about it—he even edited a collection of spy stories. But spinning yarns was also a way of presenting the CIA in a good light. An outgoing person, he made friends in the right places for generating favorable publicity. He cultivated journalists partly in order to use them as spies, but also in order to promote a positive image of himself and the CIA. According to Hugh Morrow of the *Saturday Evening Post*, senior CIA officials "flashing ID cards and looking like they belonged at the Yale Club" met correspondents as they disembarked from foreign trips. Dulles held large dinner parties for prominent journalists. His media friends included *New York Times* publisher Arthur Hays Sulzberger; CBS president William Paley; founder and chief of *Time* and *Life* magazines, Henry Luce; founding editor of *U.S. News & World Report*, David Lawrence; and *Newsweek*'s founding editor, Ernest K. Lindley. Even Walter Trohan of the Chicago *Tribune*, a fierce critic of the CIA in the 1940s, became an Allen Dulles fan.[11]

In proselytizing the cause of intelligence, Dulles did not confine himself to top people. When his schedule permitted, he spoke to a variety of potentially supportive volunteer groups. For example, in 1954 he addressed the Women's Forum on National Security, warning them to be on their guard as the Soviets had "not overlooked the vast importance of women's organizations in the field of propaganda." When the CIA came under heavy fire following the Bay of Pigs debacle in 1961, Dulles knew he could no longer rely on the press and sought support wherever he could find it. One person he turned to was E. Howard Hunt, later notorious for his involvement in the Watergate burglary. Hunt was dogmatically Right-wing and one of the CIA's most erratic and incompetent operatives, but he was a gifted and potentially popular writer. His specialty had been foreign propaganda, but, in Hunt's words, Dulles asked him in the wake of the Bay of Pigs to "respond to inquiries from various investigative bodies quickly activated by the New Frontier." Once set the task of propagandizing the CIA, Hunt continued. Under the pseudonym David St. John, he wrote a series of spy novels featuring a CIA agent, Peter Ward, who was supposed to be America's answer to James Bond.[12]

In retirement and in partial disgrace after 1961, Dulles found even more time and motivation to publicize the intelligence mission, the CIA, and himself. He made numerous appearances on television, embarked on literary activities, and cultivated popular figures such as Ian Fleming who might help cast him and the CIA in a favorable light (Fleming responded warmly, if slightly irreverently). He worked on what he intended to be the definitive tribute to his trade, *The Craft of Intelligence* (1963). Once the book was published, Dulles showed typical diligence in promoting it, badgering television producers to be allowed to talk about it on screen and demanding to know why it was not on sale at Dulles airport. Only in America did secret intelligence chiefs seek publicity in this way, and Allen Dulles stands out as a prime example.[13]

Allen Dulles (Princeton '14) was the most prominent among a group of Ivy Leaguers who, it is generally agreed, were conspicuous in the early history of the CIA.[14] Why did these patricians in charge of the CIA resort to the ungentlemanly device of self-publicity in the fifties and early sixties? After all, the aristocratic spies of U-1 had been quiet folk. Three reasons spring immediately to mind. First, the Soviet Union was mounting a powerful propaganda campaign in furtherance of the communist cause, and America had to meet the challenge, no matter who was in charge at home. Second, as the CIA had come into being by means of the legislative process, it was, in spite of the weakness of congressional oversight, democratically accountable and bound to fight its corner in the forum of public opinion. Third, in America a ready-made tradition of intelligence hyperbole lay at hand, available to those ambitious or impressionable enough to grasp it.

This leads to a fourth reason for the exhibitionism of America's clandestine gentlemen, a reason that is not so palpable, but is no less significant for that. In 1964, sociologist E. Digby Baltzell announced the death of the American ruling class and invented an acronym. He discerned in America a decline in the "authority of an establishment which is now based on an increasingly castelike White-Anglo-Saxon-Protestant (WASP) upper class." In a book written four years later, Stewart Alsop, a journalist who had close connections with the intelligence community, applied the same thesis to the CIA. He argued that in the 1950s, enterprising Ivy Leaguers, the "Bold Easterners," had led the CIA. But, after the Bay of Pigs setback, technocrats began to displace the disgraced elite and to deemphasize the use of secret agents ("human intelligence") and the more colorful aspects of public relations. Alsop referred to them disparagingly as the "Prudent Professionals." This way of looking at CIA history reflected the 1950s CIA leadership self-image of being, as William Colby so unctuously put it, "the cream of the academic and social aristocracy." According to one Soviet observer, they were just social climbers. But one could more accurately regard them as part of an elite who felt threatened—abroad by communists, and at home by tribunes of the trans-Appalachian west and by the exactions of demographic change. Like the Wilsonian Progressives, they represented a declining elite's attempt to govern anew but, in contrast to their quiet predecessors in U-1, they showed a stridency born of desperation. They were patricians who stooped to self-publicity in an attempt to prevent the setting of the Anglo-Saxon sun.[15]

The first distinct period of CIA history was the "long 1950s," extending from the agency's birth in 1947 to the Bay of Pigs operation and the resignation of Dulles in 1961. Although one might describe this period as the golden age of operations and hype, it is useful both to remember the wider context of rhetorical distortion and to visualize the "golden age" as having a beginning, a middle, and an end.

In the beginning phase of the golden age, 1947–1950, covert operations were not yet famous, but the ground was being prepared. Soon after its formation, the CIA secretly intervened in Italy and France, and unsuccessfully tried to topple the communist regime in Albania. However, none of these events captured the headlines. What did fire the

public imagination was a series of spy cases, notably the trial of Alger
Hiss, an establishment figure who had worked for President Roosevelt
both in the New Deal and in international negotiations with the Soviet
Union. The conviction of Hiss was a powerful political metaphor, not
least because it helped achieve prominence for anti-communism and its
champions, notably Congressman Richard Nixon and Senator McCarthy. Then in February 1950, McCarthy launched his anti-communist
crusade. If his claims and his tone had been more moderate, McCarthy
might not have attracted such notoriety: the subsequent declassification
of 1940s U.S. Army decrypts of Soviet intelligence messages, a program
known as the Venona Project, revealed that Soviet espionage in America in the early Cold War had indeed been startlingly widespread. But
McCarthy launched his attacks on the State Department, CIA, and
army in an indiscriminate manner that confused espionage with subversion and contributed to the hysteria of the times. McCarthy voiced the
widespread contemporary distrust of those whom he derided as "the
bright young men who are born with a silver spoon in their mouth,"
men who ran American foreign policy with the apparent aim of serving
another country.[16]

In September 1950, the nation's mounting anti-communism found
expression in the Internal Security Act, more often called the Mc-
Carran Act. This required the registration of communist organizations
and, alarmingly for American civil liberties, provided for the detention
of suspects. Congress overrode President Truman's veto of what one
White House aide called the "chamber of horrors bill." Though the law
was never implemented, it serves as a prime overt expression of Cold
War fears. However, the most significant anti-communist statement of
1950 had appeared five months earlier, in a top-secret document: Policy
Paper Number 68 of the National Security Council (NSC 68). The
author of NSC 68 was Paul Nitze, a Wall Street banker hired by the
government to work out a defense strategy following the Soviet Union's
detonation of a prototype nuclear bomb in 1949. NSC 68 addressed a
real and sobering problem in language described by one historian as
"hyperbolic rhetoric." Nitze depicted Soviet imperialism in lurid terms,
demanding that the United States match its verbal commitment to
"containment" with appropriate and, by implication, expensive measures. He advocated, in addition to military increases, "intensification of
affirmative and timely measures and operations by covert means in the

fields of economic warfare and political and psychological [meaning propaganda] warfare with a view to fomenting and supporting unrest and revolt in selected strategic satellite countries." As in the case of the McCarran Act, no attempt was made at implementation, as it was simply too dangerous to confront the Great Russian Bear by attempting to detach one of its satellites. But NSC 68 supplied important contextual rhetoric encouraging the CIA to expand and operate in other ways.[17]

Here, there arises an interpretive problem. Although NSC 68 is accepted as having been an influential statement of American foreign policy, it was a secret document, so its rhetoric affected only the coterie of government officials privileged to have sight of it—it could not influence public opinion at large or the views of congressmen empowered to increase the CIA's budget. It is to be regarded, rather, as a mirror held up to the face of America's then governing elite, for whom the document became a statement of epistolic authority. What seemed to confirm its precepts only too firmly was communist North Korea's brutal and unheralded attack on South Korea in June 1950. The forces of Marxist totalitarianism were on the march in Asia, and that seemed to confirm the prescience of NSC 68's claim that the Soviet Union was directing its efforts at the "domination of the Eurasian land mass."[18]

Against this background, CIA officials formulated their plans for covert operations. In July 1950, William Colby revealed his thoughts on the matter. Colby had been in private law practice since 1945 but was now starting a career with the CIA. He sent Donovan, his former boss at the OSS, "a few ideas . . . with regard to the Russians." He showed some restraint: the United States should try to stir up discontent among Soviet-dominated peoples but should not have any extravagant expectations of immediate success. Care should be taken, lest the hand of the United States be seen behind the operations, leading to charges that outsiders were whipping up discontent. But here, Colby began to show signs of the recklessness that stemmed from excessive enthusiasm for a single cause, anti-communism, without full consideration of the consequences. The appearance of spontaneity should be achieved by encouraging local groups to undertake subversion. Local "committees should be organized on national, racial, religious and any other lines providing a particular community of interest between groups in the free world and groups under Soviet rule."[19]

Actions taken on that basis by Colby and his colleagues were to have woeful consequences. Even before the end of the Cold War, the forces of atomistic nationalism, of ethnic and racial hatred, and of religious fanaticism—all encouraged through the blinding hyperbole of single-issue anti-communism—caused America grave problems in many parts of the world.

The events of 1950 set the scene for the middle period of the golden age of operations. In the early 1950s, the CIA busied itself with covert plans. Its Office of Policy Coordination, which had responsibility for covert action, increased its personnel from 302 in 1949 to 2,812 in 1952, with an additional 3,142 spies abroad, and these new people competed with one another to dream up schemes that would justify their salaries. Some significant initiatives took place. For example, Edward Lansdale helped defeat the Hukbalahap Left-wing insurgency in the Philippines. Lansdale was a former advertising executive from California. Like Yardley, he admired Edgar Allan Poe, especially his detective story *The Purloined Letter*. Lansdale's irrepressible instinct for self-publicity later made him one of the CIA's legendary figures, and inspired Graham Greene to immortalize him in his ironically titled novel, *The Quiet American* (1955). In the Philippine stage of his career, however, Lansdale behaved in a discreet manner and merely encouraged indigenous resistance to the Left in the manner prescribed by Colby.[20]

President Truman was a restraining factor in the early stage of the covert operational boom. He was too cautious to give the green light to the more adventurous plans. Much later, he would claim to have been against covert operations altogether, saying he would never have sanctioned the wilder schemes of the Eisenhower and Kennedy years. The truth is that as president he did agree to some operations—but, despite the increased covert action capacity at his disposal, he behaved in a restrained manner. The inauguration of President Dwight D. Eisenhower on 20 January 1953 made a difference. It was a matter of experience in two ways. As a long-serving soldier, Eisenhower had confidence in his paramilitary decision making. Second, however, Eisenhower was a political newcomer, and could not see that the operations he launched would be disastrous for U.S. foreign policy. To compound matters, he appointed the clandestine operations specialist Allen Dulles to run the CIA. Within the Republican Party, there had been a campaign for the appointment of Gen. Albert C. Wedemeyer, author of the 1941 intelligence appraisal of relative German-American military strength and a veteran of the wars in the Pacific and Korea. Donovan, in final pursuit of an ambition that had evaded him, was also pressing his claims to the directorship. But Dulles won the day. His takeover, on 26 February 1953, unleashed the covert operators and introduced a high season of intelligence hyperbole.[21]

The overthrow of the governments of Iran and Guatemala in 1953 and 1954, respectively, came to symbolize the golden age of operations. At the time, American politicians and businessmen were disturbed by a "nationalization" tendency. The governments of post-colonial countries wanted to bring local economic assets under national control—it was a way of rejecting imperialist domination. But this nationalist aspiration also was, or could appear to be, socialist in character, as national control of an asset would mean more government and less private management. In Iran, the government wished to nationalize the oil industry, hitherto owned and run by British, Dutch, and American corporations. In Guatemala, the government planned to take over some of the land owned by a Boston-based multinational, the United Fruit Company. In the latter case, venal considerations may have operated both Dulles and his predecessor at the CIA, Gen. Walter Bedell Smith, were vulnerable to charges of having a business interest in United Fruit.[22] But the general justification for intervention was anti-communism. The covert nature of the interventions arose partly from an American "good neighbor" policy—in the 1933 Montevideo pan-American conference, the United States had promised to stop interfering in Latin American countries, so the plan had to be kept secret. Additionally, covert action was preferred because policy makers were reluctant to confront the nuclear power of the Soviet Union and were already beginning to rely on the much-vaunted and apparently safer prowess of the CIA's clandestine operators.

The essential idea behind U.S. foreign policy in the 1950s was the defense of democracy. But in order to "save" Iran and Guatemala from the tendentious threat of communism, the CIA conspired to overthrow the democratic governments in those two countries, condemning the local people to decades of autocratic misrule. Not for nothing was the key CIA tactic in Guatemala called the "Big Lie." The principle behind the big lie was that if a source tells the truth concerning a host of minor issues, it will be believed when it becomes necessary to practice a major deception. In Guatemala, the big lie was disinformation to the effect that a strong force of rebels was crossing the border. Allied to Eisenhower's authorization of U.S. air support thinly disguised as a Guatemalan air force rebellion, the story helped unnerve the government in the capital, and it fled into exile.

At home, the real nature of the Guatemalan "revolution" was not immediately disclosed. Edward L. Bernays—the "father of spin," a "psywar" enthusiast, and already United Fruit's public relations man— helped mislead the American people. With Lansdale and other senior intelligence officials, notably C. D. Jackson and Gordon Gray, Bernays assembled a string of people who helped Dulles place the CIA's dirty tricks in a favorable light. But if these operations for the moment escaped censure in America, they made the name of the CIA mud throughout the rest of the world, and dragged America down with it— according to the journalist Thomas B. Morgan in his book *The Anti-Americans,* the CIA was the single greatest cause of America's unpopularity at that time. Hypothetical arguments are impossible to prove or disprove, but it is possible that these actions so discredited America and its campaign for democracy that they prolonged for decades European and Asian communist systems that would otherwise have crumbled under the weight of their own unworkability and unpopularity.

For although the operations were ostensibly secret, only the American people were kept in the dark. In Latin America, it was widely assumed that the CIA was responsible for activities in Guatemala and much else besides. In fact, it became an article of nationalist faith to insist that the CIA was responsible for all kinds of evil, even when it was not. Through its extravagant claims, the agency only strengthened this impression. Middle Eastern CIA chief Kermit Roosevelt, for example, boasted to Winston Churchill as well as to the American foreign policy establishment about the agency's role in the overthrow of the Iranian government. The irony here is that the CIA's Iran specialists knew Prime Minister Muhammad Musaddiq had strong popular support and was no ally of the Tudeh, Iran's communists—in fact, he was a standard-bearer for liberal democracy. Moreover, while the CIA's "cowboys" were present at the fall, British intelligence and the oil companies, as well as powerful factions in Iran, had more influence than did the agency in ending democracy in that nation and installing the Shah. The CIA had been a minor guest at the fatal feast, but its senior officials came away naïvely brandishing the poisoned chalice. Because of its public relations prowess at home, it claimed a brilliant success and, domestically, lived on that dubious reputation for some years.[23]

Although in later years the 1950s covert actions of the CIA were related in the memoirs of unrepentant operatives in dewy-eyed fashion, at the time they commanded admiration only within a limited circle. Had the attempt been made to broaden the debate, no doubt the CIA's covert operators would have complained about a breach in security, but perhaps they would have been forced to think of America's interests, instead of their own, narrower concerns. In the absence of such debate, hyperbole within a limited circle became part of a culture of mendacity, fusing seamlessly with disinformation campaigns at first aimed at foreigners but increasingly contaminating U.S. institutions and citizens.

The CIA was already secretly pouring money into the coffers of foreigners, some "witting" and others not, who used the funds for anti-Left purposes and declared—or pretended—that this was a campaign indigenous to their own nation. Increasingly in the 1950s, the CIA funneled money to American institutions and individuals—again, some of them aware of the source and others not—who then used the dollars to pay for international anti-Left activities and the foreign travel and boondoggling associated with them.

The cooperating individuals and institutions were numerous and covered a broad cultural spectrum, as may be briefly illustrated. The CIA used a compliant American Federation of Labor, and later the AFL-CIO, to undermine the organizing efforts of Left-wing labor unionists in foreign countries and to stir up discontent and rebellion in nations deemed unsympathetic to U.S. goals. It recruited leaders of the National Students Association to act as secret U.S. propagandists at international student conferences. Using private foundations as dummy conduits, it promoted and influenced the activities of a variety of American voluntary organizations that operated abroad. One example is the Committee of Correspondence, a women's organization patriotically named after the resistance groups formed during the American Revolution. Apparently, in 1953 Allen Dulles personally singled out this association for clandestine support, enabling it to organize meetings around the world on such themes as "The Responsibility for Freedom."[24]

Abroad, the CIA secretly funded the media in an effort to spread the view that local peoples spontaneously opposed communism. The great majority of them did oppose communism, but the efforts of the CIA clouded that fact and spread doubt as to the real sympathies of foreigners. CIA officials deemed it necessary to intervene even in Britain, a country that rivaled America in its deep hostility toward communism and was supposedly exempt from U.S. intelligence activities. The secret subsidization of *Encounter,* a magazine devoted to literature, the arts, and politics, was known to one of its editors, the American conservative Irving Kristol, but not to the other, the English Left-wing poet Stephen Spender. Even many years after the exposure of CIA funding, Spender told an interviewer that *Encounter* had once been a "good magazine."[25] Certainly, a typical issue gave few obvious clues to its anticommunist purpose. That of September 1954, for example, had an article on Africa by African American novelist Richard Wright that needs to be placed in its context for its propaganda qualities to be recognized, for its inclusion reflected a disingenuous determination on the part of the U.S. government to present black writers as equals in American society. A former communist, Wright had recanted in 1950. But the same issue carried an early letter by the unshakably socialist George Bernard Shaw defending gay brothels. The magazine seems very Left-wing—until one realizes that it was part of a grand deception to provide "cover" for an essentially anti-communist journal. No doubt Shaw would have been amused, but the eventual and inevitable exposure of secret U.S. funding caused anger and embarrassment among some of America's staunchest admirers.[26]

The catalog of the CIA's cultural blunders is endless. One of the more provocative examples is the agency's enlistment of modern art. President Truman was openly contemptuous of modern art and seemed to go along with Congressman George Dondero's view that modernism was a conspiracy to undermine American values: "All modern art is communistic." It is true that several of those loosely labeled "abstract expressionists" had communist links or were otherwise Left-leaning. But it is also true that the communist world distrusted modern art, with its libertarian and anarchistic impulses. CIA strategists calculated that if one threw money at modern art, the modernists would develop a patronage dependency syndrome and become, if not pro-American, then at least not anti-American. The money was duly channeled in this way, helped by the parallel and sympathetic philanthropy of the ultra-rich Nelson Rockefeller, a patron of New York's Museum of Modern Art

(MOMA) who now referred to abstract expressionism as "free enterprise painting." To the fury of French cultural nationalists, MOMA ended the long-inviolable ascendancy of the Parisian galleries. Modern art lost its Left-wing thrust, free expression was laundered in the name of freedom, and a generation of painters lost its authenticity.[27] Apart from well-placed U.S. art collectors and the covert-action expansionists who could luxuriate in the discovery and exploitation of a new medium, there were few winners in the cultural dimension of the Cold War.

In the years 1956–1961, the CIA showed unmistakable signs of its covert operational frailty. Notably, it tried but failed to overthrow the allegedly Left-leaning government of independence hero Achmed Sukarno in Indonesia. These efforts intensified in 1958, but the shooting down of an American pilot on a CIA bombing mission fleetingly revealed to Americans the secret hand that was already all too evident to foreigners: according to later recollection of Indonesian Foreign Minister Anak Agung, the "general opinion in Indonesia" had been "unanimous" that the CIA was trying to overthrow Sukarno, a view that "was to linger on for a long time and was the main cause of further deterioration in Indonesia-US relations."[28]

Undeterred by such considerations, and determined to propagate the can-do, appropriation-worthy qualities of the CIA, the agency's publicists continued their work. For security and political reasons it was not possible to discuss covert operations openly, but public support for the CIA's activities could be encouraged by other means. In time-honored fashion, some publicists focused on the Fifth Column menace. While anti-subversion and counterespionage at home were not the responsibility of the CIA, exhortations to be vigilant served the purpose of whipping up a siege mentality that would support the CIA's operations abroad. In an address to an annual police chiefs' meeting, CIA Inspector General Lyman B. Kirkpatrick warned that, because they were "among the foremost guardians of freedom," the police were "a major target of the Communists." He appealed to their "natural antipathy" to the Left, and by implication, to their support for the CIA.[29]

Tracy Barnes, a senior figure in covert operations and long renowned for his dash, charm, and wit, similarly ventured onto the lecture circuit to illustrate the domestic dangers of communism and thus to suggest the vital need for CIA retaliation in kind. Addressing a meeting of bankers and lawyers in August 1960, he argued that the CIA's freedom of action under executive direction was inviolate under the terms of the Constitution, though he claimed that Congress did take a "very close took." Barnes now regaled the bankers with the Abel story. Colonel Rudolph Ivanovich Abel had been an officer in the KGB, the Russian State Security system. Living under an assumed name in Brooklyn, New York, he ran an atomic spy ring in the United States, relaying the product of his work to the Kremlin's spymasters by devil-ishly cunning means: hollow pencils, microdots, cuff links, and so forth. Like all the great villains, Abel—a master of languages, an avid reader of Einstein—was clever enough to strike fear and loathing into any gather-ing of decent, ordinary citizens. For ten years, Abel escaped detection in Canada and the United States. Then, in 1957, the FBI arrested him, and he was convicted and sent to prison. Barnes related the event leading to his arrest:

> How Abel was apprehended and changed from an unknown into one of the most publicized agents of our time deserves brief mention. In May 1957, a pudgy, harried Russian named Hayhanen walked into the U.S. Embassy in Paris, showed his American passport and said that he was a Soviet agent, a member of the KGB, that he was returning to Russia on home leave, that he was afraid to do so and wanted to defect. At first he seemed a charter member of the large fraternity of crackpots. A brief association estab-lished that he was under great emotional stress and had a disturbing habit of pausing in the middle of the Champs Elysées holding up one hand as an aerial and tapping his chest with the other as if it were a transmit-ter key. He explained that he was communicating with his wife in the United States. Nevertheless, he made some statements which being spe-cific sounded genuine and were capable of being checked.[30]

Through such narratives, Barnes and a number of similarly fluent and amusing colleagues made the case for the CIA, and not least by claim-ing credit in areas where rival agencies like the FBI might have hoped to profit.

Hyperbole, often pegged to covert operations, was a feature of CIA history in the 1950s. In some of its manifestations, it degenerated into deception in a manner that tarnished the image of democracy, the principle for which the United States was fighting. In a famous article in the 1960s, CIA officer Tom Braden would proclaim "I'm glad the CIA is 'immoral,' " his argument being that the other side lacked any scruple and that one had to fight fire with fire: the ends justified the means.[31] But, too often, U.S. policy ended in support for dictatorships, with democracies being destroyed in order to save them from communism. And while the Soviet Union was just as ruthless as the United States— indeed, was often more so—it did not pay such a heavy price because it did not suffer the burden of expectations. Nobody really expected it to stand for self-determination, free discussion, and free elections.

What did all this mean for intelligence, the real business of the CIA? Here, one could argue that covert operations and hyperbole affected only limited aspects of the CIA's work. In the period from the late 1940s through the early 1960s, a major expansion took place in intelligence facilities both within the CIA and in the wider bureaucracy over which the Director of Central Intelligence had nominal control. It is true that covert operations expanded rapidly, that they damaged the reputation of the CIA within America as well as abroad, and that they helped create a climate in which it was difficult to recruit officers of ability and integrity. But covert action still took up only a very small fraction of the total budget and workforce of the U.S. intelligence community. The covert operations confidence men, or "Cowboys," as they were some- times called, did some real damage and threatened to do more, but the intelligence community as a whole served America well despite this.

An unspectacular but significant development was the expansion of the CIA's economic capability. The Soviet economy was undergoing mushroom growth. This was worrying ideologically—how could a "com- mand" economy outstrip a free enterprise economy? This point could be answered in terms of the "takeoff" factor—economies, be they 1860s America, 1950s Russia, or 1980s Asia, tend to boom when taking off from a low industrial base. But there was a more worrisome specter: Moscow's ability to direct its new resources into channels of its choosing without worrying about elections or consumer preferences. The danger was that the extra resources would build up the Red Army. But here, there was an analytical problem. The Soviet Union lacked a supply and demand mechanism, so ruble prices were meaningless and it was diffi- cult to judge real military production capabilities and even output. The Russians were as much in a fog as anyone else in attempting to analyze their own economy, so, even if one could have broken the secrecy barrier and seen their figures, one would have been little the wiser. To counter all this, the CIA's economists began to build their own models for estimating the true strength of the Soviet economy and of its military component. By 1950, the CIA had a hundred specialists working on the Soviet economy, and by 1955 the number had quintupled.[32]

Another significant area of development was scientific intelligence. During World War II, British scientist R. V. Jones had harnessed his discipline to the military effort, and in the later 1940s, events like the Soviet atomic bomb explosion added urgency to the American determination to harness science and technology to the cause of national defense. Even before the advent of the Cowboys, there was a recruitment problem, namely the irreconcilability of the spy's need for secrecy and the scientist's insistence on international, free exchange of information. But worries about advances in Soviet technology—in chemical as well as atomic warfare—encouraged scientists to cooperate with the CIA. Meanwhile, Moscow alienated scholars worldwide by suppressing genetic research for ideological reasons and by attacking Western scientists as the "learned lackeys of capitalism."[33]

The CIA's precursor, CIG, already had a scientific capability. In 1948, the CIA established an Office of Scientific Intelligence within the Intelligence Directorate. American intelligence officers alongside their British counterparts seized on a special opportunity—they interrogated returning German scientists who had been taken prisoner by the Red Army and forced to work inside Russia, where they had learned about Soviet atomic and chemical warfare research. The importance of rocketry soon became evident: in 1953, U.S. scientists realized that ballistic missiles would be able to carry the newly developed lightweight nuclear warheads vast distances. It was vital to keep an eye on Soviet advances in this area. By this time, it was becoming evident that human intelligence—spies—would in future yield only limited data on a closed society such as the Soviet Union. To fill the deficiency, rockets would deliver spy satellites into space, and in the meantime high-flying reconnaissance aircraft would at least partially remedy the informational void. The U-2 spy plane and the Corona spy satellites conspicuously affirmed the growing importance of technical intelligence. To facilitate such work and to complement developments in the armed forces, the CIA had in 1954 established a separate Directorate for Science and Technology.[34]

Although the CIA was involved in much of this scientific activity, with its director wearing his "other hat" as chief of the wider intelligence community, the agency in physical terms had only a minor involvement in the technical intelligence scene. Each of the armed services retained and expanded its intelligence capability. And the CIA was dwarfed by a new organism, the National Security Agency (NSA). Established on 4 November 1952, the NSA was meant to improve American codebreaking, to look after U.S. defense communications security, and to reduce competitive duplication, still a problem in the armed forces despite recent attempts to unify them. At first, the NSA was located in Arlington Hall, home of the Army Security Agency, renowned for its breaking of Soviet codes that had led to the Venona product. Then in 1954–1958, a new building went up at Fort Meade, in Maryland. Just as the OSS was referred to as the "Oh, So Social," the ultra-secretive NSA was known as "No Such Agency." But contemporaries were able to deduce its power and prestige from the cost of the building, $35 million, the volume and power of the pre-microchip code-breaking computers in its basement, and even the interminable length of its corridors. NSA needed listening posts worldwide, and soon it had an empire that stretched from Alaska to Okinawa, from Turkey to Taiwan. Its intelligence radar facility in Samsoun, Turkey, was able to track the test launching of missiles from the Soviet base in Kaputsin Yar.[35]

Scientific intelligence developments were not devoid of spin. To give a prominent example, President Dwight D. Eisenhower established the National Aeronautics and Space Administration (NASA) in 1958 with public relations in mind. The Soviets' launch in October 1957 of the first man-made satellite, *Sputnik,* had recently shocked an American public conditioned to believe in U.S. technological ascendancy. It is true that a distinction must here be made between the American people and their president. On the golf course, when informed of the *Sputnik* flight, the unflappable Eisenhower refused to interrupt his round. Perhaps he had heard of Sir Francis Drake's insistence on completing his game of bowls as the Spanish Armada approached. More likely, he knew that the Russians had given him a perfect excuse to spy on them from the air—a practice of relatively much greater advantage to the United States, as the USSR was a closed society.[36]

But *Sputnik* did invite a prestige war. The NASA program was designed to appeal to scientists and civilians. Like Eisenhower's own "Atoms for Peace" proposal of 1953 and President Ronald Reagan's Strategic Defense Initiative in the 1980s, it wooed the generous in spirit by offering to share American know-how with the rest of the world. Under President John F. Kennedy, in particular, NASA was presented as a pioneering agency in the American frontier tradition. Perhaps best remembered for its Apollo venture to place Americans on the moon, NASA nevertheless was to a large degree a military agency, collaborating with warhead-delivery and spy-satellite rocketry specialists. Its public image was a triumph of spin.

Nevertheless, in contrast to the calamitous covert operators, the expert intelligence researchers and analysts contributed in a positive manner to national security. To be sure, they made mistakes. Those mistakes tended to attract attention because they led to policy errors, and in a democracy people demand to know why things have gone wrong. In contrast, preventive intelligence achievements slipped quietly by in obscurity, their architects determined to shield their methods from prying and especially enemy eyes.

One criterion for measuring intelligence success is the degree to which things do not happen. To demonstrate the principle in reverse, the Berlin tunnel, dug under the city's eastern sector in 1955 to eavesdrop on communist communications and spectacularly exposed in April 1956, was a "happening" that resulted in great embarrassment. In contrast, during their occupation of Germany from 1945 to 1955, British and American intelligence officials had quietly interrogated prisoners of war returning from the communist East. Nothing "happened," but they built up an incremental picture of Soviet atomic and other scientific progress, helping to ensure that nuclear war did not occur.[37]

Another illustration may be given with regard to chemical and biological warfare. Notoriously, the CIA and army scientists explored the realm of mind-control drugs and truth drugs, an experimental program known as MK-ULTRA that culminated in the suicide, under the influence of secretly administered LSD, of army scientist Frank Olson. But this lurid story fails to disguise an underlying restraint. In the late 1940s, the CIA had started worrying about Soviet chemical warfare capabilities and mind-control drugs that might be administered to sleeper assassins (Richard Condon's novel *The Manchurian Candidate* popularized the concept in 1959). At the start of the Eisenhower administration Henry Loomis, a revolving door physicist who alternated between the CIA and Harvard University, came up with a biological and chemical warfare plan for the United States. In an oral history thirty-six years later, he recorded his colleagues' reaction: "No, no, a thousand times no. We won't do that." This was not the end of the story—the CIA's covert operators developed their own "Health Alteration Committee," dedicated to nefarious activities including assassination. However, restraint by and large prevailed, and it became American policy to spy on chemical warfare plans in foreign countries and, with no small measure of success, to try to stop them. The story is a triumph of the nonevent.[38]

Behind each covert operation, there lay an analytical intelligence assessment. Here, the CIA made mistakes. Short-term gains were allowed ascendancy over the long-term interests of the United States, and perhaps an element of subjectivity crept particularly into intelligence assessments of events in its "backyard," the Americas. Yet the lack of judgment and restraint was by no means universal, as may be seen in the case of Egypt. In the mid-1950s, Egyptian leader Abdul Nasser seemed to be leaning to the Left, and he nationalized the Anglo-French Suez Canal. In 1956 Britain, France, and Israel launched an invasion that proved disastrous not just in itself but because it coincided with the Red Army's brutal crushing of the stirrings of democracy in Hungary, and because it weakened the West's condemnation of Moscow's action there. Prior to the Suez debacle, British intelligence had, in a miasma of self-delusion, concluded that the Egyptian people would rise in support of the Anglo-French-Israeli invasion, yet plotted the assassination of Nasser just in case they did not. In fact, the Egyptians rallied to Nasser, who survived the assassination plots and became a third world hero overnight. In retrospect, the CIA's pre-Suez advice on Egypt appears to have been wise. On the basis of it, Eisenhower had concluded, "The US would be dead wrong to join in any resort to force. We should instead hold out for honest negotiations with the Egyptians." As blind to their own backyard as the Americans were to theirs, the British went ahead with the Suez invasion anyway—without telling Eisenhower. It was a disaster for democracy, but at least the CIA had counseled against it, recommending that it be a nonevent.[39]

For the greatest nonevent of all, the CIA deserves immense credit: nuclear war did not break out. In the 1950s, the U.S. armed forces greatly exaggerated the Soviet military threat. Driven by ambition to expand and with an instinct to compete with one another, the army, air force, and navy engaged in dangerous hyperbole about the tanks, missiles, and nuclear vessels being built by the enemy. Had these stories ultimately been believed, America might have been tempted into a preemptive atomic attack leading to the radioactive poisoning of the world. Had America unreasonably escalated military production to rival its phantom giant, Moscow might have been similarly tempted into a preemptive strike. But in the 1950s and early 1960s, the CIA put the pieces together—the scientific evidence, the cryptographic clues, the economic analysis. It concluded that Moscow was a powerful but not imminently dangerous enemy. Restraint and sanity prevailed. The CIA emerged in this one, vital respect as a powerfully counterhyperbolic and sensible institution.

Allen Dulles was a man of contradictions. On the one hand he was devoted to covert operations, to the dark arts of deception, and to a public relations campaign conducted on a grand scale. On the other hand he was secretive, concerning not just operational matters but any revelations about the CIA's more ruthless activities—revelations that might suggest that he was a gentleman of the gutter. In yet another twist, this very same Allen Dulles not only presided over but very actively promoted such nonsensational developments as economic, technological, and cryptographic intelligence. These developments took up most of the intelligence budget and contributed to a restrained policy, even if covert operations grabbed the imagination of Americans inside and outside government.

The massive-expenditure side of intelligence was an aspect of the onward march of the national security state. It was a milestone in a long-term shift from the private to the public domain. Although the whole intelligence effort was in defense of the principles of capitalism and free enterprise, it contributed to a shift to Big Government that was very real, and difficult to digest. The alliance with private organizations for covert operational purposes helped soothe the discomfort. So, in the short term, did the rhetoric about the CIA's derring-do. Such propaganda may have helped Allen Dulles and his allies on Capitol Hill, but, unfortunately, the rhetoric and associated actions made America a pirate on the world stage just when it was seeking to win over international opinion. Mercifully, American intelligence as a whole was not destabilized, but the tradition of the confidence man received a fillip and lived on, to inflict new damage on America in future years.

CHAPTER 11

Cuba, Vietnam, and the Rhetorical Interlude

John F. Kennedy was already a leading contender for the Democratic nomination when, on 13 March 1960, he hosted a dinner party at which Ian Fleming was a guest. The newly ascendant Fidel Castro was on the conversation menu—indeed, Kennedy was about to make an election issue of the Cuban crisis. What could America do to rid itself of this troublesome communist preening himself in its own backyard? Well, what would James Bond have done? Fleming mischievously rattled off a number of suggestions for "the James Bond treatment," among which were the exploitation of Cuban religious superstition and the emasculation of Castro's image through the removal of his beard. With one exception, all eyes were on Fleming as he rattled off his extemporaneous recipe.

That exception was Fleming's fellow guest John Gross, a senior officer from the CIA. Gross was fascinated not by the British writer but by the reactions of one very important listener. Within half an hour of the dinner party's end, Gross was on the telephone to Allen Dulles, telling how the possible future president had lapped up Fleming's suggestions.

Kennedy could see the droll side of the Bond saga, and he was quite capable of using spy mystique to enhance his own in a purely tongue-in-cheek manner. In an interview with *Life* magazine published on 17 March 1961, he included Fleming's *From Russia With Love* among his ten favorite books—as a "publicity gag" according to his staff. But the new president was in deadly earnest on the subject of the removal of

Castro. Within a month of the *Life* interview, he launched the Bay of Pigs operation to topple the Cuban leader.[1]

The Bay of Pigs operation was not just a failure in itself but also a public relations disaster that introduced a new era in intelligence history. It is an open question whether it had a purgative effect on covert operations. It is more certain that it was a setback for the culture of hyperbole that had reigned in the previous decade. The arts of spin and public relations did not die a sudden death. Indeed, in a period when the spooks fell quiet, the White House and then Congress succumbed to and in different ways promoted the American clandestine tradition. Nevertheless, there was a meaningful rhetorical interlude between the tenancies of those two great exponents of the mythology of espionage, Allen Dulles (Director of Central Intelligence, 1953–1961) and William Casey (1981–1987).

There are two ways of looking at the interlude. On the one hand, there is the pragmatic argument that the CIA and the broader intelligence community need hype. In a competitive lobbying environment, he who hypes best wins the appropriation. So, those who spin yarns about real flesh-and-blood secret agents' daring feats are essential to the intelligence community. Without them, not just romantic covert operations but the analytical intelligence effort as well would be starved of funds, to the detriment of national security. In fact, analytical intelligence needs human insights—technology and number-crunching are just not enough.

From this perspective, the CIA was left vulnerable to hostile propaganda by the demise of the Bold Easterners—Dulles and his senior colleague Richard Bissell (Yale '32) had to go after the Bay of Pigs. To continue with that line of argument, Dulles's successor, John McCone (1961–1965) was a California businessman-scientist with an aversion to publicity whose conservative and nonadventurous approach contributed to a decline in the agency's standing.[2] In 1967, an attack on covert operations initiated by *Ramparts* magazine took advantage of the CIA's exposed position, further weakening the agency. Capitalizing on this, Henry Kissinger, a secretary of state who fully appreciated that knowledge is power, silenced and all but emasculated the CIA. Finally, there occurred the disaster of Senator Frank Church's inquiry into intel-

ligence in 1975–1976, which severely demoralized the CIA. According
to the pro-publicity argument, it was only after this that a revival took
place, with DCI George Bush, President Ronald Reagan, and Casey
prominent among those who took the lead and restored the salutary
traditions of covert operations and pro-intelligence spin.

However, there is a more positive and convincing way of interpreting
the rhetorical interlude. While the intelligence community performed
dismally in the Bay of Pigs, there are signs of better performance during
the Cuban Missile Crisis and the Vietnam War, controversial though
those episodes may have been. The suggestion here is that hype is not an
essential ingredient in good intelligence performance—if anything, the
contrary is true. In 1967, the setback to intelligence was not the *Ramparts* investigation but the failure of the ensuing Katzenbach inquiry to
reform covert operations. The Church inquiry did not force intelligence
to its knees but gave it a hand up by clearing the air, reforming abuses,
and creating a new atmosphere of trust. Regarded in this light, the
interlude in spin gave America time to think about secret intelligence,
and to arrive at some sensible solutions.

The road to reform was a tortuous one, but it may still be discerned,
wending its way slowly through some of American history's most problematic thickets: Cuba in its varied ramifications, the assassination of
President Kennedy, Vietnam, *Ramparts*, Phoenix, and the Kissinger
imbroglio.

In January 1959, forces led by Fidel Castro overthrew the Batista
dictatorship in Cuba. Castro said that U.S. interference had been rife in
his nation since 1898, and that he would put an end to that. Some of his
advisers were communists, but initially, Castro's own allegiance was
unclear. Soon, however, his own communist leanings became evident.
As a result, first the Eisenhower administration and then the Kennedy
administration decided to change the Cuban regime. In one memorandum after another at the start of 1961, project coordinator Bissell
stressed on behalf of the CIA that a covert operation could succeed in
removing Castro, and that it would have to be undertaken as a matter of
urgency, before the revolutionary leader consolidated his regime.[3]

In April 1961, a brigade of Cuban exiles trained and supported by
the CIA duly landed in a remote area on the southeastern shore of the

island whose English-language name was soon to become so familiar, the Bay of Pigs. The purpose of the operation was to establish a bridge-head and then to penetrate into the interior, creating a climate that would encourage Cubans to rise in revolt and throw off the yoke of communism. Unfortunately for the Cuban brigade, it had inadequate air cover and was easy prey for the Cuban air force. The popular up-rising did not happen, and from the American viewpoint the whole scheme ended in disaster. The hand of the CIA in the affair was all too evident, and the underlying complicity of the government was obvious. President Kennedy publicly accepted responsibility for the operation, and for its failure.

The planners of covert operations were supposed to keep them covert and, failing that, to conceal the role of the United States and especially the president. But the Bay of Pigs failure was so public that this was not possible. As a result, there was an extensive and agonizing postmortem. In the spate of government reports, memoirs, and books that followed, American intelligence came in for a pounding. To be sure, President Kennedy had admitted responsibility, but people rather admired him for doing that and focused instead on the CIA and the rest of the covert operational apparatus. By the time Dulles and Bissell had been forced to resign, there was a consensus on a number of intel-ligence failings.

One of these failings was the failure of secrecy. Castro was aware of the impending operation and of the CIA's training facilities in Gua-temala for the would-be liberators. Soviet premier Nikita Krushchev knew the date of the invasion a week in advance, and he no doubt passed the information to Castro. The Soviets had four agents in the Guatemala camp, so the enemy may have had advance knowledge of even some of the details of the "surprise" attack. Secrecy appears to have been effective only in the United States. Whereas Latin American newspapers openly debated the Guatemala camp and prospective inva-sion, the U.S. press, accustomed to its supine and supportive role dur-ing the Dulles years, ignored the story. Only a single, isolated breach in the wall of silence was achieved—by Richard Dudman, a reporter for the *St. Louis Post-Dispatch*. American journalists had too much faith in the CIA. Apparently, the CIA did find out that the Soviets had dis-covered its plans—a scoop, in its way. However, the agency decided not to call off the invasion. Moreover, it did not warn the president that security had been compromised in a manner that would greatly diminish the chance of success.[4]

A second intelligence failing that received some emphasis was the oversanguine estimate of the likelihood of domestic support for the invasion. One CIA report in January 1961 is reminiscent of the racial prejudices of 1898; American soldiers were shocked to discover that some of Cuba's most patriotic soldiers were black: "A private survey made recently in Cuba showed that less than 30 percent of the population is still with Fidel. In this 30 percent are included the Negroes who have always followed the strong men in Cuba, but will not fight." Bissell received reports from unspecified "military advisers" that one Cuban province was on the verge of anarchy, that militiamen were refusing to fight in another, that only 20–25 percent of the Cuban army would fight, and that it had been "penetrated by opposition groups." But naval intelligence indicated that Castro had the support of his people—its more accurate observation was to no avail, as the CIA chose, in the interest of security, not to involve the military in its plans. Why, Gen. George H. Decker later asked, had the military come to a more sensible conclusion on a political matter than the civilian-oriented CIA?[5]

A third imputed failing was on the policy-intelligence borderline. On 16 April, the day before the invasion force arrived at the beach, Kennedy canceled an air strike that had been intended to destroy the Cuban air force on the ground, and thus its ability to bombard the incoming rebels. These strikes were to have been disguised as attacks on their own bases by defecting Cuban pilots. But the fear was that the disguise would be too thin, and that the hand of the U.S. president would be revealed. Because of this political consideration and, according to his defenders, because he had been led to believe the operation would succeed without the strikes, Kennedy at the last minute refused air support.

Those who sympathized with the CIA took a dim view of Kennedy's caution. One of these was Richard W. Rowan, an author of books on intelligence history who in 1963 agreed to look over the draft of Dulles's book *The Craft of Intelligence*. Rowan was not bound as Dulles was by residual bonds of loyalty to President Kennedy. Furthermore, the whole Bay of Pigs episode reminded him of his grievance with the Pinkerton National Detective Agency over its block on a movie he had wanted to make on its history. Rowan reminded Dulles of Allan Pinkerton's habit of counting General Lee's men "from all four sides" with the cumulative effects of inhibiting a Union attack that might have ended the Civil War, saving tremendous bloodshed: "Here overzealous intelligence worked a grave national harm. I am confident, for example, that your CIA people did or reported nothing to fit Mr Kennedy with the refrigerated socks which seem to have made inevitable the debacle of the (excusing the expression!) Bay of Pigs."[6]

The bombing issue and the cold feet allegation were the nub of the disagreement between the White House and CIA over what went wrong on 17 April. The Kennedy White House, like the FDR administration, had its talented court historians who made an effective scapegoat of the intelligence community. Its argument was that the CIA had rashly promised a successful landing and a Cuban uprising. But the CIA felt that it had had a right to expect support of the type given by President Eisenhower in the toppling of the Guatemala regime in 1954, when Ike had authorized the use of air strikes in support of the coup.

That Guatemala had served as a guiding precedent for Cuba came to be a matter of common consent, even if people differed in their opinion about how appropriate that was.[7] Here, an article written by Allan Dulles throws light on the nature of the disagreement between himself and President Kennedy. He wrote it for *Harper's Magazine* after Kennedy's death with a view to rebutting criticism of the role of the CIA in the press, in government reports, and especially in books by former White House aides Theodore Sorensen and Arthur M. Schlesinger, Jr. He felt that these aides had abused their position in using confidential information to give Kennedy's side of the story, and said he still felt inhibited in writing about the Bay of Pigs, as the DCI-presidential relationship "is a very private one." In a later draft, he defensively replaced the word "private" with "special." Then, he withdrew the article altogether—perhaps motivated in part by the dictates of operational security, in part by Kennedy's own public silence on the issue and then his sympathy-inducing tragic death, and in part by a not unwise judgment that, for once, he had been upstaged in the great American theater of public relations.

In his essay, Dulles took issue with Sorensen and Schlesinger's assertion that the CIA director (until only recently, "Mr. Dulles" to the young president) had virtually stood over Kennedy (as ever, "Jack" to Dulles) and told him that the chances for success in Cuba were "even better" than they had been in Guatemala. In each case, Dulles insisted, he had advised that the chance of success was barely more than one in five. In the case of the Bay of Pigs, even before the cancellation of the vital air strike, Dulles "had rated the prospects [only] somewhat higher than the 20 per cent I had given President Eisenhower in Guatemala in 1954." Clearly, there is a perceptual gulf here, concerning the assurances given by Dulles and their reception by Kennedy. But both Schlesinger and Dulles agree on a phenomenon that might explain that gulf. Dulles quoted with approval the following passage from the former aide's book: "Kennedy observed that the trouble with me was that I was 'a legendary figure, and it's hard to cooperate with legendary figures.'" In other words, Dulles had become not just a beneficiary but also a victim of his own spin and hyperbole. Even when he was being a good intelligence officer and giving a realistic evaluation of the risk factor, his reputation preceded him in a way that affected the judgment of the President. Because Kennedy had eyes only for Dulles the enthusiast and not for Dulles the cool appraiser, he authorized a risky operation with which, in the end, he could not cooperate.[8]

The investigations into the Bay of Pigs concentrated on tactics, minutiae, and that beloved shibboleth of the government bureaucrat, organizational structure. Notably, the Presidential Board of Inquiry on the Bay of Pigs, chaired by Gen. Maxwell D. Taylor, concluded that America "must be prepared to engage" in such operations but only when there was a "maximum chance of success." It accepted the premise that failure was the main failure at the Bay of Pigs, and that the root of that failure was to be found in the absence of an appropriate "governmental mechanism" to ensure success.[9]

However, such investigations did not confront the real nature of the failure, which may be gauged from the *consequences* of the Bay of Pigs. These consequences suggest that the real intelligence error was to counsel such a maneuver at all. For the operation consolidated Fidel Castro in power, giving both Cubans and the United States a long-term headache. It was, furthermore, merely the most emblematic of several operations that produced similar responses elsewhere, regardless of whether they "succeeded" or "failed" in narrowly defined operational terms. America's espousal of democracy may have been proclaimed in the case of Cuba, but it seemed to be a sham, as the overthrow of Left-leaning elected governments in Iran, Guatemala, Guyana, Chile, and elsewhere had made abundantly clear. The Bay of Pigs was an open invitation to any nationalist, or communist in the guise of a nationalist, to "stand up to American imperialism" in the confident expectation that his ruthlessness and mendacity would pale, in the court of international opinion, in comparison with America's actions and the apparently hypocritical words with which they were justified. Kennedy's action, inspired to an appreciable degree by CIA spin and hyperbole, provoked a siege mentality and a distrust of the United States that prolonged the Cold War and provided communist dictatorship with a new lease on life. Almost without fail, future demonstrations protesting a variety of American policies across the world would feature placards bearing that acronym of shame, "CIA."[10]

But all this was lost on the Kennedy administration. Far from absorbing the lessons of April 1961, Kennedy pressed on, compounding the errors that had by now become institutionalized in the American intelligence community. One of his earliest actions, in the wake of the Bay of Pigs, was to approve a major addition to the intelligence bureaucracy, the Defense Intelligence Agency (DIA).

There had been talk, in the Eisenhower administration, of reforming military intelligence. Each branch of the armed forces had its own intelligence unit. Indeed, proliferation had taken place in the wake of the National Security Act of 1947. This had aimed at centralization and at unification of the armed forces, and did lead to the formation of the overarching Department of Defense. But it also resulted in the addition of two intelligence agencies to the community that already existed. One of these was the CIA, and the other stemmed from the creation of the Air Force as a separate entity, and therefore Air Force intelligence, or A-2. The formation of the National Security Agency in 1952 was a step in the direction of consolidation in that it unified some of the more important communications intelligence functions of the military services. Yet, the NSA's sprawling facilities and numerous personnel did nothing to allay fears that the intelligence bureaucracy was expanding in a manner disproportionate to America's needs.

President Eisenhower liked a balanced budget and deplored wastefulness in federal spending, but there was a further reason for taking a look at military intelligence. The various agencies competed furiously

on behalf of their respective services—the navy, army, and air force—
each claiming that the Soviets threatened the area of its particular
concern. The ethos of private-profit competition with its resultant hyperbole had passed into the public sector—and no sector is more firmly
in the public domain than the military. All this was reinforced by the
testosterone factor. Generals and admirals who were keen to demonstrate their continuing virility could not be turned loose on the Soviet
Union because it was too dangerous, so to fulfill their need for combat
they turned on each other in a grand battle for appropriations. They
were vigorously abetted by members of Congress dedicated to one
service or another. For the legislators the process was partly tribal, like
supporting one's football team. In other cases it was a matter of sentiment, based on family connections with one of the services, and in still
others it was a question of job protection—for example, if one had a
navy yard in one's constituency one supported the navy's quest for appropriations, and the ONI's inflation of the threat from the Soviet navy.

The matter came to a head in the late 1950s, when A-2 claimed that
the Soviets were opening up a "missile gap" that threatened the security
of America. The USSR was a closed society, and neither the U-2 spy
plane nor the infant satellite surveillance system was, as yet, sufficiently
advanced to either prove or disprove A-2's contention that the Soviet
strike capability had suddenly assumed menacing proportions. The issue was tailor-made for Senator Kennedy, the 1960 presidential candidate. As a young and inexperienced politician and as a Democrat, he
felt vulnerable to charges of being soft on communism. Now was his
chance to berate the Republican administration for having allowed the
Russians to steal a march on America. The charge was effective, helping
him defeat Vice President Nixon in the bid for the White House. However, on becoming president, he needed to reform the intelligence
system that had slept while Moscow stole a stealthy lead. As in the
aftermath of Pearl Harbor, a system that had failed to deliver had to be
strengthened. A cynic might be forgiven for saying that those who had
failed had to be rewarded. But there was no question of asking the CIA
to assume a greater military role. That agency was in disgrace and had
to be punished despite the irrelevance of the Bay of Pigs to the missile
gap debate. So Kennedy accepted, instead, a plan to reform military
intelligence.[11]

Implementation of this plan fell to the new secretary of defense,

Robert M. McNamara. In his days with the Ford Motor Company, Mc-Namara had been a bureaucratic reformer with formidable "number-crunching" skills. When the outgoing secretary of defense, Thomas Gates, warned him that the missile gap was illusory and that a consolidation of military intelligence might be desirable, McNamara decided to accept the recommendation of a presidential study group that had reported in December 1960. In its report, the group had described the military intelligence system as "duplicatory and cumbersome," and called for the establishment of a DIA. A Department of Defense directive authorized the new agency on August 1961, and the DIA began to operate on 1 October, just two months before the resignation of Allen Dulles from the directorship of the CIA.

According to the DIA's Website in the year 2000, the agency "came of age" in the 1980s. This less than fulsome assessment of the first two decades of the agency's history accords with the judgment in successive government reviews of U.S. intelligence provision—the Whitten Report (1968), the Fitzhugh Report (1970), the Schlesinger Report (1971), and the Church and Pike reports (1976). The common criticism was that the DIA was impotent and that it failed to reduce redundancy of function and expenditure within the military intelligence community. For McNamara had decided to respect the autonomy of the three branches of the armed services—he made no attempt to make them combine, either generally or in their intelligence functions. The political difficulties in his path, should he have chosen to make the effort, would have been formidable. There was also the obstacle of the McCormack-Curtis amendment to the National Security Act of 1947, which stipulated that the armed forces could be asked to consolidate only in pursuit of efficiency and avoidance of redundancy—this continued to be the concern of the House Armed Services Committee's Special Subcommittee on Defense Agencies, when it was set up in March 1962. Ironically, the founding of the DIA in the name of efficiency merely added a layer of bureaucracy and failed to assert the hoped-for measure of civilian authority over the military intelligence branches. Its first director, Gen. Joseph F. Carroll (1961–1969), had begun his career as an assistant to J. Edgar Hoover, but thereafter rose to prominence via a career in the air force, a branch of the armed services noted for its inflationary estimates. Under his aegis, the DIA would prove to be over-responsive to pressures from the military, often representing the "sum of their fears" and at other times dithering—it was known, by the mid-1960s, as the "Old Twirling DIA."[12]

However, the DIA was a significant addition to the U.S. intelligence community. It contributed to a process that in the 1970s acquired the appellation "competitive estimating": in making his mind up about policy, the president would now have access to well-informed coordinated assessments not just from the CIA, but from the DIA as well. The voice of the DIA may have been flawed, but it was powerful. Just as the clout of the NSA and CIA could be inferred from their buildings, personnel, and rates of expansion, so the DIA prospered, acquiring substantial premises in Arlington Hall, setting up new branches such as the Defense Intelligence School, and acquiring additional functions such as the management of the defense attaché system. In the early days of Carroll's tenure, DIA analysts examined a diversity of problems ranging from China's atomic bomb program to unrest in Africa—it would be too sweeping a generalization to say that all their work was worthless.[13]

One day in September 1962, the DIA's Col. John Wright was examining pictures of ground-to-air Soviet missile sites in Cuba when he noticed a trapezoidal pattern reminiscent of those in Russia surrounding long-range nuclear missile bunkers.[14] Thus did the DIA, in conjunction with other members of the intelligence community, collect and help assemble the pieces in a jigsaw puzzle whose solution informed President Kennedy of the new Soviet offensive capability just ninety miles off the shores of Florida. The Cuban Missile Crisis is understandably cited as the most dangerous confrontation the world has yet experienced. It represented a real test for the real CIA, as distinct from its Cowboys. Although the agency's intoxicating image was ebbing—or, perhaps, precisely because it was sobering up—the CIA and its supportive intelligence network did get things right at crucial moments on this occasion.

The performance of the American intelligence community in the missile crisis may be summed up as "no prediction but discovery, and better than the adversarial competition." Its performance was initially weak in that it did not foresee that the Soviet Union would decide on and implement Operation Anadyr, the attempt to place nuclear-tipped missiles in Cuba. It seemed to subscribe to a belief that would be widely held for some years after the crisis, that Krushchev had acted irrationally and thus unpredictably. Partly because democratization in Russia has opened up previously unexamined documents, Krushchev's motives are now more understandable. The Soviet leader wanted to protect Cuba from a second American invasion. With China emerging as an atomically armed rival within the communist world, Krushchev wanted to show that he was the man to get tough with the capitalists. Like Eisenhower, he could see that atomic defense was cheaper than conventional armies, and that this could lead to better rewards for the domestic consumer, so he seized on a chance to demonstrate the potency of his weapons. Causing trouble in America's backyard gave him leverage in his own, namely the city of Berlin, which, as a legacy of World War II, was so unhappily divided between the communist and capitalist camps. The placement of missiles in Cuba would enable him to rectify the real missile gap—America was in fact well in advance of its Soviet rival in terms of nuclear strike capability. The Americans had recently placed Jupiter missiles in Turkey not far from key Soviet targets; by placing missiles within comparable range of Eastern Seaboard cities, Krushchev would achieve a valuable deterrent and bargaining chip. The move would also help bring America to the bargaining table in an attempt to limit the testing of future nuclear weapons. Lacking the means to see into the minds of the Soviet leaders, as distinct from reading their messages, the CIA and its colleagues failed to see any of this. Consequently, President Kennedy and his advisers remained blissfully ignorant of the Kremlin debate on Operation Anadyr. Until very late in the day, they also remained ignorant of the full import of the 150 round trips made by 85 ships between the Soviet Union and Cuba in the three months from mid-July 1962.[15]

The hawks on Capitol Hill grumbled loudly about the stream of imports to Cuba. DCI McCone warned on 22 August that the USSR might be preparing to place intermediate (2,000-mile) range missiles on the island, but he lacked evidence and Kennedy dismissed his view as "the suspicion of a professional anti-communist."[16] Military intelligence had cried wolf so often and Dulles had been so fallibly "legendary" that his successor, who made the correct human judgment, was not taken seriously. When Khrushchev said the buildup did not include nuclear capability, Kennedy felt he had to take the Soviet leader on trust.

Nevertheless, bits and pieces of evidence began to flow in, and the process of discovery began. There was that DIA report on the trapezoidal pattern. Further clues came in. For example, English trawlermen "fishing" north of Iceland used the cameras issued to them by British intelligence to record images of Russian freighters under very heavy naval escort heading down the western Atlantic Seaboard. By 3 October, enough evidence had accumulated for the DIA to demand aerial photographs of specific Soviet construction sites in Cuba. The U-2 spy plane delivered these. By mid-October, an angry and disillusioned president had the proof he had never wanted.[17]

With this in hand, Kennedy appealed to the nation for support and confronted the Soviet Union. Resisting pressure to launch an immediate invasion of Cuba, he explained on television that he was going to blockade the island. B-52s, the giant bombers that carried nuclear weapons, were put on alert and flew twenty-four hours a day so as to be ready to blast the heart of Russia at immediate notice. With one portion of the world on the brink of immediate destruction and the rest threatened by slow death via radioactive fallout and poisoning, Kennedy and Krushchev now came to their senses and reached agreement. Unilateral nuclear disarmament took place in Cuba. In exchange, Kennedy gave Krushchev a personal undertaking that he would not invade the island and secretly agreed to withdraw the provocative and unstable Jupiters from Turkey.[18] It was now left to posterity to debate whether Kennedy had matured into a courageous leader who remained cool and restrained under pressure, or whether Krushchev had saved mankind by having the guts to back down in a manner that threatened his political survival.

R. Jack Smith, a senior CIA analyst who helped brief Kennedy about the missiles in Cuba, thought that in the crisis, "American intelligence, and especially the CIA, experienced one of its finest hours . . . we sifted and sorted until we finally got the evidence that enabled us to target the U-2 correctly." In some respects, too much is claimed for the CIA. The role of other intelligence agencies like the DIA tends to be ignored. Furthermore, the evidence does not appear to support the claim sometimes made for the CIA's prized "defector in place," Col. Oleg Penkovsky of Soviet military intelligence: Penkovsky simply could not have supplied the vital information that the Cuban missiles would be operational by December. In other respects, though, the Smith assessment is correct. Any balanced judgment must take into account the fact that mistakes and weaknesses are inherent in all organizations— success and failure are matters of degree and are measurable in comparative terms. Thus, it is significant that Soviet intelligence in relation to the missile crisis was in utter disarray: it could not predict Kennedy's responses, and Krushchev ignored it anyway. Cuban intelligence was competent, but Castro was too single-minded about his policy agenda to take any heed of its findings. It would appear, on the evidence of the missile crisis, that the U.S. intelligence system was distinctly superior to those of America's deadliest rivals.[19]

Kennedy's stand over Cuba added luster to an already shining image summed up in the word "Camelot." King Arthur at his court in Camelot with its democratic round table conjured up images, the product of centuries of poetic spin, of a gallant Celtic warrior who held the invading English hordes at bay. First among equals in the company of men and proud companion of his lovely wife Guinevere, King Arthur wielded his phallic sword Excalibur and was a model of chivalry. Kennedy's Irish descent, his good looks, the stunning beauty and aesthetic taste of his wife, Jacqueline, and the Kennedy clan's gift for public relations made the young president an object of adulation. Substitute expansionist Russians for invading English, and the picture is complete: President Kennedy was King Arthur.

Just as Kennedy's frequent need for women was at odds with the Camelot image, so was his continuing and distinctly ungallant commitment to ruthless covert actions in pursuit of foreign policy goals.[20] While he was a master of public relations in his own right, he also seems to have been hypnotized by a type of CIA hyperbole that was going out of fashion in intelligence circles. Though the Bay of Pigs had caused others to question the magical properties of covert action, the president and his advisers—notably, his brother Robert Kennedy—pressed on. In 1962, for example, the CIA began to intervene in the politics of Latin America's oldest democracy, Chile, funneling secret slush funds to the Christian Democrats in order to prevent the election of the socialist Salvador Allende. The irony of this episode lies in its epilogue: after Kennedy's death, the covert Chile operation resumed under the guidance of the U.S. Army's Special Operations Office. This continuing U.S.

commitment to the secret subversion of democracy was code-named "Project Camelot."[21]

For Kennedy, the danger in Chile and other Latin American countries was that Castroism would take root—the Cuban leader and his comrade Che Guevara clearly had a mission to spread their revolution. Of paramount importance, therefore, was the removal of Castro himself. In the wake of the Bay of Pigs failure, the White House launched Operation Mongoose. Although counterinsurgency expert Edward Lansdale warned that the Cuban people were solidly behind Castro, the hope was that this could be changed through sabotage of the Cuban economy and other dirty tactics. Infamously, the CIA decided to use "psychological warfare" tricks including those that Ian Fleming had mentioned only as a joke, for example the application to Castro's shoes of a depilatory agent that would enter his bloodstream and make his beard fall out. The theory that this would have brought his machismo to an abrupt end never was put to the test, as the Cubans (with the assistance of Soviet security agents) carefully protected their president from the estimated thirty-two assassination plots against him in the early sixties—indeed, Mongoose may have helped provoke the arrival of Soviet weapons in Cuba, and thus the missile crisis.[22]

Both before and after the missile crisis, Castro was on the hit list of the CIA's assassination squads. At a time when Attorney General Robert Kennedy was publicly waging a war against America's mobsters, the U.S. government engaged those very same mobsters to kill "that bad Cuban." Then there was the separate plan to present Castro with a poison pen, and the ingenious plot to cripple him with an exploding clamshell while he was engaged in leisure-diving. The impression is given of confidence men elevating dirty tricks to an art form.[23]

The assassination program had not originated with President Kennedy or his brother. The Eisenhower administration had laid the groundwork. At various times under both Eisenhower and Kennedy, several prominent politicians were targeted. While the quality of the evidence varies, the following were probably on the list: Fulgencio Batista (Castro's predecessor in Cuba), Ernesto "Che" Guevara (Cuba and South America—the legendary guerrilla fighter) and Patrice Lumumba (president of the Congo, now Zaire). Curiously, the CIA never seems to have got its man. In some cases—for example, the murders of Lumumba and Guevara—this may have been only because someone else got there first. But there was also opposition inside the CIA to Castro's assassination. Sherman Kent, the nation's senior intelligence analyst, warned that "a dead Castro" would be more valuable to the communist cause as a martyr than he could ever be alive. It was not unusual for analysts to be more circumspect than operators, or more forthright than DCIs out to please a president, but in this case the DCI also seems to have been uneasy. John McCone was reluctant about the whole Mongoose program, even if he refrained from openly opposing it out of loyalty to his president.[24]

McCone's reluctance only highlights the fact that, regardless of precedent and failure, the responsibility for the decision to destabilize Cuba and to murder Castro lay with the White House. A January 1962 Department of Defense memorandum reflected the determination of the White House when it described the CIA's anti-Castro program as "a red line operation with the blessing of the President" that must not be opposed on financial or any other ground: "This is probably the most important mission we have in the government today." On 18 October at the height of the missile crisis, Kennedy's special assistant for national security affairs, McGeorge Bundy, reflected that Castro seemed to have a "daemon for self-destruction" and added, "We may have to help him with that."[25]

Kennedy's assassination on 22 November 1963 in Dallas, Texas, invites speculation that it was a preemptive strike by the Cuban supporters of Fidel Castro. But this and an abundance of other conspiracy theories have led to no firm conclusion. Certain facts are now clear: for example, the House Select Committee on Assassinations in 1977–1978 commissioned a computer-generated three-dimensional model indicating that Lee Harvey Oswald did fire the bullet that killed the president. However, because of evidential difficulties arising from still-unexplained cover-ups, it remains uncertain whether he acted alone or in concert with others.[26]

Whatever the truth is, it seems likely that Kennedy may have contributed, unwittingly, to his own death. Those who mixed in Oswald's demimonde of KGB agents and Cuban exiles were acquainted with the ruthlessness of Kennedy policy and would have felt little moral compunction in killing him. Kennedy's rhetoric on non-intelligence matters contributed further to a culture of violence. Notably, when he expounded on his campaign slogan, the "New Frontier," he conjured up and perhaps encouraged the image of a "gunfighter nation."[27]

Kennedy's death and the manner of it were of varying significance for intelligence history. Certainly, Dallas did nothing to inhibit the growth of intelligence bureaucracy. Kennedy's death affected attitudes in both the Soviet Union and in America. In Moscow, Khrushchev became nervous that America would not keep its word over the promised noninvasion of Cuba—ironically, the communist leader had come to regard his prime antagonist as a guarantor of peace. Thus the tragedy in Dallas stirred up mistrust, the oxygen of espionage. Back home, officials saw a further reason to step up intelligence— it was necessary to increase protection of the president. The Secret Service became, in the words of historian Fred Kaiser, the "organizational beneficiary" of its own failure to protect Kennedy, and received more personnel and money. While it must be remembered that federal government has expanded on all fronts throughout the twentieth century, it is notable that, after spectacular failures like Pearl Harbor and Kennedy's death, spin has resulted in the reward of the allegedly incompetent, whether the OSS/CIA/NSA or the Secret Service. In any event, the augmentation in the Secret Service did not result in more efficient preventive intelligence: of the thirteen gun attacks on presidents or presidential candidates in the 192-year era to 1981, six occurred in and after 1963— almost half the shootings in 10 percent of the time.[28]

Nevertheless, the sixties was a decade of decline for the intelligence confidence man. The operations buccaneer was obliged to take a backseat in the Vietnam War. The same conflict occasioned a flowering of analytical intelligence. Although they made rough weather of it and were not thanked for their pains, in the case of the Vietnam War the intelligence analysts issued a rare challenge to policies made in the Pentagon and White House.

U.S. covert operators had been active in Southeast Asia since World War II. In the concluding phase of the war, they helped Ho Chi Minh liberate Vietnam from the occupying Japanese forces. In one incident, they gifted him six revolvers and pronounced him OSS Agent 19. Encouraged by an OSS officer, Ho opened the Vietnamese declaration of independence by quoting the second paragraph of its U.S. precursor: "All men are created equal. They are endowed by their Creator with certain inalienable rights; among these are Life, Liberty, and the pursuit of Happiness." He declaimed the passage to a wildly enthusiastic, half-million-strong crowd in Ba Dinh square, Hanoi. As in the case of Castro later on, there was at first some doubt as to whether Ho was a communist. Was he playing along with the Americans only because the United States was in 1945 the supreme power in the Pacific arena, or was he a genuinely pro-American nationalist in an alliance of mere convenience with the communists? But then the British, nervous about rebellious stirrings in their own empire, insisted on the restoration of French colonial rule in Indochina. America emphatically if uneasily supported its wartime imperialist allies. In retrospect, it is plain that Ho was a communist. From now on, the OSS and its successors would be his enemy.[29]

America supported French attempts to reimpose colonial rule. But in 1954, military defeat forced France to give up half of Vietnam. North Vietnam became communist, while South Vietnam remained in the capitalist camp. The CIA now redoubled its efforts to frustrate communist expansion by nonelectoral means (the regime in the South was so exploitative and corrupt that there was a danger that the communists would have won an election outright). Under the regional leadership of the buccaneering, socially top-drawer Desmond FitzGerald, and the local leadership of Edward Lansdale, the agency advocated "nation-building" (an appeal to anti-communist nationalism) and a program of appealing to the "hearts and minds" of the Vietnamese people. Lansdale's operatives contaminated gasoline supplies in North Vietnam and urged Roman Catholics to flee to the South, where they were encouraged to continue to resist communism. In both Laos and Vietnam, they cultivated the montagnards, hill peoples who hated their lowland compatriots and communism in equal measure. Sectarianism and micro-nationalism, phenomena that would haunt American foreign policy after the end of the Cold War, were thus actively promoted during it.

At first, Kennedy embraced the "counterinsurgency" ideas put forward by FitzGerald, Lansdale, and William Colby, the OSS veteran who was now a senior CIA official sharing responsibility for Vietnam. But then, both he and his successor, President Johnson, turned from covert operations to other means. However, they did not do so for the correct reason. As Mongoose demonstrates, there was no sudden realization that covert operations were an albatross hung around the neck of U.S. foreign policy. Kennedy may have been partly affected by the failure at the Bay of Pigs, reasoning not that such interventions were a mistake but that the CIA could not be entrusted with them and should not be too seriously heeded in the future. At the same time, Kennedy and Johnson moved to the conclusion that Vietnam needed not the "political" solution advocated by the CIA's Asian specialists, but a military one.[30]

Most Americans approved of the decision to send combat troops to Vietnam, and the war in its early stages was more popular than any other conflict in American history, with the sole exception of World War II. Yet, with the benefit of hindsight, all serious observers agree that the decision was a mistake, even if some defend it on moral grounds.[31]

Understandably, many people who were involved in the Vietnam War later claimed to have doubted its wisdom all along—nobody likes to be associated with failure, especially one associated with untold suffering and the loss of over two million lives. Yet, the opposition of significant sections of the intelligence community is credible enough. As early as December 1953, an intelligence estimate agreed upon by the Joint Chiefs of Staff and CIA predicted that military action against the Vietnamese communists would develop into a long war of attrition with no guarantee of success. In a change of heart, the Joint Chiefs recommended intervention in October 1961, in order to interdict supplies flowing from North Vietnam to the Viet Cong communist insurgents in the South. But on this occasion, Asian specialists in both the CIA and DIA questioned the premise that the Viet Cong were a weak, nonindigenous force that could be so summarily crushed—according to one CIA estimate, the Viet Cong grew their own food, made their own weapons, and were 80 to 90 percent local. Neither of the agencies was complicit in President Kennedy's fateful decision to send the first support troops—the president did not even consult them. Desmond Fitz-Gerald could sympathize neither with McNamara's number-crunching criteria nor with his evaluation as conveyed in the defense secretary's May 1962 claim that by "every quantitative measurement . . . we are winning the war." Meanwhile, State Department intelligence (INR) reported that supporting the corrupt Saigon regime was a waste of money.[32]

As a broad generalization, it can be said that the intelligence community continued to question and to criticize, even after America became seriously engaged in the fighting. A broad qualification is also in order—the dissent was wobbly, and sometimes intelligence analysts actively supported the premises behind the war. After all, it is not easy to criticize the military policy of your government at a time when brave soldiers are being killed and wounded in action—although, of course, some patriotic critics voiced their reservations for that very reason. The phenomenon of "command intelligence" was also in evidence—not wishing to endanger their careers, analysts submitted conclusions they knew would please their superiors. Thereupon, the leaders of the intelligence community would deliver this "intelligence to please" to President Johnson and others whose displeasure they so deeply feared. Against this background, the doubts were slow to percolate through.

But they did do so in the end. For in the meantime, protest against the war was gathering pace, not just amongst the public but in the military, in Congress, and in government, too.[33] The outcome was first "Vietnamization" of the war, a forlorn attempt to restore indigeneity to the fighting, and then the American withdrawal in 1973. In their own way, the analysts contributed to this outcome.

The intelligence community responded to Rolling Thunder with typically wavering dissent. Rolling Thunder was the code name for a U.S. bombing campaign against North Vietnam from spring 1965 to fall 1968. In general, there is some doubt about the efficacy of bombing campaigns, especially against civilian targets. They can boost enemy morale. Furthermore, in being aimed at industrial targets, they can inflict only marginal damage on agricultural nations like North Vietnam. Rolling Thunder ultimately failed in its aim to force the communists to the negotiating table. Early on, the DIA supported the campaign and the CIA opposed it. Then in March 1966 the CIA supported the bombing, though with internal dissent, notably from its Vietnam specialist George A. Carver, Jr. Now, it was the DIA's turn to have doubts, and McNamara, disillusioned with the "twirling" agency he had created, turned to the CIA for an authoritative assessment. On 12 May 1967, the CIA's analytical branch delivered a searing verdict on the bombing campaign. The enemy was ingenious at repair work: "North Vietnam's ability to recuperate from the air attacks has been of a high order." Bombing had achieved only limited results in the past, and was unlikely to be more effective in the future.[34]

Both the CIA and the DIA were generally gloomy about the enemy order of battle. True, they did not always oppose the military hierarchy on this, the "numbers" issue. The issue was puzzling, because an essentially conventional American force opposed an enemy that fought a guerrilla campaign, with its soldiers attacking at one moment, only to disappear the next. The DIA at first went along with the generals, who thought the Viet Cong and other communist forces were sufficiently few in number to be defeated. Similarly, in a June 1965 memorandum, the CIA recommended an escalation in U.S. troop levels in anticipation that North Vietnam would be forced to the negotiating table—the expectation here was that the Viet Cong would be too weak to cope with an American force of 70,000 men. But this departure from pessimism was an aberration. Soon, a new analyst would arrive on the scene, an analyst who would issue a blunt challenge to the order-of-battle optimists.[35]

Sam Adams was blue-chip and bright. Everybody knew that. It was not just his Ivy League background (Harvard '55), or the fact that he was descended from the second president of the United States, but also the incisive nature of his reports once he joined the CIA and began to dissect the problem of the Viet Cong. Arriving in Saigon in January 1966, Adams researched the enemy more thoroughly than anyone previously, and discovered that they had a massive desertion rate. Add to that the heavy casualties being inflicted by American soldiers, and it was evident the Viet Cong would crumble within a year, or two years at most. This was just what President Johnson and the military top brass wanted to hear. Though just a lowly researcher, Adams was summoned personally to brief CIA director William Raborn (1965–1966). Jack Smith, by now the agency's research director, took him aside and told Adams he was "*the* outstanding analyst" in his division.[36]

They then dispatched Adams to a desk on the fifth floor of the CIA's building in Virginia and told him to carry on with the good work. There, Adams began to examine documents captured in battle from the enemy. On the afternoon of Friday, 19 August, Bulletin 689 reached his desk, a report by the Viet Cong command in Binh Dinh Province putting its guerrilla militia fighting strength at 50,000. This struck Adams as odd, because it was dramatically at odds with the official U.S. intelligence estimate of 4,500. No doubt a less confident analyst, or someone with his eye on the promotion ladder, might have left the matter there, dismissing the anomaly as a freak blip. But Adams was an intelligent, bloody-minded patriot. What if lots more enemy fighters were out there than was commonly believed?

As he furiously studied more and more figures, the picture became clear to Adams. He concluded that American intelligence had underestimated overall enemy strength by 200,000. Clearly, the Viet Cong could fight on and on—and would do so, as their high morale guaranteed that new recruitment would more than counteract the effects of desertion. Looking at the evidence in light of information generated in the course of extensive subsequent debate, it appears that Adams may well have been correct in exposing the opportunistic way in which senior officers used intelligence, though he probably confused potential recruits with actual fighting strength, and thus exaggerated enemy numbers.[37]

At any rate, Adams on 22 August set forth his prognosis in a memorandum that he thought would go straight to the president and cause a radical rethinking of American foreign policy. However, presidents rarely read memoranda by junior intelligence officers. In any case, the truth as defined by Adams was politically inconvenient. Some people believed him. Captain Barrie Williams, the order of battle specialist in the DIA, shared Adams's misgivings, and a vigorous debate took place within the intelligence community. But too many promotions were at stake for anyone to press for a thorough reassessment of the war's military premises. Nobody went public, and no senior person in the CIA or the DIA plucked up the courage to tell President Johnson of the specialists' doubts.[38]

With the numbers debate at its height, the CIA was hit by a scandal that one historian has dubbed the "Literary Bay of Pigs." On 14 February 1967 the *New York Times* and *Washington Post* ran full-page advertisements for the forthcoming issue of *Ramparts,* a West Coast Catholic magazine known for its opposition to the Vietnam War. The publicity alerted America to the fact that the CIA had long been in secret control of the international activities of the National Student Association. Touching on a very sensitive issue, *Ramparts* noted that the CIA had not only channeled hidden subsidies to compliant student leaders but also arranged draft exemptions for them. American journalists had themselves run errands for the CIA and were to do so in the future, but, for the time being, newspapers ran with the story of the hour and made further disclosures. What some people had long suspected now became irrefutable truth. The press revealed extensive CIA use of American citizens and institutions, as well as a vast international plot to bribe or subsidize people to attack communism. Abroad, America's reputation for honest dealing came in for another mauling. At home, there was outcry at the length and nature of a list of suborned institutions that included the National Education Foundation (representing 983,000 teachers), the American Newspaper Guild, the American Political Science Association, and the AFL-CIO.[39]

The scandal only confirmed the suspicions of an increasingly powerful group on Capitol Hill that the executive was taking to itself too many powers, undermining the checks-and-balances principle in the U.S. Constitution. In the coming years, congressional ire would lead to attempts to force an end to American participation in the Vietnam War by cutting off funds. More immediately, legislators fumed at what Senator Mike Mansfield described as the drift toward "big brotherism" and demanded action to curtail abuses of power by the CIA. President Johnson handed to Undersecretary of State Nicholas de B. Katzenbach the job of limiting political damage. Clandestinity was second nature to Katzenbach—on an earlier occasion, he had advised Johnson to close down the investigation into Kennedy's death in order to suppress speculation, a policy that had the reverse effect. He now recommended, "We will volunteer nothing." When that did not work, the administration pointed out that the CIA tactics under attack had not originated with the Johnson administration, promising that in the future, alternative and open sources would fund the international activities of volunteer groups like the National Students Association. In fact, the Ford Foundation did try to fill the breach. However, despite the promises made to calm public opinion in 1967, the CIA continued with business as usual—its new director, Richard Helms (1966–1973), was opposed to restrictions and to any new controls such as congressional oversight.[40]

If Johnson and Katzenbach rescued the CIA, it was at a price. Helms was a career intelligence officer with no other profession to fall back on, and Johnson's demonstration of power over *Ramparts* was frightening. Furthermore, the secret-subsidy revelations alienated from the CIA its liberal support group, making the agency ever more dependent on the White House. Against this background, Helms proved to be too self-interested to tell the president news that might have resulted in his getting fired. For example, with the huge expenditure on the Vietnam War and with Great Society spending programs under threat, Johnson did not want to have to spend substantially on nuclear defense. Moscow took advantage of this and developed its weapon systems apace, but nobody banged the table to make the president listen. Similarly, neither the DCI nor any other senior intelligence official took the risk of warning Johnson that his policies in Vietnam risked not just lack of success but political disaster.[41]

Protest against the Vietnam War was already a problem by the start of 1968. Students had risen in spectacular revolt on campuses all over the nation, and Martin Luther King, Jr., had ended the African American's love affair with the military by condemning U.S. involvement in Vietnam. Partly in reaction to this, the nation's leaders had assured the majority of Americans who still stood firm that the enemy was being worn down. Official order of battle figures seemed to offer quantifiable proof of this. However, the Tet offensive of 30–31 January brutally exposed the deficiencies in official analysis and judgment. Communist troops numbering 84,000 launched attacks throughout South Vietnam. With some of the action vividly recorded on television, the attack was as shocking to public opinion as it was surprising to the military and the White House. Johnson was thoroughly discredited, and decided not to run for reelection. Critics of the government and the military tended to overlook some aspects of Tet. For example: Why only 84,000 troops? According to the Adams figures, there should have been half a million more. Moreover, the communists failed to hold on to the areas they had targeted, and suffered huge casualties in the American and South Vietnamese counterattack. None of this, however, detracted from the political impact of the critics' argument that intelligence had failed to predict the attack and had underestimated enemy strength. It would be closer to the truth to say that American intelligence had generated the right kind of debate but failed to deliver its product to a president whose siege mentality had rendered him politically deaf in a vital domain.[42]

The Bay of Pigs debacle had to an extent discredited covert operations and did sweep away the generation associated with the swashbuckling approach. Lansdale understandably complained that McNamara was out of sympathy with his approach.[43] But covert action did continue in a more discreet vein, as the *Ramparts* episode showed. After Tet, covert operations in the shape of counterinsurgency came back into favor. Despite the success of the American counterattack, it was clear that, for political reasons back home, the United States would have to wind down its conventional military effort. At the end of the Johnson administration and continuing under President Nixon, there was an effort to "Vietnamize" the war. This was a belated attempt to restore indigeneity to the anti-communist cause. The South Vietnamese army was to do more fighting, and once again the Americans would appeal to the "hearts and minds" of the Vietnamese people. The policy was introduced against a most unpromising background, as many Vietnamese were frightened of a nation that had already rained bombs on them. But its main feature was, in fact, negative. Operation Phoenix aimed to eliminate the Viet Cong "infrastructure," its secret organization of spies, and its political commissars.

The CIA took charge of the operation, though it was executed by the Vietnamese themselves. Between 20,000 and 60,000 communists or suspected communists were assassinated in the period 1968–1972. This needs to be seen in relative perspective—it is estimated that the Viet Cong assassinated around 36,727 of their enemies in the years 1957–1972. As President Nixon is reported to have said: "We've got to have more of this. Assassinations. Killings. That's what they're doing."[44] Yet, it was an unusual moral departure for the United States. As so often happens in the case of powerful nations, there was no crimes-against-humanity trial in the wake of this mass slaughter. Thus, there was no opportunity to clear the air, achieve closure, put the matter to rest, and, by the same token, no opportunity to reclaim lost ground in the fight for world opinion once the story leaked, as it was bound to do. However, Phoenix was different from Iran '53 or Guatemala '54. Because of the scale of the bloodshed and because the communists fought on regardless, nobody trumpeted Phoenix as another great CIA achievement. If covert operations continued, they did so in muted tones, in keeping with the rhetorical interlude that had begun with that reverse on the beaches of Cuba.

The intelligence community had mixed success in the sixties. By questioning the missile gap myth they made the world a safer place, but then they failed to issue an effective warning when the USSR really did start producing missiles. The failure to predict that the Cuban people would support Castro had far-reaching consequences. Analysts in the CIA and DIA did question the premises behind U.S. participation in the Vietnam War, but only on the basis of the number-crunching criteria of the man who had escalated the war, Secretary McNamara. Though the CIA called for a political solution to that conflict, it did not see—indeed, as an exclusively foreign agency, it did not have the remit to perceive—that the Vietnamese communists would make a play for U.S. public opinion, sacrificing some of their bravest soldiers in Tet. Overall, U.S. intelligence history in the sixties may have some interesting features, but it is not an inspiring story. Yet the nuclear powers did step back from the abyss in a time of international tension. It is precisely in its dullness that the intelligence history of the sixties is so reassuring.

CHAPTER 12

Did Senator Church
Reform Intelligence?

On the afternoon of 28 April 1996, an unmanned canoe washed ashore near the confluence of the Wicomico and Potomac rivers, just south of Washington, D.C. The spot was not far from the quay at Rock Point, Maryland, where William E. Colby had his weekend home. It was known that late on the previous day, the seventy-six-year-old Colby, leaving his supper uncleared and a glass of white wine only half-consumed, had gone to the waterfront. The discovery of the empty canoe prompted a flurry of activity. Local crabbers and oystermen joined navy frogmen in a search of the area. At last, on 6 May, Mr. Colby's body washed up on shore. It became apparent that despite choppy seas on the night of his disappearance, he had not been wearing a life vest. His remains went off to Baltimore for an autopsy. The police said they did not suspect foul play.[1]

Thus ended the life of a man who had devoted his working years to American intelligence. Colby had graduated from Princeton in 1940 and then joined the OSS, serving behind the lines in France as well as in Scandinavia. After the war, he completed his law degree at Columbia, briefly went into practice, and then entered the newly formed CIA. His work with the agency took him back to Stockholm, and on to Saigon. He served as director of the agency from 1973 to 1976.

But the tributes that flowed in upon the news of Colby's death were equivocal. Richard M. Helms, Director of Central Intelligence from 1966 to 1973, managed what can only be termed a veneer of respect: "We may have had our disagreements, but no one would question Bill's

devotion to what he conceived to be the best interests of the agency."
President Clinton acknowledged there had been problems, but he put
a better face on it: Colby "led the agency through challenging times."
The serving DCI, John M. Deutch, referred to the "severe challenges"
Colby had faced.[2] A historian might be forgiven for assuming that all this
equivocation stemmed from Colby's role in Operation Phoenix, the
controversial program that led to the assassination of so many Vietnamese in the late 1960s. But it did not. Colby's unpopularity stemmed
from his actions during the congressional investigation of the CIA, FBI,
NSA, and other intelligence services in 1975—the "year of intelligence."

On the face of it, Colby was well equipped to deal with the congressional investigation. In April 1975, he traveled to New Orleans to
address the annual meeting of the Associated Press, opening with the
following words: "Fellow Publishers: I presume to address you in this
way to bring out a point which is not adequately perceived these days:
that intelligence has changed from its old image to become a modern
enterprise with many of the attributes of journalism." However, the
DCI went on to say, "Our publications have the largest staff, the small-
est circulation, and the lousiest advertising of any journalistic enterprise." Here is a hint that he feared he was in danger of losing the battle
for public opinion. For although Colby believed in publicity, he was by
no means a Bill Donovan or an Allen Dulles. No media star, he was a
quiet and retiring person.[3]

What threw these attributes into stark relief was Colby's encounter
with Frank Church, who chaired the Senate investigation into intelligence failings and abuses. Church's role gave him celebrity status and
inspired interest in his background and personality. From childhood, he
had aspired to be an actor on the public stage. A sickly youth, he had
spent numerous hours reading, giving his mind the compass necessary
to a good debater. Idaho had already sent a famous orator to the Senate,
and although William Borah had been a Republican and Church was a
Democrat, the latter modeled himself on his illustrious predecessor
and became a master of flowery, moving rhetoric. Once elected to the
Senate, Church made his mark as a determined and ambitious reformer: he opposed the Vietnam War and championed congressional
powers that were, he believed, being eroded in an age of "imperial
presidency." He was a long-standing advocate of reform of the intelligence community and of congressional oversight of the CIA. Few

doubted his sincerity—indeed, he suffered barbs for being too earnest and moralistic.

But there was another aspect to the makeup of "Frank Sunday School." His struggles with serious illness—he almost died of cancer at the age of twenty-three—made him determined to seize opportunities as they presented themselves. In the words of his former staffer Loch Johnson, he was a "high stakes player." Even before the intelligence "flap" of 1975, Church was exploring the possibility of running for president. As he came from a small state with few electoral college votes, he would need major exposure to become the Democratic contender and then win the election. With the Republicans in disgrace following Watergate and likely to lose the presidential race in 1976, opportunity beckoned. The high-profile chairmanship of the intelligence investigating committee apparently gave Church the opportunity he needed. Colby, therefore, faced an interlocutor with proven rhetorical skills, a genuine zeal for reform, and a burning ambition to travel the high road of publicity into the White House.[4]

It would be forgivable to paint the Church-Colby encounter in terms of a clash between two masters of hyperbole. The outcome, one might argue, was an era of instability—draconian reform in the first instance, and then a powerful reaction eventuating in the election of President Reagan in 1980, and the reemergence of an expansionist intelligence community. However, this ebb-and-flow scenario is too neat. While it contains more than a grain of truth, history is messier than that. For example, both Church and Colby backed off from their potentially confrontational positions, with the senator moderating his rhetoric and the DCI offering to help clear the air and to accept some reforms. All this has led to the suspicion that the Church reforms were merely cosmetic. That, however, posits an absolutist model of reform. In democracies, compromise is the rule, not the exception—without it, extremism would prevail and liberty itself might be in danger. Church was, in the words of his biographers, a man who "relished his investigative role, a role that challenged the system while working within it."[5] A review of the intelligence flap reveals a process of moderate reform underpinned by recognition of an important principle—that American intelligence agencies are accountable to Congress.

President Ford's biographer John Greene observes that the 1975 investigation of the CIA was the "most important example" of a "Power Earthquake," the gargantuan executive-legislative fight that occurred in the mid-seventies.[6] However, the fight took place in the context of long-term trends. The growth of Big Government had for decades threatened federal intrusion into every walk of life, and clandestine intrusion was an obvious danger to American liberties. Of concern to Congress, government expansion strengthened the powers of the executive, and the legislative branch of government became commensurably weak—in violation of the time-honored principle of checks and balances. In domestic as well as in foreign policy, the White House seemed to be making free with its growing powers, notably through its ability to direct the activities of secret agencies like the FBI and CIA. The FBI's investigation of anti-interventionists in the early 1940s and anti-war protesters in the late 1960s may or may not have been justifiable, but the president's authorization of these activities without consulting Congress was disturbing, and culminated in the troubles of the 1970s.

One of the reasons why the fight between Church and Colby broke out in the mid-seventies, and not earlier or later, emerges indirectly from the White House memorandum of a conversation that took place on 26 March 1974 in the Kremlin office of Leonid Brezhnev. On the agenda was the issue of how many independently variable nuclear warheads each country was attaching to its intercontinental ballistic missiles. The Soviet leader strode in and ruffled the hair of an American official, Jan Lodal. "He needs a haircut," he said. "Yes," said U.S. Secretary of State Henry Kissinger. As they joshed in this vein, tea arrived with its statutory slices of lemon. Brezhnev counted the slices: "How many warheads here? One-two-three . . . six! You tested one like this." Kissinger: "No, it was five yesterday." And so on, until the Russian concluded the badinage, declaring it was time for "very serious discussion." National leaders have things in common even in bad times, and quite often they get along together rather better than they care to admit to their constituents. But even allowing for that, it is plain from the foregoing discussion that "detente" was in full swing in 1974.[7]

According to the Ransom thesis, that explains congressional belligerence. Harry Ransom was a political scientist at Vanderbilt University who argued that there was an inverse relationship between Cold War tension and congressional disposition to oversee or investigate the

CIA.[8] Although such arguments are too neat to hold up in every circumstance, the Ransom thesis does have logic on its side: a patriotic citizen is disinclined to criticize his government when his or her nation is under threat from a foreign nation, but the very same citizen, again from love of country, may take a more critical view at a time when international relations are more cordial.

Another factor to be considered is the economic recession that set in as a result of the inflationary effects of the Vietnam War, and the oil embargo that the Arab world directed against the United States protesting American help to Israel at the time of the Yom Kippur War (1973). Senator Church thought his investigation might be sidelined because economic problems are important to people, and they might not care to focus instead on abuses by the CIA.[9] Possibly this kind of fear made him more strident than he would otherwise have been. Equally, though, the combined effects of inflation and economic stagnation (or "stagflation," to use the seventies term) may have made people more discontented than usual. In the mid-1930s, a period of intense economic depression as well as of (deceptive) international calm, the Senate had with wide approval launched the Nye investigation into the munitions industry and the La Follette inquiry into industrial espionage. The mid 1970s recession was not nearly so bad, but once again people were prepared to listen to a recitation of governmental shortcomings.

There was no shortage of short-term factors to trigger the intelligence flap. For example, Henry Kissinger's style was beginning to grate. The secretary of state's foreign policy achievements were stunning: he had negotiated peace in the Middle East, opened relations with Red China, negotiated the strategic arms limitation treaties with the Soviet Union, and, if slowly, extricated America from the Vietnam War. But peacemakers are rarely placed on the same pedestal as those who make war. And Kissinger, like that other great architect of foreign policy Thomas Jefferson, had a gift for making enemies. Among his less appealing attributes were a lack of respect for persons of modest intelligence, chauvinism toward women, and a reputation for trickery. Kissinger's pluralism made him enemies, too. President Nixon made him assistant for national security affairs in 1969, but then in September 1973 made him secretary of state as well. Kissinger came to be regarded as a power-grabbing controller with a finger in everyone's pie.

Kissinger's handling of intelligence was manipulative and calculated to deceive. As he saw it, the ends justified the means. What greater goal can a secretary of state achieve, than a more peaceful world in which his fellow citizens can live a secure and prosperous life? But his practices left an unsavory legacy for his successors (can you ever trust an American statesman?), and for the intelligence community (why deliver the facts to a man who twists them?).

Here are some illustrations of Kissinger's approach. To force the Russians to make concessions over weapons, he wanted additional bargaining chips that he would then barter away. America, he said, needed an anti-ballistic missile system to match comparable developments in the USSR. To persuade Congress to go along with the potentially expensive program, he suppressed intelligence indicating that the Soviets did not, in fact, have a working anti-ballistic missile system. Kissinger got his way, and the Soviet Union duly made concessions. In turn, there arose the question of verification of compliance with the resultant treaties. At this point, and hoping for a second round of arms-reduction negotiations, Kissinger suppressed further information from the intelligence community because it indicated that historically the Russians had a record of poor compliance with arms-limitation treaties.[10]

All this took place at a time when the CIA was already being accused of delivering intelligence to please. DCI Richard Helms lived under a cloud of suspicion in this regard. For example, under his aegis, continuing CIA skepticism about the Vietnam War had not been allowed to surface—thus, on the eve of an ill-fated and controversial American incursion into Cambodia in April 1970, Helms sat on a report that correctly predicted the raid would be ineffective as a means of interdicting communist military activity. In July 1973, the new and short-lived DCI James Schlesinger (February–July 1973) dismissed John Huizinga, chairman of the CIA's Office of National Estimates, which coordinated the product of the wider intelligence community. The *Washington Post* noted that the administration had "executed a bearer of often unwelcome tidings." This was a move that seemed to diminish the authority of the CIA and make its analysts even more vulnerable to the whims of policy makers. In 1975 one group of Republican congressmen complained that intelligence was being filtered "through a screen of policy-making officials," and an influential House committee accused Kissinger of "political control of intelligence."[11]

To the dove with less complicated thought processes than Henry Kissinger, the CIA had become a pliant instrument in the hands of the warmakers and arms-race hawks. But the real problem was that the CIA had lost its standing and was open to attack from any quarter. Indeed, it could be argued that the attack from the Right-wing hawks was more serious and damaging than that from the doves. On 4 June 1974, Roberta Wohlstetter co-hosted a dinner party in Santa Monica, California. The author of the famous Pearl Harbor study had invited NSC 68 author Paul Nitze and others with an interest in intelligence matters. While consuming a meal that included frozen zabaglione and a 1964 Clos de Vougeot, the party planned an all-out attack on detente and on what they regarded as the untrustworthy intelligence that underpinned that policy.[12]

Just a few weeks after this dinner party, the disclosure of what had taken place in Chile helped put Congress in an investigative frame of mind. In September 1973, conservative forces in Chile had overthrown their country's socialist government, and President Salvador Allende died in unverifiable circumstances during the coup. The putsch ended the longest living experiment in Latin American democracy and ushered in the harshly totalitarian regime of Gen. Augusto Pinochet. According to the disinformation of the day, the general and his colleagues had saved Chile from economic collapse and a crippling wave of strikes, just the kind of chaos one would expect from a socialist government. In reality, President Nixon had personally insisted on the deployment of a money-no-object array of clandestine dirty tricks aimed at the destabilization of the Chilean economy and the removal of Allende at any cost. As usual, Latin America perceived the not-so-hidden hand of the CIA behind the 1973 destruction of yet another democracy and, as was also the custom, the American public remained in the dark—until 8 September 1974. On that day, the *New York Times* and *Washington Post* revealed that the CIA had been implicated in attempts to remove Allende in the three years prior to his death.

Ominously, it emerged that the Nixon administration had deliberately misled Congress. There was already unease on Capitol Hill over the high-handed use of secret powers. In the wake of the Cambodian incursion, Congress had adopted a prohibition on funds for paramilitary operations, "especially" by the CIA. Congressional ire in the wake of the Chile revelation therefore came as no surprise. Senator Walter Mondale of Minnesota dismissed as "hogwash" President Ford's continuing insistence that Allende, and not the CIA, had been the real threat to Chilean democracy. Congressman Michael J. Harrington complained that the Department of State was a "patsy" to the CIA. His allegation contrasted with, and was less convincing than, other critics' fears that Secretary of State Kissinger was manipulating the CIA, but it did have one feature in common with them: a deep-seated antagonism toward the CIA and the national security power structure.[13]

A plot at a dinner party, moral revulsion at the treatment of a foreign nation—these were significant precipitants of the intelligence flap, but so far there was no popular demand for an investigation. In a very literal sense, the criticisms had not yet been brought home to the American people. This changed on 22 December, when investigative journalist Seymour Hersh published a story on the domestic activities of the CIA. On the front page of the *New York Times,* he declared: "The CIA, directly violating its charter, conducted a massive illegal domestic intelligence operation during the Nixon administration against the anti-war movement and other dissident groups in the United States."

From then on, it was open season on the CIA and the rest of the intelligence community, and both President Ford and the Congress responded. Ford summoned Colby and asked for a briefing. It is an open question whether national leaders normally *want* to know the full extent of the sordid things being done on their behalf, but on this occasion it was a question of being forewarned and forearmed. Colby was able to oblige. He showed Ford an item that lay conveniently at hand—a list of infractions, the skeletons in the CIA closet or "family jewels," as they were known. When Schlesinger had been in charge of the CIA, Colby had himself compiled this list, an action that probably reflected, in equal measure, a guilty conscience and awareness of impending trouble. According to Ford's later account, Colby (a devout Catholic) now counseled confession, and the president agreed the best policy was "to tell the truth." He established a presidential commission under the chairmanship of Vice President Nelson D. Rockefeller to investigate the domestic activities of the CIA, and to make recommendations of any necessary reforms.[14]

This was a standard maneuver. You appoint an investigative panel. As it probes the problem, months pass by. Public outrage dies down. Finally, you get away with nugatory changes. In recent intelligence history, the Katzenbach inquiry had achieved such a result. This time, however, the public mood was such that the tactic might not be fully effective. On 27 January, the Senate voted 82 to 4 to establish its own Select Committee to Study Governmental Operations with Respect to Intelligence Activities. Under the chairmanship of Frank Church, this would develop into one of the biggest-ever Senate inquiries. On 19 February, the House followed suit. Lucien D. Nedzi was the first chair of the House Select Committee on Intelligence, but his slow pace did not match the tempo of the great debate, and he gave way in July to Otis G. Pike. This New York Democrat was both a Patriot Type A and a Patriot Type B. He had flown 120 combat missions over the Pacific in World War II and supported the Vietnam War until its latter stages, but detecting a problem within the intelligence community, he saw it as his equally patriotic duty to put matters right, and he was determined to leave no stone unturned.

With the appointment of the Senate and House inquiries, the Ford administration and the intelligence community were already heading for trouble. Then, at a White House luncheon for senior *New York Times* editors, Ford let the cat out of the bag. He had placed Rockefeller in charge of the presidential probe, he said, because the nation needed a man of proven discretion who could be trusted not to make dreadful disclosures. Asked about what, he said "assassination." CBS journalist Daniel Schorr seized on this story and broadcast it. This was the first time the American public had learned that murder had been official policy, and the debate on the intelligence services now approached boiling point. As Schorr noted, in the wake of the killings of President Kennedy, Senator Robert F. Kennedy, Martin Luther King, Jr., Medgar Evers, and Malcolm X, assassination was a sensitive issue. With the CIA implicated also in the public schism over Vietnam, Ford and his advisers faced a real storm.[15]

One could paint a despairing picture of the intelligence flap. Ever since Allan Pinkerton, there had been too much intelligence hype. As a result, too much money had been poured into the business. In a profession that became one big comfort zone, there was a proliferation of functions, some of them superfluous and contrary to the national interest. With too much money floating around, there was not enough competition and the intelligence community failed to develop a sharp, critical edge. But this was not all. When, at last, Congress authorized two substantial investigations, the investigators became mesmerized by the very hype they were supposed to counter. Because of this, according to the painters of the dark picture, they lost their way, and America missed an opportunity for real intelligence reform.

Church's reputation as a hyperbolic opportunist stems largely from his reaction to a chain of events in June and July 1975. In June, the Rockefeller Commission reported. It criticized domestic abuses with startling candor and made some significant recommendations, such as the establishment of a joint congressional oversight committee. However, it avoided one thorny issue. For although it had gathered documents on assassinations and submitted these in a secret eighty-six-page supplement to the president, the Rockefeller Commission's published report skipped over the killing of John F. Kennedy with a brief and cryptic allusion: there was "no credible evidence of CIA involvement" in the incident. Once again, information on the possible revenge motive had been suppressed, fueling sensationalist speculation.[16]

Both Senator Church and the press criticized the administration for keeping the not very metaphoric skeleton in the closet. At first, the government seemed to be intransigent, and in April 1975 it ignored a plan put forward by Harvard historian Ernest May, whereby an impartial committee would decide which White House documents would go to the Church Committee. But as the days passed, it began to seem that Ford was a canny politician and that he had a plan. Just as the press was beginning to warm to Rockefeller for his nonwhitewash, Ford made it clear he was going to give the Church inquiry information it did not really want, namely the assassination file. For Church and the Democratic majority on his committee, the problem was this: some of the most shocking assassination plans, notably Operation Mongoose, the plot to get rid of Castro, had been the work of a Democratic administration. *Newsweek* speculated that Ford wanted to divest his administration of any suspicion of cover-up and may have seen the advantage in letting a Democratic Congress squirm—now that it had been presented with the nonreturnable gift of the opportunity to "investigate supposed murder plots, hatched mostly under Democratic presidents."[17]

In a press conference on 18 July, Church made the statement that branded him as a hyperbolic opportunist, and incidentally became an oft-quoted catchphrase about the CIA: "The agency may have been behaving like a rogue elephant on the rampage." The statement, which would haunt Church over the coming months, invites explanation. The notion that the CIA or other federal agencies were (or are) out of control has often been bruited, but rarely sustained. The president is a busy person and cannot watch every detail, but the record confirms that the executive decides on important matters. Church may have genuinely believed in the hypothesis. Later on, he distanced himself from the by-then-discredited rogue elephant statement, but that may have been for political reasons. One historian of the flap, Kathryn Olmsted, advances evidence to indicate that, despite his political tacking, Church continued to believe in rogue elephants. In an October hearing, for example, he opined that the president lacked "meaningful control" over the intelligence agencies.[18]

Despite this evidence of sincerity, few would disagree with the proposition that the "rogue elephant" statement was a publicity-grabbing statement. It demonstrated to Daniel Schorr that the senator was "obviously nursing presidential dreams." Olmsted suggests a contrast between Otis Pike, who was interested in conducting a "systemic" investigation of the intelligence community, and Church, who sensationalized FBI and CIA abuses. One of these abuses was the storage by the CIA/Army Special Operations Division (nicknamed the Health Alteration Committee) of lethal toxins in Fort Detrick, Maryland. Grist for Church's mill, the division had neglected to destroy them, when, in February 1970, President Nixon issued a generic instruction to destroy all toxic weapons. Thinking of the fuss Church had made about this, CIA counsel Michael Rogovin praised Pike in terms that put the senator in a poor light: "He knew what he was looking at, and he wasn't going to be deflected by poisoned dart guns and shellfish toxins and the silliness of the moment."[19]

Church at least half-believed what he was saying, and he could also see the advantage of saying it. By alleging CIA abuse of power, he not only gained personal publicity but also diverted attention from presidential malpractices. This released Republican presidents from the hook, and also the still-iconic John F. Kennedy. The tactic not only saved face for the Democrats but appeared to be the kind of nonpartisan and statesmanlike conduct the voters would expect in a presidential candidate.

The tactic was, however, doomed to failure. The Ford administration effectively countered it with the flashback technique, that is, the practice of supplying Church with information flashing back to the Kennedy years in a way that sullied the Camelot myth. The technique is evidence of a determined counterattack by the administration and the Republicans against both the Church and the Pike committees.

In September, the Pike Committee felt the brunt of the counterattack. This committee wanted to review the analytical and especially the predictive performance of the intelligence community in selected crises, with the objective of reaching overall conclusions and making recommendations for improvement. One of its chosen cases was the surprise attack on Israel, by Egypt and other neighbors, that initiated the Yom Kippur War. The Ford administration supplied the Pike Committee with secret documents to assist it in its task. One of these was a CIA postmortem revealing several American intelligence agencies had failed to predict Egypt's move. In fact, these agencies had said there was no prospect of war. To alert the public to the seriousness of this mistake, Pike wanted to release the text of the CIA document, but the Ford administration stalled and then requested the deletion of some words. The words themselves were not crucial to national security, but both sides now dug in, on the principle of executive privilege, in a way that was reminiscent of the recent Watergate scandal when President Nixon had abused his constitutional position in furtherance of his infamous cover-up.[20]

At first, the press was sympathetic to Pike, but Kissinger now took up the cudgels on behalf of the administration. Already, the administration was censoring some of the documents sent over to the Hill and had failed to comply with subpoenas requiring the delivery of a series of National Security Agency and Defense Intelligence Agency documents connected with the Yom Kippur War. Kissinger's specially constituted committee threatened withdrawal of cooperation from Pike. At a press conference on 11 September, a defiant Pike revealed the contents of the Yom Kippur report anyway. The next day, the Ford administration refused further cooperation, and Assistant Attorney Gen. Rex E. Loe demanded the "immediate return" of the classified materials in the committee's possession. Ford and Kissinger had correctly anticipated that the chairman of the House committee would no longer be seen as a deep-flowing river of truth. Other topographical features sprang to mind. In its editorial headed "Pike's Pique," the *Washington Star* depicted him as rashly inquisitorial.[21] Kissinger still had friends as well as enemies, especially in the media, and less conservative newspapers began to sing a similar tune.

But Ford now faced a tactical dilemma. Kissinger was prepared to enforce secrecy, but Colby, albeit in a restrained and qualified manner, was ready to help clear the air. Perhaps a selective release of information, a kind of disinformation by omission, would be a compromise and would best serve the interests of the administration. The possibilities of this calculated flashback technique were becoming widely recognized. In part because he was fearful of its political effect, Church had already resorted to the distraction tactic of demonizing the CIA. Now, in the wake of the Pike-Kissinger clash, Export-Import Bank Chief William J. Casey sent the president a clipping from the *Washington Star*. The OSS veteran was struck by the *Star* reporter's observation that "an ambitious fellow like Church" would not wish to be "the intrepid investigator who pointed the finger and cried assassin at the martyred John F. Kennedy." To Casey, the Kennedy campaign against Castro was "an astonishing story of an unauthorized war, dwarfing anything that may have been done in Chile." He thought it was well authenticated and was "amazed that it [had] raised so little attention in the press and, apparently, also on the Hill." It is not always easy to deduce which letters presidents do or do not read, but this one from Casey was marked "THE PRESIDENT HAS SEEN. . . ."[22]

In a move that reflected his compromise tactic, Ford now half-punished the concealer and removed the half-divulger. In the "Halloween Massacre" of 2 November 1975, he stripped Kissinger of his responsibilities as national security affairs adviser, retaining him as secretary of state only, and dismissed Colby altogether, bringing in George H. W. Bush to be the new CIA director (he would serve from January 1976 to January 1977). Largely because of the passions aroused over the intelligence debate, both Kissinger and Colby had become political liabilities, even if Kissinger remained an asset because of his experience and immense ability. At the same time, the president had asserted his authority and opened the way for an initiative by his counsel and adviser Philip W. Buchen. In negotiation with the Church Committee, Buchen offered to release full documentation on any one of a number of cases of covert operations. The committee chose Chile. Buchen and the

White House continued to obstruct even this investigation to a certain extent, and also tried unsuccessfully to block publication of the Church report on assassinations. To what degree this was political posturing by an administration that secretly desired to surrender the secrets remains a matter for conjecture.[23]

To a perceptible degree, things were moving the administration's way, and now its fortunes received a boost from yet another assassination. Two days before Christmas, masked killers gunned down Richard S. Welch, the CIA's station chief in Athens, as he returned home with his wife from a party. The reasons for the attack and the identity of its perpetrators remain obscure, although a Leftist/nationalist group called November 17 later claimed responsibility. In fact, the notoriety of the CIA would have been deemed reason enough by any number of terrorist groups, and it turned out that security in Athens had been lax: Welch had occupied the same house as his predecessor, he was known to be the CIA man in Greece, his name and address had been published in the newspapers in that country, and he refused the services of a bodyguard. This was not, however, the chosen perspective of the *Washington Star*, which proclaimed that the murder was "a direct consequence of the stagy hearings of the Church Committee." Heated allegations circulated, some to the effect that Church had incited the assassination, others more specifically alleging that investigative reporters had betrayed Welch's identity and therefore his life. Actually, a communist publication had named him as long ago as 1967, but the opportunity to calumnify the CIA's detractors was too good to miss. Colby never ceased to claim that Welch died because of the "sensational and hysterical" congressional investigations. Welch's funeral at Arlington National Cemetery was conducted, the *Washington Post* reported, with "a show of pomp usually reserved for the nation's most renowned military heroes." The event was not important enough to bring about a reversal in Republican fortunes and a serious prospect of Ford's retention of the presidency, but it was a significant reversal for the critics, and it set the scene for compromise over the intelligence issue.[24]

In the meantime, the Pike Committee was about to report after holding a series of hearings in fall 1975. These hearings had focused on selected issues, such as the closely guarded secret of the intelligence budget. Was that budget, after years of unscrupulous hype, simply far too large? The Pike Committee suspected the budget was double the assumed amount and that this inflated expenditure stemmed, at least in part, from misuse of funds. For example, the FBI was purchasing bugging equipment through corporations in which its agents had an interest, while the CIA was buying golf equipment. But an increasingly confident White House, determined to preserve the secrets of the budget, placed obstacles in the inquiry's way. Citing national security, the executive told its witnesses not to testify on putters and golf hats.[25]

The committee was more successful in eliciting a response on the issue of who controlled covert operations. Ever since the 1940s, the White House had insisted on a system of "plausible deniability" whereby the "hidden hand" presidency would escape responsibility for operations that went wrong or were exposed. In disasters like the Bay of Pigs, the DCI would ultimately have to be the scapegoat for executive error, and in less serious cases a "circuit-breaking" committee would take the blame—a system that encouraged presidential rashness on the one hand, and on the other deceived Church into alleging that the CIA was out of control. But on 30 October 1975, the Pike Committee held hearings that led its chairman to conclude, "The CIA does not go galloping off conducting operations by itself." The next day, Kissinger gave unambiguous testimony on the point: "Every operation is personally approved by the President." Representative James V. Stanton (Dem., Ohio) now interjected a partisan question, trying to fix executive malpractice on Republican President Nixon: "In other words, during the period of 1972 to 1974, any covert decision that was made was approved by the President of the United States?" Kissinger replied: "At any time, not just in that period."

To be sure, Kissinger was trying to protect the Republicans and so testified in a way that furthered the flashback tactic, but documentary evidence shown to the Pike Committee confirmed that Democratic presidents in the 1960s had given direct covert operations orders. Pike later said he formed the impression that the CIA had sometimes tried to hold the president back from rash courses of action. In fact, the more he learned about this, the more he respected the agency. While that may be a controversial view, Kissinger's testimony is significant. Yet, as historian Frank Smist observes, at the time it went "virtually unnoticed." Nothing could compete with Senator Church's inaccurate but mesmeric remark about the "rogue elephant."[26]

Partly because of Pike's confrontational approach and partly because of a changing public mood, the House of Representatives voted to suppress the report prepared by his committee. However, at this point Daniel Schorr, having obtained a copy from an undisclosed source, leaked it. Some revelations had already appeared in the *New York Times* on 26 January 1976, but in February *The Village Voice* published substantial extracts from Schorr's smuggled copy. CBS fired Schorr over this affair, but the report was ultimately published in its entirety.[27]

These events placed the Pike inquiry in a poor light, making it appear leak-prone, irresponsible, even unpatriotic. The House Committee on Standards of Official Conduct held hearings on the leak, President Ford offered the services of the FBI to track down the identity of Schorr's informant, and former Pike Committee member Ron Dellums quipped, "The investigator has now become the investigatee."[28] But America was still listening, and the Pike report's findings and recommendations were to be influential.

The Pike Committee enumerated various instances of failure in foreign intelligence. It had held hearings on Tet, paying particular heed to Colby's testimony and reaching the conclusion that enemy numbers had been underestimated, the intelligence community having prior to Tet come under intense pressure "to generate numbers, less out of tactical necessity than for political purposes." Its report condemned intelligence failings over the Yom Kippur War and was scathing on Kissinger's political control over intelligence at the time of the arms-limitation negotiations, noting that his "comments on this situation are at variance with the facts."[29]

Taxpayers were not getting value for their intelligence dollar, according to the Pike Committee. The DIA, set up in the 1960s in the name of efficiency, was in fact "duplicative, expensive." In general, the foreign intelligence community collected too much pointless information and then failed to make sense of it. On the domestic front, the FBI wasted money on pointless investigations such as that into the Socialist Workers' Party. The CIA's gratuitously extensive relations with the media were a threat to the free press, though the committee accepted that Colby was trying to reform matters here. The National Security Council was not properly supervising the activities of the foreign intelligence community.[30]

The recommendation from the Pike Committee was for a standing House intelligence committee. In keeping with the distribution of powers arranged in the U.S. Constitution, it would have "exclusive jurisdiction for budget authorization for all intelligence activities and exclusive jurisdiction for all covert action operations." Pride of place went to this idea. The report also proposed a number of ideas for better financial management. Some recommendations, such as the separation of the posts of director of the CIA and director of central intelligence, or the prohibition of any future subornation of the American press or educational institutions, were not budget-related. Others, like the call for the abolition of the DIA, were made with cost savings only partly in mind. But perhaps most symptomatic of the committee's overall outlook was its demand for budgetary disclosure. The findings of the Pike Committee were a slap in the face of the intelligence expansionists who had met with such success since 1941.[31]

By the time the Senate investigation reported on 26 April 1976, it was evident that it had enjoyed a smoother ride than its House equivalent. Nevertheless, Church failed in his ambition to secure the presidential nomination and then, having been kept waiting by Jimmy Carter, found he had been turned down for the vice presidential ticket as well. To a degree, the Idaho senator had been too publicity conscious for his own good, had made so obvious a play for higher office that he alienated potential supporters. What compounded this was that his commitment to publicity at intelligence hearings seemed to be intellectual rather than instinctive. He did not preen for the cameras, slumping half-hidden behind the chairman's dais, hiding his face behind his hand. A *Village Voice* reporter observed that Church was "relatively oblivious to the impression he was making on the TV audience."[32] While it was certainly a time for reform, and while "Church" became practically synonymous with the political struggles of 1975 and early 1976, the opportunity evaded the western prodigy both because he was overcommitted to publicity and because he did not know how to play to the camera.

Nothing can take away from Senator Church and his colleagues their achievement in ventilating some long-standing abuses in the U.S. intelligence community. Yet, like other great Senate inquiries before it, the Church probe was open to criticism from a variety of perspectives. Its publication of evidence on assassination plots as well as contemporary disclosures about sexual activity in the White House all but destroyed the reputation of John F. Kennedy. Perhaps that corrective was politically healthy—but it was a reluctant achievement, forced upon Church by his partisan opponents because he himself had been partisan in his approach. In addition, Church and the majority of his colleagues on the select committee could be accused of liberal bias in their investigation of the FBI's surveillance programs known as COINTELPRO. The committee investigated four of these programs, affecting the Communist Party of the United States, white hate groups, the black nationalist movement, and the New Left at the time of its opposition to the Vietnam War. It offered a convincing exposé of the bureau's violation of citizens' rights through such means as anonymous mailings, harassment of individuals, and promotion of marital discord. But it seemed harsher in its judgment of FBI harassment of the New Left and black militants than in its condemnation of the persecution of racists and communists, giving rise to the suspicion that its implicit agenda ranged wider than concern for the impartial enforcement of the law.[33]

Yet, this liberal bias was rather toothless. Compared with the Pike investigation, the Church inquiry was mild. To be sure, the Senate committee investigated assassination, but in effect it limited its probe to plots against high officials, all of them unsuccessful or never implemented. In later years, a pair of prominent lawyers wondered why "the Church Committee publicly considered five incidents of alleged political assassination but did not consider the so-called Phoenix program in Vietnam." The Church inquiry into infringements of personal privacy also seemed less than forceful. Certainly, it produced reports on abuses by the Internal Revenue Service, U.S. Postal Service, and the National Security Agency, whose SHAMROCK operation had since the 1940s routinely spied on and recorded American citizens' international communications. It transpired that, as in the World War I/1920s era, major corporations had cooperated with the latter program. But it was left to Congresswoman Bella Abzug, in a House hearing weeks after Church had reported, to grill the NSA's batch of cooperating corporations. L. Britt Snider—later CIA inspector general but in 1975–1976 on the Church Committee staff—recalled that RCA Global, ITT International, and Western Union International were on one particular day in summer 1976 "red meat" to the New York Democrat and feminist: "Her hearings brought to mind the days of Nero, when Christians were thrown to the lions for sport." Clearly, a contrast with the Church style had suggested itself to Snider.[34]

The Church Committee's recommendations differed in some ways from those of its legislative cousin in the House. For example, instead of demanding the abolition of the DIA, it wanted a revision of the intelligence clauses of the 1947 National Security Act, with new charters being drawn up for the DIA, CIA, and NSA. Like the Pike Committee, Church objected to the politicization of intelligence, but he focused on the responsibility of former DCI Richard Helms for this, faulting him, in particular, for allegedly exaggerating the Soviet threat to appease administration hawks. In common with its House equivalent, the Church Committee wanted a ban on assassinations. It further demanded, after scrutinizing 900 major covert operations since 1961 and thousands of minor ones, that the U.S. government refrain from propping up governments with poor records on civil rights—a rap on the knuckles of those who would overthrow Leftist regimes while supporting Rightist dictatorships.

There was one significant area of concurrence. The Church Committee faulted the intelligence community for duplication and overexpenditure. Too much money was being spent on collection, too little on analysis. This was partly because of huge military intelligence budgets that produced informational overkill, but the CIA also contributed to the problem by spending too much of its budget on covert operations. These operations were too often pointless and counterproductive, and also drained away resources that would have been better spent on analysis. With all these points in mind, the Church report recommended the creation of a permanent Senate intelligence oversight committee, with powers to supervise the foreign intelligence budget.

As its critics noted, the Senate report used circumspect language. Its call for a permanent committee to give "further consideration" to the "prudent" disclosure of budgetary details was hardly a ringing endorsement of the principle of open government, and the report's section on the intelligence budget was tucked away in the penultimate section on the list of findings. Its call for oversight only of foreign intelligence was similarly more cautious than Pike's aspiration to oversee the entire clandestine budget. On the other hand, this simply reflected the Senate's constitutionally vested foreign policy prerogative.

Its concern over the bloated nature of intelligence expenditure did mirror that expressed in the House committee.[35]

Many in the intelligence community were demoralized by the Pike and Church investigations and developed quite apocalyptic views on the whole process of inquiry. Other commentators, however, took a radically different view. They took note of the change in the political climate after December 1975, of the discrediting of Pike, of the temporizing instincts of Frank Church, and of the relative timidity of his committee's report. Historians with this perspective have suggested that despite the great fuss, not much change took place. One such historian, Frank Smist, applied institutional theory to explain this postulated nonevent. This is a reincarnation of that familiar scenario in which the labor leader sits down once too often with the employer, develops a cozy relationship, and ends up signing a "sweetheart contract." Just so, once the intelligence investigator starts having coffee, lunch, and cocktails with the investigatee, he becomes too friendly to perform his function properly. As the years passed, oversight committee staff members and intelligence officials even began to exchange functions, on the "revolving door" principle so familiar in federal government and so conducive to sleepy toleration. According to Smist, investigative as distinct from permanent oversight committees are less likely to fall into the comfort-zone trap because they do not operate for long enough to develop bad habits, although the investigative Church inquiry did display some "institutional" tendencies.[36]

It is possible to take a profoundly skeptical view of the reform process, not least regarding those centerpieces of reform, congressional oversight committees. The Senate approved a permanent committee in May 1976, and the House authorized is own equivalent in July. It could be argued that both these permanent committees showed signs of becoming part of the institutions they were supposed to be scrutinizing. By 2000, for example, they were criticizing the executive for underfunding the intelligence agencies. On the other hand, a principle had been established. The same can be said about the prohibition on clandestine support for dictatorships of the Right as well as of the Left—a principle observed only in the breach before the flap, but increasingly respected after it. It was frustrating for contemporary reformers that not all their ideas were accepted with immediate effect, but the legislative probes had a long-term impact. In 1997, for example, the budget of the intelligence community was for the first time officially disclosed—to the horror of leading intelligence officials, who still saw it as a dangerous concession.[37]

Church's intelligence reforms need to be put perspective. For one thing, he was not the only reformer at work. Representative Pike had prepared much of the ground for a change in perceptual context, and how people thought about intelligence mattered just as much as the detail of particular laws or regulations. Other members of Congress, too, made their contributions to reform: Senator Clifford P. Case secured the prohibition on Cambodian funds in 1971, Senator Harold F. Hughes and Representative Leo J. Ryan in 1974 secured passage of the Hughes-Ryan resolution, requiring the executive discreetly to consult Congress before launching significant covert operations, and in December 1975 Senator Richard Clark won support for an amendment cutting off funds from a CIA operation in Angola. Taking a broader perspective still of the legislative campaign against secret government, in 1974 Congress strengthened the 1966 Freedom of Information Act in a way that potentially opened up national security documents, and in 1976 it tried to give greater transparency to its own proceedings through the Government in the Sunshine Act.[38]

Such was the prominence of the 1970s constitutional struggle between the executive and the legislative branches of government that the executive's own interest in and contribution to intelligence reform is sometimes overlooked. By the beginning of the decade, the 1960s affinity for recreational drugs like marijuana had given way to concern about a hard-drug addiction problem that was spreading out of the ghetto and into white, middle-class homes. There was a pressing need to address the problems of cocaine processing in South America and heroin refining in Southeast Asia, and the existing intelligence resources did not seem adequate. By executive order, though with the support of Congress, President Nixon on 1 July 1973 established within the Department of Justice the Drug Enforcement Administration (DEA). Its initial budget was small, at $74.9 million, but it inherited personnel from earlier anti-drug agencies and immediately put 1,470 special agents in the field. The DEA would be a significant if controversial newcomer to the intelligence community.[39]

For President Ford, it was politically imperative to do something about intelligence reform. With Kissinger a dominant personality in his administration, he had to place his own stamp on policy in a way that would show he was in charge, and not just a Kissinger poodle or a Nixon clone. At the same time, he knew that executive reform was one way of taking the sting out of congressional attacks. Finally, like any president, he needed an effective intelligence capability, and America manifestly had a few problems in that quarter.

So Ford introduced a number of intelligence reforms, including tighter management procedures and a ban on assassination. But his administration's most dramatic intervention concerned the analytical process, which was, after all, a far more important function than covert operations or domestic surveillance. For some time there had been a demand for "competitive estimating." This demand arose from deep-seated concerns about the apparent disarray of the established estimating process and malleability of its practitioners. There were worries, too, about methodology: the unreliability of ruble costing of defense projects in the USSR's command economy, the disjunctures of costing and actual weaponry, the dangers of mirror-imaging (the assumption that Russians were just Americans in fur coats and would behave in a similar manner), and the supremacy of technology in the estimating process as distinct from a "human intelligence" attempt to understand the collective mind of the Kremlin. There was a conservative, hawkish thrust to the critique—its exponents argued that politicization of the estimates had led to an underestimation of the Soviet threat. They expected that an independent, competitive estimate would demonstrate this. In other words, they had a political agenda of their own.

A formidable ginger group led the attack. Not long after the zabaglione dinner party in Santa Monica, Roberta Wohlstetter's husband, Albert, published an influential article alleging systematic underestimation of Soviet missile production. As the debate developed, support came from leading intellectuals—an innovation in American politics, as the intelligentsia had traditionally inclined to the Left. The famously anti-Soviet atomic scientist Edward Teller was one prestigious ally. Another was Richard Pipes, a professor of Russian history at Harvard University who wanted a more humanistic approach to intelligence. The DIA weighed in on the side of the "neoconservative" critics. Meanwhile, those defending the CIA's estimates were on weak ground not just because of the flap, but because the CIA in 1972 had itself been complicit in the Kissinger plot to exaggerate the Soviet threat in the pursuit of bargaining chips and peace. In the words of Lawrence Freedman, a leading authority on the Soviet estimate, "The main problem for the administration . . . was that having raised the bogey of . . . vulnerability [to missile attack] it could not bury it."[40]

Despite the fact that his agency was under siege and vulnerable, DCI Colby held out against the proposal that an independent panel should be engaged to review the evidence derived from intelligence gathering and to reach its own conclusions in competition with the usual team of analysts. With a new round of strategic arms limitation treaty talks (SALT II) under way, Bush was not much more enthusiastic about the idea. But the new DCI decided to cooperate, perhaps in the belief that it was one way of silencing the critics. The Ford administration set up a "Team B" that would operate in competition with "Team A," the CIA-led analysts, and with equal access to relevant data. In August–December 1976 Team B, with Pipes taking a leading role, wrote a critical review of past intelligence estimates on the Soviet Union. Team B would be a difficult legacy for the next administration, and the issues raised by the neoconservative critics set the agenda for debate until the end of the Cold War. An important and controversial reform had, therefore, come from within the Ford administration.[41]

At first, it seemed as if reforms of the congressional variety would continue in the Carter presidency. Intelligence abuses were still a salient issue at the time of the 1976 presidential election, and Carter recalled having been "deeply troubled," at the time, by the "CIA's role in plotting murder and other crimes."[42] A newcomer to Washington politics, the former governor of Georgia broke with the tradition that the DCI should be a nonpolitical appointment—Carter released George Bush and chose in his stead Adm. Stansfield Turner (1977–1981), a man whose preference for technological as distinct from human intelligence alarmed people of Team B disposition. Fred Hitz, legislative counsel to the CIA in the Carter presidency, later summed up what came to be a common perception of the intelligence problem at the time:

> It must be noted that Carter came in as an outsider, and did not realize what the agency could do for a president of the United States. Of course, he changed his mind later in his presidency. Then, another problem was that Democrats who had served on the Church Committee such as Vice-

President [Walter] Mondale were members of the Carter administration. As to Turner, he in some ways misunderstood the nature of the work that the agency did. He distrusted clandestine operations. His attitude had an effect within the agency, and . . . he released a substantial number of people, especially from operations, and in an insensitive manner.[43]

Did Carter change his mind? Were there two Carters? Or, in fact, was there just one all along? It could be argued that the supposedly naïve peanut farmer shrewdly adopted a stance, in the 1976 campaign, to capitalize on the post-Vietnam, anti-CIA, anti-Washington public mood. After all, Carter's son Jack had served in Vietnam, Jimmy had supported the military effort there, and he delivered the nominating speech at the 1972 Democratic convention for the prominent Vietnam hawk, Henry "Scoop" Jackson. Even at the very beginning of his presidency, Carter temporized over the vexing issue of covert operations. They could be "legitimate and proper," and, in the interest of security, he thought that not too many members of the Congress should know about them. The inner Jimmy Carter may have been more consistent than his political exterior.[44]

Nevertheless, dramatic events persuaded the president to adjust the emphasis in his public stance on intelligence, finally prompting the remark by New York's Senator Daniel P. Moynihan: "Carter has now discovered that it is *his* CIA!"[45] The most disturbing of these events took place in Iran. On 16 January 1979 the shah, twenty-six years after the CIA-assisted coup that had given him autocratic power, fled into exile. Within a month, a charismatic seventy-nine-year-old cleric, the Ayatollah Khomeini, returned from a fourteen-year exile to impose on Iran a more traditional, and emphatically anti-American, style of government. On 4 November, a student mob bearing the usual anti-CIA placards stormed the American embassy in Teheran, taking its staff members hostage. The Iranians refused to release the hostages until Carter, defeated in the 1980 election, had left the White House.

These events were hurtful to the Carter administration, for earlier developments had made Iran an apparently indispensable ally in the Middle East. America had needed a new friend in the region in the wake of the collapse of British power, and of the alienation of the Arab world over Yom Kippur. Iran had seemed a doubly suitable choice because of the Arab oil embargo—the world's second-largest oil producer, Iran was in a position to help. Iran, moreover, stood as a bulwark between the Soviet Union and the Indian Ocean—the Red Army's occupation of neighboring Afghanistan on Christmas Day 1979 did nothing to calm the nerves of those who feared Soviet domination of the oil-rich Arabian Gulf, as well as of South Asia and the horn of Africa. Nor was this all. Iran under the shah had hosted U.S. intelligence listening posts, within 600 miles of missile-testing stations inside the USSR. These listening posts would be useful in any effort to verify Soviet compliance with SALT II. The loss of Iran and the accompanying hostage crisis were a real problem for President Carter.

Leading officials in the Carter administration blamed the Iranian crisis on the intelligence community, claiming it had not delivered adequate warning of the impending fall of the shah, and had left the policy makers unprepared to take preemptive action or to deal with the consequences. Here, the indictment of the intelligence community is doubly deadly: it failed to predict Yom Kippur, causing the oil crisis, then failed to warn of the collapse of America's main petroleum ally. Certainly, intelligence on Iran was deficient in some regards. For example, U.S. military attachés in Teheran had been more interested in selling weapons to the oil-rich regime than in assessing its stability. On 28 September 1978, the DIA had reported that the shah was "expected to remain actively in power over the next 10 years." But this was an exceptional piece of wishful thinking, and, in truth, there had been intelligence competence and intelligence warnings for a long time. Analysts in the CIA and in State Department intelligence (INR) had not been convinced of the need to remove Iran's Premier Mossadeq in 1953; a national intelligence estimate in 1962 had warned of the inherent instability of the shah's regime; during the unrest in the months leading up to the fall of the shah, INR had consistently taken a pessimistic view of his survival chances, and the CIA had moved steadily closer to that position. In November 1978, for example, the CIA warned that the shah could no longer rely on the military's support, and in December it poured cold water on the notion that the shah's opponents were controlled by Moscow-directed outsiders. For anyone familiar with Pearl Harbor, the story had a familiar ring: there had been warnings, but nobody listened. The response would also be similar: blame intelligence, and then bolster it.[46]

The SALT II debate underlined the need to have a capable and respected CIA. In June 1979 at a ceremony in Vienna, the Americans and the Soviets penciled their initials on a new agreement. Its wide-ranging provisions included a brake on the development of destabiliz-ing weapons systems—for example, missiles with independently tar-getable multiple warheads, and subradar cruise missiles. Article XV recognized the legitimacy of satellite surveillance as a means of verifica-tion. But the Team B critique had taken its toll. In retrospect, Team B appears to have been wrong on the productive capacity of the Soviet military economy and on the aggressive nature of the Kremlin's inten-tions. But the loss of Iran and its listening posts sewed doubt about verification and, indeed, about the resolve of the Carter administration in standing up for American interests. In January 1980 Carter withdrew the SALT II treaty from the Senate, knowing that it would not be ratified in that chamber. It could be argued that Team B had won the battle but lost both the argument and the war—both the Americans and the Soviets honored the terms of the nonratified treaty.[47] However, it had become plain that it was no easy matter to conduct an effective foreign policy with the CIA in low esteem.

Accordingly, Carter began to send out signals emphasizing what he had probably believed all along. There was a need, he declared in January 1980, "to remove unwarranted restraints on America's ability to collect intelligence." Admiral Turner dutifully chimed in with the observation that Hughes-Ryan was too restrictive—covert operations should not have to be disclosed to so many legislators. But by now it was too late, as other hunters were in the field. Running in the Republican primaries in February, Bush advocated "moves to beef up the CIA." But even his rhetoric was no match for that of Ronald Reagan, who promised that if elected, he would "unleash" the CIA.[48] The eventual Reagan-Bush ticket came to stand for intelligence expansion, whereas Carter-Mondale, despite its changed emphasis, seemed a hangover from the restrictionist phase of the Church era. By 1980, intelligence was not such a burning issue as it had been in the previous election, but the Republican victors had made no secret of their message to restore secret intelligence, and they were true to their promise.

Looked at in its long-term context, the inquiry spearheaded by Sen-ator Church did help reform American intelligence. Quite apart from convincing America of the need for congressional oversight and inspiring particular reforms, the congressional investigators educated the public about both the problems that can stem from a secret state and the need for an efficient foreign intelligence service. On the other hand, certain qualifications are in order. First, the Church Committee was not the only body committed to reform. Among the others were President Ford, DCI Colby, and that determined group of zabaglione gourmands that spawned Team B. Second, the Iran debacle proved, once again, that in the world of intelligence nobody has a magic wand. While intelligence successes occurred every day and went unnoticed, intelligence mistakes happened, and, after many months of urgent congressional inquiry, they showed no signs of being eradicated. Finally, there is the question of whether Church and his fellow reformers managed to dispel that great and abiding illusion, the belief in the confidence man as intelligence leader. A resounding "No" to that question is suggested by a review of the stewardship of Ronald Reagan and William Casey in the 1980s.

CHAPTER 13

The Casey-Reagan Era
From History to Victory

President Ronald Reagan injected new life into an old and paradoxical conspiracy: he used the cloak of clandestinity to achieve his ends, yet, at the same time, he hyped the role of secret intelligence. Trust me, he told the American people, to twist the truth in your interest.

Reagan's skill as a salesman was legendary, and his elevation to the White House was bound to boost intelligence because of his past affinities with secret service and deception.[1] He had acted in B movies for Warner Brothers in the late 1930s, a time when the government was urging moviemakers to stop making heroes of gangsters and to glamorize federal agents instead. An obliging Hollywood issued a string of espionage films. Humphrey Bogart and Edward G. Robinson accepted some of the lead roles, but there was room also for lesser actors. As Brass Bancroft, Secret Agent J-24, Reagan achieved the pinnacle of his filmic career. The young actor played parts that supported the work of the newly formed House Committee on Unamerican Activities, and of America's counterintelligence agencies. For example, in a movie that took its cue from the 1938 radio adaptation of H. G. Wells's novel *War of the Worlds* (1898), the celluloid Reagan saved the nation from the effects of the potential theft of America's top-secret "death ray projector."

Once America had entered World War II, the young actor threw himself into the officially orchestrated Hollywood fakery effort designed to improve American morale, to mislead the foe, and to promote confidence among America's allies. At this point, Reagan was still something of a liberal and a New Dealer; he was sympathetic to the principle of labor unionism and, indeed, would become president of the Screen Actors' Guild.

But then, in the dead of one fateful night, Reagan received a visit. The year was 1946, and the three agents were from the FBI. They warned him of the danger of communism in his union and appealed to him to inform on his fellow actors. Reagan at first refused, insisting that he was no Red-baiter. The agents persisted. Their targets were not just communists, they said, but "spies and saboteurs" like those German agents in the recent war. Reagan finally succumbed. He became FBI informer number T-10 and was issued a handgun for his personal protection.[2]

Although three and a half decades would elapse before he ran for the White House, the heady days of these early Hollywood experiences colored Reagan's outlook permanently. The "Gipper's" movie memories affected his political vocabulary and governed his attitude toward secret service and defense matters. His determination to "unleash" the CIA followed, as it were, a preordained script.

Once elected president, Reagan boosted intelligence in another vital way—he appointed William J. Casey to preside over the CIA. Casey would invent a new line of hyperbole to support the expansion of intelligence not just during his tenure but long after his death in 1987. In doing so, he drew on his perceptions of history. Here, it is important to note that he had not always been a career intelligence officer and that his interpretation of the past for this reason transcended the usual story of the CIA in the Cold War.

Bill Casey had spent most of his life not sitting behind a government desk but acting out the American Dream. His grandfather had been a refugee from the Irish potato famine, and the family still lived in relative poverty in Queens, New York, when Casey gained his education from the Jesuits at Fordham University. He then embarked on an imaginative and successful business career—it was he who invented the "tax shelter." Having made one fortune, he proceeded to make another, by writing texts advising others how to make theirs.

Like the new president, Casey was an outsider who had made good. Age was another factor they had in common: at the time of his inauguration, Reagan was sixty-nine, and Casey sixty-seven. Thus, the men shared yet another characteristic: memories of World War II. Like Reagan, Casey cherished recollections of secret service during that period, and, as they were his only personal memories of clandestine action, they were especially important to him.

In 1944, Bill Casey had been made chief of the Special Intelligence Branch in the European theater of operations, OSS London. Commenting on his relationship with the OSS's social elite, one colleague later said Casey was "with them" but not "*of* them." Yet, as independently minded as he was in other ways, Casey did absorb the "Bold Easterner" OSS-CIA propaganda line that was at the heart of post–World War II intelligence expansion. His enthusiasm stemmed in part from the fact that he had enjoyed what is known as a "good war." OSS London had been in bad shape when he took charge of it, but his improvements in training and organization had yielded results. U.S. agents infiltrating Germany sent back information that helped the Allies in their final push for victory. On Casey's watch, the OSS accomplished 102 penetration missions—three times as many as its British counterparts.[3]

Casey could and did look back in pride. In the post-war years, he conducted a regular and mutually admiring correspondence with Allen Dulles. In his unsuccessful bid for the 1966 Republican congressional nomination from Nassau County, New York, he dwelled on his Cold Warrior and intelligence credentials despite the liberal temper of the times and the low standing of the CIA in the post–Bay of Pigs years. The very first sentence of his campaign biography identified "William J. Casey, one of the architects of America's intelligence services." Comments on his activities as president of Veterans of the OSS took up an imprudently large amount of space in the four-page statement, which was, after all, aimed at voters who probably had more pressing concerns. So Casey failed electorally, an experience he shared with both Donovan and Dulles, and one that perhaps made all three men disrespectful of election results. Dulles could only sympathize with Casey on his failed bid, in an exchange that illustrates neatly the apostolic succession of empathetic intelligence leaders.[4]

In December 1974, President Ford sent Casey a note congratulating him on the receipt of the William J. Donovan Award, an honor periodically bestowed by Veterans of the OSS. Thanking him, Casey sent the president a copy of his speech at the Veterans' dinner. In it, he praised Donovan, a man "ready to approve any operation that had half a chance," and noted the role of the British who, with the advantage of three years' prior war experience, took on the unprepared Americans "as junior partners and . . . generously taught us all they knew." Here, Casey was subscribing to the well-worn expansionist parable, the view that U.S. intelligence had been unready for the challenge in World War II, had to be rescued by the British, and—by implication—could not afford to contract in the future. It is significant that, according to a note by his aide, Ford read Casey's speech and took it seriously.[5]

That the "neoconservative" political vocabulary of intelligence expansion was in gestation even in the midst of the flap crisis is confirmed by the tone of Casey's recollection of the December 1975 assassination of Richard Welch, the incident that helped reverse the critical tide for the CIA and the rest of the intelligence community:

> You will recall that [in the mid-1970s] renegade Americans seeking to destroy the nation's intelligence capability were revealing the identities, locations, and addresses of officers and agents serving our nation around the world. Each person named in the publications they sent around the world became a potential target, along with his family and colleagues, for assassination or other forms of terrorist attack. Dick Welch, our station chief in Greece, was fingered by these traitors and assassinated in the driveway of his home as he was getting out of his automobile.[6]

But although Casey subscribed, when it suited him, to some of intelligence history's more comforting and conformist mythologies, he was still capable of an imaginative historical leap, a leap that would mark him as the twentieth century's last great intelligence confidence man. For Casey took a broad view of history. In the bicentennial year of 1976, he wrote about one of his profound interests in a book called *Where and How the War Was Fought: An Armchair Tour of the American Revolution*. This volume was peppered with anecdotes about intelligence. Some were just entertaining, like the story of how Quaker Lydia Darragh smuggled messages across the lines to the Continental Army on bits of paper pressed into the buttons on her fourteen-year-old son's coat. But Casey's light touch did not conceal his interpretive approach. Seeking to explain how the American Revolutionaries won against overwhelming odds, he pointed to General Washington's disinformation skills and to his wisdom in resorting to "irregular, partisan, guerrilla warfare," here making a parallel with the recent tactics used by Vietnamese communists in defeating the United States. Time and again, in his extensive writings, Casey would return to the theme of George Washington as an intelligence leader, noting, for example, how the Revolutionary general read deeply into French military scholarship on espionage and irregular warfare. Making an unfortunate comparison, he praised the irregular tactics of a group the CIA had trained. These were Afghanistan's Islamic militants, anti-Soviet then, but anti-American later.[7]

The significance of all this is twofold. On the one hand, it indicates a continuing dedication to covert action and to the belief that America should "unleash" the CIA. On the other hand, his fascination with the American Revolution points to his ability to liberate himself from the Manichean constraints of the Cold War vision of intelligence history. The communists had not been America's only foes and, by implication, would not be the last.

Casey made this point frequently and explicitly. In May 1981, not long after taking the helm at the CIA, he told a group of businessmen in Hot Springs, Virginia: "Our first priority is still the Soviet Union—its military capability and economic strength. . . . However, there are many other problems of concern to intelligence. For example: nationalism, terrorism, and resource dependency." In 1986, he appealed for breadth of vision by stating that the competition between the United States and the USSR was just "the latest chapter of the same conflict that pitted Athens against Xerxes and the Persians, and Medieval Europe against Genghis Khan and the Mongols." But the day when the USSR had been America's "principal adversary" was "long past," and America now faced a proliferation of new enemies and problems. Lecturing at Fordham, Casey maintained that the intelligence community had a responsibility for "scouting the future" and for identifying a "broad spectrum" of problems stretching "past the year 2000."[8]

This perspective indicates Casey's appreciation of the ahistoricity of pinning U.S. intelligence history too firmly to the Cold War years. Casey's perspective marks him as a pragmatist and spin doctor who wanted the CIA to stay in business. It pointed a way forward for intelligence expansionists after his death and after the demise of the Soviet Union, by showing that their agenda could be wider than the containment of communism. Casey's claim to paternity of the CIA pales by comparison with his patently clear fatherhood of the child he never lived to see, the post–Cold War intelligence community.

◆ ◆ ◆ ◆

Hyperbole played a prominent part in the Reagan administration's defense policy, and the actor in the White House had the skills needed to massage the message. For the first time, the director of the CIA was given a seat in the presidential cabinet. Such advantages were certainly needed in the long term, because administration hype was self-contradictory. Hyping *for* victory in the Cold War meant exaggerating the Soviet threat in order to procure larger defense appropriations. Yet, Casey simultaneously wanted to refocus intelligence and downplay the role of Moscow as the chief rogue confronted by the United States. After communism's demise, the latter goal would be further threatened by the hyping *of* victory, a form of propaganda that threatened Casey's hoped-for intelligence continuity, as it seemed to imply that the CIA had accomplished its goal and was no longer needed. These inconsistencies did not help when critics turned their heavy guns on the intelligence community during and after the Reagan presidency.

Casey's publicity and diversification programs nevertheless succeeded, as is borne out by events both during and after his tenure at the CIA. In the first few years of the two-term Reagan administration, "unleashing" the CIA meant attacks on open government, a renewed surge in covert operations, and a larger budget. All this was made easier by the cooperation of the third member of the pro-CIA, Cold Warrior triumvirate, the septuagenarian Senator Barry Goldwater. Republican gains in the 1980 election meant that this former presidential candidate would now chair the Senate Intelligence Committee—he remained at the head of that oversight body until 1985. Goldwater was no admirer of Bill Casey, and came to distrust him ever more deeply, but his negative views on oversight perversely ensured that Reagan and Casey could proceed with the unleashing process. As a member of the Church inquiry in 1975–1976, Goldwater had called for a cessation of its activities and then attacked its final report. Later, he voted against the establishment of the oversight committee it had recommended, and which he himself came to chair. Assuming his new post in January 1981, the senator declared, "I think the CIA is going to find a very cordial reception here." In May 1981, he stated, "When it comes to covert operations, it would be best if they didn't have to tell us anything," adding, a couple of months later, "I don't even like to have an intelligence committee."[9]

Liberated from the constraints of close inspection by that branch of the legislature having chief responsibility for foreign policy, the CIA had greater scope for action. That is not to say that it was out of control, however, for the White House exerted a tight grip. The intelligence community's Soviet estimates were politically controlled. The National Security Council took over some particularly sensitive covert operations, bringing them even more tightly into the White House orbit. Casey personally controlled delicate policy areas without heeding or even informing his colleagues in the CIA and wider intelligence community.

Still, there is ample evidence of the unleashing process. In February 1981, the administration began a propaganda campaign against the Left-leaning "Sandinista" government of Nicaragua, committing itself to the Contra movement dedicated to its overthrow. By November, it was evident that a covert operation to this end had been set up, and that Congress was being bypassed. In vain did Norman Mineta of the House Intelligence Committee complain, "We are like mushrooms, they keep us in the dark and feed us a lot of manure."[10]

As in the 1950s, the public rhetoric was once again about rolling back communism worldwide. In another similarity to the earlier decade, the clandestine services were expected to play a major role. Casey was said to be unhappy with the CIA's Harvard-Yale-Princeton establishment, which, in spite of its acronym (HYPE) and its lineal descent from the 1950s Ivy League Bold Easterners, was too cautious for his taste. He insisted on more action, and, according to one estimate, the number of U.S. covert operations increased fivefold in the period 1980–1986. Spook-watchers assumed that the overall intelligence budget increased dramatically, even more rapidly than the booming military budget of the Reagan years. Attempts at quantification yielded different conclusions, as, for reasons of national security, no official figures were released. According to Senator Goldwater's biographer, the CIA's authorized expenditure rose by 50 percent in the first two years of the Reagan administration. But investigative journalist Bob Woodward reported Reagan's approval of a much bigger increase in the aggregate intelligence budget—from $6 billion in 1980, to $20 billion in 1985.[11]

On the first day of 1982, the *New York Times* reported two cases, each illustrative of the Reagan administration's determination to clamp down on unwanted disclosures. In one, former CIA director William Colby agreed to pay a $10,000 fine in order to avoid being sued for breaking the secrecy agreement he had signed as a CIA employee. He was deemed to have made some unauthorized disclosures, in his autobiography *Honorable Men* (1978), about an expensive failure in the Nixon administration, the attempt to recover a sunken Soviet submarine using Nixon's financial backer Howard Hughes as an intermediary. The message seemed to be that it was necessary to silence a liberal Director of Central Intelligence who had cooperated with the Church inquiry and who had advocated open government in his book. The other *Times* story concerned Frank Snepp, a former CIA employee who had published a book exposing U.S. insensitivity and incompetence when Saigon was evacuated upon the communist triumph in 1975. In this case, Snepp was ordered to turn over to the government the $140,000 profit made from his book.[12]

Administration supporters in Congress now launched a campaign to secure two pieces of intelligence legislation, statutes to exempt the CIA from the provisions of the Freedom of Information Act, and to protect the identities of U.S. intelligence officers and prevent a repetition of the Welch affair. In June, large majorities in both houses of Congress passed the Intelligence Identities Protection Act. But although Goldwater argued strenuously for the other measure, the defenders of open government fought back. It was not until October 1984 that the CIA was given exemption from the Freedom of Information Act, and then only partly. Even in Reagan's first term, then, the unleashers did not find everything going their way. Edward P. Boland chaired the House Permanent Select Committee on Intelligence from 1977 to 1985, and he and his colleagues consistently asked what were known as "hardball" questions. Nor was the House committee toothless. In December 1982, the Boland amendment prohibited the CIA from arming the counter-revolutionary movement in Nicaragua, and in varying forms the prohibition remained effective until October 1986.[13]

However, officials at the heart of the administration and possibly the president himself set out to circumvent the Boland amendment. Their ploy was to unleash, not the CIA itself, but a CIA surrogate, an ad hoc group of officials headed by former U.S. Marine Oliver North. This group organized support for the Contras with logistical help from the CIA, but using money derived from private or unofficial sources and channeled through cooperating foreign countries. For example, in 1983 Casey approached Israel and South Africa to see if they would act as third parties when the Boland amendment took effect. According to some accounts, Israel was supplying weapons to the Contras by the end of that year.[14]

It did not unduly worry the Reagan administration that some individuals saw through its surrogacy and other concealment strategies. Reagan and Casey took their anti-communist crusade directly to the people, hoping that members of the House would repent in their opposition to a popular policy. In January 1984, the CIA mined the harbors of Nicaragua, an act of state terrorism that led to the conviction of the United States in the international court at the Hague. Although it must have been obvious that the American hand could not be hidden, the administration had not sought prior consultation with Congress about the policy. Senator Goldwater, though still struggling to be loyal to the principles of lax oversight and active covert operations, on this occasion lost his composure and venomously attacked Casey over the mining. Then, in October 1984, it emerged that the CIA had been instructing the Contras in the art of assassination. President Reagan had routinely reissued the government's ban on assassination as an instrument of state policy. But John Kirkpatrick, a contract CIA agent hitherto known only to a few colleagues and mainly for his love of drink and propensity to weep, was revealed to have written a Contra manual on how to murder people on one's own side and then blame the opposition. The revelation and its timing seemed custom-made for the 1984 election campaign, when Reagan was seeking a second term. The Democratic candidate was Church Committee veteran Walter Mondale. His running mate, Geraldine Ferraro, had launched an attack on the proposition that "refining the murder techniques of Central Americans will advance our national interests." However, the issue had no adverse effect on Reagan's chances for electoral reendorsement, and the president won in convincing style. Intelligence expansion and intelligence spin seemed set to continue.[15]

Intelligence spin lay at the root of the Reagan administration's Strategic Defense Initiative (SDI), otherwise known as "Star Wars." The program was designed to operate on the frontiers of technology, yet it was based on a simple idea. It would develop a space-based defense shield. If the Soviets attempted a nuclear attack, their incoming rockets would be destroyed by satellite-launched laser beams. Though more sober analysts considered it to be, at best, a means of protecting America's missile silos, physicist Edward Teller and the president euphorically promoted the idea that the American people would be protected forever.

It is tempting to see in the program the enactment of one of Reagan's movie dreams, an initiative by a confused septuagenarian who could not separate in his mind the defense requirements of the 1980s and the need to protect America from the "death ray projector" of the Warner Brothers film. But SDI had, in fact, serious objectives. Reagan looked on technology not just as the ultimate nuclear shield but also as an ideal. It would end the arms race and bring peace not for America alone but for the world—like Eisenhower, he offered to share American technology with the enemy in pursuit of this great end. In the meantime, though, the hope was that the Soviets would try to compete by producing their own version of SDI, an effort that would ruin their economy and bring about the end of communism in Europe. The hope that the arms race would bring the Russian economy to its knees went back to the classic Cold War policy statement, NSC 68. The circumstances that prevailed in the early 1980s seemed to furnish some hope for success.

In the meantime, SDI would also perform a role similar to that of America's mythical anti-ballistic missile program in the early 1970s. Secretary of State George Shultz saw SDI as, in the words of journalist/historian Garry Wills, "the ultimate 'bargaining chip' that was not played."[16] Like the earlier program, it would need to be predicated on plausible expenditure plans. That meant congressional approval, which in turn meant the necessity of inventing a new Soviet menace. To be plausible, the depiction of a dire military threat from Moscow had to be based on intelligence estimates. Once again, intelligence and politics were to be intertwined.

In January 1982, Casey asked CIA experts for their view on an embryonic Star Wars plan. They replied that it would be very expensive, and that the Soviet Union would regard it as a provocation. In May, National Security Adviser William Clark nevertheless signaled a new thrust in defense strategy, stating that it was President Reagan's intention to use economic means to weaken the Soviet Union and roll back communism worldwide. In the months ahead, the government used various means of weakening the Soviet economy: a reduction of oil prices to curtail Moscow's currency earnings; covert support to Solidarity in Poland, fundamentalists in Afghanistan, and other opposition movements that strained the communist purse; a boycott on the export of technology that would have helped the Soviet economy; and so on. But both Reagan and his defense secretary, Caspar Weinberger, were determined to play their economic ace. In March 1983, Reagan attacked the Soviet Union as an "evil empire," warning of a massive communist military buildup and then, in a televised address, calling for a facility that "could intercept and destroy strategic ballistic missiles before they reached our own soil." The whole program was launched in the following year, with Congress agreeing to appropriate money despite the $26 billion price tag for start-up research costs alone. In the final Reagan budget, this price tag ballooned to $40 billion for the fiscal period 1990–1994, with the actual expenditure amounting to $60 billion by 1999 in spite of continuing CIA criticism.[17]

That the administration achieved this result was in some measure due to its ability to persuade Congress and the public of the gravity of the Soviet menace. Intelligence estimates inevitably played a role in this exercise in persuasion. The CIA had been analyzing the Soviet economy and military production capacity since 1951 and had enjoyed some success. On the other hand, following the creation of the Defense Intelligence Agency in 1961, the CIA had come under fire for underestimating Soviet capabilities, a discernible element of chaos had entered the estimating process, and Kissinger's manipulations had raised fears about the politicization of intelligence. The Team B neoconservatives of the Ford-Carter years had questioned the reliability of the estimating process, and this had helped prepare the way for Reagan's successful election campaign. The problem, here, was that the neoconservatives had shot themselves in the collective foot. In order to persuade the United States to part with more defense dollars in the 1980s, they now needed to restore the very faith in the estimating process that they had conspired to destroy in the 1970s. Like Carter in the 1970s, the Reagan neoconservative of the 1980s had to swallow the unpalatable fact that it was *his* CIA.[18]

In any event, it proved sufficient to generate a debate. After all, even if there was a possibility that Moscow *might* threaten U.S. national security, a legislator mindful of his or her duties to constituents would think twice about voting down new defense appropriations. Whether or not because of Team B pressure, the CIA had already revised its estimate of the 1975 Soviet defense budget from 152 billion to 234 billion rubles. Led by the DIA, in the 1980s a group of analysts hammered away on the theme that America faced a major new threat from the communist world. Not everyone agreed with this view. Robert Gates, who had taken over as the CIA's chief Soviet analyst in 1980, from the outset argued that Moscow's bark was worse than its bite—its saber-rattling masked a consciousness of consumer discontent, even of potential economic collapse, within a sprawling Soviet empire that had overspent on armaments. In 1983, Gates accused the Department of Defense of exaggerating Soviet military expenditure, and in January 1985 the department's spokesman had to admit that Soviet military expenditure had been stagnant since the mid-1970s.[19]

By this time, however, the SDI bargaining chip was in place. It is also worth noting the deployment, within conservative circles, of a piece of casuistry reminiscent of taxation in the days of Henry VII of England and Wales (if you are spending money, you are rich and can be taxed; if you are not, you must be saving money and again can afford to pay taxes). The news that the communist economies were not doing well was really, of course, welcome to those who believed in the market economy, and they found a way of reconciling their economic principles with their foreign policy ambitions. In the words of Philip Zelikow, who had been an NSC staffer: "The conservatives maintained that since the Soviet economy was really smaller than previously thought, Moscow must have been spending an even larger share of resources on defense, thus revealing its confrontational priorities. Further, a smaller Soviet economy would be less able to sustain a competition with Reagan's defense buildup."[20]

In 1991 congressional hearings, critics opposed Gates's confirmation as DCI, arguing that he had conspired to twist intelligence to suit the hard-line policy of the Reagan administration.[21] In Reagan's first term, Gates did limit himself to internal expressions of disagreement, no doubt with an eye to the continuation of his career, and hoping that it would be more effective to argue from within than after a soon-forgotten public breach and resignation. By the time the hawks had

been forced to admit their error, his public dissent was less damaging to
the administration. In any case, the whole issue now went backstage,
making way for the intelligence drama of the decade, the Iran-Contra
affair.

Looking backward from the Olympian heights of the twenty-first
century, it is now possible to place into perspective a scandal that, at the
time, seemed to rock America and to carry the distinct possibility of
impeachment of the president. For the truth is that Iran-Contra was a
debacle that failed even as a debacle. While it discomfited the Reagan
administration and took some of the shine off an administration accustomed to basking in unqualified optimism, it produced no great
upheaval, and President Reagan and his Republican successor, George
H. W. Bush, were able to survive their terms in office with more than a
hint of triumph.

In fall 1984, a conspiracy was hatched to deliver American weapons
to Iran. Since September 1980, that nation had been at war with its
neighbor Iraq. America had equipped Iran's armed forces in the days of
the shah, and new equipment and spares were needed to continue the
war. Israel, which feared the military might of Iraq and also wanted to
please America, acted as an intermediary, and through this channel Iran
received substantial quantities of missiles and other equipment. For its
part, officials in the Reagan administration saw two advantages in the
deal. One was that, by opening a channel to Teheran, the Iranians' good
offices might be sought to induce terrorist groups over which they had
influence to release a number of Americans who had been taken hostage and were being held in unknown locations in Lebanon. The second
advantage was that the sales would generate profits that could be secretly diverted to the support of the Contras in Nicaragua, at a time
when the Boland amendment threatened to starve those counterrevo-
lutionaries of funds.

There were, however, problems with the Iran-Contra ploy. It ran
contrary to declared U.S. policies—America was committed to an arms
boycott of Iran following the embassy hostage crisis, and had also vowed
to make no concessions to kidnappers, for the reason that such weakness would only encourage extremists to snatch more Americans. This
was reason enough to keep the policy under wraps, but the Nicaraguan

dimension to the plot made secrecy even more vital. As Congress had banned American aid to the Contras, the use of American assets to help them, even indirectly, was illegal. The funds diversion therefore opened the way to possible criminal prosecutions, and to impeachment of the president.[22]

In fall 1986, things looked promising for the Iran-Contra conspirators. The Contra movement had survived, Congress was in a more cooperative mood, and the Boland ban on aid to the anti-Sandinista movement ran out on 17 October. But then, on 2 November, disaster struck. On that day, the Lebanese journal *Al-Shiraa* ran an exposé of the missiles-for-hostages swap.

This news shocked America, and the White House had to respond. Having in mind preemption and what one journalist called "a show of purification," the Reagan administration established two inquiries.[23] John Tower, a former senator who had sat on the Church Committee, would conduct an investigation into the National Security Council's role in the affair. Deputy Attorney General Lawrence E. Walsh was appointed independent counsel and given the task of investigating the arms sales and the Contra diversion, ostensibly with a view to prosecution. But this kind of response, reminiscent of the earlier "whitewash" inquiries by Nicholas Katzenbach and Nelson Rockefeller, did not satisfy the administration's critics. In a move on 4 December that apparently threatened the administration, the Senate and House jointly resolved to set up their own inquiry.

Iran-Contra was a news story with compelling ingredients. One of them was a kind of human-interest detective thriller, though less a whodunit than a whoknewit—some person or persons in the administration must have known what was going on and should have stopped it. Predictably, if not very convincingly, the phrases "out of control" and "rogue elephant" once again emerged in public discourse. The complicity in the affair of National Security Council officials gave a novel twist to the old debate about the Constitution, intelligence, and foreign policy. Academia as well as Congress agonized anew over the issue of legislative oversight of secret intelligence, and especially covert action.[24]

But in terms of outcome, Iran-Contra was ineffective. As a policy, it simply did not succeed. Even if some Americans were released in the wake of the Iranian arms deal, Washington had revealed itself to be a soft touch on hostages, leaving American citizens at risk in the future. Relations with oil-rich, strategically placed Iran remained as frosty after the affair as before it. The Contras lost not just their illegal funding but also the promised renewal of legitimate support—Congress cut off all further military assistance early in 1988. To cap it all, in the Nicaraguan general election in February 1990, the Sandinistas were quite peacefully voted out of office and replaced by a government more acceptable to the Bush administration. Election analysis suggests that the Nicaraguan people voted for a more conservative party partly because they thought it could end the war, but partly also because they wanted more friendly relations with the United States. The election result illustrates how counterproductive covert operations can be: Nicaraguans had supported the Left-wing Sandinistas only so long as they were fighting the CIA.[25]

Iran-Contra was similarly ineffective as a goad to reform. The attempt to find out who had authorized lawbreaking fizzled out, partly because of secrecy and obfuscation, but perhaps partly also because it was obvious that too many public figures, members of Congress included, were complicit. In the wake of the Church inquiry, most informed observers realized that the president controlled secret intelligence initiatives, so there was extensive speculation about Reagan's role. To describe the behavior of a chief executive who forgot what he had said or feigned forgetfulness, his friends coined new euphemisms like "passively decisive." Vice President Bush similarly escaped censure by claiming ignorance. Casey slipped out of the firing line when he died of prostate cancer on 6 May 1987. Investigative journalist Bob Woodward had been interviewing him on his deathbed. His last question was, did Casey know about the Contra diversion? According to Woodward, the dying DCI nodded his assent. Others had already made the assumption of guilt, taking advantage of Casey's death and inability to answer back to make him a special scapegoat—he had become, in the words of another journalist, "usefully deceased." North, of course, was guilty but, though photogenic and interesting, too small a fish to satisfy the scapegoat hunters.[26]

Other officials were pursued and perhaps paid an indirect price: Robert Gates, for example, was interrogated and deemed it prudent to assume a low and perhaps quiescent profile in order to keep his career alive. However, few suffered the full consequences of lawbreaking.

Though convicted of falsification of documents and lying to Congress, North and National Security Adviser John Poindexter won their appeals. Then, on Christmas Eve 1992, President Bush pardoned six former officials who had participated in the Iran-Contra scam. The only conspirator to serve a prison sentence was a minor figure: Thomas G. Clines, a former CIA employee who had served as procurement officer for the Contras and was convicted on charges of tax evasion.[27]

As for the three inquiries, they told a tale of human error and seemed to concur in the view that Iran-Contra had been an "aberration." The congressional inquiry's insistence on stronger oversight was not new and did not carry the authority it might have, because oversight mechanisms had been in place throughout the scam—having chosen not to scrutinize the executive too closely, the intelligence committees had no clean hands to throw up in horror—and who would trust them to do a better job in the future? Nevertheless, in August 1991, after some resistance Bush did sign a law to the effect that the president should henceforth give the oversight committees advance intimation in writing of all covert activities, though he hinted that he might sometimes ignore it. Possibly of greater significance was Bush's agreement to another recommendation by the congressional panel, that the office of CIA inspector general be put on a statutory basis and that the person appointed to that office should be subject to Senate approval. The office had existed in the CIA since 1952, and some inspectors had been sharply critical, as in the case of Lyman Kirkpatrick's report on the Bay of Pigs fiasco. However, the congressional panel felt that under existing arrangements inspectors general lacked the "tenacity" to do an effective job. In 1990, Bush appointed lawyer and former CIA officer Frederick P. Hitz to the newly strengthened post, in which he served for eight years.[28]

Iran-Contra did not stop intelligence expansion and diversification. At the height of the flap, for example, the DIA reported on Pakistan's nuclear industry, noting that power stations in Karachi and elsewhere had serious maintenance problems, that there was "paranoia" about India's development of nuclear weapons, and that Pakistan had the theoretical expertise and fuel enrichment capacity to develop a small nuclear arsenal of its own. The report was proto-post–Cold War, in that it pointed no accusing finger at the Russians or other communists. In this way, it mirrored Casey's conviction that serious problems lay in the future that had little to do with American-Soviet rivalry.[29]

While nuclear proliferation was a worrying problem, it paled in political significance compared with another that, in the 1980s, snaked out into America's middle-class suburbs, that of addiction to banned substances. The war against crack cocaine and other drugs was emblematic of both the hyperbole and the intelligence diversification that had taken place in the Reagan years. President Clinton in 1997 emphasized the issue as one of the main challenges facing the intelligence community, and it would be tempting to see it as a post–Cold War phenomenon. But the issue and its irrationalities had been present for decades, and the high-profile treatment they received during the Reagan presidency had already pushed them onto center stage.[30]

American attitudes toward addictive substances, including alcohol, have long been ambivalent—Will Rogers once quipped that "Mississippi would vote dry as long as the voters could stagger to the polls." In some ways, the period after World War II became a second era of Prohibition; America, free in so many ways, seemed almost subliminally to seek the artificial lash of federal repression to give zest to its rebellious recreational urges. Comparing the modern nation with its 1920s counterpart, it is possible to discern a similar enthusiasm for both drugs and their suppression, similar opportunities for the rise of organized crime, ensuing opportunities for police and intelligence work, and an all-too-familiar scope for the former to corrupt the latter. In the meantime, three distinct strands of thought developed on how best to cope with the drug problem. The libertarians advocated the legalization of drugs, for reasons that varied from resource diversion (spend money on rehabilitation, not enforcement) to the view that legalization would cause a rise in supply, a drop in prices, and a collapse in criminals' income and motivation. But although the libertarians included the fashionable supply-side economist Milton Friedman and Secretary of State George Schultz, they could not combat the populist puritanism of the Reagan presidency. Nor was there support for the potential middle way—international regulation of the narcotics trade with sympathetic treatment of users and addicts. Instead, prohibition won the day. This was a recipe for intelligence expansion.[31]

At first, America had been keen on an international approach to drug control. At conferences in Shanghai and The Hague between 1909 and 1914, the United States undertook to cooperate in the control of the international trade in opium, morphine, cocaine, and Indian hemp. Playing its part within this framework, Congress passed the Harrison Act in 1914, outlawing the importation, sale, and use of opium, morphine, heroin, and cocaine. Previously, the patent medicine industry had incorporated some of these substances in cordials taken mostly by unsuspecting middle-aged white women, but from 1914 to the 1950s consumption declined—except in the black ghettoes. But the Senate's nonratification of American membership of the League of Nations ushered in a more unilateralist era, with America trying to cajole rather than cooperate with other nations. In 1930, the government established the Federal Bureau of Narcotics. Harry J. Anslinger was in charge of this for the next thirty-two years. Anslinger was a former consular official and anti-Bolshevik agent, had a nativist tendency to blame foreigners for the drug problem, distrusted the League of Nations and its successor, the United Nations, and wanted a prohibitionist approach. However, in the Cold War he undermined his chances of success by subordinating the war on drugs to the war on communism, which he believed was the greater threat. He and his colleagues collaborated with the OSS, turned a blind eye to the use of heroin profits to finance Chinese anti-communists, and even helped the CIA with its MK-ULTRA program, the accident-prone effort to develop mind-changing drugs as an instrument of the Cold War.[32]

The enforcement apparatus was therefore shaky and discredited when after World War II the mafiosi, hitherto restrained by the Catholic Church, turned to narcotics smuggling and distribution. The 1950s intelligence effort was further hindered by J. Edgar Hoover's refusal to entertain the proposition that the Mafia may have been operating as a coordinated network—still a debatable point today, and an issue on which an open mind would have been more appropriate. To compound matters, a real problem lay in waiting for the law enforcers, for new lifestyles and the effects of the Vietnam War made the sixties a decade when heroin users increased in number from 50,000 to 500,000. When the habit spread into the white suburbs, politicians at last sat up, and promised tough-sounding reforms. The publication in 1969 of Mario Puzo's bestselling *The Godfather* and the success of the movie based on the novel concentrated attention anew on organized crime. A spate of bureaucratic shake-ups ended with the establishment, in 1973, of the Drug Enforcement Administration (DEA).[33]

In the 1980s, the "victory" culture took root in the war on drugs, just as it did in the rivalry with the Soviet Union. On the local level, Rudy Giuliani was one of those who took the lead. The New York district attorney and future Republican mayor secured the conviction of prominent mobsters like John Gotti, "Fat Tony" Salerno, and Tony "Ducks" Corallo, who locally, at least, allegedly operated an integrated crime network. On the national level, President Reagan announced his intention to "end the drug menace and cripple organized crime." First Lady Nancy Reagan took the lead in the drug prohibitionists' campaign, promoting the slogan "just say no." That she and her fellow campaigners struck a chord is confirmed by the DEA's increase in personnel and budget. The Federal Bureau of Narcotics had never employed more than 300 agents, but in 1973, the DEA boasted 2,898 employees, 1,470 of whom were special agents. Its budget that first year was $74.9 million. The number of special agents rose in the Nixon/Ford years, then declined under Carter: by 1982, there were 1,896 special agents, and the budget was $244.1 million. Then came two spurts in expenditure, the first in Reagan's first term, and the second during the Bush (senior) presidency. The figures by 1992 were 7,277 employees, 3,672 agents, and a budget of $1,004.8 million.[34]

This 1992 budget figure was only about one-ninth the overall anti-drug budget spread around different agencies. The great bulk of the money was spent on intelligence and enforcement, as distinct from education and rehabilitation. As this indicates, the prohibitionists and intelligence expansionists were politically victorious. The Democrats and Republicans vied with each other in the period 1986–1988 to bring forward the most severe anti-drug legislation, and a public opinion poll in 1989 suggested that a majority of Americans saw drugs as the most serious problem facing the nation. The federal anti-drug budget increased by almost 800 percent in the decade 1981–1990, a period when the rise in prison population from 329,821 to 771, 243 was largely due to the greater numbers of convictions of drug dealers and users. Clearly, the Reagan-Bush years were a bonanza both for the DEA, and for other agencies involved in the war on drugs.[35]

Mission corruption was a major problem for those agencies that climbed on the anti-drug bandwagon. In his days in charge of the FBI,

Hoover insisted that his agents dress in smart suits and never touch alcohol, practices that impeded undercover work in the seedy world of drug trafficking. After his death, the bureau "reformed" its ways. Its director in 1978–1987, William Webster, who made drugs a top FBI priority and had ambitions to take over the DEA, testified to a congressional committee: "I hope we won't go back to the days, Mr. Chairman, when our agents walked into bars and ordered glasses of milk." But inevitably, as casually attired agents from the FBI and local police forces lived in the gutter and engaged in dubious practices such as the "sting," corruption followed.[36]

In foreign affairs, Cold War priorities had induced U.S. intelligence agents to deal with drug traffickers who were useful as couriers, as paymasters, or as guerrilla fighters. These activities, with their moral relativism, were sometimes abhorrent to the agents involved. Periodically, they also tarnished the names of America and the CIA. For example, in 1972 the CIA sparked adverse publicity when it unsuccessfully attempted to suppress a book by Alfred McCoy—a book that detailed the agency's transportation of opium grown by "anti-communist" Laotian tribesmen. The constraints of national security secrecy made it difficult to defend publicly the agency's long-standing involvement in the world's prime heroin-producing regions, the "Golden Crescent" (Afghanistan, Iran, and Pakistan), as well as the "Golden Triangle" (Laos, Burma, and Thailand).[37]

In Panama, General Manuel Noriega was on the CIA payroll while serving the KGB and the notorious Colombian cocaine cartels. He was the channel for the diversion of drug-trafficking profits to the support of the Contras, a particularly explosive issue at the time of Iran-Contra and the constitutional clash over control of U.S. foreign policy. Noriega's overthrow of the democratically elected government in 1985 and his continuing profiteering from narcotics that ruined the lives of American families finally forced President Bush to act, despite having been Noriega's paymaster when in charge of the CIA in the mid-1970s. In a special operation in December 1989, the American military arrested Noriega, and in 1992 he was imprisoned after a trial in the United States. In this unusual case, morality had triumphed over expediency, but the outcome did nothing to resolve the clash between conflicting missions occasioned by the prohibitionist regime.[38]

If mission corruption was one problem for the intelligence war on drugs, mission failure was another. In 1975 Otis Pike, chair of the House investigation into intelligence, had criticized the DEA for interdicting only 10 percent of the heroin being imported into the United States. Yet, DEA figures for the Reagan-Bush years and their aftermath did give some grounds for hope. For example, the number of Americans who were regular users of illicit drugs declined from 25.4 million in 1979 to 13.6 million in 1998. But in the 1990s, despite the money lavished on the DEA and other drug interdiction agencies, a whole segment of young America fell prey to the pushers of hard drugs. The number of heroin users almost doubled to 130,000 by 1998, heroin-related deaths "rocketed," and the new victims were mainly children and youths: the heroin user's average age dropped from 26.6 years old in 1990 to 17.6 years old in 1997. When President Clinton suggested he might charge the CIA with taking on international drug traffickers, Senator Daniel P. Moynihan observed that "several dozen federal agencies" were already addressing the drugs and crime problem, "none of them with notable success."[39]

The anti-drug campaign in America had long been emotional, moralistic, and subject to hyperbole. In the 1980s, the hyperbole reached a crescendo, and money was thrown at the DEA and other agencies shrewd enough to muscle in on a crusade that was fashionable and yielded political benefits to its makers. As one student of the problem observed, "The term 'underworld' could hardly be more misleading since the 'upperworld' has gained more from organized crime activity."[40] The campaign was ineffective, except as another illustration of the prowess of the American confidence man. Like other covert operations, the intelligence war against drugs may, further, have been counterproductive, diverting much needed resources from education and rehabilitation and, in being corrupted, adding to the income and motivation of the traffickers. In the end, the Holy Grail of Victory in the drug war proved to be a chimera—a point that invites comparison with the fate of the crusade against communism.

In 1987, the Intermediate-Range Nuclear Force Treaty promised an end to the Soviet-American arms race. In 1989, Soviet troops withdrew from Afghanistan, Hungary, and Mongolia. On 9 November of that year, the Berlin Wall was breached, sounding the death knell of

European communism. In December, General Secretary Mikhail Gorbachev and President George Bush met on the island of Malta and declared an end to the Cold War.

These dramatic developments inspired the "victory" claim. According to this claim, America had won the Cold War. Events unfolding to the east of the former Iron Curtain meant a triumph of democracy over totalitarianism, and of the free market over socialist planning. America had contributed significantly to this outcome, and conservatives claimed particular credit for Republican administrations. They argued that the foundations for an effective national security policy had been laid during the Eisenhower years. The triumphalists were agreed that secret intelligence, especially covert operations and the estimative underpinnings of Star Wars, had played a key role in the triumph—and never more so than in the latest incarnation of Republican excellence, the Reagan and Bush presidencies.[41]

The "victory" claim can be—and has been—challenged from several perspectives. For one thing, the biggest winners were the citizens of Russia, Poland, and other countries who had suffered under the yoke of communism. Those citizens had struggled for democracy often at great personal risk. They sometimes bridled at the suggestion that foreigners, sitting comfortably behind their desks in far-off places, had helped them. Books written by non-Americans on the fall of communism in eastern Europe do not, by and large, attribute a significant role to the United States, let alone to the CIA.[42]

Russian scholar Alexei Filitov was joined in the early 1990s by distinguished western European colleagues in claiming that Germany and Japan had won the Cold War at the expense of both the Soviets and the United States. These countries had benefited economically from being nonparticipants in the arms race. Since the fall of communism, the U.S. economy has boomed, but it could be argued that, in earlier times, the strain of arms competition forced America to give up social improvements in such areas as education and health.[43]

To focus more closely on the 1980s, it is by no means clear that the Reagan administration won the battle of wits against its Soviet counterparts. On 8 December 1995, CIA director John M. Deutch released a report on Soviet disinformation in the period 1985–1994. Moscow had deceived Washington about the nature of Soviet military dispositions, and, in an effort to match the myths, America had wasted money.

Apparently, the Soviets were trying to ruin the U.S. economy just as America was sabotaging theirs. The disinformation also presented a puffed-up image of Soviet military might.[44] Bluff, as ever, was part of Moscow's arsenal. But damaging to claims that the Star Wars stratagem succeeded is the fact that just when the CIA was being pressured to exaggerate Soviet might, the Russians were only too happy to oblige, with their intelligence service distorting the truth in precisely the same way as its U.S. counterpart.

A credible if prosaic case can be made for the view that communism ended because Europeans hated it, and that the arms race ended because Gorbachev was a sensible man who could see that it was damaging both sides.[45] The idea that the White House, Pentagon, and Langley had pursued a cunningly concealed and devastatingly effective victory strategy needs to be treated with caution—in fact, Robert Gates diplomatically claimed in his 1996 memoir that there had been "no sense of victory" in the Bush White House.

Yet, Gates refers to the outcome of the Cold War as "the greatest of American triumphs."[46] His attitude is testimony to the survival of Casey's reputation and inspirational powers. Of course, both Casey and Gates lost some face over Irangate. But it could be argued that, when he died, Casey was more in favor than Donovan, Dulles, and Hoover when they had left office. Casey's two-pronged, if inconsistent, strategy became an inheritance—according to the hype, he had battled the beast of communism and defeated it, conferring everlasting glory and appropriations-worthiness on the intelligence community. Yet, he had retasked the CIA and its intelligence siblings to combat drugs, nuclear proliferation, and other alternative "menaces" lying conveniently at hand. Victory and diversification would be potent companions in the great rhetorical carpetbag of the post–Cold War intelligence confidence man.

CHAPTER 14

The Real American Century?

University College, Oxford, 1969. Nestling in privileged proximity to All Souls, Oriel, and the jumble of other colleges making up the heart of the ancient university, the place seemed a peaceful haven in a noisy and contentious world. The young Rhodes scholar made friends, and had a good time.

But Oxford's tranquillity did not calm Bill Clinton's every worry. He had a problem that seven centuries of college tradition could do nothing to erase—he wanted out of the Vietnam War.

Clinton had secured the suspension of his 28 July induction order by promising Willard Hawkins, the Selective Service head in Arkansas, that he "would serve his country in another capacity later on."[1] However, the martial sword of Damocles still hung over his head, suspended by the thinnest of threads. How could he extricate himself from military service without paying the price, without seeming unpatriotic, without harming his career?

Enter the CIA. The *Ramparts* revelations of 1967 had indicated how the CIA fixed draft exemptions for students who were prepared to cooperate with its aims. On 9 September 1969, Bill Clinton wrote to Richard Stearns about his problem. Stearns was known as the person who had organized CIA-funded international activities on behalf of the National Student Association (NSA). Magically, Clinton's draft worries evaporated—even before President Nixon's announcement of a draft lottery on the eve of Thanksgiving 1969 and Clinton's luck in the

1 December draw, when he received a number far down the list, rendering it very unlikely he would have to serve.

For this reason, there has been speculation about what the CIA did for Clinton then and since—and about what he did for the CIA in return. Anonymous intelligence sources claimed that he was an agency "asset" at Oxford, and on the international student conference circuit. His duties might have included promoting official American policy while pretending to be an independent-minded student. He possibly informed on the people he met. Maybe the future president owed the agency a longer-term favor, too, and maybe the agency was in a position to threaten him with the dark secret from his past—namely, the precise mechanism of his avoidance of the draft.[2]

It appears more likely that the agency simply provided him with an "insurance" policy, a means of draft exemption in case he ran out of luck and was drafted. But what is really significant about all this is that Clinton appears to have had faith in the agency and its ability to fix his problem. It seems that Clinton believed—then and later—in the "can-do" image of the CIA. He was not so much hooked by the agency as sold on it.

In the 1990s, this revelation caught some people unawares. After a decade in which conservatives had championed intelligence, it might have seemed likely that a former critic of the Vietnam War would abandon the CIA to its enemies. But, in reality, the Right was a relatively new supporter of the agency. Bill Clinton fit into the older tradition of liberal promotion of and reliance on the CIA.

However, at the beginning of his term, Clinton, like other presidents before him, was preoccupied with domestic policy. His first director of central intelligence, R. James Woolsey (1993–1995), reputedly experienced difficulties in gaining access to the chief executive—when a small aircraft crashed onto the White House lawn in 1994, it was said to be "Woolsey trying to get an appointment." But then, again like so many of his predecessors, Clinton found that Congress would not enact his grand domestic plan, or at least would approve only a watered down version of it. With an eye to his historical reputation, he devoted more attention to foreign policy. He persuaded Woolsey's successor, John M. Deutch, to serve at the helm of the CIA (1995–1997) with a promise of a place in the cabinet. The only other DCI to achieve this status had been William Casey. Now, *Washington Post* journalist Mary McGrory suggested that Clinton "dares not lift a finger against the spooks. He is too insecure about national security matters." Her assumption was that Clinton would instinctively curb the intelligence people, if only he dared. To the contrary, however, the president had no innate hostility toward the intelligence establishment and, as time passed, came to support it in a more active manner. Increasingly rocked by scandals culminating in his impeachment and trial in 1998–1999, Clinton needed the CIA to help him achieve something. For its part, a CIA similarly under siege needed the president, and received that support.[3]

Thus, the recent history of the intelligence community can be seen to have been part of a longer-term continuum. In an article that proved to be prophetic about the rise of U.S. power and influence, the publishing mogul Henry Luce had in 1941 proclaimed the "American Century." During the Cold War, Luce used his resources to promote that dream and to support its cast of actors, including the CIA. The clandestine promotion of power seemed to go hand in hand with the endless march of American prosperity. Ironically, however, the collapse of communism, even as it vindicated the old equation, appeared to render it obsolete. Even in the midst of "victory" euphoria, a faltering economy suggested that America had been weakened by the long struggle against the Soviets. Dangerous economic rivals like Germany and Japan had emerged, taking advantage of the economic giant's indisposition. Meanwhile, there were strident calls for the dissolution of the CIA.

But the prophets of doom were to be disappointed. Freed of Cold War worries and burdens, America boomed once again. Cynics had quipped that the American Century had finished early, but now it could be imagined that the Real American Century was only just beginning. A review of the Clinton years shows that, by the time of the advent of the George W. Bush administration in 2001, Casey's vision for the CIA had triumphed—if only after a fight.

In the wake of the Cold War, there took place a debate on the future of secret intelligence. The CIA, as the standard-bearer of the intelligence community, came under close scrutiny. The debaters divided into opponents of the CIA, supporters of the agency, and moderates who sought a compromise. These contending camps had already staked out their ground during the Bush presidency, and the debate between them rumbled on through President Clinton's second term.[4]

At first, the critics, including some who wanted to abolish the CIA outright, seemed to hold the advantage. Their prominence perhaps owed something to the outbreak of Russo-American harmony, which made it seem less unpatriotic to attack the national security bureaucracy. Nobody doubted that the collapse of communism in Europe was final, so it seemed an especially apt moment to call for the abolition of the CIA. As Casey had foreseen in advocating task diversification, the agency seemed to have lost its role. The fact that Casey was no longer around to make his case in person further strengthened the hand of the critics—and no reincarnation of the Donovan/Dulles/Casey type of leader emerged in the 1990s. At the end of several decades of great military and intelligence expenditure, it seemed reasonable to seek a "peace dividend"—money could be spent on other things, such as improved health care services (Hillary Clinton's ambition), or taxes could be reduced (the conservatives' ambition). For such reasons as these, the attack on the intelligence community was more serious than the Iran-Contra criticisms and was the CIA's most challenging crisis since the difficult days of the 1975 intelligence flap.

The reinvigorated critics came from a variety of backgrounds— intelligence, journalism, the military, academia, as well as politics. The criticism could be weighty. For example, in 1997 former President Ford claimed the 1960s CIA had been "180 degrees wrong" in advising that the Soviet Union would overtake the United States economically and militarily within ten years. Just as demoralizing were doubts that came from within, especially right at the beginning of the debate. Vincent Cannistraro was one such doubter. Cannistraro had served as chief of counterterrorism operations for the CIA and as director of intelligence programs at the National Security Council. In 1991 he wondered, "Is the CIA relevant in the contemporary world?" Journalists were even less respectful. During the 1991 hearings into Robert Gates's nomination as DCI, Mary McGrory reflected widespread suspicions that the CIA official had not been candid about his role in the Iran-Contra affair. He was, she wrote, "secretive, sycophantic, loyal and incurious."[5]

Both Cannistraro and McGrory supported Senator Daniel P. Moynihan's intelligence-reform campaign. A distinguished scholar and diplomat, Moynihan had represented New York in the Senate as a Democrat since 1977, and had served for eight years on the Senate Intelligence Committee. Radical and unpredictable yet respected, he had opposed aid to the Contras and U.S. participation in the Gulf War of 1990–1991. He wanted to abolish the CIA, and, in the interim, to lift the veil of secrecy and at least to publish the agency's budget. Moynihan was not only an ardent advocate of open government but a critic of the CIA's performance. He was scornful, for example, of the agency's contention in the 1980s that per capita income in communist East Germany was higher than that in democratic West Germany. He thought the agency had overestimated the size of the Soviet economy by 300 percent. Now that *glasnost* (openness) prevailed in Russia, there was no need for a secret organization to penetrate its recesses. In the final years of the Bush presidency and the Clinton administration, Moynihan campaigned for the foreign intelligence functions of the CIA to be transferred to the State Department.[6]

Moynihan's anti-secrecy campaign, which continued to the end of the century, was a direct challenge to the power of the confidence man, who had habitually sheltered behind the veil of secrecy so vital to the promotion of false alarms and invented menaces. In January 1993, he changed the angle of his attack, calling for a bipartisan inquiry into the problem of government secrecy. He chaired the Commission on Protecting and Reducing Government Secrecy, established by Congress the following year. The commission took evidence from the CIA, FBI, and ninety-four other organizations and, in March 1997, recommended the closer guarding of a reduced number of essential national security secrets and the declassification of vast amounts of less vital documents. Hoping to achieve a result before his retirement from the Senate in 2001, Moynihan pressed on with this campaign. The release of more information, he argued, would demystify the spooks, making them seem less sinister. He gave as an example the Warren Commission's failure to release enough information on the assassination of President Kennedy, as a result of which three-fourths of Americans still believed there had been a "conspiracy involving the CIA"—indeed, the "Grassy Knoll continues to cut a wide path across our national consciousness." With the support of some prominent historians, Moynihan pressed, in the teeth of opposition from the intelligence agencies, for a law requiring the mandatory declassification of all but the most sensitive materials that were more than twenty-five years old. Failing in that goal, he continued to campaign for the expedition of open government. His very presence on the Hill hampered the efforts of those who continued to promote the twin cults of secrecy and intelligence.[7]

Moynihan's moderation of his campaign over the years reflected a more widespread retreat from absolutism. Moral objections to under-cover work continued but were less pervasive than a more pragmatic belief that things would have to change and that institutions would need to adapt. In the early stages of the debate, Harvard's Ernest May had likened CIA headquarters in Langley, Virginia, and the even more monumental federal office buildings across the Potomac to those archi-tectural relics of past imperial might that are found in European capi-tals: "Before long, if not already, Washington, D.C., may also seem a capital where form and function are not in kilter."[8]

The challenge, then, was not to demolish the structure, but to change its form. Attacks on the CIA typically focused neither on its immorality nor on its right to exist, but on its alleged ineffectiveness. They were no less savage for that. Because of the second oldest profes-sion's secret nature, there tends to be a time lag between its acts of alleged incompetence and news stories about them. Thus, much of the criticism of the agency's involvement in Nicaragua, its alleged twisting of Soviet estimates, its failure to predict the rise, actions, and fall of Gorbachev, and its involvement in international drug trafficking became headline news just when people were asking why so much money was being spent on intelligence now that the Cold War was over.

As if that were not enough, intelligence failings in the Gulf War came in for a roasting. General H. Norman Schwarzkopf, America's commander of the United Nations forces in the Gulf War, complained in a joint hearing of the House and Senate Armed Services Committees on 12 June 1991 about the poor quality of intelligence in the war. In the effort to expel Iraq from occupied Kuwait, the DIA and other intel-ligence agencies had been coordinated by the CIA; Schwarzkopf com-plained that the resultant interpretation of data from satellite recon-naissance had been "caveated, footnoted and watered down" to such a degree as to make it almost useless. Gulf War controversy, like earlier scandals, was destined to simmer in the pot. In the course of the war, American troops blew up ammunition depots not knowing that they had contained chemical weapons. When it later emerged that the CIA had known about the chemicals but not warned the soldiers about the danger, the story produced a reaction from Gen. Colin L. Powell, who had been chairman of the Joint Chiefs of Staff at the time: "If I was still in office, I would be raping and pillaging throughout the intelligence and operational community to get to the bottom of this."[9]

The post–Cold War attack on the intelligence community took its toll. In 1992, the FBI shifted 300 agents from counterespionage work to the investigation of domestic crimes of violence. As things turned out, this was premature: the number of people arrested for espionage in the United States increased in the following few years, and the FBI soon resumed its hiring of counterspies. But, at the time, the move was symptomatic of concern over the apparent end of the decades-long Cold War gravy train. Another symptom was a new outbreak of intelligence "turf wars." Both the DIA and the FBI targeted the CIA and tried to invade its former territory, in this way protecting the size of their domain at the expense of a rival. The old distinction—the CIA doing foreign work and the FBI domestic work—began to blur. In 1996, for example, FBI director Louis J. Freeh (1993–2001) requested money to establish ten overseas offices, and Congress gave him enough for five.[10]

The overall intelligence budget declined in the aftermath of the Cold War. An accidental disclosure in 1994 confirmed the accuracy of deductions made by a voluntary watchdog, the Federation of American Scientists. The total amount was $26.7 billion, with most of it going to high-technology Pentagon agencies like the DIA, NSA, National Reconnaissance Office, and the military, and about $4 billion to the CIA. Critics of the intelligence community could argue that the intelligence budget was distinctly generous compared with expenditures in the Carter years, and that a comparison with the expansionist Reagan-Bush presidencies was inappropriate: CIA Inspector General Frederick P. Hitz thought that "on the personnel front," Casey had "vastly increased the numbers, perhaps by as much as 33 percent, but, in too many cases, at the expense of quality." Nevertheless, the decline from $30 billion in 1989–1991 was depressing for those involved. The further decrease to $26.6 billion in 1997 made people even more nervous—certainly in "real dollar" terms the budget was gently declining at a time when developments in information technology had caused the cost of espionage to spiral upward.[11]

CIA director James Woolsey contributed to internal demoralization.

He subscribed to Casey's view that America had lost one enemy only to gain many: "We live now in a jungle filled with a bewildering variety of poisonous snakes." But his shrill attempts to sell the CIA alienated potential supporters in the Senate. Necessary though the reform may have been, CIA morale dropped further when Woolsey effected, in 1993–1994, a 24 percent reduction in agency personnel. Working for the CIA had become an insecure and unattractive option. Even the job of leading the CIA had lost its charm—there were no fewer than five directors between 1991 and 1997.[12]

Yet, although no agency had produced a "super-spinner" of Casey's caliber to defend the intelligence community in the 1990s, there were plenty of people around who had been versed in the Casey school of discourse. Intelligence veterans had always been available to put the CIA in a better light, and they stepped forward once again when the end of the Cold War threatened their erstwhile colleagues with redundancy. Former DCIs Richard Helms and James Schlesinger attacked the post–Iran-Contra proposal for an independent CIA inspector general. In a 1990 article in the journal *Foreign Affairs*, CIA veteran George Carver, Jr., argued against cuts. The intelligence budget, he estimated, constituted only about 8 percent of the $300 billion spent on defense in 1990. Stating that George Washington had spent 12 percent of the entire federal budget on intelligence in 1792, he concluded that the 1990 intelligence budget was "an enormous bargain indeed."[13]

Reflecting on the CIA's ability to resist serious change, Senator Moynihan suggested it had become part of an institutional "iron triangle," as unassailable as its diplomatic and military partners. He described some of the internal resources at the agency's disposal. The agency had always benefited from legislative counsel, but in 1966 it set up a special office for that purpose, then increased its personnel to thirty-two during the seventies flap, and by the 1990s had a staff of forty-five attached to its Office of Congressional Affairs.[14]

The mid-seventies intelligence flap had inspired the development of further lobbying and propaganda assets. The Association of Retired Intelligence Officers attracted a substantial membership, lobbied Congress, engaged in publicity, and inspired the formation of other groups with similar aims. And, as Moynihan pointed out, there was also an official organism handling publicity. This was the CIA's Center for the Study of Intelligence. The agency had since its earliest days engaged in-house historians, who had produced many detailed studies. Almost all this research had remained classified, but now the new center began to reach out to the public by publishing some studies, and by creating a host of other publicity vehicles, such as newsletters and conferences. These endeavors intensified in the 1990s. Perhaps of two minds—he favored open discussion, yet he suspected the center of creating and disseminating pro-CIA propaganda—Moynihan saved his barbs for a comment on the dichotomy between CIA erudition and CIA mistakes concerning practical matters. But it could be argued that by making available selected information, the center helped calm fears about secrecy in government.[15]

Diversification was ever the watchword of those who defended the intelligence bureaucracy or called for its expansion. Carver thought that many of America's future challenges had an intelligence dimension, and that this would "dramatically increase" the need for services of the type supplied by the CIA and its partners, a need "that must be met at whatever cost." He listed terrorism, economic espionage, environmental treaty monitoring, narcotics trafficking, and immigration violations as specific future problems requiring the intelligence community's attention.[16] A mission statement issued in the mid-nineties by the CIA's current staff similarly identified a new range of special targets. Called "A New Direction, A New Future," it identified China and Russia as problem nations, but it also called for intelligence resources to be concentrated on "rogue" states like North Korea, Iran, and Iraq, and on transnational threats such as terrorism and nuclear proliferation.[17]

Between those who wanted to abolish or severely diminish the CIA and those who wanted no change or expansion lay the moderates. Prominent among them was Senator David L. Boren, to date the longest-serving chair of the Senate Select Committee on Intelligence (1987–1993). Although the abolitionist McGrory accused him of being "starry eyed" about the CIA, Boren could be said to have represented, in some ways, an embryonic consensus. Like the promoters of intelligence, he spoke of diversification. However, there was a hint of realism in his observation that nonideological regional conflicts like that in the Middle East showed "no signs of abating." In other words, these conflicts had not magically materialized to justify indefinite new leases on life for the CIA but had been there all along. Boren wanted an end to promotional intelligence hype. New problems did not justify new resources, he argued. Existing resources previously devoted to the threat from Moscow could be diverted to new purposes.[18]

In an article for *Foreign Affairs* in 1992, Boren attacked both the expansionists and the abolitionists. Those who were nostalgic for the practices of the Cold War would have to be resisted if the CIA were not to become an "expensive and irrelevant dinosaur." But Moynihan was wrong to advocate the abolition of the CIA and the transfer of its intelligence function to the Department of State, because, in the interest of objective assessment, it was vitally important to separate the policy and intelligence functions. Boren did not strike a consensual chord with all his proposals. For example, in 1993 he teamed up with his fellow Oklahoma Democrat Dave McCurdy, chair of the House Permanent Select Committee on Intelligence, to introduce legislation creating a new intelligence "czar," an idea that won gathering support for a couple of years but then fell victim to the stony resistance that had always greeted such proposals in the past.[19] However, Boren had potentially identified a middle way, giving America a varied menu from which to choose.

Boren, moreover, struck an appealing note when he stressed that the new CIA would have to act in accordance with the "fundamental values of the American people," and with proper congressional oversight. A new era of accountability did seem to be dawning. For example, in 1993, 1,512 meetings took place between the CIA's legislative liaison staff and members of Congress, a 29 percent increase over the previous year. There seemed grounds for optimism among those who believed that reform would triumph at the expense of abolition and expansion.[20]

As America is a democracy, the future of secret intelligence depended in good measure on wider opinion. Such opinion was informed by debates in Congress and among public officials, but drew also on other sources. Take, for example, Tom Clancy, a popular writer whose novels—and the movies derived from them—both influenced and reflected public taste. During the Reagan presidency, Clancy published *The Hunt for Red October* (1984), a Cold War submarine thriller that attained the number three spot on the *New York Times* best-seller list and inspired a well-received movie. But in 1990, Clancy's *Clear and Present Danger* (1989) achieved the number one position, establishing itself as the best-selling novel published in the entire decade of the 1980s. It showed an awareness of Reagan-Bush fallibilities, such as a certain weakness in the office of the national security adviser for the "glamour of field ops. It was known in the trade as the *Mission: Impossible* Syndrome. Even professionals could confuse a TV drama with reality."[21] The novel was about the CIA's anti-narcotics operations in Colombia, and thus appealed to a nation deeply worried about the drug problem. At the same time, in *Clear and Present Danger* Clancy referred to the Cold War only to achieve ambiance, and effectively in the past tense. He wrote about post–Cold War intelligence diversification into major anti-drug operations in a manner that suggests the American people had come to terms with such changes at a relatively early stage.

In the Clinton administration, public opinion was affected by an event that had its origins in some sinister disappearances midway through the Reagan presidency. In all, thirty-six American and allied secret agents were lost. Gradually, it emerged that ten CIA spies had been executed. All of them had been agents "in place," that is, locally recruited people who had stayed in post and transmitted information to their U.S. controllers. Three had been in the GRU, or Soviet military intelligence, and six in the KGB, the communist political intelligence organization. The tenth, Adolf G. Tolkachev, executed on 24 September 1986, had been a Soviet defense researcher in Moscow.

Although the full extent of all this damage was unknown even inside the CIA, the pattern of betrayal suggested early on that something was amiss, and strongly indicated that there was a "mole," or double agent, inside the CIA. The CIA's chief of counterintelligence, Gus Hathaway, appointed a four-person team to investigate, under the direction of Jeanne Vertefeuille. However, although she pursued her task diligently and was in at the kill at the very end, for years Vertefeuille received few resources and even less cooperation. Her colleagues' sluggish responses stemmed from human factors. Some remembered the long and futile search for a mole conducted in an earlier era by counterintelligence chief James Jesus Angleton—they scented similar paranoia in the latest quest. Another problem, later articulated by DCI Woolsey, was that the Directorate of Operations (which ran foreign espionage) was run as "a fraternity . . . a white male one."[22]

On 22 February 1994, the FBI arrested a senior CIA official and charged him with betraying CIA agent names and other secrets to the

KGB and to its successor, the Russian Intelligence Service. His name was Aldrich Hazen Ames, and he had been chief of the CIA's Soviet counterintelligence branch when the agent names were betrayed in the mid-1980s. With the wisdom of hindsight, those who studied Ames's profile wondered how his colleagues could possibly have missed the signs that he was the traitor. His father had also been a career CIA officer, and had worked with Angleton in that officer's legendary search for a nonexistent mole: it was almost as if Ames, out of subliminal filial duty, had given material form to a self-fulfilling prophesy. Ames was an alcoholic, a condition especially at odds with reliable intelligence work—in fact, his career did eventually stall and, at the time of his arrest, he was working in the agency's anti-narcotics division. Rosario, Ames's second wife and his accomplice toward the end of his period of treason, had a spending habit. The couple indulged this habit to an extent that was incompatible with Ames's final salary of $69,800—it was remotely possible that they could have afforded the cash purchase of their $540,000 house in Arlington, but not while spending $50,000 per annum on credit cards.[23]

Why did Ames betray his colleagues and his country? His attempts to explain that he was leveling the playing field between East and West or striking a blow for world peace were feeble and unconvincing. Clearly he was not driven by ideological imperatives—here, he was very different from members of England's notorious Cambridge spy ring in the 1930s, or some of the U.S. traitors of the 1940s and 1950s, whose allegiance to Moscow sprang from the fact that they were committed communists. Psychological considerations undoubtedly played their part. And perhaps in the Margaret Thatcher–Ronald Reagan era, assertions that only competitive individualism mattered, and that society effectively did not exist rendered loyalty to the nation-state anachronistic. Harvard sociologist Robert Putnam argues that capitalism is not at the root of post-1960s civic disengagement: America has been capitalistic for a long time, and "A constant can't explain a variable." But together with other causes of social disintegration, *individualistic* materialism of the Adam Smith–Chicago School variety seems to have played a role in the betrayals by Ames and others in recent years. Like H. O. Yardley, in whose treason alcohol and psychology also played a role, Ames was a spy who knew no side except that dictated by the dollar, yen, or ruble. In this sense, it might be argued that the motive of the American spy-traitor mirrors that of the nonbetraying spy or private detective, who played on the fears of his clients to win more contracts or appropriations. In recent times money has played a determining role, not just in the Ames case but in a string of other betrayals stretching from the navy's John Walker in 1985 to the FBI's Robert Hanssen, who, by the time of his arrest in 2001, had received $600,000 in cash and diamonds from his masters in Moscow and a promise of $800,000 more. Just as in the world of the confidence man, profit can and not infrequently does take precedence over loyalty.[24]

The Ames affair shocked America and its allies. A British newspaper, the *Independent,* reported it to be "one of the most damaging spy scandals to hit the United States." David Wise, a seasoned and respected reporter on intelligence affairs, judged Ames to have been the CIA's "most damaging mole" ever, and the case to be evidence that the agency was "a tired bureaucracy, living in the past." The House Intelligence Committee agreed that the affair was "the most serious operational disaster" to have befallen the CIA. Estimates of the extent of the damage were disturbing. Along with the tragic fate of agents who had trusted the United States, there was the matter of the loss of almost all the CIA's significant human intelligence assets in Russia. It became apparent that in the 1980s, at precisely the time when the CIA was being upheld as an effective thorn in the side of world communism, literally hundreds of its operations had been betrayed to the Soviet Union. Even more disturbing was the realization that at a time when the Reagan administration had believed it was outwitting the Soviet Union, Moscow had been privy to American secrets and had been running an effective disinformation program, as a result of which the CIA gullibly forwarded thirty-five "tainted" reports to the White House and Pentagon.[25]

The Ames affair had a devastating effect on a CIA already reeling from the effects of the end of the Cold War and years of budgetary and personnel cuts: the *New York Times* journalist Tim Weiner described CIA morale at the end of the year as "lower than Death Valley."[26] Not the least worrying dimension of the affair were the facts that the CIA's rival, the FBI, had played a conspicuous role in the operation set up in May 1993 to ensnare Ames, and that the agency had, prior to that date, withheld from the FBI information that might have led to an earlier arrest. When the CIA becomes suspicious, its instinct is to let the suspect run, hoping he or she will calumnify others and open useful intelligence leads; the FBI, on the other hand, has a law enforcement ethos and is interested in making arrests—indeed, it had to make the Ames arrest because the CIA does not have the authority to perform that domestic function. The CIA's persistent Jeanne Vertefeuille had never given up, and she debriefed Ames after his arrest. Nevertheless, in terms of public perception, the FBI emerged from the Ames affair looking better than the CIA, a state of affairs that lasted until the discovery, in 2001, that the bureau had itself been harboring a double agent.

On 28 December 1994, DCI Woolsey announced his resignation, becoming "the eleventh victim of Aldrich Ames."[27] His departure reflected and also enhanced a gloomy view of the impact of the great betrayal. Another pessimist was CIA Inspector General Frederick P. Hitz, who issued a critical report on the Ames affair. Interviewed for this book in 1998, he still saw its impact as catastrophic. Asked whether the CIA had survived the ending of the Cold War, he gave a qualified answer: "Not exactly. Just because the CIA has not been abolished, that does not mean it has 'survived.' There is a reluctance, in America, to abolish agencies. Rather, they are left to wither on the vine. The CIA is still there, but it no longer has the influence it once had."[28]

The Ames debacle finally prompted President Clinton to intervene in the intelligence debate. Favorably inclined toward the CIA though he may have been, he was already worried by its inconsistent performance. In his administration's first foreign policy challenge, he authorized an American peacekeeping intervention in Somalia, a nation that was falling prey to tribal warfare. But the intelligence community's inability to establish the location of the tribal leader Gen. Muhammad Farah Aideed contributed to an unsatisfactory U.S. performance. After Ames, the president knew something had to be done, and decided on an inquiry. As in the case of earlier probes by Nicholas Katzenbach, Nelson Rockefeller, and John Tower, Clinton's aim may have been preemption and procrastination. However, the proposal that there should be a presidential commission on intelligence was robust enough to alarm Senator John Warner. The CIA's Langley headquarters employed a substantial number of people and was located in the Virginian Republican's constituency. Warner was a senior member of the Senate intelligence committee and wanted to scotch any possibility of a commission that would recommend the CIA's abolition and the loss of thousands of jobs in Fairfax County.[29]

The Commission on the Roles and Capabilities of the United States Intelligence Community was, in any event, a compromise—a joint inquiry by the executive and Congress. Clinton put Les Aspin in charge of it. Aspin had been a Robert McNamara "whiz kid," had both liberal and conservative attributes (he had opposed the Vietnam War but supported the Contras), and was, by common consent, a leading authority on defense. He had had to resign, recently, from his post as secretary of defense because of criticism of his handling of the Somalia crisis, and because of opposition to his advocacy of gay and women's rights in the armed forces. Nevertheless, he was greeted as an appropriate choice to head the biggest inquiry into the intelligence community for twenty years. On May 1995, three months into the inquiry, Aspin died suddenly of a massive stroke. He was replaced by President Carter's secretary of defense, Harold Brown. Thus, it seemed reasonable to expect that the Aspin-Brown commission would chart a firm course for the future of the intelligence community.[30]

The Aspin-Brown commission reported in March 1996. It recommended that the size of the intelligence community should be reduced, that coordination should be improved between the producers and consumers of intelligence as well as between the several agencies engaged in high-technology information gathering, that the job of DCI should be made more secure and apolitical through the introduction of a six-year term, and that, in the interest of greater openness and accountability, the intelligence budget should be publicly disclosed. The commission recommended, however, that the CIA should continue to function as an independent agency and should be given an enhanced coordinating role with increased authority over the intelligence branches of other agencies—but without spawning an intelligence "czar." The *New York Times* welcomed these proposals and carried sanguine reports anticipating personnel cuts. Yet, its editorial complained that the "anodyne" report "lacked imagination and courage" and contained "no bold ideas for overhauling the government's espionage empire." Loch Johnson, a veteran member and observer of governmental intelligence inquiries, concluded that the commission's report was timid in that it "largely met Warner's objective."[31]

On one level, the Aspin-Brown report could be seen as a victory for the moderates in the post–Cold War intelligence debate. On the other hand, it is significant that the intelligence-community advocates had managed to change the question being asked, from "How can we curb the CIA or even abolish the agency?" to "How can we make the CIA and the rest of the intelligence community more effective?"

Even in the hour of its affliction, the CIA was bullish. For example, DCI John Deutch in July 1995 went a little further than usual in announcing the CIA's plans for diversification. The agency would hunt down international criminals, terrorists, and drug traffickers and would, in addition, coordinate multi-source intelligence to inform U.S. military operations. A former undersecretary of defense, Deutch had in mind both the Gulf War and recent problems with the U.S. contribution to the peacekeeping forces in Bosnia, where micro-nationalism had resulted in what was euphemistically called "ethnic cleansing" but was in reality genocide, and where, in the home of Balkanization, it took a massive learning effort to understand what was going on and who should be forcibly restrained. Expanding on the CIA's new military intentions, Deutch explained that "a singular purpose of this effort is to [ensure] that we provide future military commanders with dominant battlefield awareness."[32] This mission statement reflected the Aspin-Brown commission's recommendation for better coordination, as well as the perception that America, more than ever the world's policeman, would continue to be involved in local small-scale wars needing good battlefield intelligence.

However, the statement also laid down the gauntlet to one of the CIA's oldest and most dangerous turf rivals, the U.S. military. Deutch, in fact, had little choice but to react to the diversification plans of the DIA. Testifying to the Senate Armed Services Committee in January, DIA director Lt. Gen. James R. Clapper, Jr., said his intelligence analysts did not just work on traditional targeting and order of battle problems. They now reported on infrastructure and geography in Rwanda, tuberculosis and clan structure in Somalia, and so forth.[33]

The CIA preservationists and expansionists were determined not to be beaten. In fact, they came out fighting. One of the most prestigious among a cluster of nongovernmental inquiries into intelligence was that by a Council on Foreign Relations panel that included Brent Scowcroft, national security adviser in the Ford and Bush administrations. Its report positively bristled with aggressive intelligence salesmanship. Its compiler, Richard N. Haass, had also served on the NSC under Bush. In an article for the press, he called for the resumption of assassinations and coups d'état as instruments of U.S. policy, and the empowering of the CIA to use the Peace Corps as cover for its agents—a practice previously resisted.[34]

Intelligence affairs can be complex and dull; public debate therefore tended to focus on simple, even crude emblems. One of these was the idea of an intelligence "czar," the notion that one, all-powerful official would be able to whip the intelligence community into shape, eliminating duplication and wasteful expenditure, coordinating the overall effort, and putting an end to turf wars. The super-DCI would not necessarily be the director of the CIA—indeed, later the Department of Defense bid for a "fusion center" that would coordinate intelligence and operations under its own control, with the CIA as an ancillary inferior. But, in the Clinton administration, it continued to be more widely assumed that the CIA would house any super-mechanism. In April 1996, the Senate went further than the Aspin-Brown commission when it declared itself in favor of a DCI/CIA director who would control the entire intelligence budget, most of which had been administered from the Pentagon. In May, the House also demanded a more powerful DCI, though it refused to support proposals for a merger of CIA and Pentagon components into a National Imagery and Mapping Agency.[35]

In reality, the idea of an all-powerful intelligence chief was no more than a pious wish. It had been mooted over many decades, and as often resisted—because of its presumed threat to civil liberties, and because it ran afoul of the very turf allegiances it sought to eliminate. Once again, in the mid-nineties, the intelligence super-boss failed to materialize. However, active discussion of the notion was another indication of the bullish intelligence spirit that prevailed despite the Ames affair.

If "intelligence czar" was one emblem, "Venona" was another. Venona was an intelligence imbroglio that lived, died, then lived again as a political issue when disclosed many years later. Rumors about it had circulated since 1981. On 11 July 1995, the CIA officially confirmed the existence of the program at a public ceremony at its Langley headquarters conducted jointly with the NSA and FBI, and with Senator Moynihan in attendance. Then, in summer 1996, the agencies ran a full-blown conference to publicize Venona.[36]

"Venona" was a codeword stamped on certain documents in the 1940s in order to limit access to information about a U.S. cryptanalytic breakthrough. Codebreakers at the NSA's institutional precursors had broken certain Soviet codes, a circumstance that enabled an FBI agent, Robert J. Lamphere, to track down individuals in the United States who were spying for the Soviet Union. The information was fairly extensive, 2,900 documents in all, amounting to 5,000 pages of text. A number of people were arrested, tried, and convicted on espionage charges, including British atomic scientist and spy Klaus Fuchs and Americans Judith Coplon, Harry Gold, and, most infamously, Julius and Ethel Rosenberg, who were convicted of the theft of nuclear secrets and executed in 1953.[37]

While Venona was operationally significant in the 1940s, for many years it was not a political issue. This was because its existence was a tightly kept secret. While Moynihan may have been mistaken in his charge that even President Truman had been kept in the dark about the program, it is certain that very few officials were in the know, and many years passed before it was acknowledged publicly. One effect of this delay was that the spy prosecutions of the Cold War years were less convincing and, perhaps, less effective than they might have been, as, for fear of compromising its effectiveness, the Venona evidence was not used in court. This had the further effect of hiding from the public the degree to which the Communist Party of the United States of America had been involved in espionage. Like its antecedent, the Industrial Workers of the World, it had often been *accused* of being under foreign control. The difference in this case was that it *was* controlled from abroad, but definitive proof of that fact was not made available for years.[38]

The operational reasons for keeping Venona secret after the mid-1950s are not entirely convincing, as the Soviets would have known about it by then. Soviet spy Kim Philby, courteously shown around Arlington Hall when he was working for British intelligence, would already have told the Russians, and they changed their encryption methods, ending Venona's utility. Possibly, an FBI memorandum drafted in 1956 and released in 1999 hints at a further reason for nondisclosure. Its

author, senior FBI man Alan H. Belmont, pointed to problems in interpretation, transcription, and accuracy that, in his view, rendered the
Venona decrypts unacceptable as evidence in court. As Venona release
would not have assisted the FBI in its prosecutorial role, Lamphere—
who left the bureau in 1955 to pursue a humdrum career in insurance—
had to wait until 1986 for the story of his triumph to be told in a book
that even then did not specifically mention Venona. Inertia combined
with the culture of secrecy ensured this long delay in publicizing what
had been, in the 1940s, a notable counterintelligence success.[39]

By the 1990s, the need to keep Venona secret seemed less urgent.
Glasnost played its part, and not only by inspiring a worldwide campaign for open government. When the USSR collapsed in December
1991, the new government of Boris Yeltsin seized the records of the
Communist Party of the Soviet Union, which, for a tantalizingly brief
spell, were opened to historians. A pair of American researchers, John
Haynes and Harvey Klehr, traveled to Moscow and came across the
Russian end of the documentation on the recruitment of American
spies. The evidence prompted them, in light of what they already suspected, to seek confirmation of America's ability to read the traffic.
These two scholars began an extensive program of publication.[40]

By 1996, Venona had escaped into the public realm and was a
sensational issue that inflamed one of the Cold War's rawest nerves.
Liberals and civil libertarians who had long defended the innocence of
the Rosenbergs and others were rocked back on their heels. Here, in
the Venona files, was laid bare the story of Soviet espionage and of U.S.
communists' treason in all its perfidiousness. No matter that Moscow
did not think highly of its U.S. operation: Soviet operatives complained
in a 1951 memorandum of their "lack of agents in the State Department, intelligence service, counterintelligence service and the other
most important U.S. government institutions." Despite such evidence,
Venona had become a potent "counterrevisionist" symbol in politics, a
reminder of the past excellence of American espionage and an encouragement to those who would once again lift aloft the torch of intelligence expansion.[41]

On the other side of the debate, keepers of the liberal flame perceived in the spate of Venona publications a well-financed Right-wing
conspiracy. The Ames case and a cluster of lesser ones seemed to indicate that the root cause of treason against the American capitalist

state had been the very materialism and greed engendered by the market economy. Venona was a timely reminder that ideologically motivated treason had once been a potent threat to national security. But Haynes and Klehr offered a more mundane yet quite persuasive explanation of the government's decision to release the Venona materials: it could not have been "lost on senior security officials that Senator Moynihan hoped to persuade the Congress to support a bill mandating a drastic reduction in government secrecy. If government officials refused to voluntarily lift the secrecy on a project involving Soviet cables that were more than forty years old, they would appear intransigent and unreasonable and would risk having Congress mandate a more sweeping reduction in secrecy." Moynihan, the advocate of open government, could only applaud the Venona releases, and he accordingly attended the events publicizing them. But by celebrating the achievement of one of his cherished reforms, he undermined another. For his endorsement of the Venona release helped publicize a past intelligence triumph, and that publicity undermined the prospects for future intelligence curtailment.[42]

The question of whether the intelligence budget should be published was another emblematic issue, and again inspired preemptive tactics from the Clinton administration. On 3 October 1993, President Clinton had issued an executive order requiring all federal agencies to end their routine obstruction of requests they received under the terms of the Freedom of Information Act. But the White House, exempt from the new requirement, did not set a good example and voluntarily release information. In his first year in office, Clinton's administration stamped "secret" on 60,000 more documents than had been so stamped in Bush's final year in office. Steven Aftergood, director of the American Federation of Scientists government secrecy project, protested that "unless you are a Russian spy, there is more and more information becoming inaccessible." Although former DCI Robert Gates and the U.S. Senate of 1991–93 had been in favor of disclosure of the intelligence budget, Woolsey and the administration were not. The sticking point was not the bottom-line figure itself, which had already been leaked and did not really provide a clue to what was going on in operational terms. For Woolsey and his supporters, it was a point of principle: if you conceded one point, the floodgates would open. Woolsey seemed ready to make concessions on historical documents. He repeated Gates's promise to declassify records on past CIA operations in Indonesia and Guyana. But it turned out that these had already been destroyed, and Woolsey showed no sign of departing from his abrasive defense of current budgetary secrecy.[43]

When Deutch took over as DCI in 1995, he declared himself "in favor of as much declassification and as much openness as possible." Tim Weiner of the *New York Times* described it as a "remark never heard from any of the agency's 16 previous directors." But historians who wanted access to intelligence records to help them supply the "missing dimension" in the scholarly record of foreign affairs remained unimpressed. Staff from the CIA's history office met with representatives appointed by the historical profession, but problems persisted. For example, the agency would release certain documents, but without citations. As record descriptions remained classified, it was impossible to tell whether the released documents were representative or a means of disseminating disinformation by selection. After working with the CIA's Historical Review Panel from 1990 to 1996, George C. Herring wrote: "The Agency had done such a brilliant public relations snow job, ... that in numerous conversations with people in and outside academia I was frequently told how the CIA was moving toward openness, a carefully nurtured myth that was not at all easy for me to dispel."[44]

Despite his soothing statements about open government, Deutch never did publicly announce the intelligence community's budget. In October 1997, it fell to his successor, George J. Tenet (1997–), to confirm the figure of $26.6 billion. Steven Aftergood had filed a suit under the terms of the Freedom of Information Act, and, to resist official confirmation of a fact already known, Tenet would have had to risk ridicule by testifying under oath that disclosure would damage national security. Under these circumstances, President Clinton authorized disclosure. Tenet said it did "not jeopardize" national security, and "serves to inform the American people." Although Tenet hinted that the disclosure would not necessarily set a precedent, in 1998 he again divulged the amount, $26.7 billion, this time under no pressure, and House Speaker Newt Gingrich (Rep., Georgia) was able to demand openly that a further $260 million be added to the appropriation request.[45]

Tenet's appointment to head the intelligence community brought to an end, at least for a few years, the quest for a DCI able to survive politically and withstand the abuse consistently aimed at the director of the CIA. A former staff director for the Senate Select Committee on Intelligence, he showed himself to be an adroit Washington insider when, newly installed as DCI in July 1997, he appointed a blend of Cold War espionage veterans and former White House and congressional staffers to assist him at the agency. He may have been helped, too, by public sentiment that it was time to end what had been seen as brutal partisan attacks on Clinton's CIA: the president's first choice to succeed Deutch, former national security adviser Anthony Lake, had been savaged by Republican critics, and withdrew from the confirmation procedure, describing it as "nasty and brutish without being short."[46]

Tenet's political instincts no doubt told him that it would be timely to divulge budget figures for 1997 and 1998. But preemption need be only a temporary expedient, deployed to hush opposition until the fuss dies down. Continued disclosure risked making enemies of those whose power and standing stemmed from privileged access to information kept secret from all but the chosen few. For example, the chairman of the Senate intelligence committee, Richard C. Shelby (Rep., Ala.) had from the outset opposed budget disclosure, which he denounced as being "of little use to anyone except our nation's enemies." In 1999, Tenet withheld budget information once again. Challenged in court by Aftergood, he argued that changes in the budget since 1998 "could add to the mosaic of other public and clandestine information acquired by our adversaries about the intelligence budget in a way that could reasonably be expected to damage the national security." On the same ground, the CIA continued to withhold budget information in 2000.[47]

Budget secrecy aspirations, czarist dreams, and Venona publicity were all symptoms of a resurgence in expansionist ambition. But the debate swirling around them did not take place in a vacuum. It was affected by contemporary perceptions of intelligence performance. In the second half of the nineties, the business of intelligence continued as usual, and indeed diversification proceeded apace. As ever, there were some embarrassing tales of incompetence. However, the major scandals of the nineties—the alleged twisting of SDI-related evidence and the Ames treason—had been postmortems on the Reagan administration, not adverse reflections in themselves on the way in which things were run under Clinton. So far as the public was aware, no great new disasters had befallen the intelligence community during the remainder of the century. This helped ensure that the CIA would survive the inevitable criticism of its inevitable minor errors.

In 1996, a CIA-supported attempt to overthrow Iraq's President Saddam Hussein foundered. It did not take long for details to emerge, as Saddam took his bloody revenge on the agency's collaborators and launched a genocidal attack on his nation's Kurdish minority, a group the CIA was known to have supported in the past. While news of these developments was bad publicity for the CIA, it was not serious. For Saddam was an unpopular figure in the West. He was the instigator not only of the bullying invasion of Kuwait and repression of the Kurds, but also of the earlier, and immensely more bloody, war against Iran, in the course of which Baghdad had deployed chemical weapons. The press represented him as the Hitler of modern times. Criticism of the CIA tended to be directed at its incompetence rather than its objective. That the clandestinely supported coup d'état had survived as an instrument of American foreign policy was confirmed in 1998, when the press openly and without any sense of impending scandal reported an attempt to remove Yugoslav President Slobodan Milosevic. Until his downfall in 2000, the orchestrator of ethnic cleansing in Bosnia and Kosovo was a favorite bugbear of the Western media, and it seemed perfectly in order when President Clinton convened a meeting of CIA and DIA officials to discuss removal plans.[48]

In 1999, the United States played a major role in air strikes directed against Yugoslav forces in Serbia and Kosovo, designed to secure their removal from the latter province and an end to ethnic cleansing there. The campaign was a testing ground for new weapons, notably "smart" bombs designed to inflict military damage without "collateral" destruction of civilian lives and facilities. Equally, it was a test of the way in which the intelligence community had adapted to the high-technology requirements of America's role in its latest phase as a global military policeman. Controversy broke out over the accuracy and effectiveness of the bombing campaign in Kosovo, which seemed to have been blunted by the deployment of dummy tanks as decoys, and impaired by the effects of bad weather. An even more virulent debate broke out over the bombing of the Chinese embassy in Belgrade on 7 May, an incident that threatened the Beijing-Washington trading axis and embarrassed the CIA, which had recommended the target and supplied the bombing coordinates. Variously described as incompetence and as a deliberate accident (to destroy communications assistance being given to the Yugoslav forces), CIA performance in the embassy incident was again discussed in the context of efficiency and of ends, not means. The point is even more graphically illustrated by the fact that the press reported the bombing of Milosevic's home as a routine news item, whereas in the mid-1970s it might have screamed "assassin."[49]

One of the time-honored practices in the history of U.S. intelligence has been to reward failure. This is based on the principle that shortcomings must stem from a lack of resources and that it is dangerous to fire incompetent insiders who know too much and might talk. By 2000, according to the *Washington Post*'s Vernon Loeb, the CIA was recovering—at "about $30 billion," the annual U.S. intelligence budget was larger than that of the entire Russian military. But Walter Millis, who had left the CIA for Congress in 1993 and now chaired the House Permanent Select Committee on Intelligence, stated, "We're in big trouble." Despite unambiguous evidence, the U.S. intelligence community had failed to detect preparations for India's 1998 testing of a nuclear bomb, an event that destabilized the politics of the subcontinent. It just showed, said Millis, how the DCI needed more authority over the intelligence community—as well as more latitude to use journalists as spies, to engage in covert operations, and to counter the Russians, who had many more secret agents than did America, and "still use all the tricks—and more."[50]

By the beginning of the twenty-first century, there were indications that the intelligence Old Guard were back in control. Yet, in the dying years of the past millennium, there had been signs of change. For example, multiculturalism and political correctness arose, like ghosts from the 1960s, to haunt the secret establishment. The idea of white male patrician domination of intelligence was open to criticism from three perspectives. First, it was operationally questionable. For example, now that Africa had been decolonized, it was ludicrous to expect a white man with a Harvard accent to work undercover on that continent. Second, confinement of recruitment to a narrow segment of the population deprived the intelligence world of talent—a commodity that past investigations of the intelligence community had suggested was in short supply. Finally, discrimination against "minorities," who collectively made up the majority of the U.S. population, was undemocratic. While some aspects of sixties radicalism became unfashionable with the passage of time, the idea of an all-inclusive society had come to be accepted by liberals and conservatives alike. The intelligence community might have returned to some of its old habits, but it could not entirely turn the clock back, and it was no longer able to get away with discriminatory practices.

In 1991, a CIA "Glass Ceiling Study" initiated by the Bush (senior) administration had found that 45 percent of the agency's female personnel complained of sexual harassment and of being denied promotions. Within the Directorate of Operations, 300 women now charged that out of a total of 2,000 employees of whom 450 were female, only 10 women held responsible positions in this espionage branch of the agency. In 1995, the CIA settled out of court with all but ten of the women, offering retroactive promotions and $990,000 in back pay. Meanwhile, DCI Deutch appointed Nora Slatkin to the number three job in the agency, the post of executive director, stating that her appointment would "make the glass ceiling the glass floor."[51]

Within months, CIA officers identified in the *Washington Post* as the "old guard" were complaining about Slatkin. She had taken on the unpopular task of disciplining seventeen officers for negligence in the Ames affair. But underlying causes of the resentment were also her mission to remove promotion barriers for women, her reluctance to authorize covert operations, and the mere fact that she was in a position to give men orders in this traditionally macho realm. According to the rumor mill, she had an improper relationship with Deutch—a third-hand story in the press had her sitting next to the DCI at a meeting with British intelligence, "slipping her hand into his pocket, taking out jelly beans and feeding them to John." But the rumors proved to be unfounded and, in the 1996 presidential election, America's female voters showed their preference for Clinton and their appreciation of his efforts on behalf of women. The reelected president made a number of female appointments, including that of Madeleine K. Albright, the first woman to serve as secretary of state. This did not spell sudden death for male chauvinism in the intelligence community, but the principle of gender equality could no longer be ignored.[52]

On 4 August 1995, President Clinton issued an executive order on security clearance that banned discrimination against homosexuals, enabling those who were openly gay to work in the intelligence community. Now that attitudes on homosexuality had changed, foreign intelligence services would no longer be able to recruit gay double agents by using blackmail. (Whether this had ever been the case is open to question—Aldrich Ames was only the latest in a long line of spies who have proved the point that heterosexual persons can be traitors.) Within a year, a group within the CIA had organized the Agency Network of Gay and Lesbian Employees (ANGLE), while, across the way at Fort Meade, NSA workers formed a chapter of Gay, Lesbian and Bisexual Employees (GLOBE), in honor of Alan Turing, the British World War II codebreaker who killed himself after being forced to undergo "treatment" for his homosexuality in the 1950s. In 2000, Representative Barney Frank (Dem., Mass.) addressed a gathering at the CIA during Gay and Lesbian Pride Month. He was an open-budget advocate and at variance with the agency's leadership on that issue, but he recognized the nature of open secrets when he quipped, "Your budget by now is about as big a secret as my sexuality." Prejudice against gays, like that against women, was on the retreat.[53]

In May 2000, Vernon Loeb noted the changes taking place as a result of "affirmative action" within the CIA. The Directorate of Operations, he reported, saw diversification of personnel as essential to the successful accomplishment of diversification of function. He quoted Jack Downing, a CIA veteran who had been station chief in both Moscow and Beijing, as saying that America had a "competitive advantage" in being "a nation of nations." America's linguistically and culturally diverse population was an ideal source of intelligence recruits. Loeb noted that 18 percent of the CIA's approximately one thousand case officers were now women, and 11 percent were members of minority groups.[54]

However, according to Loeb, CIA officials thought they had "image problems" in trying to recruit minorities. Some potential recruits were put off by the agency's history of coups in Latin America and the Middle East. Others had been alienated by a 1996 story in the *San Jose Mercury News* that, during the Reagan years, the CIA had diverted drug profits to the illegal support of the Nicaraguan Contra movement. While crack cocaine is to some extent a classless drug, it has a particularly catastrophic effect in the black ghettoes, where its effects were compounded by many other problems. According to the *San Jose Mercury News* story, the Contra-supportive hard drugs had gone on sale in Los Angeles's troubled black quarter, a story that provoked outrage and allegations among some African Americans that the U.S. government was promoting genocide.[55]

Another serious racial problem stemmed from the arrest, in March 1999, of Wen Ho Lee on a charge of spying at the Los Alamos National Laboratory in New Mexico. The allegation against the Taiwanese-born scientist was that he had betrayed to Red China U.S. expertise on miniaturized nuclear warheads. The case rapidly escalated into a scandal when a congressional inquiry chaired by Representative Chris Cox reported a catalog of alleged Chinese American security lapses stretching back to the 1950s. A Chinese spy scare broke out in the press, and the liberals hit back. The Federation of American Scientists accused the main U.S. newspapers of racism. *The Nation* portrayed Lee "as the victim of neo-McCarthyite Republicans who see the Chinese menace everywhere and hope to use the 'China Threat' as a bludgeon against Democrats in the upcoming presidential election." Robert Vrooman, a former counterintelligence chief at Los Alamos, now revealed that "racial profiling" had been "a crucial component of the FBI's identifying Dr. Lee as a suspect." Lee's lawyers filed a "selective prosecution" motion, claiming discriminatory treatment of Chinese Americans. In Chinese espionage, a new "menace" had been discovered that could be used to justify intelligence budgets—but it was a potential setback for the future recruitment into the CIA of talented Asian Americans.[56]

In spite of setbacks, the CIA and other parts of the intelligence bureaucracy were becoming a "broad church," setting aside traditional barriers born of prejudice. But care should be taken not to assume that the beast itself had changed, as distinct from the way it looked. A social group that is breaking through may well adopt normative culture as the price of that achievement—indeed, it may be frightened into doing so by events like the Chinese spy scare. Multiculturalism did not spell an end to hyperbole in the history of American intelligence—it was actually part of the American Dream that had contributed to the hype.

Multiculturalism did, however, open the possibility of intelligence cooperation with the rest of the world. There was a dawning recognition that this might make good political sense, now that Cold War rigidities no longer prevailed. From the U.S. point of view, there was also a

prospect of savings to the taxpayer. The mounting expense of intelligence became evident in the case of the National Security Agency,
which ran into a storm of criticism in early 2000. On the one hand, the
NSA had again been criticized for being an overintrusive Big Brother,
snooping on private citizens the world over. Yet, the NSA was also
accused of not being intrusive enough. It was beginning to look de-
crepit, bowing under the burdens of informational overload and anti-
quated equipment that was unable to keep up with rapid, worldwide
developments in information technology. In its prime, the NSA had
been one of the driving forces behind computer technology; it employed 95,000 people; it listened to Soviet leaders chatting in their
limousines as they drove to and from the Kremlin. But by century's end,
it had fallen behind global developments in satellite-proof fiber-optic
communications and computer-aided encryption—shortcomings cru-
elly exposed in a *New Yorker* article by journalist Seymour Hersh, who
depicted NSA leadership as a smug, "self-licking ice-cream cone."[57]

In January, the NSA's computers crashed, and its problems could no
longer be denied. Barbara A. McNamara, the agency's number two
official, depicted by Hersh as an inflexible defender of the status quo,
had to appeal to the British for help. Known by her initials "BAM"
because her brusque speech was reminiscent of the "sound of a gun-
shot," she at least achieved her goal, and Britain kept America informed
for a period of seventy-two hours while computer repairs were made. In
time-honored fashion, the recently appointed NSA director Michael V.
Hayden said more money would fix the problem: "The price tag for new
information capabilities is high, but the alternatives are unthinkable."[58]

However, international cooperation was, in theory at least, a possible alternative solution. As BAM's experience shows, cooperation could
work bilaterally. It could also be accomplished through collective en-
tities, such as the North Atlantic Treaty Organization (NATO). The fact
that France and other countries resented American domination of
NATO only reinforced the case for intelligence sharing. Another developing possibility was the growth of intelligence capabilities in the
European Union. According to one estimate, at the turn of the century
the entire European intelligence expenditure (including that of nation-
states) was only in the region of $5 billion to $8 billion—a fraction of the
U.S. budget.[59] Nevertheless, a stronger Europe held forth the possibil-

ity of both cost-sharing and competitive estimating—a practice that had reassured U.S. skeptics in the past and remained attractive to those outside the United States who were nervous about American hegemony.

An improved intelligence capability for the United Nations was potentially popular in nations that resented European/American domination, and the idea commanded support, also, in Europe and America themselves. The recent history of peacekeeping operations indicated a desperate need for improved U.N. secret intelligence. In the 1990s, for example, genocide took place under the noses of a U.N. peacekeeping force in Rwanda, whose French commander admitted he had been "deaf and blind" to what was going on. Meanwhile, in Bosnia, Scandinavian observers used open radio to comment on the bombardment of a Moslem town; listening in, Serbian gunners used the information to improve the accuracy of their fire.[60]

While America could and did supply U.N. forces with intelligence on a need-to-know basis, international politics demanded that the U.N. capability be more independent. In 1994, President Clinton issued a directive promising that the United States would "share information, as appropriate, while ensuring full protection of sources and methods." It now fell to the DIA to supply the United Nations with information related to field operations. U.S. intelligence support to the United Nations in areas like refugee policy, peacekeeping, and nonproliferation reached, in the words of one authority, "an unprecedented level." But Clinton's directive also called for the United Nations to set up an information and research unit, which was established, albeit with a staff of only four. Both intelligence-sharing and U.N. intelligence capability remained under discussion: for example, at a U.N. global information technology summit in New York in July 2000. Shortly after that, U.N. Secretary General Kofi Annan backed the idea of a new U.N. peacekeeping department with stronger intelligence as its keystone. Potentially, all this was of benefit to the American taxpayer and a setback to the promoters of ever-larger intelligence budgets.[61]

There were, however, obstacles to the United Nations' fulfillment of its potential. For many of its supporters and officials, the organization was a noble dream, not to be sullied by the realities of everyday politics. In the words of a quasi-official U.N. handbook, "Intelligence, having covert connections, is a dirty word," and officials preferred to use the word "information."[62] U.N. opposition to espionage began to crumble under the weight of new, post–Cold War peacekeeping responsibilities and a campaign for improved awareness, but it remained a significant factor.

Walter Dorn, a Canadian campaigner for and student of U.N. peacekeeping, thus summed up another obstacle: "The major nations have been reluctant to give the U.N. a greater intelligence mandate because to many of them, intelligence is power." In spite of President Clinton's support, there was opposition in the United States itself. Although President Woodrow Wilson had pressed for the establishment of the League of Nations and his successors Franklin D. Roosevelt and Harry Truman has presided over the foundation of its successor, America had always suffered from "mood swings" on the general subject of the United Nations. In 1987, a minority of senators had specifically objected to the establishment of a U.N. information office, and, although they were defeated, objections lingered. Doubts arose because of fears that the American taxpayer would end up footing the intelligence bill anyway, and would in the process lose control over intelligence not just because of shared responsibility, but because there was no provision for oversight—a goal won at home only after a hard-fought battle. When they looked at the prospect of enhanced U.N. intelligence, isolationists and unilateralists did not tremble with joy.[63]

A rash of revelations about economic espionage among democratic allies encouraged nationalist, hence anti-internationalist feeling. Once the Moscow bogey man had gone, nations felt more free to compete with old friends, or at least to talk about that competition openly, and to complain in a manner that would be faintly comical in its hypocrisy were it not for its effect of undermining global comity. In 1991, American businesspeople were warned that French airline seats were bugged in an effort to glean secrets that would benefit Gallic capitalists. For its part, the CIA passed on clandestinely obtained information to the American business community, giving about 20,000 briefings annually by the century's end (the agency scrupulously avoided giving one U.S. firm an advantage over another, but it could help U.S. industry compete with foreign businesses). In 1995, the *New York Times* interpreted U.S. espionage against the Japanese automobile industry as the "CIA trying to get a new life." Two years later, the press was full of indignation about Japanese economic espionage in the United States. In the same year, the European Parliament began its protracted inquiry into Echelon. This was the NSA's vastly expensive program, started in the mid-1970s, of mopping up worldwide nonencrypted telephone, fax, and email communications. Objections to the program were on civil libertarian grounds, and because it gave U.S. corporations a competitive edge (for example, in 1993 Boeing allegedly won a $3.7 billion Saudi Arabian contract against the European consortium Airbus using secretly obtained inside information). Echelon recriminations continued into the new century, each side indignant about the other side's indignation and both sides ignoring the fact that Echelon could not cope with twenty-first-century encryption.[64]

This climate of distrust helped the cause of those who wanted to boost America's own intelligence capabilities. The mood in Congress as the Clinton administration drew to a close was quite different from the one that had prevailed in the mid-1990s. Although the *Washington Post* reported that the once again secret intelligence budget had increased for the fifth year in a row, both the House and Senate intelligence committees concluded that intelligence was underfunded. The Senate committee claimed its "number one priority was the recapitalization of the National Security Agency." There were other straws in the wind. Moves were afoot in Congress to exempt U.S. intelligence agencies from any obligation to obey the laws of foreign countries, to restrict the money available to finance government agencies' responses to freedom-of-information declassification requests, and to exempt the DIA entirely from the provisions of the Freedom of Information Act. While Congress no doubt remained alert to intelligence abuses, it was in significant ways acting as the guardian of the expansionists' interests.[65]

The advent of George W. Bush to the White House seemed to signal a continuity in this kind of approach. For one thing, Bush retained the services of Democratic appointee George Tenet. It was the first time since the 1970s that a DCI had kept his job under such circumstances. For this triumph, there were special reasons. Before Jimmy Carter's election, the DCI job had been regarded as apolitical. Then the Democrat Carter had removed the Republican Bush (senior) from his CIA post in 1977 amid protest that he was politicizing—and slapping down—intelligence. There did seem to be a need to negate that precedent, and no doubt the Bushes felt strongly about it. Another reason for Tenet's continuance was that the DCI had assiduously cultivated Bush, father and son, while Clinton was still in office. His personal acceptability continued to be evident as he became a frequent caller at the Bush (junior) White House.[66]

But the welcome afforded to the bearer of secret tidings was not merely symbolic. From the beginning, senior members of the new administration made it clear that intelligence, along with national missile defense, would receive a boost. Defense Secretary Donald H. Rumsfeld had, with Bush (senior), helped lead the intelligence community's fight back in the Ford administration. He now declared robust intelligence to be one of his "key objectives." The expansionists received further encouragement from the 31 January 2001 report of the U.S. Commission on National Security. Set up in the previous administration and co-chaired by two former senators, the commission now concluded that the intelligence community had responded well to previous reforms and that no more change was necessary—except that the overall intelligence budget would need to be increased. Meanwhile, both the House and the Senate oversight committees reiterated their support for a bigger dollar injection into the intelligence community. Senator Bob Graham (Fla.), the Democratic vice chairman of the Senate committee, expressed the bipartisan view: "We have a special responsibility to represent the interest of the intelligence community before those who will make these budgetary decisions."[67]

With even the watchdogs on their side, the expansionists had cause for optimism, and events in the first weeks of the Bush (junior) administration helped their cause. Moscow and Washington each claimed to have discovered the other's spies at work in its bailiwick, and a round of tit-for-tat expulsions took place. In a separate development, Sino-American relations came close to a hostage crisis. Under Clinton, the United States had stepped up the number of spy-plane missions it flew up and down the Chinese coast. One of these planes accidentally collided with a Chinese fighter and made a forced landing on the island of Hainan, where the communist authorities held its crew for a short but tense period. In the Cold War, these espionage-related stand-offs with Moscow and Beijing would have been regarded as routine. In modern times, they threatened to reintroduce grit into the machinery of international harmony. Yet, they once again raised the profile of espionage and even enhanced its prestige.

The debate on the scale of intelligence continued. According to

British intelligence expert Nigel West, the Americans, Russians, and Chinese all appreciated that in the age of dwindling defense expenditure, successful espionage could give one a vital technological edge. Consequently, in this context more spying was needed, not less. On the other hand, there was support in both America and Russia for the idea that the powers were spying too much. In 1996, former diplomat Robert E. White had proposed the negotiation of espionage treaties, extending to other countries the arrangement whereby America, Canada, Australia, and Britain supposedly did not spy on one another (untrustworthy countries would still have to be watched). Against the background of the Hainan episode, former Soviet foreign minister Boris Pankin supported the idea. The proposed reliance on honorable abstention and idealistic treaties was reminiscent of an earlier Republican era, the 1920s.[68]

In the early months of the Bush (junior) presidency, the U.S. intelligence community was heir to a tradition of hyperbole and spin that stretched from Allan Pinkerton to William Casey. Together with a deserved reputation for past successes, this had helped it to survive the Cold War's end and, in due course, to continue its expansion. To use the language of the Cold War triumphalists, the real American Century was by the summer of 2001 well and truly under way, underpinned in no small measure by the CIA and its siblings. Incipiently, the United Nations had begun to emerge as an alternative world policeman and global intelligence officer. But foreign nationalisms as well as nationalist intelligence spin in the United States held this process back, and an "America First" spirit prevailed in the intelligence community.

The terrorist attacks of 11 September 2001 were a severe blow to America's sense of security. A ruthless hand had struck at the Pentagon and New York's World Trade Center (WTC) and had caused four civilian passenger aircraft to crash. Thousands were killed and injured, and thousands more suffered desperate grief.

The effectiveness of this surprise attack prompted government officials and journalists to conclude that there had been a catastrophic intelligence failure. Certainly, there had been shortcomings, with indications of clues being ignored and of a lack of coordination and proper analysis within the American intelligence community. At the same time, it was evident that the intelligence community contained many dedicated and capable officers. Well-planned surprise attacks are notoriously difficult to predict, and no system can permanently guard against a mode of aggression that is by definition countersystemic. It is a time-honored tradition for politicians to make a scapegoat, in such circumstances, of the intelligence community.

Equally encrusted in tradition were the immediate appeals for a boost to the intelligence community, accompanied by ill-founded complaints that it had been financially squeezed since the end of the Cold War. The situation was custom-made for the intelligence confidence man and his political allies. Once again, the cries were heard: give them more money, unleash the CIA. Once again, it was tempting to reward failure, and to resort to expensive, static, and home-based solutions. In the wake of the WTC clamor, the need remains for the United States intelligence community to become more a part of the wider world that has inspired and continued to invigorate the great nation of immigrants.

Abbreviations to Notes

Locations

AMHI	U.S. Army Military History Institute, Carlisle Barracks, Pennsylvania
CCC	Churchill College, Cambridge, England
FLP	Firestone Library, Princeton University, Princeton, New Jersey
GRF	Gerald R. Ford Library, Ann Arbor, Michigan
GUL	Georgetown University (Lauinger Memorial) Library
HST	Harry S. Truman Library, Independence, Missouri
LC	Library of Congress, Washington, D.C.
NA	National Archives, Washington, D.C.
NRC	National Records Center, Suitland, Maryland
PAC	Public Archives of Canada, Ottawa, Ontario
PRO	Public Records Office, London, England
SGM	Seeley G. Mudd Library, Princeton University, Princeton, New Jersey
UM	University of Michigan Libraries, Ann Arbor, Michigan
WL	State Historical Society, Madison, Wisconsin
YUL	Yale University Library, New Haven, Connecticut

Collections

ACUE	American Committee on United Europe Papers, GUL
AWD	Allen W. Dulles Papers, SGM
CHM	Charles H. McCall Files, GRF
CM	Charles McCarthy Papers, WL
ELB	The Papers of Edward L. Bernays, LC
EMH	E. M. House Collection, YUL

JV	Jan Valtin Papers, FLP
LH	Leland Harrison Papers, LC
MID	Records of the War Department General Staff Military Intelligence Division, 1917–1941, NA
OC	Records of the office of the counselor, Department of State, NA
ONI	Records of the Office of Naval Intelligence, NA
PGS	Philip G. Strong Collection on Espionage, SGM
PNDA	Papers of the Pinkerton National Detective Agency: Letterpress copybooks, 1872–1883, LC
RJB	Russell J. Bowen Collection, GUL
RSS	Records of the U.S. Secret Service, NRC
USDS	Records of the undersecretary, Department of State, NA
WD	Walter Drew Papers, UM
WEC	William E. Colby Papers, SGM
WHCF	White House Central Files, presidential libraries
WJD	William J. Donovan Papers (on microfilm), CCC
WLP	Sir Wilfrid Laurier Papers, PAC

Notes

Chapter 1. The American Spy Considered as a Confidence Man

1. Carver, "Intelligence," 148–49; Walker quoted in Dobson, "The USA, Britain, and the Question of Hegemony," 134. Carver underestimated both the U.S. intelligence expenditure in 1990 (see Chapter 14) and the dangers confronted by America in Washington's first term, when Britain, the nation's most-dangerous-ever enemy, seemed poised to attack, and when the Western (Indian) Confederacy seemed to pose a threat. It could also be argued that he overestimated the role of federal expenditure in the 1790s, when intelligence accounted for a large proportion of only a small sum.

2. *Washington Post,* 6 March 2000; Valladsen, "Prospects," 87.

3. Luc Sante in his introduction to the 1999 edition of David Maurer's *The Big Con* observes (p. ix) that there were confidence tricksters in ancient Mesopotamia. Scadder's description of "The City of Eden" in Charles Dickens' novel *Martin Chuzzlewit* (1848) foreshadowed the real estate scam, and immediately preceded one of the first literary uses of the term "Confidence Man," in the account of William McGrath's arrest in the *New York Herald,* 8 July 1849 (see the Norton critical edition of *The Confidence-Man,* ed. Hershel Parker, 227, 246). For a study of mainly non-American individual cases of intelligence tricksters in World War II, see Nigel West, *Counterfeit Spies* (London: St Ermin's Press, 1998). On Frémont: Robin W. Winks, *Frederick Billings: A Life* (Berkeley: University of California Press, 1998), 120.

4. *The Civil War Papers of George B. McClellan: Selected Correspondence, 1860–1865,* ed. Stephen W. Sears (New York: Ticknor and Fields, 1989), 617.

5. Cook, *FBI,* 56; Yardley, *Education,* 7; Kahn, *Codebreakers,* 355.

6. John Godfrey, "Intelligence in the United States," 7 July 1941, CAB 122/ 1021 S4206, kindly supplied to the author by Bradley F. Smith, and later reproduced in Smith, "Admiral Godfrey's Mission"; Colby, "Intelligence and the Press: Address to the Associated Press Annual Meeting," 7 April 1975, Box 2, WEC; Gates, *From the Shadows,* 552.

7. Melville, *Confidence-Man,* 44–46, 373.

8. Yardley, *American Black Chamber,* 167; Currey, *Lansdale,* 19.

9. Jack Downing quoted in the *Washington Post,* 31 May 2000.

10. Washington (at Camp at Fort Cumberland) to Colonel Henry Bonquet, 16 July 1758, *The Papers of George Washington. Colonial Series,* ed. W. W. Abbot (Charlottesville: University Press of Virginia, 1988), 5, *October 1757-September 1958,* 291–92.

11. Rose, "Civil War," 73–80.

12. J. Anthony Lukas, *Big Trouble: A Murder in a Small Western Town Sets off a Struggle for the Soul of America* (New York: Touchstone/Simon & Schuster, 1998), 14 (see also Slotkin, *Gunfighter Nation,* 139 ff); F. W. Cohen to Walter Drew, 26 October 1910, Walter Drew Papers, University of Michigan Libraries, Ann Arbor, Michigan.

13. Williams, "Without Understanding," 24–25.

14. Vance Packard, *The Hidden Persuaders* (Harmondsworth: Penguin, 1960 [1957]), 215.

Chapter 2. The Washington Style

1. O'Toole, *Honorable Treachery,* 25–26, 36–37.

2. Howard H. Peckham, *The War for Independence: A Military History* (Chicago: University of Chicago Press, 1958), 58–60; John E. Ferling, *The First of Men: A Life of George Washington* (Knoxville: University of Tennessee Press, 1988), 193–94.

3. O'Toole, *Honorable Treachery,* 37; Douglas Southall Freeman, *George Washington: A Biography,* Vol. 4, *Leader of the Revolution* (London: Eyre and Spottiswoode, 1951), 384, 384 -85nn19–23.

4. Washington (at Headquarters, Morristown) to Capt. Allen McLane, 28 March 1777, in *The Writings of George Washington from the Original Manuscript Sources 1745–1799,* vol. 7, *Jan. 13, 1777-April 30, 1777,* ed. John C. Fitzpatrick (Washington, D.C.: USGPO, 1932), 328.

5. Washington (at Headquarters, Morristown) to Col. Elias Dayton, 26 July 1777, photocopy of the original in folder "Washington, George. Copies of five letters," Box 3, PGS. Judging from the handwriting, the letter on file in the Strong collection was written or copied by one of Washington's clerks. For an example of Washington's own hand, see his letter to Major Benjamin Tallmadge (one of his spymasters from 1778), sent from Morristown on Nov. 28, 1780, and photographically reproduced in Morton Pennypacker, *General Washington's Spies on Long Island and in New York* (Brooklyn, N.Y.: Long Island Historical Society, 1939), facing p. 192. On Strong: McWilliams, "Covert Connections," 665.

6. Knott, *Secret and Sanctioned,* 14; expenditure percentage estimate in Rowan, *Secret Service,* 162, 711n12; Washington (at Headquarters, Pennybacker's Mill) to "Sir," 29 September 1777, typed copy in folder "Washington, George. Copies of five letters," Box 3, PGS. The unpublished original of this letter, in the hand of Tench Tilghman, is located in the Houghton Library, Harvard University, under the shelf-mark "Autograph file." This was traced because the photocopy of the typescript in the Strong collection is, like all photocopies of similar provenance, stamped on the reverse "Harvard College Library." The other letters in the folder

are not so stamped and would appear not to be located in the Harvard libraries, but their authenticity is implied by the proven provenance of the Houghton item. On the "daring and skillful" character of John Clark's activities, see Freeman, *Leader,* 304n8.

7. Anonymous (from an unstated location) to "Sir," n.d. (though in a clerk's hand, its authoritative tone and its location indicate the author of this letter was George Washington), in folder "Washington, George. Copies of five letters," Box 3, PGS.

8. In the inventory of the Autograph file in the Houghton Library, the commentaries are designated "Notes on intelligence, apparently derived from reports of spies." The attributability of the text to George Washington was confirmed in Jennie Rathbun (Houghton Reading Room) to author, 23 August 1999. Publication is by permission of the Houghton Library, Harvard University. These notes as well as the Strong collection documents were kindly dated on the basis of their contemporary references by the author's colleague Francis D. Cogliano, author of *Revolutionary America, 1763–1815: A Political History* (London: Routledge, 2000). See also George Washington, "Instructions for Spies Going into New York," ca. September 1790, in John Rhodehamel, *George Washington: Writings* (New York: Library of America, 1997), 389–90.

9. Rowan, *Secret Service,* 154; Morton Pennypacker, *The Two Spies: Nathan Hale and Robert Townsend* (Boston: Houghton Mifflin, 1930). Pennypacker hinted rather unconvincingly that his book had demythologized Hale: "Until 1930 the most talked about character of Revolutionary days was Nathan Hale. Then when the hidden documents that revealed Robert Townsend as the chief spy of General Washington were discovered they occasioned a mild sensation": Morton Pennypacker, *General Washington's Spies on Long Island and in New York,* vol. 2 (East Hampton, Long Island, N.Y.: special edition printed privately for Morton Pennypacker, 1948), 32.

10. Washington (at Camp at Fort Cumberland) to Colonel Henry Bonquet, 16 July 1758 in *The Papers of George Washington. Colonial Series,* vol. 5, *October 1757-September 1758,* ed. W.W. Abbot (Charlottesville: University Press of Virginia, 1988), 291–92. In a letterbook copy of this letter, the word "Spies" was substituted for "Scalping Partys."

11. Bryan, *Spy in America,* 15. Bryan's parentheses.

12. Of interest here in light of the "special relationship" in intelligence and other matters that had by 1943 developed between America and Britain, is the suggestion by historian Don Higginbotham "that English settlers were most unorthodox and barbaric in their conflicts with Indians throughout the colonial era, that they were more restrained in their confrontations with the French and Spanish, and that they were more civilized (if war can be that) in their struggle for independence against the British motherland": Higginbotham, *War and Society in Revolutionary America: The Wider Dimensions of Conflict* (Columbia, S.C.: University of South Carolina Press, 1988), 264.

13. Marcus Cunliffe, *George Washington: Man and Monument* (London: Collins, 1959), 27; Mason L. Weems, *The Life of Washington,* ed. Marcus Cunliffe (Cambridge, Mass.: Harvard University Press, 1962 [1809]), xxxv, 12.

14. Hannah Adams, *History of New England* (1799), quoted in Pennypacker, *Washington's Spies,* 22. Adams may have drawn on an earlier account in Timothy

Dwight's epic poem, "Conquest of Canaan" (ca. 1785): Pennypacker, *Washington's Spies,* 21.

15. Whether it was Hale or Adams who garbled Addison's Cato, it was not a bad choice: Cato was the Roman republican who killed himself rather than submit to Caesar. See Pennypacker, *Washington's Spies,* 22n and Miller, *Spying for America,* 19n.

16. Pennypacker, *Washington's Spies,* v, 33; Alan Taylor, *William Cooper's Town: Power and Persuasion on the Frontier of the Early American Republic* (New York: Knopf, 1995), 409; Cooper, *The Spy,* 326.

17. Unpaginated 1849 introduction, Cooper, *The Spy.*

18. Ameringer, *U.S. Foreign Intelligence,* 37–38; Jeffreys-Jones, *American Espionage,* 25–26.

19. Henry M. Wriston, "Executive Agents in American Foreign Relations" (Ph.D. diss., Harvard University, 1922), 132.

20. Knott, *Secret and Sanctioned,* 5–6. See also Jack Rakove, *Original Meanings: Politics and Ideas in the Making of the Constitution* (New York: Knopf, 1996).

Chapter 3. Allan Pinkerton's Legacy

1. Stephen W. Sears on Pinkerton's estimate of the strength of General Joseph E. Johnstone's Confederate army in Manassas and Centreville, Virginia, in late October 1861: Sears, *Landscape Turned Red: The Battle of Antietam* (New Haven, Conn.: Ticknor & Fields, 1983), 23. Sears also notes that McClellan accepted a triple-strength estimate of Robert E. Lee's army in September 1862, but that Pinkerton was not the only source of misinformation on which he based his calculation: *The Civil War Papers of George B. McClellan: Selected Correspondence, 1860–1865,* ed. Stephen W. Sears (New York: Ticknor & Fields, 1989), 433.

2. For a summary of the literature expounding these views, see Fishel, *Secret War,* 615–16n1.

3. Fishel, *Secret War,* 104–7.

4. Sears, *Landscape Turned Red,* 24; Bruce Catton, *The Coming Fury* (Garden City, N.Y.: Doubleday, 1961), 225. Edwin Fishel argues that Pinkerton's intelligence estimates improved as time went on and as he became free of the fear of underestimating the enemy before he had found his feet: Fishel, *Secret War,* 102.

5. Gorbals parish register cited in Mackay, *Pinkerton,* 20; watercolors of Gorbals in the 1840s painted by William Simpson (Glasgow Corporation Galleries of Art Register, checklist numbers 892c, 892d, 892e, 892v); *Collins Encyclopaedia of Scotland,* ed. John Keay and Julia Keay (London: HarperCollins, 1994), 445; Pinkerton to a recipient, possibly David Gallacher but written in an illegible hand, residing in Gordon Street, Glasgow, 12 September 1872, Reel 3, Container 8, p. 86, PNDA.

6. David Williams, *A History of Modern Wales* (London: John Murray, 1950), 238.

7. Pinkerton to Mrs. Alex Campbell, Leeds, England, 1 September 1873, Reel 3, Container 8, p. 414, PNDA.

8. Horan, *Pinkertons,* 8. Horan is one of the few reliable authorities on Allan Pinkerton, but his documentation is erratic. From his confused endnotes, it would

appear that the quotation is from one of two letters written by Allan to his son Robert on, respectively, 22 May 1879 and 28 April 1883.

9. Horan, *Pinkertons*, 10–11; Pinkerton to "My Dear Little Wife," 28 March 1878, Reel 3, Container 7, p. 141, PNDA.

10. Pinkerton letter reproduced in Gutman, "Five Letters," 388–91. Pinkerton did not stress his abolitionist sympathies in private correspondence. However, as Horan notes, "Pinkerton commented many times in his books and pamphlets on his rabid abolitionist sentiments": Horan, *Pinkertons*, 521, ch. 5, n. 1. For some evidence on his actual involvement, see Morn, *The Eye*, 211n13. Although Pinkerton gave anti-communism a recognizably modern form, hostility toward socialism was already prevalent in America. See Heale, *American Anticommunism*, 14–15.

11. On Pinkerton and violence, see Horan, *Pinkertons*, 9. The poverty expert and socialist Robert Hunter was one of many who deplored the violence of the Pinkertons: Hunter, *Violence and the Labor Movement* (New York: Macmillan, 1922 [1914]), 281 ff. But see Jeffreys-Jones, "Profit Over Class," 233–48.

12. Alexander Richmond, *Narrative of the Conditions of the Manufacturing Population and the Proceedings of Government Which Led to the State Trials in Scotland* (1824), Peter Mackenzie, *Exposure of the Spy System Pursued in Glasgow during the Years 1816–1820* (1833); admissions of the spymaster Kirkman Finlay, M.P., in the *Glasgow Evening Post* (28 September 1833) recorded in Thomas Johnston, *The History of the Working Classes in Scotland*, 2d ed. (Glasgow: Forward Publishing Co., 1929), 238n; David Williams, *John Frost: A Study in Chartism* (Cardiff: University of Wales Press, 1939), 240, 311; William A. Pinkerton to Mrs. Carrie Pinkerton McEwen, 10 June 1908. This last letter outlines the Pinkerton family's history to a woman who had asked if she might be a relative. Its author refers to his grandfather, in reality a turnkey, as "a Sergeant of Police in Glasgow, Scotland," an item of family mythology sometimes accepted by historians at face value. The Africa story may be true, but perhaps it more likely belongs to the same category of family mythology as the Sergeant of Police claim, and to have been the invention of a man disguising something murky in his past. The letter is in the Pinkerton archives and was photocopied and made available by kind courtesy of Jane Wilson Adler at a time when the documents were still located in Encino, California. Mrs. Adler was the Pinkerton archivist in the three years prior to the donation of the collection to the Library of Congress, in spring 2000.

13. Pinkerton to Herndon, 5 August 1866, in Cuthbert, ed., *Baltimore Plot*, 2.

14. Pinkerton to Herndon, 23 August 1866, in Cuthbert, ed., *Baltimore Plot*, 4–10. Further details of Pinkerton's account are taken from Pinkerton, "History and Evidence," 299, and *Spy of the Rebellion*, 81–113.

15. Pinkerton to Herndon, 23 August 1866, in Cuthbert, ed., *Baltimore Plot*, 11 (see also pp. xvii, 114–15); Pinkerton, *Spy of the Rebellion*, 61.

16. Pinkerton, *Spy of the Rebellion*, 60. Pinkerton's payroll for December 1861 was $4,486, but out of that he had to pay twenty-four operatives. See Fishel, *Secret War*, 113, 596; Mackay, *Pinkerton*, 180.

17. *McClellan Correspondence*, 617; Pinkerton to Herndon, 23 August 1866, in Cuthbert, ed., *Baltimore Plot*, 11.

18. Owsley, "Sanford," 212, 226–27. For accounts of the intelligence history of the Civil War that range more broadly than the activities of Pinkerton and his

agents, see Fishel, *Secret War;* Knott, *Secret and Sanctioned,* 139–48; Robin W. Winks, *Canada and the United States: The Civil War Years* (Baltimore: Johns Hopkins Press, 1960), 132–35; and Bulloch, *Secret Service.* The writing on Civil War espionage is extensive. For a selection of 175 books, articles, and other items, see Petersen, comp., *American Intelligence,* 34–42.

19. Vaughan Shelton, *Mask for Treason: The Lincoln Murder Trial* (Harrisburg, Pa.: Stackpole, 1965), referred to in Hanchett, *Lincoln Murder Theories,* 219–20.

20. William A. Tidwell was with the CIA, James O. Hall was with the DIA, and David W. Caddy was the assassination "specialist." They admitted their case was "largely circumstantial" but claimed their study benefited from the deployment of the "analytical tools that a modern intelligence officer would use." See Tidwell, Hall, and Caddy, *Come Retribution,* xiii, 4–5, 159, and, on the provenance of the authors, a review by Stephen W. Sears, *Washington Post,* 19 December 1988. Another example of the application of contemporary spook-talk to the Civil War era is Milton, *Abraham Lincoln and the Fifth Column:* "Even before the outbreak of the war, Washington had seemed to offer the perfect place of concealment and field of operations for Confederate spies" (p. 40).

21. Pinkerton to George H. Bangs, 2 September 1872, Reel 3, Container 7, pp. 1–8, PNDA.

22. Baker, *History,* 34, 40.

23. Pinkerton, *General Principles,* 5–7, 12. (Capitalization as in the original.)

24. Pinkerton, *Thirty Years,* 19.

25. George Bangs to Allan Pinkerton, 21 December 1872, Reel 3, Container 6, pp. 238–39, PNDA; *Chicago Tribune,* 12 August 1882, quoted in Morn, *Eye,* 66. On the nine children: William A. Pinkerton to Mrs. Carrie Pinkerton McEwen, 10 June 1908, cited above.

26. Maurer, *Big Con,* 19.

27. Maurer, *Big Con,* xi, 19; Lindberg, *Confidence Man,* 61–62, 127, 306n4; Melville, *The Confidence-Man;* Edgar Allan Poe, "Diddling: Considered as One of the Exact Sciences" (1843), widely reproduced, for example in Poe, *The Fall of the House of Usher and other Tales* (New York: New American Library, 1960); Walt Whitman, *Democratic Vistas* (1871); Mark Twain, *The Gilded Age* (1873). Richard Slotkin advances a different explanation of the American roots of Pinkerton's detective propaganda, portraying the literary Eye as the descendent of the Hawkeye western genre: Slotkin, *Gunfighter Nation: The Myth of the Frontier in Twentieth-Century America* (Norman: University of Oklahoma Press, 1998), 139–43.

28. Morn, *Eye,* 83, 221n56; publicity fliers issued by Chicago publishers, W.B. Keen, Cooke & Co., to promote three of Pinkerton's books in 1875 (*The Expressman and the Detective, Claude Melnote as a Detective,* and *The Detective and the Somnambulist*), all the fliers from the Pinkerton archive, and photocopied and made available by kind courtesy of Jane Adler. On Pinkerton's indirect methods of publicizing the PNDA, Jane Adler to author, 16 September 1998.

29. Quotation from Pinkerton's preface to *The Detective and the Somnambulist* quoted in Ken, Cooke flier; Pinkerton, *Thirty Years,* 7, 19; Horan, *Pinkertons,* 238.

30. This account of the PNDA and the Mollies and the following account of the attack on the O'Donnell family are taken from Kenny, *Making Sense,* 202–8.

31. Kenny, *Making Sense,* 199–200, 231–33. According to Jane Adler, McParlan "was enraged that a woman had been killed" in the O'Donnell tragedy, and "offered his resignation." She believes that behind that particular episode were probably Allan Pinkerton and Franklin P. Gowen, president of the Philadelphia and Reading Railway Company and of the Philadelphia and Reading Coal and Iron Company: Adler to author, 1 November 2000.

32. Quotation attributed to Franklin Gowen in Pinkerton, *Molly Maguires,* 14. For varying accounts, see Mackay, *Pinkerton,* 212; Kenny, *Making Sense,* 203; Morn, *Eye,* 95; and, authoritatively, Horan, *Pinkertons,* 204.

33. Charles Loring Brace, *The Dangerous Classes of New York and Twenty Years' Work Among Them* (New York: Wynkoop and Hallenbeck, 1872), 25.

34. Pinkerton, *Strikers, Communists,* xi–xii, 13, 14, 67, 80–82, 386.

35. Quoted in J. B. Frantz, "The Frontier Tradition: An Invitation to Violence," in *The History of Violence in America: Historical and Comparative Perspectives,* ed. H. D. Graham and T. R. Gurr (New York: Bantam, 1969), 128.

36. Horan, *Pinkertons,* 198–202; Gary L. Roberts, "James, Jesse and Frank," in *The New Encyclopedia of the American West,* ed. Howard R. Lamar (New Haven: Yale University Press, 1998), 564–65.

37. Williams, "Without Understanding," 26; Morn, *Eye,* 72.

38. U.S. Senate, Committee on Education and Labor, *Violations of Free Speech and the Rights of Labor,* 76 Cong., 1st sess. (1939), Rept. no. 6, Part 1, *Strikebreaking Services,* 14; *New York Times,* 17 August 1892. The House investigation of the role of the Pinkertons in the lockout resulted in the report, "Investigation of the Employment of Pinkerton Detectives in Connection with the Labor Troubles at Homestead, Pa.," *House Miscellaneous Document,* 52 Cong., 1st sess., no. 335 (1892).

39. P. K. Rose (of the CIA's Directorate of Operations), "The Civil War," 73–80. Over the years, Pinkerton's career inspired a genre of children's literature and several books for adults, including Sigmund A. Lavine, *Allan Pinkerton: America's First Private Eye* (New York: Dodd, Mead, 1963), and Arthur Orrmont, *Master Detective: Allan Pinkerton* (New York: J. Messner, 1965).

Chapter 4. Did Wilkie Crush the Montreal Spy Ring?

1. Don Wilkie, *Agent,* 18.

2. Raymond Carr, *Spain 1808–1939* (Oxford: Clarendon Press, 1966), 385; Ernest R. May, *Imperial Democracy: The Emergence of America as a Great Power* (New York: Harcourt, Brace, & World, 1961), 218.

3. *London Spectator,* 28 May 1898; anonymous, undated copy of telegram attributed to "Writer" (apparently an American or Canadian secret agent) sent to the Treasury Department from Canada; "Lena Huhn me Aguirra" of Houston, Texas, to General Ramon Blanco (Spanish commander in Cuba), 29 May 1898 (copy of intercepted letter); anonymous to Lieutenant Commander A. V. Wadhams, U.S. Customhouse, New Orleans, 8 June 1898; Capt. W. S. Scott (in charge of Bureau of Military Intelligence, Tampa) to George D. Meiklejohn, assistant secretary of war, 29 June 1898, all in RSS; editorials in *Cigar Makers' Official Journal,* 26 (15 August 1901ff); "Tampa's Capitalistic Banditti," *American Federationist,* 10 (May 1903); Wilkie, "Secret Service," 430.

4. Harrison to Sagasta, 20 April 1898; dispatch, dated 28 April 1898, of Washington correspondent of *Brooklyn Eagle,* both in RSS; Don Wilkie, *Agent,* 16; Orestes Ferrara, *The Last Spanish War,* trans. W. E. Shea (New York: The Paisley Press, 1937), 136.

5. Wilkie, "Secret Service," 425.

6. Unidentified newspaper clippings, bearing the dateline Montreal, 21 May, RSS.

7. Special report to *Toronto Star,* dateline 23 May 1898, RSS.

8. Wriston, *Executive Agents,* 132; Kaiser, "Origins," 108–9.

9. Kaiser, "Origins," 110; *Who Was Who in America* (Chicago: A.N. Marquis, 1943), I; Wilkie, "Catching Spain's Spies," *Boston Sunday Herald,* 2 October 1898; Wilkie, "Secret Service," 424, 425; Don Wilkie, *Agent,* 17; Kaiser, "Origins," 112.

10. Wilkie, "Secret Service," 433. See also Wilkie, "Catching Spain's Spies."

11. Wilkie, "Catching Spain's Spies"; M. W. Twitchell, U.S. consul, Kingston, Canada, to J. B. Moore, assistant secretary, State Dept., 11, 21 May 1898; G. W. Cridler, 3d assistant secretary, State Dept., to secretary of the treasury, 24 May 1898, both in RSS.

12. J. G. Foster, U.S. consul general, Halifax, Nova Scotia, to Moore, 27 May 1898; Cridler to secretary of the treasury, 2 June 1898; both in RSS. Foster's reference to "the Secret Service of the Dominion of Canada" is puzzling. The Canadian Northwest Mounted Police had a file on Mellor, according to the (Regina, Northwest Territories) *Leader:* clipping enclosed with letter from D. L. Cavan, Canadian govt. agent, Bad Axe, Mich. to "The Chief of the Detective Department," Washington, D.C., 6 June 1898, RSS. But the Royal Canadian Mounted Police had no jurisdiction in eastern Canada in 1898. There is no reference to the Montreal spy ring in the RCMP and Dominion Police files in the Public Archives of Canada.

13. Wilkie, "Secret Service," 432; *Montreal Star,* 8 July 1899.

14. Wilkie, "Secret Service," 432, 436; Sir Julian Pauncefote to Lord Aberdeen, 10 June 1898, WLP.

15. A. E. Campbell, *Great Britain and the United States 1895–1903* (London: Longmans, 1960), 5.

16. Chamberlain to Aberdeen, 6 June 1898, Laurier to Aberdeen, 7 June 1898, and Du Bosc to Saint-Pierre, 23 June and 2 July 1898, all in WLP; *Boston Evening Transcript,* 8, 10 July 1899.

17. Pauncefote to Aberdeen, 10 June 1898, WLP.

18. Opinion of Richard Webster and Robert B. Finlay, 10 June 1898, Salisbury to Wolff, 11 June 1898, and Wolff to Salisbury, 12 June 1898, all in files on "Spanish Espionage in U.S.A.," PRO.

19. Chamberlain to Aberdeen, 12, 13 June 1898, Du Bosc to H. C. Saint-Pierre, Q.C., 23 June 1898 and Saint-Pierre to Laurier, 23 June 1898, all in WLP; Wolff to Foreign Office, 16 June 1898, PRO; (London) *Times,* 17 June 1898.

20. The *Montreal Star* of 8 July 1899 published the full text of both "Carranza letters," one called "George F. Bell's version" and the other the "Washington version." In a full discussion of the Tupper St. theft, the *Star* tended to give credence to Bell, despite the Englishman's record as an alleged if unconvicted counterfeiter and his admission that he had offered his services to Spain as a double agent. The *Star* was inclined to accept Bell's version of the Carranza letter because it seemed

to be confirmed in a textually exact manner by Carranza's original allegations concerning interpolation. *The Boston Evening Transcripts* of 8 and 10 July 1899 preferred the Redfern story and the "Washington version."

21. Wilkie, "Secret Service," 432, 436.

22. Mount, *Canada's Enemies*, 9; A. W. Greeley, chief signal officer, signal office, War Dept., to assistant secretary of war, 16 July 1898 and Owens to Wilkie, 6 February 1899, both in RSS.

23. O'Toole, *Honorable Treachery*, 195. The foregoing description of U.S. intelligence activities is also taken from O'Toole: chap. 16, "Espionage in the War with Spain," 188–200, and Mount, *Canada's Enemies*, 3. For a more extensive discussion of the ONI's war plan, see David F. Trask, *The War with Spain in 1898* (Lincoln: University of Nebraska Press, 1997 [1981]), 74–80. The mythologization was assisted by Elbert Hubbard's oft-reprinted *A Message to Garcia, being a preachment by Elbert Hubbard* (East Aurora, N.Y.: The Roycroft Shop, 1899).

24. Trask, *War with Spain*, 63. For a contrary assessment, see Mount, *Canada's Enemies*, 9–10.

25. M. Kastle to Wilkie, 13 June 1898, passenger list for Prince line sailing, New York-Azores-Gibralter-Naples-Genoa, 11 June 1898, both in RSS.

26. Kastle to Wilkie, 13 June 1898, RSS.

27. Lincoln Steffens, *The Autobiography of Lincoln Steffens* (New York: Harcourt, Brace, 1931), 285–91.

28. Don Wilkie, *Agent*, 14.

29. Kaiser, "Origins," 116. See also Kaiser, "Presidential Assassinations," 546–47, and Sidney Fine, "Anarchism and the Assassination of McKinley," *American Historical Review*, 60 (July 1955).

30. Kaiser, "Origins," 110–13; *Chicago Inter-Ocean*, 3 January 1904, quoted in Williams, "Without Understanding," 33.

Chapter 5. U-1

1. William Jennings Bryan, *British Rule in India* (Westminster: British Committee on the India National Congress, ca. 1906), quoted in Paul W. Glad, *The Trumpet Soundeth: William Jennings Bryan and His Democracy 1896–1912* (Lincoln: University of Nebraska Press, 1960), 70.

2. William R. Polk, *Polk's Folly: An American Family History* (New York: Doubleday, 2000), xxvii, 360.

3. Confidential diary of Frank Polk, 16 June 1916, 3 March 1917, EMH. A more extensive treatment of U-1, and of American intelligence activities in World War I, is in Jeffreys-Jones, *American Espionage*, from which some of the details in the present account are taken.

4. For information on Wiseman, see Fowler, *British-American Relations*, and R. Jeffreys-Jones, "Wiseman, Sir William George Eden (1885–1962)" in *The New Dictionary of National Biography* (Oxford University Press, forthcoming).

5. John Morton Blum, *Woodrow Wilson and the Politics of Morality* (Boston: Little, Brown, 1956), 10; Popplewell, *British Intelligence*, 248, 250.

6. Blum, *Wilson*, 170. But Wilson was capable of being pragmatic toward Irish Americans (whose support was needed by the Democratic Party), and his administration made occasional gestures acknowledging the justice of the Irish

nationalist cause. See Francis M. Carroll, *American Opinion and the Irish Question, 1910–23* (Dublin: Gill & Macmillan, 1978), 81–82.

7. Witcover, *Sabotage at Black Tom*, 12, 20.

8. Jones, *German Spy in America*, 38, 88–91.

9. See Alan J. Ward, *Ireland and Anglo-American Relations 1899–1921* (London: Weidenfeld & Nicolson, 1969), 108, 155.

10. Kahn, *Codebreakers*, 145.

11. In another link in the Anglo-American elitist intelligence chain, one of Bell's daughters married David K. E. Bruce, who became chief of the World War II Office of Strategic Services office in London, and the U.S. ambassador to Britain after the war. See Kahn, "Bell," 143, 146–47.

12. The words are those of Walter Hines Page, the American ambassador in London, paraphrasing for President Wilson's eyes a concocted Anglo-American version of events, and quoted in Tuchman, *Zimmermann Telegram*, 161. See also Doerries, *Imperial Challenge*.

13. Ambrosius, "Secret German-American Negotiations," 288–309.

14. Henry W. Wriston, "Executive Agents in American Foreign Relations" (Ph.D. diss., Harvard University, 1922), 132.

15. Wiseman memo, 5 June 1928, reproduced in Charles Seymour, ed., *The Intimate Papers of Colonel House*, 4 vols. (London: Ernest Benn, 1928), vol. III, 176.

16. Confidential diary of Frank Polk, 12 April 1920, EMH.

17. E. R. Warner McGabe (assistant chief of staff, G-2), "The Military Intelligence Division, War Department General Staff" (typescript of lecture delivered at the Army War College, Washington, D.C., 1940), 11–12.

18. W. J. Flynn, memo for secretary of the treasury (transmitted via Harrison), 10 May 1915, in "Human Espionage Activities" file, OC; Tuchman, *Zimmermann Telegram*, 74.

19. Insertion in "Lost and Found" section of *New York Evening Telegram*, 27 July 1915; press release no. 31–83, 31 May 1942, in general records of the Department of the Treasury, office of the secretary, general correspondence, NA; Daniel M. Smith, *Robert Lansing and American Neutrality* (Berkeley: University of California Press, 1958), 98.

20. Polk diary, 8 August, 30 November 1918, EMH.

21. Polk diary, 4 October 1918, EMH; Peter G. Filene, *Americans and the Soviet Experiment, 1917–1933* (Cambridge, Mass.: Harvard University Press, 1967), 47–48.

22. John M. Keynes, *The Economic Consequences of the Peace* (London: Macmillan, 1920); J. W. Hiden, *The Weimar Republic* (London: Longmans, 1974).

23. Notes of a conversation between Gen. T. H. Bliss and Captain Emanuel Voska, 26 February 1919," LH.

24. Dulles to Grew, 25 February 1919, and Voska to secretary of state, attention Harrison, 19 March 1919, both in LH. See also Dulles, *Craft*, 11.

25. Voska to secretary of state, attention Harrison, 19 March 1919, LH.

26. Harrison to Crane, 24 March 1921, LH.

27. Wiseman to Auchincloss, 26 January 1918, Wiseman papers, EMH.

28. Maugham, *Ashenden*, 157; Maugham, *A Writer's Notebook* (London: Heinemann, 1949), 140.

29. Robert L. Calder, *W. Somerset Maugham and the Quest for Freedom* (London: Heinemann, 1971), 273–74; Gordon Auchincloss diary, 20 November 1917, YUL.

30. Maugham, *Stories,* 44; Calder, *Maugham,* 200, 205.

31. Maugham, *Stories,* 224.

32. Memos to the British embassy at St. Petersburg, 22 August 1917 and 18 January 1918 in Calder, *Maugham,* 277, 286–87; Jeffreys-Jones, *American Espionage,* 87–101.

33. Wilson, quoted in Robert C. Hilderbrand, *Power and the People: Executive Management of Public Opinion in Foreign Affairs, 1871–1921* (Chapel Hill: University of North Carolina Press, 1981), 109; Stephen L. Vaughan, *Holding Fast the Inner Lines: Democracy, Nationalism, and the Committee on Public Information* (Chapel Hill: University of North Carolina Press, 1980), 77, 81, 141.

34. Robert Lansing, *The Peace Negotiations: A Personal Narrative* (New York: Houghton Mifflin, 1921), 217, 221.

35. Daniel T. Goggin and H. Stephen Helton, *General Records of the Department of State* (Washington, D.C.: National Archives; General Services Administration, 1963), 116 17.

36. Departmental order no. 414, (17?) June 1927, signed by Frank B. Kellogg, in anachronistically labeled "Office of the Counselor" record section, National Archives, which survived until June 1927 and Kirk to Hoover, Hepburn, and Ford, 22 June 1927, both in OC.

37. Kirk to Hoover, Hepburn, and Ford, 22 June 1927, OC.

38. Joseph C. Grew, *Turbulent Era: A Diplomatic Record of Forty Years, 1904–1945,* 2 vols. (London: Hammond, 1953), vol. 1, 699, 705.

39. Kirk to Hoover, Hepburn, and Ford, 22 June 1927, OC.

40. Berle, *Navigating the Rapids,* 320.

Chapter 6. Burns, Hoover, and the Making of an FBI Tradition

1. Burns, *Masked War,* 83–84. On Burns in Tacoma: Fisher, "Home Colony," 137, 140.

2. Adams, "Burns," 27–28.

3. The U.S. Commission on Industrial Relations published an account of the National Dynamite Campaign and of the background to it: Luke Grant, *The National Erectors' Association and the International Association of Bridge and Structural Ironworkers* (Washington, D.C., 1915).

4. F. W. Cohen of the Pennsylvania Steel Company to Walter Drew, commissioner of the National Erectors' Association, 26 October 1910, WD; Burns to Charles McCarthy (director, Research Division, Commission on Industrial Relations), 16 February 1915, CM; Jeffreys-Jones, *Violence and Reform,* 73, 215n48.

5. Michael J. Heale warns against "accepting those interpretations of anticommunism that emphasize its hysterical, irrational and aberrant features": *American Anticommunism,* xiii.

6. A useful book could be written on the origins of the FBI. The details here are drawn from Williams, "Without Understanding," 25, 26, 30, 34–37; Torres, *Handbook,* 136; Kaiser, "Origins," 118; and Kessler, *FBI,* 573.

7. Knott, *Secret and Sanctioned,* 50–60, 202–3n7; Lowenthal, *Federal Bureau,* 3–12.

8. David Graham Phillips, *The Treason of the Senate,* ed. George E. Mowry and Judson Grenier (Chicago: Quadrangle, 1964 [1906]) (President Roosevelt thought this book went too far, and applied John Bunyon's term "muckraker" to Phillips and similar investigative journalists); Williams, "Without Understanding," 29.

9. John Messing, "Public Lands, Politics, and Progressives: The Oregon Land Fraud Trials, 1903–1910," *Pacific Historical Review,* 35 (February 1966), 56. Lincoln Steffens published his exposés in *American Magazine* in 1907, and one of the convicted swindlers used his time in jail to pen a lurid confession that appeared the following year: Stephen A. Douglas Puter (with Horace Stevens), *Looters of the Public Domain* (Portland, 1908)—references in Jerry O'Callaghan, "Senator Mitchell and the Oregon Land Frauds, 1905," *Pacific Historical Review,* 21 (August 1952), 255–261.

10. Don Wilkie, *Agent,* 67; Williams, "Without Understanding," 39; Kaiser, "Origins," 117–18; O'Callaghan, "Mitchell," 261; Cook, *Nobody Knows,* 52.

11. Williams, "Without Understanding," 48.

12. Lowenthal, *Federal Bureau,* 14–15; Williams, "Without Understanding," 50.

13. Lowenthal, *Federal Bureau,* 14–15; Cook, *Nobody Knows,* 56.

14. Cook, *Nobody Knows,* 57–58; *Concise Dictionary of American Biography* (New York: Charles Scribner, 1990), 4th ed., 569; Williams, "Without Understanding," 52.

15. Cook, *Nobody Knows,* 60–63; Williams, "Without Understanding," 82.

16. Murray, *Red Scare,* 30.

17. Military intelligence officer turned historian William R. Corson wrote of the 6 March 1918 meeting: "The central intelligence proposal was shelved for forty years, when the Central Intelligence Agency was sanctioned in language very similar to McAdoo's": Corson, *Armies,* 59.

18. Martin R. Ansell, "William Gibbs McAdoo," *American National Biography* (New York: Oxford University Press), vol. 14, 806–8. On McAdoo's prewar achievements, see John J. Broesamle, *William Gibbs McAdoo: A Passion for Change, 1863–1917* (Port Washington, N.Y.: Kennikat Press, 1973).

19. Cook, *Nobody Knows,* 64–67.

20. Powers, *Secrecy and Power,* 6. Unless otherwise indicated, details on Hoover's career are taken mainly from this source, and from Theoharis and Cox, *The Boss.*

21. Murray, *Red Scare,* ix; James K. Libbey, "New Study Areas for Soviet-American Relations: The Case of Russian Gold," *The Society for Historians of American Foreign Relations Newsletter,* 6 (June 1975), 17. In 1920, the Radical Division was renamed the General Intelligence Division. On Flynn, see Corson, *Armies,* 58, 590.

22. See the interpretation of the *New York Times* story of 28 July 1919 in Ellis, "Hoover and the Red Summer," 44.

23. For a critical encapsulation of some of the key points in the Hoover debate, see Garrow, *FBI and King,* 221–24.

24. On the gay charge, see Summers, *Official and Confidential.* Athan Theoharis notes that serious commentators did not accept Summers's claims, and at the

conclusion of a lengthy analysis he questions them himself: Theoharis, *Hoover, Sex, and Crime,* 15, 55.

25. Theoharis and Cox, *The Boss,* 67–69; Powers, *Secrecy and Power,* 126, 128. See also Ellis, "Hoover and the Red Summer."

26. McKnight, *Last Crusade,* 6. Hoover sometimes proceeded less strenuously than he would have liked against black radicals because he could not carry with him his fellow officials in the Justice Department: see Carson, *Malcolm X,* 65. According to William A. Little, Senator Frank Church's 1970s inquiry into FBI abuses showed a politically correct tendency to focus on harassment of Black Nationalists and the New Left in spite of the bureau's more questionable tactics in pursuit of the White Hate movement: Little, "Radicals and Racists," 49, and see U.S. Congress, Senate, Select Committee to Study Governmental Operations with Respect to Intelligence Activities, *Hearings,* Vol. 6, *Federal Bureau of Investigation,* 94th Cong., 2d sess., GPO, 1976.

27. McKnight, *Last Crusade,* 5.

28. Warren G. Harding, quoted in Williams, "Without Understanding," 218.

29. Burns testimony, quoted in Williams, "Without Understanding," 234; Andrew Sinclair, *The Available Man: The Life Behind the Masks of Warren Gamaliel Harding* (New York: Macmillan, 1965), 258–59, 262; Dorwart, *Conflict of Duty,* 3–4.

30. Charles, "Informing FDR," 213–14; Bureau of Investigation, Department of Justice, "Weekly Bulletin of Radical Activities (26 June and 3 July 1920) and "General Intelligence Bulletin" (weeks ending 25 September and 16 October 1920, and 17 September 1921), all in the files of the "Radical Division," OC.

31. Williams, "Without Understanding," 315–19.

32. On the role of FBI agent Leon G. Turrou in the arrest and trial of German spy Gunther Gustav Rumrich and on the accompanying publicity, see Miller, *Spying for America,* 228.

33. Charles, "Informing FDR," 218, 223; Charles and Rossi, "Lindbergh Investigation," 844.

34. Rout and Bratzell, *Shadow War,* 36–37, 88; Raat, "Covert Action in Mexico," 629–30.

35. Theoharis, *FBI Reference Guide,* 4, 5, 182. While noting Hoover's bureaucratic resilience, María Emilia Paz suggests that FBI reporting on Mexico lacked depth and would have been less valuable without supplementation from other sources: Paz, *Strategy, Security and Spies,* 192, 202.

36. For a variety of views on American Communism and the FBI, see Lamphere, *FBI-KGB War;* Barron, *Operation Solo;* Weinstein and Vassiliev, *Haunted Wood;* Haynes and Klehr, *Venona;* Edward P. Johannsmeier, *Forging American Communism: The Life of William Z. Foster* (Princeton, N.J.: Princeton University Press, 1994); Whitaker, "Cold War Alchemy," 177–210, and Powers, *Secrecy and Power,* 333.

37. Garrow, *FBI and King,* 221; Moynihan, *Secrecy,* 62, 154.

Chapter 7. H. O. Yardley

1. Yardley, *Education,* 7; *Surveillant* 2 (January/February 1992): 99.
2. Fleming in Yardley, *Education,* 11; Ian L. Fleming, *Casino Royale* (Lon-

don: Cape, 1954). The main problem with Fleming's claim is that central intelligence had been advocated and fought over within the U.S. intelligence establishment since World War I. For a critical assessment of the more immediate circumstances of the 1941 Fleming memoranda on the improvement of U.S. intelligence, see Troy, *Wild Bill and Intrepid,* 127.

3. Dulles, *Craft,* 76.

4. Farago, *Broken Seal,* 55–57, 359–60; Lewin, *American Magic,*19; *Surveillant,* 2 (January/February 1992): 99.

5. Denniston, "Yardley's Diplomatic Secrets," 89.

6. Kahn, *Codebreakers,* 355.

7. Yardley, *Education,* 17–18.

8. Yardley, *Black Chamber,* 2; Kahn, *Codebreakers,* 352.

9. Yardley, *Black Chamber,* 14, 149–50.

10. Yardley, *Education,* 77; Kahn, *Codebreakers,* 354.

11. Yardley, *Black Chamber,* 164–67; Denniston, "Yardley's Diplomatic Secrets," 92; Kahn, *Codebreakers,* 355.

12. Denniston, "Yardley's Diplomatic Secrets," 92.

13. Shidehara document in H. O. Yardley, "Japanese Diplomatic Secrets," quoted in Denniston, "Yardley's Diplomatic Secrets," 109.

14. H. O. Yardley, "Japanese Diplomatic Secrets," cited in Denniston, "Yardley's Diplomatic Secrets," 111. "Japanese Diplomatic Secrets" (JDS) largely consists of transcripts of Japanese diplomatic messages. These are presumably reliable textually, even if there may be doubt as to the criteria for selection. But there is a question mark over the authorship of the rest of JDS, as the title page bears the name Marie Stewart Klooz. Denniston argues that Klooz helped the uneducated Yardley write the manuscript, that it was more satisfying to praise himself in the third person in someone else's name, and that the stratagem protected Yardley against prosecution. In truth, the text of JDS is stylistically turgid and uncharacteristic of Yardley's published writings. Yet, Yardley's was probably the prime influence on the text of JDS. On balance, it does seem likely that he speculated about the smile on Hughes's face.

15. Yardley, *Black Chamber,* 221. For an assessment of the naval conference from both the American and the Japanese perspectives, see Walter Lafeber, *The Clash: A History of U.S.-Japanese Relations* (New York: Norton, 1997), 138–41.

16. Alastair Denniston, "Code and Cypher School," 55–56; Farago, *Broken Seal,* 32; Lafeber, *The Clash,* 139.

17. Bamford, *Puzzle Palace,* 34–35.

18. Alvarez, *Secret Messages,* 15–16.

19. Quoted in Miller, *Spying for America,* 213.

20. William Friedman, "A Brief History of the Signal Intelligence Service" (n.d., unpublished), 175, quoted in Denniston, "Yardley's Diplomatic Secrets," 89n15.

21. Washburn to secretary of state, 26 May 1925, USDS; Kellogg to Amlegation, Vienna, 26 May 1925, USDS.

22. Kellogg to Amlegation, Vienna, 27 May 1925, USDS; Kahn, *Codebreakers,* 385.

23. Yardley, *Education,* 77.

24. Although he probably did not utter these words at the time, they did appear later in Stimson and Bundy, *Active Service,* 188.

25. Alastair Denniston, "Code and Cypher School," 48; excerpt from the microfilm edition of the Stimson diaries in Yale University Library, quoted in Fischel, "Mythmaking," 5.

26. Farago, *Broken Seal,* 55–57.

27. Farago, *Broken Seal,* 58.

28. Pennypacker, *General Washington's Spies on Long Island and in New York,* vol. 2, 32.

29. Kahn, *Codebreakers,* 363; Denniston, "Yardley's Diplomatic Secrets," 115–16.

30. Yardley, *Education,* 77; Kahn, *Codebreakers,* 363; Lafeber, *The Clash,* 170.

31. Bamford, *Puzzle Palace,* 40–46; Reinhard R. Doerries, "Introduction" to Captain Von Rintelen (Franz Rintelen von Kleist), *The Dark Invader: Wartime Reminiscences of a German Naval Intelligence Officer* (London: Frank Cass, 1997 [1933]), xxx; Stafford, *Silent Game,* 86.

32. Denniston quoted in Budiansky, "Difficult Beginnings," 51; Denniston, "Yardley's Diplomatic Secrets," 118n118.

33. See Mangold, *Angleton,* 45; and Haynes and Klehr, *Venona,* 333.

Chapter 8. Pearl Harbor in Intelligence History

1. Prange, *At Dawn We Slept,* 499–503.

2. The texts of the 1941–1946 Pearl Harbor government reports and congressional hearings are available on the Internet. The Net addresses keep changing, and it is best to use a Web crawler and key in the words "Pearl Harbor."

3. The Democrats may have had a special partisan motive in portraying Pearl Harbor as an intelligence failure and they did lead the way in the 1946 hearings, yet Republican supporters of the CIA proposal sometimes subscribed to the same view. For a summary of the debate, see Jeffreys-Jones, "Why Was the CIA Established in 1947?" 25–29. It has been established that, possibly because he did not trust his rivals with full knowledge of his sources, the director of the FBI withheld from both the president and naval intelligence indications based on a German secret service document that the Japanese had identified Pearl Harbor as a prime target: John F. Bratzel and Leslie B. Rout, Jr., "Research Note: Pearl Harbor, Microdots, and J. Edgar Hoover," *American Historical Review,* 87 (1982): 1342–51.

4. Haines, "CIA History Program," 203.

5. Transcript, Langer lecture at the State Department on "Research and Intelligence," 31 May 1946, 13–15, Box 5, PGS.

6. Dulles to Souers, 7 December and Souers to Dulles 9 December 1948, Box 52, folder 33, AWD; Langer, *In and Out of the Ivory Tower,* 210, 212; W. L. Langer and S. E. Gleason, *The Challenge to Isolation: The World Crisis of 1937–1940 and American Foreign Policy,* 2 vols. (New York: Harper and Row, 1952); pamphlet, Harry Elmer Barnes, *The Court Historians versus Revisionism* (no further particulars given), cited in Waller, ed., *Pearl Harbor and the Coming of the War,* 111.

7. Charles A. Beard, *President Roosevelt and the Coming of the War, 1941: A Study in Appearances and Realities* (New Haven: Yale University Press, 1948); William H. Chamberlin, *America's Second Crusade* (Chicago: Regnery, 1942). For overviews of the debate, see Waller, *Pearl Harbor* and Donald Goldstein, "Pearl Harbor," in Bruce W. Jentleson and Thomas G. Paterson, eds., *Encyclopedia of U.S. Foreign Relations*, 4 vols. (New York: Oxford University Press, 1997), vol. 3, 378–80.

8. George Morgenstern, *Pearl Harbor: The Story of the Secret War* (New York: Devin-Adair, 1947); Charles C. Tansill, *Back Door to War: The Roosevelt Foreign Policy, 1933–1941* (Chicago: Regnery, 1952). For discussion of the debate on Stimson's famous paraphrase, see Current, "How Stimson Meant to 'Maneuver' the Japanese," 67–74; transcript, Walter Trohan oral history interview, 7 October 1970, by Jerry N. Hess for the Harry S. Truman Presidential Library, HST; Husband E. Kimmel, *Admiral Kimmel's Story* (Chicago: Regnery, 1955).

9. Roberta's husband, Albert, an authority on strategy associated with the University of Chicago and one source of inspiration for her book, spent much of the next twelve years criticizing the CIA for underestimating the Soviet threat, and, in the mid-1970s, he launched a determined attack on the agency for that reason. See Cahn, *Killing Detente*, 11–15.

10. Wohlstetter, *Pearl Harbor*, xi, 382–401.

11. Cline, *CIA Under Reagan Bush and Casey*, pp. 21, 27, 38.

12. David Kahn, "United States Views," 477, 500.

13. Before the Pearl Harbor attack, Foreign Minister Shigenori Togo "recalled the [Yardley] episode and checked to see whether Japanese communications were then secure": Kahn, *Codebreakers*, 364. See also Goldstein, "Pearl Harbor," 379; Stafford, *Roosevelt and Churchill*, 116–17; Budiansky, "Difficult Beginnings," 49–73.

14. Edward L. Beach, "Who's to Blame," *United States Naval Institute Proceedings* (December 1991): 39–40.

15. Beach, *Scapegoats;* Clausen and Lee, *Pearl Harbor: Final Judgement;* Edwin Dorn, memo for the deputy secretary for defense, "Advancement of Rear Admiral Kimmel and Major General Short," 15 December 1995, 4, 6, taken from the Internet.

16. Rusbridger and Nave, *Betrayal at Pearl Harbor,* 28; Stinnett, *Day of Deceit,* 2–3.

17. Stinnett, *Day of Deceit,* 182–209. While some of Stinnett's evidence commands serious attention, his theory that Roosevelt followed a plan drawn up by a junior naval intelligence officer to manipulate Japan into making the Pearl Harbor attack is improbable. For an exposition of some of the weaknesses in Rusbridger's book, see Aldrich, "Conspiracy or Confusion?" 335–46. According to Gill Bennett, chief historian at the Foreign and Commonwealth Office, Britain is just as willing as America to open its historical intelligence files: Bennett lecture in Edinburgh, 13 December 2000. U.S. historians Warren Kimball and Bruce Lee believe the full Pearl Harbor story awaits the opening of the British files: Lee, *Marching Orders*, x.

18. Historical branch, G-2, "Materials on the History of Military Intelligence in the United States, 1885–1944" (unpublished document, 1944), Part I, Exhibit B: "Headquarters Personnel and Funds Military Intelligence Activities," in USA Cen-

ter of Military History Library, Forrestal Building, Washington, D.C.; F. H. Lincoln (assistant chief of staff, G-2), "The Military Intelligence Division, War Department General Staff" (typescript of 1937 lecture), 3, MID; "Duties of Intelligence Officers, U.S. Army," *Army and Navy Journal* (1 September 1923); Andrew, *For the President's Eyes Only,* 68; *Naval Investigation: Hearings before the subcommittee of the Committee on Naval Affairs . . . Printed for the use of the Committee on Naval Affairs* (Washington, D.C.: Government Printing Office, 1921), 2716; Dorwart, *Conflict of Duty,* 11–14.

19. Wark, *Ultimate Enemy,* 233, 240; Angevine, "Gentlemen," 7, 24; B. F. Smith, "American Road," 6, 13.

20. "Scope of Intelligence," penciled notes, undated but apparently pre–World War II, in folder "Notes," Box 1, PGS; Dorwart, *Conflict of Duty,* 3–5, 45.

21. Stanley S. Ford, "The Military Intelligence Division, War Department General Staff" (typescript of War College lecture, 1928), 5, 7, MID. A book on U.S.-British anti-subversive intelligence cooperation is being written by Bradley F. Smith, Eunan O'Halpin, and Keith Jeffreys. See B. F. Smith, "American Road," 12, 19n32.

22. Angevine, "Gentlemen," 9–10.

23. A. W. Johnson, "Duties of Naval Attaché" (Navy Department: n.d., but c. 1930), 28–30, 32, 44, 63, 64, 68, ONI.

24. Zacharius, *Secret Missions,* 13; Rhodri Jeffreys-Jones, "Roscoe C. Hillenkoetter," in John A. Garraty and Mark C. Carnes, eds., *American National Biography* (New York: Oxford University Press, 1999), vol. 10, 812–13.

25. Angevine, "Gentlemen," 6, 8, 21; Kahn, "United States Views," 482; Budiansky, "Difficult Beginnings"; Antony Best, " 'This Probably Over-Valued Military Power': British Intelligence and Whitehall's Perception of Japan, 1939–41," *Intelligence and National Security,* 12 (July 1997): 67–94.

26. Niblack (director, ONI), *History and Aims,* 12, 24; S. Heintzelman (assistant chief of staff, G-2), "Report of the Military Intelligence Division for the Fiscal Year Ending June 30, 1922," 4, MID; Ford, "Military Intelligence Division," 6.

27. E. R. Warner McGabe, "The Military Intelligence Division, War Department General Staff" (typescript of lecture delivered at the Army War College, Fort Humphreys, Washington, D.C., 1940), 1, MID.

28. Kahn, "United States Views," 493; Lowenthal, "Searching for National Intelligence," 737–38.

29. Lowenthal, "Searching," 742. The Wedemeyer estimate, "Ultimate Requirements Study: Estimate of Army Ground Forces," appears as an appendix in Charles E. Kirkpatrick, *An Unknown Future and a Doubtful Present: Writing the Victory Plan of 1941* (Washington, D.C.: Government Printing Office, 1990), 125–38.

30. Lowenthal, "Searching," 740. Historian David Kahn notes that when President Roosevelt tasked his army and navy intelligence chiefs in June 1940, he did not even ask them to find out in any detail about Axis plans or strength. It is distinctly possible that he was tired of doom-and-gloom intelligence estimates, and refrained from asking questions that would produce unpalatable answers. See Kahn, "United States Views," 478.

31. Kendall, "Function of Intelligence," 549.

Chapter 9. Hyping the Sideshow

1. Asbjørn Øye to Colby, 5 April 1995, Box 5, WEC. This and the quotations of William Colby below published with permission of the Princeton University Library.

2. Colby, "V-E Day in the Norwegian Mountains," typescript in Box 5, WEC.

3. This detail is omitted from a later account by Colby, which also differs from the typescript in a number of other respects that are not relevant here, as the point under discussion is not minutiae but the artifact of memory as testimony to the glamorization of the OSS: Colby, "Skis and Daggers."

4. Colby's ten "greatest" spies, all of them twentieth-century, were, in descending order of greatness: Donovan, Reginald V. Jones, Freidman, Sorge, the Rosenbergs, Philby, Penkovsky, Kelley Johnson (who developed the U-2 plane), Arthur Lundahl (Cuban missile crisis photo-interpreter), and Lansdale: Colby, "Who Were the Greatest Spies of All Time?" typescript supplied for the *Rand McNally Almanac of Adventure* in response to a request from the editor-in-chief of the Rand McNally trade division, Robert Garloch, 6 October 1981, Box 2, WEC.

5. For a critical discussion of this idea, see Rudgers, *Creating the Secret State*, 2–3.

6. Dunlop, *Donovan*, 9; Cave Brown, *Last Hero*, 12; Ford, *Donovan of OSS*, 11–12; *Buffalo Evening News*, 9 February 1959.

7. Cave Brown, *Last Hero*, 115.

8. Cave Brown, *Last Hero*, 122–25; Ford, *Donovan*, 75–76.

9. Bernays, "Biography of an idea—Notes—Donovan, William J.," ELB, Part 1, Box 458.

10. Cave Brown, *Last Hero*, 134, 141–42, 168.

11. Troy, *Donovan and the CIA*, 13; Berle, *Navigating the Rapids*, 320.

12. Troy, *Donovan*, 34; David Stafford, "A Myth Called Intrepid," *(Toronto) Saturday Night* (October 1989), 33–37.

13. Stafford, "Myth," 33–37; Cave Brown, *Last Hero*, 147–48; B. F. Smith, *Shadow Warriors*, 33; Troy, *Donovan*, 36; Troy, *Wild Bill and Intrepid*, 41–42; West, *British Security Coordination*, 9.

14. According to Mowrer, Donovan did not take up the Fifth Column idea until Prime Minister Winston Churchill suggested it to him in London, while OSS officer and future CIA director Allen Dulles thought the Fifth Column investigation was just a "cover": transcript, Edgar Ansel Mowrer conversation with Allen Dulles, n.d. (ca. 1962), AWD, Box 17, Folder 18, 6.

15. B. F. Smith, *Shadow Warriors*, 33; Troy, *Donovan*, 31; Troy, *Wild Bill and Intrepid*, 42.

16. Rhodri Jeffreys-Jones, "Lord Lothian and American Democracy: An Illusion in Pursuit of an Illusion," *Canadian Review of American Studies*, 17 (Winter 1986): 411–22; Cave Brown, *Last Hero*, 150–51.

17. MacDonnell, *Insidious Foes*, 3–4; James V. Compton, *The Swastika and the Eagle: Hitler, the United States and the Origins of the Second World War* (London: Bodley Head, 1968), 17–18.

18. "Statement of General Donovan Before Foreign Relations Committee, 1948," ACUE, Box 1, Folder 1, 712; transcript, Edgar Ansel Mowrer conversation with Allen Dulles, n.d. (ca. 1962), AWD, Box 17, Folder 18, 2–3. Jan Valtin was the

pseudonym of Richard Julius Herman Krebs. Valtin had been in prison in Germany until 1937; his best-selling novel *Out of the Night,* about both Nazi and communist subversion, was written between January and October 1940 and published in February the following year: Valtin to "Lillian," 27 February 1943 (written from prison on Ellis Island, Valtin himself having fallen under suspicion), JV, Box CO 731. See also MacDonnell, *Insidious Foes,* 64, 78–79.

19. Donovan and Mowrer, *Fifth Column Lessons,* 3–6, 8, 10, 16.

20. Cave Brown, *Last Hero,* 153; Miles to Marshall, 8 April 1941, quoted in Troy, *Donovan,* 42 (emphasis in the original).

21. John Godfrey, "Intelligence in the United States," 7 July 1941, in B. F. Smith, "Admiral Godfrey's Mission," 445–50. On Wiseman's role, see Cave Brown, *Last Hero,* 163.

22. Andrew, *Secret Service,* 453–55; Jeffreys-Jones, "Role of British Intelligence," 5–19.

23. Troy, *Wild Bill and Intrepid,* 115, 125; Cave Brown, *Last Hero,* 165.

24. Wilhelm F. Flicke seemed to believe that although the OSS had more money and more men than their German counterparts, they still lost out in some key conflicts. For example, he related how in May 1944 German agents won a gunfight against the OSS's Organatione Resistenzia Italia, consequently taking control of Milan: Flicke, "War Secrets in the Ether. Part III," trans. Ray W. Pettengill (Washington, D.C.: National Security Agency, 1954), 269, 297, in folder "Flicke, Wilhelm F.," Box 5, PGS. The official organ of the Polish Peasant Party admitted that the OSS had tried to "paralyze" German armies of occupation but charged that its main aim in the war was not to fight Hitler's forces but to spy on the Soviet Union and establish reactionary post-war regimes: "Actual Role of American Intelligence Service During the War against Hitlerism," *Gazeta Ludowa,* 9 November 1949, translated transcript in Folder 18, Box 17, AWD.

25. B. F. Smith, *Shadow Warriors,* 141; Drea, *MacArthur's ULTRA,* 231–35; Budiansky, "Difficult Beginnings," 69–70.

26. W. L. Rehm, Special Funds Branch, memo for the director, DeWitt C. Poole, Foreign Nationalities Branch, memo for Donovan, H.S. Morgan, CD Branch, memo for Donovan, all dated 13 November 1944 and in Reel 118, Box 5, WJD.

27. Watts Hill, Research and Development, memo for Donovan, William L. Langer, Research and Analysis branch, memo for Donovan, Paul Roberts, Personnel Procurement Branch, memo for the director, all dated 13 November 1944 and in Reel 118, Box 5, WJD.

28. Roosevelt, *War Report,* v, 1, 248; Leahy, *I Was There,* 21, 114, 338.

29. W. L. Langer, "Research and Intelligence," transcript dated 31 May 1946, in folder "Research and Intelligence," Box 5, PGS; Katz, *Foreign Intelligence,* 137–64, 196–98.

30. Laidlaw, "The OSS and Burma Road," 104, 116; Yu, *OSS in China,* 103–5, 265–67; Ernest Volkman and Elaine Bagget, *Secret Intelligence* (London: W.H. Allen, 1989), 40.

31. Walker, "Democracy Goes to War," 60–61.

32. OSS biography of K prepared by "M.I.G.," 17 December 1942, Anon. to Assistant Secretary of State G. Howland Shaw, June 1943, "Details Sur la Mission de A. Kouyoumdjisky en Turquie du 17 Novembre 1943 au 22 Mars 1944 Adressés

Au 'Secretary of State' par l'Aimable entremise de Mr Cavendish Cannon," Annexe No. 1, p. 7, all in Reel 123, Box 15, WJD. Background details here and hereafter are taken from an account that appeared before the release of the Donovan papers containing further information on K Project: Jeffreys-Jones, *American Espionage,* ch. 13: "The OSS and K Project."

33. OSS biography of K prepared by "M.I.G.," Reel 123, Box 15, WJD; Rubin, *Istanbul Intrigues,*180; B. F. Smith, *Shadow Warriors,* 237.

34. B. F. Smith, *Shadow Warriors,* 238; Toulmin to Whitney Sheppardson, 7 February 1944, Reel 123, Box 15, WJD.

35. "Details Sur la Mission de A. Kouyoumdjisky en Turquie du 17 Novembre 1943 au 22 Mars 1944 Adressés Au 'Secretary of State' par l'Aimable entremise de Mr Cavendish Cannon," 1, memo, K to Donovan, 27 March 1944, "Aperçu Sur la Situation Politique, Militaire et Economique de la Bulgarie," 2 and Donovan to Spencer Phenix, 1 April 1944, all in Reel 123, Box 15, WJD.

36. Mosley, *Dulles,* 88–91; Grose, *Gentleman Spy,* 81.

37. Allen W. Dulles's account of Operation Sunrise appeared in *The Secret Surrender.* See also Grose, *Gentleman Spy,* 242, and Dulles, *Germany's Underground,* 197.

38. Anon. (but bearing the imprint of Donovan's thinking), "Memorandum on the Need for a Permanent Independent Intelligence Organization for the United States," 10 September 1943, Anon. (but bearing the imprint of Donovan's thinking), "The Basis for a Permanent, United States Foreign Intelligence Service," 10 October 1944, FDR, memo for General Donovan, 31 October 1944, all in Reel 117, Box 15, WJD; Donovan, memo for the President, 18 November 1944, in Folder 18, Box 17, AWD.

39. W. L. Langer, "Research and Intelligence," transcript dated 31 May 1946, in folder "Research and Intelligence," Box 5, PGS; Steward Alsop and Thomas Braden, *Sub Rosa,* 8; "The Clandestine War in Europe (1942–1945): Remarks of William J. Casey on receipt of the William J. Donovan Award at Dinner of Veterans of O.S.S., December 5, 1974," printed text in RJB; *By Safe Hand: Letters of Sybil and David Eccles 1939–42* (London: Bodley Head, 1983), 243, 266; Dunlop, *Donovan,* viii–ix, 421.

40. The three films were *13 Rue Madeleine* (Twentieth-Century Fox), *OSS* (Paramount Pictures), and *Cloak and Dagger* (Warner Bros. Pictures). See Deutsch, " 'I Was a Hollywood Agent,' " 88–89.

Chapter 10. Allen Dulles and the CIA

1. Dulles, *Germany's Underground,* 196. On the book's sell-out (and the publisher's subsequent decision not to reprint), see R. L. DeWilton (editor-in-chief, Macmillan) to Dulles, 13 February 1952, Folder 5, Box 40, AWD. On Wolff and the early surrender plan, see Dulles, *Secret Surrender* and Grose, *Gentleman Spy,* ch. 10.

2. Narrative from *13 Rue Madeleine* (Twentieth Century Fox), quoted in Deutsch, "I Was a Hollywood Agent," 85; *New York Times,* 16 July 1946; *New York Sun,* 17 December 1946; *Washington Post,* 11 April 1947; *Washington Evening Star,* 11 April 1947; *St. Louis Post-Dispatch,* 11 May 1947.

3. Leffler, *Preponderance of Power,* 15; Souers memo, "Development of In-

telligence on the USSR," 29 April 1946, in Thorne and Patterson, *FRUS: Emergence,* 344. See also Jeffreys-Jones, "Why Was the CIA Established in 1947?" and B. F. Smith, *Ultra-Magic Deals.*

4. Rudgers, *Creating the Secret State,* 101–5; Pettee, *Future,* 1, 4–7, rear dust jacket; introduction to Pettee lecture ca. 1947 by Dr Reichley, Box 22, PGS; Williams, *Legislative History,* 141, 144; Hogan, *Cross of Iron,* 288–89.

5. Ameringer, *U.S. Foreign Intelligence,* 196–97; Pforzheimer quoted in Braden, "Birth of the CIA," 11; Rudgers, *Secret State,* 114; Vandenberg, private memorandum for the Secretaries of State, War, and the Navy and for Adm. William D. Leahy, 29 April 1947, Document No. 232, CIA Collection, Special Collections, Department of State Electronic Reading Room (http://foia.state.gov), the collection being a supplement to Thorne and Patterson, *FRUS: Emergence.*

6. Section 102 of the National Security Act, reproduced in Leary, *History and Documents,* 128–30; Jeffreys-Jones, *CIA and American Democracy,* ch. 4.

7. William J. Casey, speeches in 1981 and (on Pearl Harbor) in 1986, in Casey, *Scouting the Future,* 20, 32.

8. Allen W. Dulles, foreword to the embryonic, 37-page manuscript of an unpublished autobiography, "The View from Henderson Harbor" (3 April 1962), Folder 3, Box 80, AWD; Grose, *Gentleman Spy,* 13.

9. "Notes on the New York Conference, Sept. 13, 1962" (publicizing a forthcoming article by Allen Dulles), Folder 12, Box 70, AWD.

10. Grose, *Gentleman Spy,* 127–29; Polk-Dulles correspondence, 17 July 1917 to 29 November 1919, Folder 4, Box 45, AWD; Dulles, *Secret Surrender,* 10.

11. Dulles, *Great True Spy Stories;* Morrison, "Journalists," 55–56; Trohan to Dulles, 1 December 1961, Box 55, AWD.

12. Allen W. Dulles, "CIA and Its Role in Maintaining the National Security," *Ladies Auxiliary Veterans of Foreign Wars National Bulletin* (March 1954), 21; Hunt, *Undercover,* 132; McCormick and Fletcher, *Spy Fiction,* 143–44.

13. Dulles-Fleming correspondence, 1962–1965, in Folder 14, Box 25, AWD; Dulles to James Nelson (producer, NBC), 27 March 1963, and Dulles to Sally Williams (Harper and Row, New York), 31 October 1963, both in Folder 13, Box 70, AWD.

14. Winks, *Cloak and Gown,* 25, 64; Hersh, *Old Boys,* 4; Thomas, *Very Best Men,* 10; Bissell, *Reflections,* 5.

15. Colby, *Honorable Men,* 180; E. Digby Baltzell, *The Protestant Establishment* (New York: Random House, 1964), 9; Alsop, *The Center,* 228–29, 233; Yakovlev, *CIA Target,* 302. Although Alsop captured an important shift in attitudes, the reality may have been different: a disproportionate number of top CIA people in the early 1980s still came from an Ivy League background: Jeffreys-Jones, "Composition of the CIA Elite," 421–24.

16. Pisani, *CIA and Marshall Plan,* 99; Jeffreys-Jones, *CIA and American Democracy,* 49–52; Haynes and Klehr, *Venona,* 331–32; McCarthy quoted in Richard H. Rovere, *Senator Joe McCarthy* (New York: Harcourt, Brace, 1959), 69.

17. White House aide quoted in William R. Tanner, "McCarran Internal Security Act of 1950," in Donald C. Bacon and others, eds., *The Encyclopedia of the United States Congress,* 4 vols. (New York: Simon & Schuster, 1995), vol. 3, 1323–24; "NSC 68: United States Objectives and Programs for National Security (April 14, 1950)," in Joseph M. Siracusa, *Into the Dark House: American Diplomacy and*

the Ideological Origins of the Cold War (Claremont, Calif.: Regina, 1998), 211–63; Leffler, *Preponderance,* 355; NSC 68/Siracusa, program point 7, 257.

18. NSC 68/Siracusa, program point 7, 214. The author is here grateful to Marilyn B. Young, who offered the privacy-of-rhetoric critique in discussion following his paper at the Department of History, New York University, 28 September 1998.

19. Colby, memorandum, 12 July 1950, enclosed with Colby to Donovan, 14 July 1950, both in Box 2, WEC.

20. Ambrose, *Ike's Spies,* 176; Currey, *Lansdale,* 19.

21. Harry S. Truman, "Truman Deplores Change in CIA Role," *Evansville Courier,* 21 December 1963; Grose, *Gentleman Spy,* 336.

22. The United Fruit Company was an important client of Allen Dulles's law firm, Sullivan and Cromwell. Displaying insensitivity to the potential charge of reward for services rendered, Smith joined United Fruit's board of directors after the coup. See Claude Julien, *L'Empire américain* (Paris: B. Grasset, 1968), 330, 333; Ambrose, *Ike's Spies,* 223; Schlesinger and Kinzer, *Bitter Fruit,* 23, 91–93, 97. An overview of American clandestine policy is Immerman, *The CIA in Guatemala,* and the subsequently declassified official history of the coup is Cullather, *Secret History.*

23. CIA Secret Special Estimate, "The Current Crisis in Iran," 16 March 1951, cited in Donovan, "Intelligence and Policy on Iran," 44–45; Tye, *Bernays,* 155–57; Phillips, *Night Watch,* 48; Roosevelt, *Countercoup,* 3, 7, 83; Morgan, *Anti-Americans,* 9–10. See also James Goode, *The United States and Iran: In the Shadow of Musaddiq* (New York: St Martin's Press, 1997).

24. Helen Laville, "The Committee of Correspondence," 111.

25. Stephen Spender to Lynne Morrison, 5 July 1991, quoted in Morrison, "Journalists," 64.

26. George Bernard Shaw, "The Cleveland Street Scandals" (unpublished letter dated 26 November 1889) and Richard Wright " 'What Is Africa to Me ?' " in *Encounter,* 3 (September 1954), 20–31. On Shaw's capacity to be amused by America: Rhodri Jeffreys-Jones, "Shaw and the U.S.," *New Edinburgh Review,* 29 (April 1975), 32–34.

27. Saunders, *Who Paid the Piper?,* 253, 258; Serge Guilbaut, *How New York Stole the Idea of Modern Art: Abstract Expressionism, Freedom, and the Cold War* (Chicago: University Press of Chicago, 1983).

28. Robert J. McMahon, *The Limits of Empire: The United States and Southeast Asia since World War II* (New York: Columbia University Press, 1999), p. 89; *Washington Post,* 30 October 1994.

29. Lyman B. Kirkpatrick, Jr., address to the 67th Annual Conference of the International Association of Chiefs of Police, Inc., Washington, D.C., 4 October 1960, in Folder "Speech: Lyman B. Kirkpatrick," Box 7, PGS.

30. Press release of address by C. Tracy Barnes, "Some Thoughts about Intelligence," to the Corporation, Banking and Business Law Section, American Bar Association, 29 August 1960, in Folder "Speech by C. Tracy Barnes," Box 7, PGS. On Barnes, see Thomas, *Very Best Men,* 75 ff.

31. Tom Braden, "I'm Glad the CIA is 'Immoral'," *Saturday Evening Post,* 20 May 1967.

32. Ernst, "Economic Intelligence in CIA," 306; Zelikow, "American Economic Intelligence," 167.

33. Doel and Needell, "Science, Scientists, and the CIA," 67.

34. Maddrell, "British-American Intelligence Collaboration," 74, 76, 83; Richelson, "Wizards of Langley," 82; Kenneth E. Greer, "Corona," in Ruffner, *Corona*, 3.

35. Bamford, *Puzzle Palace*, 87; Andrew, *For the President's Eyes Only*, 217; Prados, *Soviet Estimate*, 35.

36. According to documents released in 1996, Eisenhower had delayed the launch of an American satellite until, as anticipated, *Sputnik* overflew the United States, thus establishing the principle of satellite surveillance. The United States could now reciprocate without offending domestic or international opinion, which was still queasy on the subject of espionage: BBC News report, 25 October 1996.

37. Maddrell, "British-American Scientific Collaboration," 74, 76–77.

38. Transcript, Henry Loomis oral history interview, 25 February 1989, by G. Lewis Schmidt for the Foreign Affairs Oral History Program, Association for Diplomatic Studies, 1, 18, GUL; Mosley, *Dulles*, 459.

39. Lucas and Morey, "CIA and MI6 Before and After Suez," 104, 106, 109.

Chapter 11. Cuba, Vietnam, and the Rhetorical Interlude

1. Pearson, *Life of Fleming*, 322–23, 327; Schlesinger, *Thousand Days*, 105.

2. McCone refused to go on television to explain the intelligence community's role during the Cuban Missile Crisis—Secretary of Defense Robert McNamara did the job instead: Mescall, "A Function of Command," 156.

3. Richard M. Bissell, memorandum for an 11 March 1961 meeting with the president, "Proposed Action against Cuba," *FRUS: 1961–1963*, vol. 10, *Cuba: 1961–1962* (1997), 137–42. See, also, the same FRUS volume, pp. 14, 55, 85, 101–2.

4. Manuel Galich, "Playa Giron desde Buenos Aires, hace dos decades," *Casa de las Américas*, 21 (March–April 1981), 55–56; Victor Bernstein and Jesse Gordon, "The Press and the Bay of Pigs," *The Columbia University Forum*, 10 (Fall 1967): 7; Testimony of Jacob L. Esterline (a CIA official who was involved in the planning of the Bay of Pigs operation but pleaded for its cancellation on the ground of likely failure), in memorandum for the record, Paramilitary Study Group Meeting, Pentagon, 22 May 1961 (this portion of the Taylor inquiry into the Bay of Pigs [see below] was excised from earlier published versions but released in March 2000 and put on the Web by the National Security Archive: www.gwn.edu/nsarchiv/); Blight and Kornbluh, *Politics of Illusion*, xiv.

5. Wyden, *Bay of Pigs*, 93–94; Bissell, *Reflections*, 180–81; transcript, George Decker oral history interview, 18 December 1972, by Dan H. Ralls, 12–14, AMHI.

6. Commentary enclosed with Rowan to Dulles, 19 April 1963, Folder 13, Box 70, AWD.

7. See, for example, Welch, *Response to Revolution*, 72; Bar-Joseph, *Intelligence Intervention*, 145; Bissell, *Reflections*, 152.

8. Allen W. Dulles, "My Answer on the Bay of Pigs" (1965), 2, 4, 8, 9, 22, 25, 41, 47, and Dulles to John Fischer (of Harper and Row in New York), 12 October

1965, both in Folder 15, Box 62, AWD; Schlesinger, *Thousand Days,* 226–97; Sorensen, *Kennedy,* 276.

9. *Operation Zapata,* 43. CIA Inspector General Lyman Kirkpatrick also deplored the structural weaknesses exposed by the Bay of Pigs operation: for his findings, see Kornbluh, *Bay of Pigs*.

10. Kennedy's adviser Arthur M. Schlesinger, Jr., claimed in a memorandum to the president that Europeans had had high hopes of Kennedy, but that they had disappeared in the wave of "acute shock and disillusion" caused by the Bay of Pigs; the CIA had given bad advice, would be blamed by foreigners for all kinds of ills in the future, and should be shaken up and subordinated: "Reactions to Cuba in Western Europe," 3 May 1961, *FRUS: 1961–1963,* vol. 10, *Cuba: 1961–1962* (1997), 423–28.

11. Opinions vary on the causal relationship or otherwise between the Bay of Pigs and the birth of the DIA. For a discussion of the literature by a disbeliever in that theory, see Mescall, "Birth of the Defense Intelligence Agency," 163.

12. Mescall, "Function of Command," 50–51, 70, 72, 108, 154; "DIA—A Brief History—35 Years": http://140.47.5.4/foia/foia.html; Roger R. Trask and Alfred Goldberg, *The Department of Defense, 1947–1997: Organization and Leaders* (Washington, D.C.: Historical Office, Office of the Secretary of Defense, 1997), 32, 78.

13. "DIA—A Brief History"; Fursenko and Naftali, *"One Hell of a Gamble,"* 221.

14. Prados, *Soviet Estimate,* 137–38.

15. White, *Missiles in Cuba,* 30–51. After the event, James R. Killian, chairman of the president's Foreign Intelligence Advisory Board, produced a report enumerating the intelligence errors made during the crisis itself—perhaps he missed the point that, as in the case of the Bay of Pigs, the real omissions were those of longer-term intelligence overview: Killian, memo for the president, 4 February 1963, in McAuliffe, *CIA Documents,* 362–71. Although Krushchev may be more understandable in light of information now available, his judgment still appears to have been dangerously fallible. For example, far from feeling pressured over Berlin, President Kennedy responded that he could not afford to give ground over Cuba, because that would be interpreted as a sign of weakness over Berlin: Kennedy's tape-recorded account of an Oval Office meeting with senior officials just before midnight on 18 October 1962, in May and Zelikow, *Kennedy Tapes,* 172.

16. Kennedy quoted in Allison, *Essence of Decision,* 190.

17. *Guardian,* 9 November 1996; Killian report in McAuliffe, *CIA Documents,* 364.

18. The Jupiters were provocative in that they were parked aboveground and within easy range of Russian targets; they were unstable in that there were insufficient safeguards against unauthorized firing: see Nash, *Other Missiles,* 83, 86.

19. R. J. Smith, *Unknown CIA,* 161; Fursenko and Naftali, "Soviet Intelligence and the Cuban Missile Crisis," 64–87; Amuchastegui, "Cuban Intelligence and the October Crisis," 88–119; Wirtz, "Organizing for Crisis Intelligence," 120–49. The claim on behalf of Penkovsky appeared once again in the microfiche supplement to "Proposed Action against Cuba," *FRUS: 1961–1963,* vol. 10, *Cuba: 1961–1962* (1997), and is shown to be chronologically untenable in Garthoff, "Documenting the Cuban Missile Crisis," 299.

20. For general evidence of Kennedy's ruthlessness and on the president's sex life, see Hersh, *Dark Side of Camelot*.

21. "Covert Action," *Hearings Before the Select Committee to Study Governmental Operations with Respect to Intelligence Activities of the United States Senate*, 94 Cong., 1st sess., pursuant to S. Res. 21, 7 vols., vol. 7, 4 and 5 December 1975, 151, 161–63, 204; Horowitz, *Rise and Fall of Project Camelot*, 4–5.

22. Lansdale testimony in "Alleged Assassination Plots Involving Foreign Leaders" (an interim report of the Select Committee to Study Governmental Operations with Respect to Intelligence Activities), *Senate Report*, 94 Cong., 1st sess., no. 94–465 (20 November 1975), 140; Kaiser, "Review Essay," 192. Evidence emerged in the late 1990s to suggest that the CIA alone concocted 33 plots to kill Castro: *New York Times*, 29 September 1998.

23. Peter Collier and David Horowitz, *The Kennedys* (London: Pan, 1984), 368–69; "Alleged Assassination Plots," 71–90, Hinckle and Turner, *The Fish Is Red*, chs. 2, 4, 5; Hersh, *Camelot*, 306–10.

24. Sherman Kent, memo for Allen Dulles, "The Situation and Prospects in Cuba," 3 November 1961, *FRUS: 1961–1963*, vol. 10, *Cuba: 1961–1962* (1997), 672. In the wake of the missile crisis, McCone reported that, not wishing the CIA to act unilaterally, he had "stood down" an operation to infiltrate ten teams into Cuba by submarine. President Kennedy responded by saying the plan should be further discussed, and by suggesting that Operation Mongoose should be "reconstituted": Summary Record of the Sixth Meeting of the Executive Committee of the National Security Council, 26 October 1962, *FRUS: 1961–1963*, vol. 10, *Cuban Missile Crisis and Aftermath* (1996), 221. Kent's warning was in his memo for Allen Dulles, "The Situation and Prospects in Cuba," 3 November 1961, in ibid., 672.

25. Memorandum for record: "Guidance from the Deputy Secretary of Defense and His Reaction to Original Proposed Policy for CIA Support . . . 30 January 1962," being one of a number of documents released by the JFK Assassination Review Board in 1998, reproduced in Anna K. Nelson, "JFK Assassination Review Board, OAH, Foster Release of Top Secret Documents," Organization of American Historians *Newsletter* (February 1998), 10; Bundy quoted in Philip Zelikow, "US Intelligence and the Cuban Missile Crisis," an H-DIPLO Web posting (5 May 2000) in which the author discussed the contents of forthcoming volumes to supplement May and Zelikow, *The Kennedy Tapes*.

26. For reviews of some of the extensive literature on the Kennedy assassination, see Kaiser, "Review Essay," 165–95, Posner, *Case Closed*, 404–23, and Geoffrey C. Ward, "The Most Durable Assassination Theory: Oswald Did It Alone," *New York Times Book Review*, 21 November 1993. The Assassination Records Review Board, created in 1992 to examine secret documents on the Kennedy assassination, contributed 4 million pages of additional evidence to the public domain, concluding that Oswald had been the sole assassin but that there had been an unwarranted cover-up regarding the plots to kill Castro and their possible connection with Dallas: *New York Times*, 29 September 1998.

27. See Slotkin, *Gunfighter Nation*, 2, 511–12.

28. Kaiser, "Presidential Assassinations," 545, 556; *Report of the President's Commission on the Assassination of President John F. Kennedy* (Washington, D.C.: GPO, 1964), 461.

29. Marilyn B. Young, *The Vietnam Years, 1945–1990* (New York: Harper-

Collins, 1991), 10–11; Marvin E. Gettleman, Jane Franklin, Marilyn B. Young and H. Bruce Franklin, *Vietnam and America: A Documented History,* 2d ed. (New York: Grove, 1995), 26; Jacques Portes, *Les Americains et la Guerre du Vietnam* (Brussels: Editions Complexe, 1993), 28–31.

30. Gerard J. DeGroot, *A Noble Cause? America and the Vietnam War* (Harlow: Longman, 2000), 63; McIntyre, "Kennedy Administration's Diplomatic and Clandestine Responses"; Warner, *Back Fire,* 35, 116; Thomas, *Very Best Men,* 44, 327; Ellen Baker, "Montagnards," in Stanley I. Kutler, ed., *Encyclopedia of the Vietnam War* (New York: Scribner's, 1996), 340.

31. Rhodri Jeffreys-Jones, *Peace Now! American Society and the Ending of the Vietnam War* (New Haven: Yale University Press, 1999), 15, 236n; DeGroot, *Noble Cause?,* 2, 11.

32. Mescall, "Function of Command," 93–94; Usofsky, "Kennedy and the Central Intelligence Agency," 376–77; Robert Buzzanco, *Masters of War: Military Dissent and Politics in the Vietnam Era* (Cambridge: Cambridge University Press, 1996), 39; Thomas, *Very Best Men,* 286; DeGroot, *Noble Cause?,* 76.

33. On the military critique, see Buzzanco, *Masters of War,* 342 ff.

34. Mescall, "Function of Command," 216; Sandra C. Taylor, "Central Intelligence Agency," in Kutler, ed., *Encyclopedia,* 109; Robert J. McMahon, *The Limits of Empire: The United States and Southeast Asia since World War II* (New York: Columbia University Press, 1999), p. 131; intelligence memorandum by the Directorate of Intelligence, CIA, 12 May 1967, in Gareth Porter, ed., *Vietnam: The Definitive Documentation of Human Decisions,* 2 vols. (London: Heyden, 1979), vol. 2, 466.

35. Mescall, "Function of Command," 217; CIA memorandum, originating office not specified, "US Options and Objectives in Vietnam," 10 June 1965, in *FRUS: 1964–1968,* vol. 2, *Vietnam: January–June 1965* (1996), 749–51.

36. Adams, "Vietnam Cover-Up," 42.

37. Wirtz, "Intelligence to Please?" 254.

38. Adams, *War of Numbers,* 215.

39. Saunders, *Who Paid the Piper?* 369; *Washington Post,* 18, 22, 23 February 1967.

40. Jeffreys-Jones, *CIA and American Democracy,* 157–64.

41. According to historian Walter Laqueur, U.S. analysts had the data on Soviet missile development in the second half of the 1960s but did not aggregate it to provide the evidence of a trend. This could have been simple negligence, but it is just as likely that a culture of intelligence to please had taken hold. See Laqueur, *World of Secrets,* 188–89.

42. Melvin Small, *Johnson, Nixon, and the Doves* (New Brunswick, N.J.: Rutgers University Press, 1988), 225–26; Wirtz, "Intelligence to Please?" 253.

43. Currey, *Lansdale,* 2.

44. Moyar, *Phoenix and the Birds of Prey,* 167, 173. See also Guenter Lewy, *America in Vietnam* (Oxford: Oxford University Press, 1978), 272.

Chapter 12. Did Senator Church Reform Intelligence?

1. *New York Times,* 7 May 1996. Chief Medical Examiner John Smialek found that Colby had died from drowning and hypothermia, having possibly suf-

fered a heart attack that caused him to fall into the water: Associated Press report, 11 May 1996, captured on the Intelligence Forum Website, 31 May 2000.

2. All quotations from *New York Times*, 7 May 1996.

3. Colby, "Intelligence and the Press: Address to the Associated Press Annual Meeting," 7 April 1975, Box 2, WEC.

4. Johnson, *Season of Inquiry*, 16–22; Olmsted, *Challenging*, 53.

5. Ashby and Gramer, *Life of Frank Church*, 453.

6. John Robert Greene, *The Presidency of Gerald R. Ford* (Lawrence: University Press of Kansas, 1995), 101.

7. Quotations from Cahn, *Killing Detente*, 8–9.

8. Harry H. Ransom, "Secret Intelligence in the United States," 205, 225–26.

9. Johnson, *Season of Inquiry*, p. 17.

10. Henry Kissinger, *White House Years* (Boston: Little, Brown, 1979), 535; Freedman, *U.S. Intelligence and the Soviet Strategic Threat*, 168; G. Smith, *Doubletalk*, 111, 114–15, 173; Prados, *Soviet Estimate*, 230.

11. Seymour Hersh, *The Price of Power: Kissinger in the White House* (London: Faber and Faber, 1983), 187n; Johnson, *Season of Inquiry*, 225; Freedman, *U.S. Intelligence*, 54; Paul N. McCloskey, Edwin B. Forsythe, and John N. Erlenborn to President Gerald R. Ford, April 17, 1975, folder "Intelligence June 24, 1975," Subj. ND6, WHCF, GRF; *CIA: Pike Report*, 249–53.

12. Cahn, *Killing Detente*, 9.

13. Costa, *Legislation*, 35; Mondale quoted in Welch, "Secrecy, Democracy and Responsibility," 170; Transcript, Martin Agronsky TV interview with Michael Harrington and Ray S. Cline, 11 September 1974, folder "9.13 CIA (3)," Box 33, CHM.

14. Colby to Ford, 24 December 1974, in "Oversize Attachment 4595," WHCF, GRF; Gerald R. Ford, *A Time to Heal: The Autobiography of Gerald R. Ford* (New York: Harper, 1979), 324–25.

15. Transcript in WHCF Name File under Schorr, GRF; Schorr, *Clearing the Air*, 153.

16. *Report to the President by the [Rockefeller] Commission*, 15, 42.

17. Orton, "Reorganizing," 70; *Newsweek* (23 June 1975), quoted in Ashby and Gramer, *Fighting the Odds*, 474; Olmsted, *Challenging*, 84.

18. Olmsted, *Challenging*, 96. For a none-too-complimentary affirmation of presidential control over a long period, see Andrew, *For the President's Eyes Only*.

19. Schorr, *Clearing the Air*, 156; Rogovin interview with Kathryn Olmsted, 24 March 1992, in Olmsted, *Challenging*, 112. See also "Unauthorized Storage of Toxic Agents," *Hearings before the Select Committee to Study Governmental Operations with Respect to Intelligence Activities of the United States Senate*, 94 Cong., 1st sess., pursuant to S. Res. 21, 7 vols., vol. 1, 16, 17, and 18 September 1875, pp. 189–90, and Moseley, *Dulles*, 457.

20. Olmsted, *Challenging*, 121–23.

21. *CIA: Pike Report*, 34–35, 39; memo, Ford to secretary of state and others, 19 September 1975, folder "Central Intelligence Agency 7/1/75–9/30/75," FG 6-2, Subj. WHCF, GRF; *Washington Star*, 29 September 1975, quoted in Olmsted, *Challenging*, 128.

22. *Washington Star*, 10 September 1975; Casey to Ford, 13 September 1975, in folder "Church, Frank (Sen.) 1975," Name File, WHCF, GRF.

23. Jeffreys-Jones, *CIA and American Democracy,* 209.

24. *Christian Science Monitor,* 20 April 1976; Mader, *Who's Who in the CIA,* 411; *Washington Star,* 29 December 1975, and *Washington Post,* 7 January 1976, both quoted in Johnson, *Season of Inquiry,* 161–62; Colby, *Honorable Men,* 451. By 2000, the November 17 group had claimed responsibility for more than twenty further killings; critics accused the Greek government of tolerating the activities of terrorists with a "Robin Hood" reputation: *Washington Post,* 9 June 2000.

25. Smist, "Congress Oversees," 313.

26. Smist, "Congress Oversees," 404–6.

27. Olmsted, *Challenging,* 162–65.

28. Dellums quoted in Smist, "Congress Oversees," 283.

29. *CIA: Pike Report,* pp. 133, 141–45, 251.

30. *CIA: Pike Report,* pp. 168–78, 182, 222.

31. *CIA: Pike Report,* pp. 257–63.

32. Quoted in Ashby and Gramer, *Fighting the Odds,* 465.

33. "Alleged Assassination Plots Involving Foreign Leaders" (an interim report of the Select Committee to Study Governmental Operations with Respect to Intelligence Activities), *Senate Report,* 94 Cong., 1st sess., no. 94–465 (20 November 1975), 74–90, 117; "The Investigation of the Assassination of President John F. Kennedy: Performance of the Intelligence Agencies" (final report of the Select Committee to Study Governmental Operations with Respect to Intelligence Activities, 5 Books, Book V), *Senate Report,* 94 Cong., 2d sess., no. 94–755 (23 April 1976), 84; Johnson, *Season of Inquiry,* 123–24; Little, "Radicals and Racists," 15, 49. For detailed accounts of the New Left COINTELPRO and of FBI harassment of different types of black leaders, see Davis, *Assault on the Left,* Garrow, *FBI and King,* Kenneth O'Reilly, *"Racial Matters": The FBI's Files on Black America, 1960–1972* (New York: Free Press, 1989), and Carson, *Malcolm X: The FBI File.*

34. Reisman and Baker, *Regulating Covert Action,* 70; Snider, "Unlucky Shamrock," 49.

35. "Foreign and Military Intelligence" (final report of the Select Committee to Study Governmental Operations with Respect to Intelligence Activities, 5 Books, Book I), *Senate Report,* 94 Cong., 2d sess., no. 94–755 (26 April 1976), 425, 469–71. For summaries and discussions of the Church Committee's five-volume final report, see Johnson, *Season of Inquiry,* 224–25, Smist, "Congress Oversees," 158–59, and Olmsted, *Challenging,* 174.

36. Smist, "Congress Oversees," 164, 549. Cf. Johnson, *Season of Inquiry,* 227, and Olmsted, *Challenging,* pp. 3, 178.

37. In May 2000, both the House Permanent Select Committee on Intelligence and the Senate Select Committee on Intelligence criticized the Clinton administration for underfunding the CIA, NSA, and other intelligence agencies: *Washington Post,* 28 May 2000. DCI George J. Tenet testified that the disclosure of the total figure for the 1999 intelligence budget "could reasonably be expected to cause damage to national security": quoted in the Federation of American Scientists' *Secrecy and Government Bulletin,* Net edition, no. 84 (June 2000). Loch K. Johnson, a political scientist at the University of Georgia who served as a senior staff member on the Church Committee, has defended the accountability process both against the attacks of those who think oversight has been too soft and against

the criticism of those who think it was irresponsible, and went too far: Johnson, "CIA and the Question of Accountability," 183–90.

38. John D. Lees, "Open Government in the USA: Some Recent Statutory Developments," *Public Administration* (Autumn 1979): 340–41.

39. Information from the DEA Website.

40. Wohlstetter, "Is There a Strategic Arms Race?"; Cahn, *Killing Detente,* 11–12. Freedman was referring to the Nixon administration, but the problem persisted in the Ford presidency: Freedman, "CIA and the Soviet Threat," 133.

41. Cahn, *Killing Detente,* 138, 163; Freedman, "CIA and the Soviet Threat," 123.

42. Jimmy Carter, *Keeping Faith: Memoirs of a President* (New York: Bantam, 1982), 143.

43. Author's interview with Frederick P. Hitz, Princeton, N.J., 24 September 1998, 3.

44. Kenneth E. Morris, *Jimmy Carter: American Moralist* (Athens: University of Georgia Press, 1996), 220; Carter's comment in a question-and-answer session with State Department employees, 24 February 1977, in *Public Papers of the Presidents of the United States. James F. Carter, 1977* (Washington, D.C.: GPO, n.d.), 242.

45. Moynihan quoted in Ransom, "Secret Intelligence," 220.

46. Brzezinski, *Power and Principle,* 368n1; Sick, *All Fall Down,* 14; Turner, *Secrecy and Democracy,* 114; Bill, *Eagle and Lion,* 258; Donovan, "U.S. Political Intelligence and American Policy on Iran," 44, 68, 122–23, and "National Intelligence and the Iranian Revolution," 144, 145, 152, 156.

47. For assessments of the debate on Team B's findings, see Freedman, "CIA and the Soviet Threat," 138 and, by a pair of former CIA experts on the Soviet economy, Firth and Noren, *Soviet Defense Spending,* 64–65.

48. Carter's State of the Union address of 23 January 1980 quoted in Cline, *CIA Under Reagan Bush and Casey,* 275; Turner's 21 February 1980 testimony before the Senate Intelligence Committee in *Congressional Digest,* 59 (May 1980): 152; Allan J. Mayer and others' paraphrase of Bush in "Bush Breaks out of the Pack," *Newsweek* (4 February 1980): 35; Reagan quoted in Morton H. Halperin, "The CIA's Distemper," *New Republic* (9 February 1980): 21–22.

Chapter 13. The Casey-Reagan Era

1. One tribute to Reagan's salesmanship is implicitly conveyed in the main title of Frances FitzGerald's study, *Way Out There in the Blue: Reagan, Star Wars and the End of the Cold War* (2000), which is a quotation from Arthur Miller's *Death of a Salesman* (1947).

2. Vaughan, "Spies, National Security, and the 'Inertia Projector,'" 354–58, 366, 370; Andrew, *For the President's Eyes Only,* 457; Wills, *Reagan's America,* 193, 293, 298.

3. Walter Lord quoted in Persico, *Casey,* 85; MacPherson, "Inspired Improvisation," 716.

4. "WILLIAM J. CASEY. Candidate for Congress" (n.d. [1966]), Dulles to Casey, 29 July 1966, and a selection of Casey-Dulles correspondence from 1951 to 1966, all in Folder 7, Box 12, AWD.

5. "The Clandestine War in Europe (1942–1945); Remarks of William J. Casey on receipt of the William J. Donovan Award at Dinner of Veterans of O.S.S., December 5, 1974," enclosed with Casey to President, 16 January 1975 (stamped "The President has seen"), in turn enclosed with Jerry H. Jones to Bob Linder, 21 January 1975 (stating "The attached has been seen by the President and should be handled appropriately"), in folder "William J. Casey," Name File, WHCF, GRF.

6. Casey address at Ashland College, Ohio, 27 October 1986 in Casey, *Scouting the Future*, 31–32.

7. Casey, *Where and How the War Was Fought*, 1, 23, 135, and "Learning from History" (address to the OSS/Donovan Symposium, Washington, D.C., 19 September 1986) in Casey, *Scouting the Future*, 239.

8. Casey, *Scouting the Future*, 20, 32, 128–29.

9. Goldwater quoted in Edwin Warner, "New Day for the CIA?" *Time* (19 January 1981): 27; Goldberg, *Goldwater*, 316.

10. Mineta quoted in David M. Alpern and others, "America's Secret Warriors," *Newsweek* (10 October 1983): 30.

11. Schweizer, *Victory*, 18; Goldberg, *Goldwater*, 318; Woodward, *Veil*, 180.

12. *New York Times*, 1 January 1982; Colby, *Honorable Men*, 465–66; Frank Snepp: *Decent Interval: The American Debacle in Vietnam and the Fall of Saigon* (London: Allen Lane, 1980).

13. Dempsey, "CIA and Secrecy," 48; Johnson, *Secret Agencies*, 102–3; *Report of the Congressional Committees Investigating the Iran-Contra Affair*, 100 Cong., 1st sess., H. Rept. no. 100–433, S. Rept. no. 100–216 (13 November 1987), 3–4; Walsh, *Iran-Contra* (Final Report of the Independent Counsel for Iran/Contra Matters, 1993), 10.

14. London *Guardian*, 5, 13 December 1986; Draper, *Thin Line*, 71–73.

15. *Time* (23 April 1984), 6; Edgar Chamorro and Jefferson Murphy, "Confessions of a 'Contra,'" *New Republic* (5 August 1985), 23; Christopher Dickey, *With the Contras: A Reporter in the Wilds of Nicaragua* (New York: Simon & Schuster, 1985), 254; Ferraro quoted in *Facts on File*, 44 (1984), 809.

16. Wills, *Reagan's America*, 462. On the politics of SDI, see FitzGerald, *Way Out*, and Simon J. Ball, *The Cold War: An International History, 1947–1991* (London: Arnold, 1998), 190.

17. Gates, *From the Shadows*, 263–64; Schweizer, *Victory*, 82; FitzGerald, *Way Out*, 478, 480–81; *New York Times*, 5 July 2000; *Washington Post*, 6 July 2000. The new end-of-century acronym was NMD, standing for National Missile Defense.

18. Firth and Noren, *Soviet Defense Spending*, 13, 37, 41. For a brief critique of the Soviet economic estimate suggesting that the CIA itself overestimated Soviet strength, see Philip Zelikow, "Intelligence and World Economy," 167–70.

19. Firth and Noren, *Soviet Defense Spending*, 60; Jeffrey T. Richelson, "Old Surveillance, New Interpretations," *Bulletin of the Atomic Scientists*, 3 (February 1986): 18; *Washington Post*, 22 February 1985, 10 April 1986.

20. Zelikow, "Intelligence and the World Economy," 168.

21. Gates, *Shadows*, 547.

22. According to Fred Kaiser of the Congressional Research Service, the Nicaraguan diversion infringed the Continuing Appropriations Act for FY 1985 (the

Boland amendment) and "contradicted the spirit, if not the letter," of the 1980 Intelligence Oversight Act: Frederick M. Kaiser, "Causes and Conditions of Interbranch Conflict: Lessons from the Iran-Contra Affair" (paper given at the American Political Science Association annual meeting in Augusta, Ga., 1989, and supplied by kind courtesy of the author), 3.

23. Draper, *Thin Line*, 552.

24. Cockburn, *Out of Control;* Treverton, *Covert Action*, 228. Entire issues of two law journals were given over to these problems: "Symposium: Legal and Policy Issues in the Iran-Contra Affair: Intelligence Oversight in a Democracy," *Houston Journal of International Law*, 11 (Fall 1988), and "Intelligence Oversight, National Security, and Democracy," *Harvard Journal of Law and Public Policy*, 12 (Spring 1989).

25. Kagan, *Twilight Struggle*, 716–17.

26. Menges, *Inside the National Security Council*, 385; Woodward, *Veil*, 507; Cockburn, *Out of Control*, 247.

27. Walsh, *Final Report*, xxiii–xxv, 223–32.

28. Leslie Cockburn applied the word "aberration" to the congressional premise: Cockburn, *Out of Control*, 247. There was widespread implicit concurrence on the view that transient human error was to blame, not the system. See *Tower Commission Report*, 4–5, and Walsh, *Final Report*, 561, 566. See also Robert J. Havel, "Iran-Contra Committees," in *The Encyclopedia of the United States Congress* (New York: Simon & Schuster, 1995), ed. Donald C. Bacon and others, 1159–61; *Report of the Congressional Committees Investigating the Iran-Contra Affair*, 425; Kaiser, "Watchers' Watchdog," 55; author's interview with Frederick P. Hitz, Princeton, N.J., 24 September 1998, 1–2.

29. Partly redacted (i.e., censored) report, "[Redacted word, probably 'Pakistan's'] Nuclear Industry," dated 1987 in National Security Archive Electronic Briefing Book No. 34 (2000): www.gwu.edu/nsarchiv.

30. Moynihan, *Secrecy*, 215.

31. Will Rogers quoted in Andrew Sinclair, *Prohibition: The Era of Excess* (Boston: Little, Brown, 1962), 46; Woodiwiss, *Crime, Crusades and Corruption;* Bewley-Taylor, *United States and International Drugs Control;* De Grazia, *DEA*, 201; Milton and Rose Friedman, *Free to Choose* (Harmondsworth: Penguin, 1980), 267–69.

32. De Grazia, *DEA*, 2–3; Walker, "Drug Control"; McWilliams, "Covert Connections," 372–73; 658–59, 661, 665, 674; Bewley-Taylor, *Drugs Control*, 114.

33. De Grazia, *DEA*, 7–8; Torres, *Handbook*, 126–27.

34. Reagan statement, 14 October 1982, quoted in Woodiwiss, *Organized Crime*, 30; McWilliams, "Covert Connections," 658; "DEA Staffing and Appropriations FY 1973–1999" (DEA Website, accessed in 2000).

35. De Grazia, *DEA*, 200; David F. Musto, "Drugs," in *The Reader's Companion to American History* (Boston: Houghton Mifflin, 1991), ed. Eric Foner and John A. Garraty, 297–99.

36. Webster quoted in Marx, *Undercover*, 1; Kessler, *FBI*, 117; Woodiwiss, *Organized Crime*, 33, 35.

37. Bewley-Taylor, *Drugs Control*, 114, 125; McCoy, *Politics of Heroin;* Mackenzie, *Secrets*, 52–54.

38. CIA Inspector General, "Report of Investigation: Allegations of Connections Between CIA and the Contras in Cocaine Trafficking in the United States" (8 October 1998), accessed on the Internet; Cockburn, *Out of Control*, 152–88.

39. Smist, "Congress Oversees," 409; DEA, "Overview of Drug Use in the United States" (DEA Website, accessed in 2000); Moynihan, *Secrecy*, 215.

40. Woodiwiss, *Organized Crime*, 36.

41. Schweizer, *Victory*; Wells, "Nuclear Weapons and European Security," 63, 66.

42. John Gooding, *Rulers and Subjects: Government and People in Russia 1801–1991* (London: Arnold, 1996); Robert Service, *The History of Twentieth Century Russia* (Harmondsworth: Penguin, 1998). But J. N. Westwood thought that Star Wars had a severe effect on the Soviet Union: Westwood, *Endurance and Endeavor: Russian History, 1812–1992*, 4th ed. (Oxford: Oxford University Press, 1993), 492.

43. Filitov, "Victory in the Postwar Era," 78; Lundestad, "End of the Cold War," and Reynolds, "Beyond Bipolarity"; Cahn, *Killing Detente*, 196; Alperovitz and Bird, "The Fading of the Cold War," 211–12.

44. *Washington Post*, 9 December 1995.

45. See FitzGerald, *Way Out*, 471.

46. Both Gates quotations from Gates, *Shadows*, 552.

Chapter 14. The Real American Century?

1. Morris, *Partners in Power*, 88–89.

2. Morris, *Partners in Power*, 102–5, 406–15; "Clinton's CIA Connection," *NameBase Newsline* (October–December 1996), 6–7; Walker, *The President We Deserve*, 67–68.

3. *Economist*, 22 February 1997; *Washington Post*, 14 March, 10 December 1995; Walker, *The President We Deserve*, 266.

4. The categorization is taken from Winterhalt, "Debate on the Future."

5. Ford quoted in *New York Times*, 20 July 1997; Vincent Cannistraro, "The CIA Dinosaur," *Washington Post*, 5 September 1991; Mary McGrory in *Washington Post*, 26 September 1991.

6. Winterhalt, "Chapter Two—Abolitionist Sentiment," in "Debate on the Future." On Moynihan and his career, see Hodgson, *The Gentleman from New York*.

7. Richard Gid Powers, "Introduction" to Moynihan, *Secrecy*, 9–12; Moynihan quoted in the *Washington Post*, 1 November 1999.

8. May, "U.S. Government," 217.

9. Schwarzkopf quoted in *Facts on File*, 1991, 535; Powell quoted in *New York Times*, 18 April 1997.

10. Gary T. Marx, "Some Reflections on *Undercover*: Recent developments and enduring issues," *Crime, Law and Social Change: An International Journal*, 18 (September 1992): 199; Cavanagh, "Individuals Arrested 1993–1998"; *Washington Post*, 18 March 1996.

11. Author's interview with Frederick P. Hitz, Princeton, N.J., 24 September 1998, 4.

12. Woolsey quoted in Johnson, *Secret Agencies*, 49–50; Treverton, *Reshap-*

ing, 55, 235. See also *Washington Post*, 25 April 1996; *New York Times*, 16 October 1997, 21 March 1998.

13. Richard Helms and James Schlesinger, "C.I.A. Watchdog or Mole?" *New York Times*, 22 November 1989; Winterhalt, "Chapter Three—Maintaining the Status Quo," in "Debate on the Future"; Carver, "Intelligence in the Age of Glasnost," 148–49.

14. Moynihan, *Secrecy*, 76–77. Loch Johnson gives different figures apparently because of changing bureaucratic nomenclature, although these, too, confirm the upward trend: in 1994, 65 in the Office of General Counsel and "over a dozen" in the Office of Congressional Affairs: Johnson, "CIA and the Question of Accountability," 194.

15. Moynihan, *Secrecy*, 76–77; Johnson, "CIA and the Question of Accountability," 193.

16. Carver, "Intelligence in the Age of Glasnost," 156, 166.

17. Martin Walker, "Mission Implausible," *The Guardian*, 14 April 1997.

18. McGrory quoted in Winterhalt, "Chapter Four—Reform and Moderation," in "Debate on the Future"; David L. Boren, "New World, New CIA," *New York Times*, 17 June 1990.

19. Boren, "Intelligence Community," 53–55; *New York Times*, 17 February 1993.

20. Boren, "New World"; Johnson, "CIA and the Question of Accountability," 190.

21. Clancy, *Clear and Present Danger*, 140. Information on sales culled from the *New York Times Book Review* Best Sellers List and presented in an appendix to Richell, "Trends in Contemporary American Spy Fiction."

22. Woolsey statement, 18 July 1984, quoted in Wise, *Nightmover*, 317.

23. *Independent*, 23 February 1994; *New York Times*, 10 July 1995.

24. For a slightly apologetic exposition of the anti-societal view, see Margaret Thatcher, *The Downing Street Years* (New York: HarperCollins, 1993), 626. When Yardley was growing up in Worthing, Indiana, America was, according to Putnam, going through an earlier phase of social disintegration: Putnam, *Bowling Alone*, 282–83, 382–83. Money motivated or helped motivate John A. Walker, the navy spy arrested on 20 May 1985; the former CIA officer Edward L. Howard, who escaped the clutches of the FBI in 1986 after betraying submarine secrets; and Harold James Nicholson, a CIA training officer arrested in 1996 for revealing to the Russians the names of his trainees and of businessmen who performed services for U.S. intelligence. Nicholson's arrest, according to the *Washington Post*, 21 November 1996, once again had a "devastating effect" on CIA morale. On Robert Philip Hanssen: *Washington Post*, 20 February 2001; FBI affidavit (in relation to his arrest) in the U.S. District Court for the Eastern District of Virginia, Alexandria Division, posted on the Web 23 February 2001.

25. *Independent*, 23 February 1994; Wise, *Nightmover*, 315, 317, 334; *Washington Post*, 10, 17 November, 9 December 1995.

26. Weiner in *New York Times*, 1 January 1995.

27. Picture caption, Wise, *Nightmover*, opposite page 183.

28. Author's interview with Frederick P. Hitz, Princeton, N.J., 24 September 1998, 5.

29. Johnson, "CIA and the Question of Accountability," 192.

30. David Usborne, "Les Aspin" (obituary), *Independent*, 23 May 1995.

31. Commission on the Roles and Capabilities of the United States Intelligence Community (Aspin-Brown Commission), *Preparing for the Twenty-First Century: An Appraisal of U.S. Intelligence* (Washington, D.C., 1996): http://www.access.gpo.gov/int; *Washington Post*, 1 March 1996; *New York Times*, 3 March 1996; Johnson, "Accountability," 193.

32. Deutch quoted in *Washington Post*, 13 July 1995. The *Post* printed the word "assure" instead of "ensure."

33. Clapper quoted in Treverton, *Reshaping Intelligence*.

34. *Washington Post*, 30 January 1996; Johnson, "CIA and the Question of Accountability," 194–95.

35. *Washington Post*, 25 April, 10 May 1996. Supporters of the proposed National Operations and Analysis Hub (NOAH) included Representative Curt Weldon (Rep., Penn.), chair of the Military R&D Subcommittee of the House National Security Committee. Details of NOAH appeared in an article by Clarence Robinson in *Signal* (April 2000), synopsis retrieved on the Internet.

36. Haynes and Klehr, *Venona*, 3, 6.

37. Benson and Warner, *Venona*, vii.

38. Benson and Warner, *Venona*, xxxviii; Moynihan, *Secrecy*, 71; Hodgson, *The Gentleman*, 388.

39. Moynihan, *Secrecy*, 16; Lamphere, *FBI-KGB War*, 230, 237–8; Walter and Miriam Schneir, "Cables Coming in from the Cold," *Nation*, 5 July 1999: 26.

40. Haynes and Klehr, *Venona*, 3.

41. Soviet intelligence document, 1 March 1951, erroneously described as of "KGB" provenance (the KGB was not established until 1954), quoted in Ellen Schrecker and Maurice Isserman, "The Right's Cold War Revision," *Nation*, July 24/31, 2000, 22; Jacob Weisberg, "Cold War Without End," *New York Times Magazine*, 28 November 1999, 121.

42. Schrecker and Isserman, "Right's Revision," 24; Haynes and Klehr, *Venona*, 6.

43. Aftergood quoted in Mackenzie, *Secrets*, 196; *New York Times*, 30 May 1997.

44. *New York Times*, 16 May 1995; George C. Herring, "My Years with the CIA," *Organization of American Historians Newsletter* (May 1997), 5; Page Putnam Miller, "Capitol Commentary," *Organization of American Historians Newsletter* (May 2000), 12.

45. *New York Times*, 16 October 1997, 21 March 1998.

46. *New York Times*, 22 July 1997; *Washington Post*, 18 March 1997.

47. Shelby quoted in *New York Times*, 21 March 1998; declaration of George J. Tenet, 6 April 1999, in the United States District Court for the District of Columbia, Civ. No. 98–2107, in the case Steven Aftergood on behalf of *Federation of American Scientists v. Central Intelligence Agency*, and *Secrecy & Government Bulletin*, 84 (June 2000), both accessed on the Federation of American Scientists Web pages.

48. *Sunday Times*, 2 April 2000; *Observer*, 29 November 1998.

49. *Observer*, 17 October 1999; *Washington Post*, 10 April 2000.

50. Millis quoted in Vernon Loeb, "Portrait of a Pessimist," *Washington Post,* 6 March 2000. On the missed evidence, see the *New York Times,* 17 May 1998.

51. *New York Times,* 16 May, 6 June 1995.

52. *Washington Post,* 22 June, 10 December 1995, 3 December 1996; Powers, "Whizz Kid."

53. *Washington Post,* 5 August 1995; 8, 9 June 2000. It should be noted that policy on gays began to be rethought in 1991, the year in which the problem of women's inequality of opportunity was also addressed. At the time, Republican president Bush was in office

54. *Washington Post,* 31 May 2000.

55. *New York Times,* 3 June 1997.

56. Bill Mesler, "The Spy Who Wasn't," *The Nation,* 9/16 August 1999, 13; Gertz, *China Threat;* Report by Steven Aftergood in *Secrecy & Government Bulletin,* 79 (June 1999), accessed on the Federation of American Scientists Web page; Vrooman quoted in *Washington Post,* 4 July 2000.

57. Sir David Hannay (formerly British representative to the European Union and United Nations), "Intelligence and International Agencies," 173–181; Barbara Crossette, "Panel Recommends Overhaul of U.N. Peacekeeping Department," *New York Times,* 24 August 2000; anonymous intelligence source quoted in Hersh, "Intelligence Gap," 62; Levy, *Crypto;* Treverton, *Reshaping,* 88.

58. Michael V. Hayden, address at American University, 17 February 2000, press release accessed on NSA Website; *New York Times,* 27 April 2000.

59. Roper, "Intelligence and International Agencies," 189.

60. Dorn, "The Cloak and the Blue Beret," 415–16.

61. Presidential Decision Directive 25, May 1994, quoted in Treverton, "Intelligence Since Cold War's End," 116; Perry L. Pickert, "Introduction," in Pickert and Swenson, eds., *Intelligence for Multilateral Decision and Action,* xxiii; Crossette, "Sweeping Overhaul."

62. International Peace Academy, *Peacekeeper's Handbook* (New York: Pergamon Press, 1984), p. 39, quoted in Johnson, "No Cloak and Dagger Required," 103. See also Dorn, "Cloak and Blue Beret," 414–15, Treverton, "Intelligence Since Cold War's End," 116, and Air Marshall John Walker, chief of British defense intelligence, quoted in Mark Urban, *UK Eyes Alpha: Inside British Intelligence* (London: Faber and Faber, 1996), 214.

63. Dorn, "The Cloak and the Blue Beret," 433, 442; Stanley Michalak's review, on the H-DIPLO Internet forum, of Gary B. Ostrower, *The United Nations and the United States* (New York: Twayne Publishers, 1998).

64. *Sunday Times,* 6 August 2000; Loch K. Johnson, "Economic Espionage," address at St. Antony's College, Oxford, 26 September 1999; *New York Times,* 21 October 1995, 1 November 1999; Peter G. Gosselin, in the *New York Times Book Review,* 16 February 1997, on John J. Fialka, *Economic Espionage in America* (New York: Norton, 1997); *Washington Post,* 17 April 2000.

65. United States Senate Select Committee on Intelligence press release, 4 May 2000, accessed on the Senate's Website; *Washington Post,* 29 May 2000; *Secrecy & Government Bulletin,* 84 (June 2000), accessed on the Federation of American Scientists Web pages.

66. *Washington Post,* 4 February 2001.

67. *Washington Post,* 22 January 2001; *Secrecy News* (accessed on the Internet from the Federation of American Scientists Project on Government Secrecy), 1, 14 February 2001.

68. Nigel West (the pen name of Rupert Allason), *Observer,* 8 April 2001; "Too Many Spooks?" *Economist,* 29 March 2001; Fiona Morgan, "Does the U.S. Spy Too Much?" Salon.com/News, 26 April 2001; Boris Pankin, "An Espionage Treaty," themoscowtimes.com, 12 April 2001.

Bibliography

Adams, Graham, Jr. "William J. Burns," in *American National Biography*, ed. John A. Garraty. Vol. 4. New York: Oxford University Press, 1999.

Adams, Sam. "Vietnam Cover-Up: Playing War with Numbers." *Harper's* (May 1975): 41–44, 62, 64–66, 68, 70–73.

——. *War of Numbers: An Intelligence Memoir*. South Royalton, Vt.: Steerforth Press, 1994.

Aid, Matthew M. "The Time of Troubles: The U.S. National Security Agency in the Twenty-First Century." *Intelligence and National Security* 15 (Autumn 2000): 1–32.

Aldrich, Richard J. "Conspiracy or Confusion? Churchill, Roosevelt and Pearl Harbor." *Intelligence and National Security* 7 (July 1992): 335–46.

Allison, Graham T. *Essence of Decision: Explaining the Cuban Missile Crisis*. Boston: Little, Brown, 1971.

Alperovitz, Gar, and Kai Bird. "The Fading of the Cold War—and the Demystification of Twentieth-Century Issues," in *End of the Cold War*, ed. Hogan.

Alsop, Stewart. *The Center: The Anatomy of Power in Washington*. London: Hodder and Stoughton, 1968.

Alsop, Stewart, and Thomas Braden. *Sub Rosa: The OSS and American Espionage*. New York: Reynal and Hitchcock, 1948.

Alvarez, David. *Secret Messages: Codebreaking and American Diplomacy, 1930–1945*. Lawrence: Kansas University Press, 2000.

Ambrose, Stephen E. *Ike's Spies: Eisenhower and the Espionage Establishment*. Garden City, N.Y.: Doubleday, 1981.

Ambrosius, Lloyd E. "Secret German-American Negotiations during the Paris Peace Conference." *Amerikastudien* 24 (1979): 288–309.

Ameringer, Charles D. *U.S. Foreign Intelligence: The Secret Side of American History*. Lexington, Mass.: D.C. Heath, 1990.

Amuchastegui, Domingo. "Cuban Intelligence and the October Crisis," in *Intelligence and the Cuban Missile Crisis*, ed. Blight and Welch.

Andrew, Christopher. *For the President's Eyes Only: Secret Intelligence and the*

American Presidency from Washington to Bush. London: Harper Collins, 1995.

———. *Secret Service: The Making of the British Intelligence Community*. London: Heinemann, 1985.

Andrew, Christopher M., and David Dilks, eds. *The Missing Dimension: Governments and Intelligence Communities in the Twentieth Century*. London: Macmillan, 1984.

Angevine, Robert G. "Gentlemen Do Read Each Other's Mail: American Intelligence in the Interwar Era." *Intelligence and National Security* 7 (April 1992): 1–29.

Ashby, LeRoy, and Rod Gramer. *Fighting the Odds: The Life of Frank Church*. Pullman, Wash.: Washington State University Press, 1994.

Baker, Lafayette C. *History of the United States Secret Service*. Philadelphia: L.C. Baker, 1867.

Ball, Simon J. *The Cold War: An International History, 1947–1991*. London: Arnold, 1998.

Bamford, James. *Body of Secrets: Anatomy of the Ultra-Secret National Security Agency from the Cold War Through the Dawn of a New Century*. New York: Doubleday, 2001.

Bar-Joseph, Uri. *Intelligence Intervention in the Politics of Democratic States: The United States, Israel and Britain*. University Park: University of Pennsylvania Press, 1995.

Barron, John. *Operation Solo: The FBI's Man in the Kremlin*. London: Robert Hale, 1997.

Beach, Edward L. *Scapegoats: A Defense of Kimmel and Short at Pearl Harbor*. Annapolis, Md.: Naval Institute Press, 1995.

Beard, Charles A. *President Roosevelt and the Coming of the War, 1941: A Study in Appearances and Realities*. New Haven: Yale University Press, 1948.

Benson, Robert Louis, and Michael Warner, eds. *Venona: Soviet Espionage and the American Response, 1939–1957*. Washington, D.C.: NSA and CIA, 1996.

Berle, Beatrice B., and Travis B. Jacobs, eds. *Navigating the Rapids 1918–1971: From the Papers of Adolph A. Berle*. New York: Harcourt Brace Jovanovich, 1973.

Bewley-Taylor, David R. *The United States and International Drugs Control, 1909–1997*. London: Pinter, 1999.

Bill, James A. *The Eagle and the Lion: The Tragedy of American-Iranian Relations*. New Haven: Yale University Press, 1988.

Bissell, Richard M., Jr. *Reflections of a Cold Warrior: From Yalta to the Bay of Pigs*. New Haven: Yale University Press, 1996.

Blight, James G., and David A. Welch, eds. *Intelligence and the Cuban Missile Crisis*. London: Frank Cass, 1998.

Blight, James G., and Peter Kornbluh, eds. *Politics of Illusion: The Bay of Pigs Invasion Reexamined*. Boulder, Colo.: Lynne Rienner, 1998.

Boren, David L. "The Intelligence Community: How Crucial?" *Foreign Affairs* (Summer 1992): 52–62.

Braden, Tom. "The Birth of the CIA." *American Heritage* 28 (February 1977): 4–13.

Bryan, George S. *The Spy in America*. Philadelphia: J.B. Lippincott, 1943.

Brzezinski, Zbigniew. *Power and Principle: Memoirs of the National Security Advisor, 1977–1981*. New York: Farrar, Straus and Giroux, 1983.

Budiansky, Stephen. *Battle of Wits: The Complete Story of Codebreaking in World War II*. New York: Free Press, 2000.

——. "The Difficult Beginnings of U.S.-British Codebreaking Cooperation," in *American-British-Canadian Intelligence Relations 1939–2000*, ed. Stafford and Jeffreys-Jones.

Bulloch, James D. *The Secret Service of the Confederate States in Europe, or, How the Confederate Cruisers Were Equipped*. 2 vols. New York: Thomas Yoseloff, 1959 (1883).

Burns, William J. *The Masked War: The Story of a Period that Threatened the United States by the Man Who Uncovered the Dynamite Conspirators and Sent Them to Jail*. New York: George H. Doran, 1913.

Cahn, Anne Hessing. *Killing Detente: The Right Attacks the CIA*. University Park: Pennsylvania State University Press, 1998.

Carson, Clayborne. *Malcolm X: The FBI File*. New York: Ballantine, 1995.

Carver, George A., Jr. "Intelligence in the Age of Glasnost." *Foreign Affairs* (January/February 1990): 148–49.

Casey, William J. *Scouting the Future: The Public Speeches of William J. Casey*, comp. Herbert E. Meyer. Washington, D.C.: Regnery Gateway, 1989.

——. *Where and How the War Was Fought: An Armchair Tour of the American Revolution*. New York: William Morrow, 1976.

Cave Brown, Anthony. *The Last Hero: Wild Bill Donovan*. New York: Times Books, 1982.

Charles, Douglas M. "Informing FDR: FBI Political Surveillance and the Isolationist-Interventionist Foreign Policy Debate, 1939–1945." *Diplomatic History* 24 (Spring 2000): 211–232.

Charles, Douglas M., and John Rossi. "FBI Political Surveillance and the Charles Lindbergh Investigation, 1939–1944." *The Historian* 59 (Summer 1997): 831–47.

CIA: The Pike Report. London: Spokesman Books, 1977.

Clancy, Tom. *Clear and Present Danger*. New York: Berkley Books, 1990.

Clausen, Henry C., and Bruce Lee. *Pearl Harbor: Final Judgement*. New York: Crown, 1992.

Cline, Ray S. *The CIA Under Reagan Bush and Casey*. Washington, D.C.: Acropolis, 1981.

Cockburn, Leslie. *Out of Control: The Story of the Reagan Administration's Secret War in Nicaragua, the Illegal Arms Pipeline, and the Contra Drug Connection*. New York: Atlantic Monthly Press, 1987.

Colby, William. *Honorable Men: My Life in the CIA*. London: Hutchinson, 1978.

——. "Skis and Daggers." *Studies in Intelligence* (Winter 1999–2000): 53–60.

Cook, Fred J. *The FBI Nobody Knows*. London: Jonathan Cape, 1965.

Cooper, James Fenimore. *The Spy; or, A Tale of the Neutral Ground*. New York: Dodd, Mead, 1946 (1821).

Corson, William R. *The Armies of Ignorance: The Rise of the American Intelligence Empire*. New York: Dial, 1977.

Costa, John. *Legislation Introduced Relative to the Activities of the Intelligence Agencies, 1947–1972*. Washington, D.C.: Congressional Research Service, 1972.

Cullather, Nick. *Secret History: The CIA's Classified Account of Its Operations in Guatemala, 1952–1954*. Stanford, Calif.: Stanford University Press, 1999.

Current, Richard N. "How Stimson Meant to 'Maneuver' the Japanese." *Mississippi Valley Historical Review* 40 (June 1953): 67–74.

Currey, Cecil B. *Edward Lansdale: The Unquiet American*. Boston: Houghton Mifflin, 1988.

Cuthbert, Norma B., ed. *Lincoln and the Baltimore Plot, 1861, From Pinkerton Records and Related Papers*. San Marino, Calif.: Huntington Library, 1949.

Davis, James Kirkpatrick. *Assault on the Left: The FBI and the Sixties Antiwar Movement*. Westport, Conn.: Praeger, 1997.

De Grazia, Jessica. *DEA: The War against Drugs*. London: BBC Books, 1991.

Dempsey, James X. "The CIA and Secrecy," in *Culture of Secrecy*, ed. Theoharis.

Denniston, Alastair. "The Government Code and Cypher School Between the Wars." *Intelligence and National Security* 1 (January 1986): 48–70.

Denniston, Robin. "Yardley's Diplomatic Secrets." *Cryptologia* 18 (April 1994).

Deutch, James I. " 'I Was a Hollywood Agent': Cinematic Representations of the Office of Strategic Services in 1946." *Intelligence and National Security* 13 (Summer 1998): 85–99.

Dobson, Alan P. "The USA, Britain, and the Question of Hegemony," in *No End to Alliance,* ed. Lundestad.

Doel, Ronald E., and Allan A. Needell. "Science, Scientists, and the CIA: Balancing International Ideals, National Needs, and Professional Opportunities," in *Eternal Vigilance?* ed. Jeffreys-Jones and Andrew.

Doerries, Reinhard R. *Imperial Challenge: Ambassador Count Bernstorff and German-American Relations, 1908–1917*. Chapel Hill: University of North Carolina Press, 1989.

Donovan, Michael P. "National Intelligence and the Iranian Revolution," in *Eternal Vigilance?* ed. Jeffreys-Jones and Andrew.

——. "U.S. Political Intelligence and American Policy on Iran, 1950–1979." Ph.D. diss., Edinburgh University, 1997.

Donovan, William, and Edgar Mowrer, Fifth Column Lessons for America. Washington, D.C.: American Council on Public Affairs, n.d. (1940).

Dorn, A. Walter. "The Cloak and the Blue Beret: Limitations on Intelligence in UN Peacekeeping." *International Journal of Intelligence and Counterintelligence* 12 (Winter 1999–2000): 414–47.

Dorwart, Jeffery M. *Conflict of Duty: The U.S. Navy's Intelligence Dilemma, 1919–1945*. Annapolis, Md.: Naval Institute Press, 1983.

Draper, Theodore. *A Very Thin Line: The Iran-Contra Affairs*. New York: Hill and Wang, 1991.

Drea, Edward J. *MacArthur's ULTRA: Codebreaking and the War against Japan, 1942–1945*. Lawrence: University Press of Kansas, 1992.

Dulles, Allen W. *The Craft of Intelligence*. London: Weidenfeld and Nicolson, 1963.

——. *Germany's Underground*. New York: Macmillan, 1947.

——, ed. *Great True Spy Stories*. New York: Harper and Row, 1968.

———. *The Secret Surrender*. New York: Harper, 1966.

Dunlop, Richard. *Donovan: America's Master Spy*. Chicago: Rand McNally, 1982.

Ellis, Mark. "J. Edgar Hoover and the 'Red Summer' of 1919." *Journal of American Studies* 28 (April 1994): 39–59.

Ensign, Eric S. *Intelligence in the Rum War at Sea, 1920–1933*. Washington, D.C.: Joint Military Intelligence College, 2001.

Ernst, Maurice C. "Economic Intelligence in CIA," in *Inside CIA's Private World*, ed. Westerfield.

Farago, Ladislas. *The Broken Seal: The Story of "Operation Magic" and the Pearl Harbour Disaster*. London: Mayflower, 1969 (1967).

Filitov, Alexei. "Victory in the Postwar Era: Despite the Cold War or Because of It?" in *End of Cold War*, ed. Hogan.

Fine, Sidney. "Anarchism and the Assassination of McKinley." *American Historical Review* 60 (July 1955): 777–799.

Firth, Noel E., and James H. Noren. *Soviet Defense Spending: A History of CIA Estimates, 1950–1990*. College Station: Texas A&M Press, 1998.

Fischel, Edwin C. "Mythmaking at Stimson's Expense: What Did the Secretary Say (or Not Say)?" *Foreign Intelligence Literary Scene* 5 (October 1985): 4–6.

———. *The Secret War for the Union: The Untold Story of Military Intelligence in the Civil War*. Boston: Houghton Mifflin, 1996.

Fisher, David. "Home Colony: An American Experiment in Anarchism." M.Litt. diss., Edinburgh University, 1971.

FitzGerald, Frances. *Way Out There in the Blue: Reagan, Star Wars and the End of the Cold War*. New York: Simon & Schuster, 2000.

Ford, Corey. *Donovan of OSS*. Boston: Little, Brown, 1970.

Fowler, W. B. *British-American Relations 1917–1918. The Role of Sir William Wiseman*. Princeton, N.J.: Princeton University Press, 1969.

Freedman, Lawrence. "The CIA and the Soviet Threat: The Politicization of Estimates, 1966–1977," in *Eternal Vigilance?*, ed. Jeffreys-Jones and Andrew.

———. *U.S. Intelligence and the Soviet Strategic Threat*. London: Macmillan, 1977.

Fursenko, Aleksandr, and Timothy Naftali, *"One Hell of a Gamble": Khruschev, Castro, and Kennedy, 1958–1964*. New York: Norton, 1997.

———. "Soviet Intelligence and the Cuban Missile Crisis," in *Intelligence and the Cuban Missile Crisis*, ed. Blight and Welch.

Garrow, David J. *The FBI and Martin Luther King, Jr.* New York: Penguin, 1983.

Garthoff, Raymond L. "Documenting the Cuban Missile Crisis." *Diplomatic History* 24 (Spring 2000): 297–303.

Gates, Robert M. *From the Shadows: The Ultimate Insider's Story of Five Presidents and How They Won the Cold War*. New York: Simon & Schuster, 1996.

Gertz, Bill. *The China Threat*. Washington, D.C.: Regnery, 2000.

Goldberg, Robert A. *Barry Goldwater*. New Haven: Yale University Press, 1995.

Goldstein, Donald M. "Pearl Harbor," in *Encyclopedia of U.S. Foreign Relations*, 4 vols., ed. Bruce W. Jentleson and Thomas G. Paterson. New York: Oxford University Press, 1997.

Grose, Peter. *Gentleman Spy: The Life of Allen Dulles*. Boston: Houghton Mifflin, 1994.

Gutman, Herbert G. "Five Letters of Immigrant Workers from Scotland to the United States." *Labor History* 9 (1968): 384–408.

Haines, Gerald. "The CIA's Own Effort to Understand and Document Its Past: A Brief History of the CIA History Program, 1950–1995," in *Eternal Vigilance?*, ed. Jeffreys-Jones and Andrew.

Hanchett, William. *The Lincoln Murder Theories*. Urbana: University of Illinois Press, 1983.

Hannay, David. "Intelligence and International Agencies," in *Agents for Change*, ed. Shukman.

Haynes, John Earl, and Harvey Klehr. *Venona: Decoding Soviet Espionage in America*. New Haven: Yale University Press, 1999.

Heale, Michael J. *American Anticommunism: Combating the Enemy Within, 1830–1970*. Baltimore: Johns Hopkins University Press, 1990.

Herring, George C. "My Years with the CIA." *Organization of American Historians Newsletter* (May 1997): 5–6.

Hersh, Burton. *The Old Boys: The American Elite and the Origins of the CIA*. New York: Scribner's, 1992.

Hersh, Seymour M. *The Dark Side of Camelot*. Boston: Little, Brown, 1997.

——. "The Intelligence Gap: How the Digital Age Left Our Spies Out in the Cold." *New Yorker* (Dec. 6, 1999): 58–76.

Hinckle, Warren, and William W. Turner. *The Fish Is Red: The Story of the Secret War against Castro*. New York: Harper, 1981.

Hodgson, Godfrey, *The Gentleman from New York: Daniel Patrick Moynihan: A Biography*. Boston: Houghton Mifflin, 2000.

Hogan, Michael J. *A Cross of Iron: Harry S. Truman and the Origins of the National Security State 1945–1954*. Cambridge: Cambridge University Press, 1998.

——, ed. *The End of the Cold War: Its Meaning and Implications*. Cambridge: Cambridge University Press, 1992.

Horan, James D. *The Pinkertons: The Detective Dynasty that Made History*. New York: Crown, 1967.

Horowitz, Irving L., ed. *The Rise and Fall of Project Camelot*. Cambridge, Mass.: MIT Press, 1967.

Hunt, E. Howard. *Undercover: Memoirs of an American Secret Agent*. New York: Berkeley/Putnam, 1974.

Immerman, Richard H. *The CIA in Guatemala: The Foreign Policy of Intervention*. Austin: University of Texas Press, 1982.

In From the Cold: The Report of the Twentieth Century Fund Task Force on the Future of U.S. Intelligence. New York: Twentieth Century Fund, 1996.

Jeffreys-Jones, Rhodri. *American Espionage: From Secret Service to CIA*. New York: Free Press, 1977.

——. *The CIA and American Democracy*. 2d ed. New Haven: Yale University Press, 1998.

——. "Profit Over Class: A Study in American Industrial Espionage." *Journal of American Studies* 6 (December 1972): 233–48.

——. "The Role of British Intelligence in the Mythologies Underpinning the OSS and Early CIA," in *American-British-Canadian Intelligence*, ed. Stafford and Jeffreys-Jones.

——. "The Socio-Educational Composition of the CIA Elite: A Statistical Note." *Journal of American Studies* 19 (December 1985): 421–24.

——. *Violence and Reform in American History*. New York: New Viewpoints, 1978.

——. "Why Was the CIA Established in 1947?" in *Eternal Vigilance?*, ed. Jeffreys-Jones and Andrew.

Jeffreys-Jones, Rhodri, and Christopher Andrew, eds. *Eternal Vigilance? 50 Years of the CIA*. London: Frank Cass, 1997.

Jeffreys-Jones, Rhodri, and Andrew Lownie, eds. *North American Spies: New Revisionist Essays*. Lawrence: University Press of Kansas, 1991.

Johnson, Loch K. "The CIA and the Question of Accountability," in *Eternal Vigilance?*, ed. Jeffreys-Jones and Andrew.

——. *A Season of Inquiry: The Senate Intelligence Investigation*. Lexington: University Press of Kentucky, 1985.

——. *Secret Agencies: U.S. Intelligence in a Hostile World*. New Haven: Yale University Press, 1996.

Johnson, Paul. "No Cloak and Dagger Required: Intelligence Support to UN Peacekeeping." *Intelligence and National Security* 12 (October 1997): 102–12.

Jones, John P. *The German Spy in America: The Secret Plotting of German Spies in the United States and the Inside Story of the Sinking of the Lusitania*. London: Hutchinson, 1917.

Kagan, Robert. *A Twilight Struggle: American Power and Nicaragua, 1977–1990*. New York: Free Press, 1996.

Kahn, David. *The Codebreakers: The Story of Secret Writing*. London: Weidenfeld and Nicolson, 1966.

——. "Edward Bell and His Zimmermann Telegram Memoranda." *Intelligence and National Security* 14 (Autumn 1999): 143–59.

——. "United States Views of Germany and Japan in 1941," in *Knowing One's Enemies*, ed. May.

Kaiser, David. "Review Essay: Intelligence and the Assassination of John F. Kennedy." *Intelligence and National Security* 12 (October 1997): 165–95.

Kaiser, Frederick M. "Origins of Secret Service Protection of the President: Personal, Interagency, and Institutional Conflict." *Presidential Studies Quarterly* 18 (Winter 1988): 101–27.

——. "Presidential Assassinations and Assaults: Characteristics and Impact on Protective Procedures." *Presidential Studies Quarterly* 11 (Fall 1981): 545–58.

——. "The Watchers' Watchdog: The CIA Inspector General." *International Journal of Intelligence and Counterintelligence* 3 (Spring 1989): 55–75.

Katz, Barry M. *Foreign Intelligence: Research and Analysis in the Office of Strategic Services 1942–1945*. Cambridge, Mass.: Harvard University Press, 1989.

Kendall, Wilmoore. "The Function of Intelligence." *World Politics* 1 (1948–49): 542–52.

Kenny, Kevin. *Making Sense of the Molly Maguires*. New York: Oxford University Press, 1998.

Kessler, Ronald. *The FBI*. New York: Pocket Star/Simon & Schuster, 1993.

Knott, Stephen F. *Secret and Sanctioned: Covert Operations and the American Presidency*. New York: Oxford University Press, 1996.

Kornbluh, Peter, ed. *Bay of Pigs: The Secret CIA Report on the Invasion of Cuba*. New York: New Press/Norton, 1998.

Laidlaw, Richard B. "The OSS and the Burma Road, 1942–45," in *North American Spies*, ed. Jeffreys-Jones and Lownie.

Lamphere, Robert J. *The FBI-KGB War: A Special Agent's Story*. New York: Random House, 1986.

Langer, William L. *In and Out of the Ivory Tower*. New York: Watson, 1977.

Laqueur, Walter. *A World of Secrets: The Uses and Limits of Intelligence*. New York: Basic, 1985.

Laville, Helen. "The Committee of Correspondence: CIA Funding of Women's Groups 1952–1967," in *Eternal Vigilance?*, ed. Jeffreys-Jones and Andrew.

Leahy, William D. *I Was There*. New York: Whittlesey House/McGraw-Hill, 1950.

Leary, William M., ed. *The Central Intelligence Agency: History and Documents*. University, Ala.: University of Alabama Press, 1984.

Lee, Bruce. *Marching Orders: The Untold Story of World War II*. New York: Crown, 1995.

Leffler, Melvyn P. *A Preponderance of Power: National Security, the Truman Administration, and the Cold War*. Stanford, Calif.: Stanford University Press, 1992.

Levy, Steven. *Crypto: Secrecy and Privacy in the New Code War*. London: Allen Lane, 2001.

Lewin, Ronald. *The American Magic: Codes, Ciphers and the Defeat of Japan*. Harmondsworth: Penguin, 1983 (1982).

Lindberg, Gary. *The Confidence Man in American Literature*. New York: Oxford University Press, 1982.

Little, William A. "Radicals and Racists: The Church Committee's Investigation of the FBI's COINTELPRO." M.Sc. diss., Edinburgh University, 1995.

Lowenthal, John. "Venona and Alger Hiss." *Intelligence and National Security* 15 (Autumn 2000): 98–130.

Lowenthal, Mark M. "Searching for National Intelligence: U.S. Intelligence and Policy Before the Second World War." *Intelligence and National Security* 6 (October 1991): 736–47.

Lowenthal, Max. *The Federal Bureau of Investigation*. New York: Harcourt Brace Jovanovich, 1950.

Lucas, W. Scott, and Alistair Morey. "The Hidden 'Alliance': The CIA and MI6 Before and after Suez," in *America-British-Canadian Intelligence*, ed. Stafford and Jeffreys-Jones.

Lundestad, Geir. "The End of the Cold War, the New Role for Europe, and the Decline of the United States," in *End of the Cold War*, ed. Hogan.

——. "'Imperial Overstretch,' Mikhail Gorbachev, and the End of the Cold War." *Cold War History* 1 (August 2000): 1–20.

——, ed. *No End to Alliance: The United States and Western Europe: Past, Present and Future*. New York: St. Martin's Press, 1998.

MacDonnell, Francis. *Insidious Foes: The Axis Fifth Column and the American Home Front*. New York: Oxford University Press, 1995.

Mackay, James. *Allan Pinkerton: The Eye Who Never Slept*. Edinburgh: Mainstream, 1996.

Mackenzie, Angus. *Secrets: The CIA's War at Home*. Berkeley: University of California Press, 1997.

MacPherson, B. Nelson. "Inspired Improvisation: William Casey and the Penetration of Germany." *Intelligence and National Security* 9 (October 1994): 695–722.

Maddrell, Paul. "British-American Intelligence Collaboration during the Occupation of Germany," in *American-British-Canadian Intelligence Relations,* ed. Stafford and Jeffreys-Jones.

Mader, Julius. *Who's Who in the CIA.* East Berlin: Julius Mader, 1968.

Mangold, Tom. *Cold Warrior: James Jesus Angleton, the CIA's Master Spy Hunter.* London: Simon & Schuster, 1991.

Marx, Gary T. *Undercover: Police Surveillance in America.* Berkeley: University of California Press, 1988.

Maugham, W. Somerset. *Collected Short Stories.* Vol. 3. Harmondsworth: Penguin, 1971 (originally published in 1928, in slightly different form, as *Ashenden*).

Maurer, David W. *The Big Con: The Classic Story of the Confidence Man and the Confidence Trick.* London: Century, 1999 (1940).

May, Ernest R., ed. *Knowing One's Enemies: Intelligence Assessment Before the Two World Wars.* Princeton, N.J.: Princeton University Press, 1986.

——. "The U.S. Government, a Legacy of the Cold War," in *End of the Cold War,* ed. Hogan.

May, Ernest R., and Philip D. Zelikow. *The Kennedy Tapes: Inside the White House During the Cuban Missile Crisis.* Cambridge, Mass.: Harvard University Press, 1997.

McAuliffe, Mary S., ed. *CIA Documents on the Cuban Missile Crisis, 1962.* Washington, D.C.: CIA, 1992.

McCormick, Donald, and Katy Fletcher. *Spy Fiction: A Connoisseur's Guide.* New York: Facts on File, 1990.

McCoy, Alfred W. *The Politics of Heroin in Southeast Asia.* New York: Harper and Row, 1973.

McIntyre, Catherine C. "The Kennedy Administration's Diplomatic and Clandestine Responses to the Laotian Crises of 1961 and 1962." M.Sc. diss., Edinburgh University, 1997.

McKnight, Gerald D. *The Last Crusade: Martin Luther King, Jr., the FBI, and the Poor People's Campaign.* Boulder, Colo.: Westview, 1998.

McWilliams, John C. "Covert Connections: The FBN, the OSS, and the CIA." *Historian* 53 (1991): 657–78.

Melosi, Martin V. "National Security Misused: The Aftermath of Pearl Harbor." *Prologue* 9 (1977): 75–89.

——. *The Shadow of Pearl Harbor: Political Controversy over the Surprise Attack, 1941–1946.* College Station: Texas A&M University Press, 1977.

Melville, Herman. *The Confidence-Man: His Masquerade.* New York: Russell and Russell, 1963 (1857).

Menges, Constantine C. *Inside the National Security Council: The True Story of the Making and Unmaking of Reagan's Foreign Policy.* New York: Touchstone, 1989.

Mescall, Patrick N. "The Birth of the Defense Intelligence Agency," in *North American Spies,* ed. Jeffreys-Jones and Lownie.

——. "A Creature of Compromise: Postwar Military Intelligence and the Defense Intelligence Agency." *International Journal of Intelligence and Counterintelligence* 7 (Fall 1994): 251–74.

——. "A Function of Command: The Defense Intelligence Agency, 1961–1969." Ph.D. diss., Edinburgh University, 1995.

Miles, Anne Daugherty. *The Creation of the National Imagery and Mapping*

Agency: Congress's Role as Overseer. Washington, D.C.: Joint Military Intelligence College, 2001.

Miller, Nathan. *Spying for America: The Hidden History of U.S. Intelligence.* New York: Paragon House, 1989.

Milton, George Fort. *Abraham Lincoln and the Fifth Column.* New York: Collier, 1962 (1942).

Morgan, Thomas B. *The Anti-Americans.* London: Michael Joseph, 1967.

Morn, Frank. *"The Eye that Never Sleeps": A History of the Pinkerton National Detective Agency.* Bloomington: Indiana University Press, 1982.

Morris, Roger. *Partners in Power: The Clintons and Their America.* New York: Macrae/Henry Holt, 1996.

Morrison, Lynne G. P. "Journalists and American Intelligence 1947 to 1955, with particular reference to the CIA." M.Sc. diss., Edinburgh University, 1992.

Mosley, Leonard. *Dulles: A Biography of Eleanor, Allen, and John Foster Dulles and Their Family Network.* London: Hodder and Stoughton, 1978.

Mount, Graeme S. *Canada's Enemies: Spies and Spying in the Peaceable Kingdom.* Toronto: Dundurn Press, 1993.

Moyar, Mark. *Phoenix and the Birds of Prey: The CIA's Secret Campaign to Destroy the Viet Cong.* Annapolis, Md.: Naval Institute Press, 1997.

Moynihan, Daniel P. *Secrecy: The American Experience.* New Haven: Yale University Press, 1998.

Murray, Robert K. *Red Scare: A Study in National Hysteria, 1919–1920.* Minneapolis: University of Minnesota Press, 1955.

Nash, Philip. *The Other Missiles of October: Eisenhower, Kennedy, and the Jupiters 1957–1963.* Chapel Hill, N.C.: University of North Carolina Press, 1997.

Niblack, A. P. *The History and Aims of the Office of Naval Intelligence.* Washington, D.C.: Government Printing Office, 1920.

O'Callaghan, Jerry. "Senator Mitchell and the Oregon Land Frauds, 1905." *Pacific Historical Review* 21 (August 1952): 255–61.

O'Reilly, Kenneth. *"Racial Matters": The FBI's Files on Black America, 1960–1972.* New York: Free Press, 1989.

O'Toole, G. J. A. *Honorable Treachery: A History of U.S. Intelligence, Espionage, and Covert Action from the American Revolution to the CIA.* New York: Atlantic Monthly Press, 1991.

Olmsted, Kathryn S. *Challenging the Secret Government: The Post-Watergate Investigations of the CIA and FBI.* Chapel Hill: University of North Carolina Press, 1996.

Operation Zapata: The "Ultrasensitive" Report and Testimony of the Board of Inquiry on the Bay of Pigs. Frederick, Md.: University Publications of America, 1981 (13 June 1961).

Orton, J. Douglas. "Reorganizing: An Analysis of the 1976 Reorganization of the U.S. Intelligence Community." Ph.D. diss., University of Michigan, 1994.

Owsley, Harriet Chappell. "Henry Shelton Sanford and Federal Surveillance Abroad, 1861–1965." *The Mississippi Valley Historical Review* 47 (September 1961): 211–28.

Paz, María Emilia. *Strategy, Security and Spies: Mexico and the U.S. as Allies in World War II.* University Park: Pennsylvania State University Press, 1997.

Pearson, John. *The Life of Ian Fleming*. London: Jonathan Cape, 1966.

Pennypacker, Morton. *General Washington's Spies on Long Island and in New York*. Brooklyn, N.Y.: Long Island Historical Society, 1939.

——. *General Washington's Spies on Long Island and in New York*. Vol. 2. East Hampton, Long Island, N.Y.: special edition printed privately for Morton Pennypacker, 1948.

——. *The Two Spies: Nathan Hale and Robert Townsend*. Boston: Houghton Mifflin, 1930.

Persico, Joseph E. *Casey: From the OSS to the CIA*. New York: Viking, 1990.

Petersen, Neal H., comp. *American Intelligence, 1775–1990: A Bibliographic Guide*. Claremont, Calif.: Regina, 1992.

Pettee, George S. *The Future of American Secret Intelligence*. Washington, D.C.: Infantry Journal Press, 1946.

Phillips, David A. *The Night Watch*. New York: Atheneum, 1977.

Pickert, Perry L., and Russell G. Swenson, eds. *Intelligence for Multilateral Decision and Action*. Washington, D.C.: Joint Military Intelligence College, 1997.

Pinkerton, Allan. *General Principles of Pinkerton's National Detective Agency*. Chicago: Fergus, 1873

——. "History and Evidence of the Passage of Abraham Lincoln from Harrisburg to Washington, Feb. 22–23, 1861." *The Magazine of History* 8, extra number 32 (1914): 271–305.

——. *The Molly Maguires and the Detectives*. New York: Dover, 1973 (1877).

——. *The Spy of the Rebellion: Being a True Story of the Spy System of the United States Army*. Lincoln: University of Nebraska Press, 1989 (1883).

——. *Strikers, Communists, Tramps and Detectives*. New York: Arno Press, 1969 (1878).

——. *Thirty Years a Detective*. Montclair, N.J.: Patterson Smith, 1975 (1884).

Pisani, Sallie. *The CIA and the Marshall Plan*. Lawrence: University Press of Kansas, 1991.

Popplewell, Richard J. *British Intelligence and the Defence of the British Empire 1904–1924*. London: Frank Cass, 1995.

Posner, Gerald. *Case Closed: Lee Harvey Oswald and the Assassination of JFK*. New York: Random House, 1993.

Powers, Richard Gid. *Secrecy and Power: The Life of J. Edgar Hoover*. New York: Free Press, 1987.

Powers, Thomas. "The Whizz Kid vs. the Old Boys." *New York Times Magazine*, 3 December 2000.

Prados, John. *The Soviet Estimate: U.S. Intelligence Analysis and Soviet Strategic Forces*. Princeton, N.J.: Princeton University Press, 1986.

Prange, Gordon. *At Dawn We Slept: The Untold Story of Pearl Harbor*. New York: Penguin, 1982.

Putnam, Robert D. *Bowling Alone: The Collapse and Revival of American Community*. New York: Simon & Schuster, 2000.

Raat, W. Dirk. "U.S. Intelligence Operations and Covert Action in Mexico, 1900–47." *Journal of Contemporary History* 22 (October 1987): 615–38.

Ransom, Harry H. "Secret Intelligence in the United States, 1947–1982: The CIA's Search for Legitimacy," in *The Missing Dimension*, ed. Andrew and Dilks.

Reisman, W. Michael, and James E. Baker. *Regulating Covert Action: Practices, Contexts, and Policies of Covert Coercion Abroad in International and American Law*. New Haven: Yale University Press, 1992.

Report to the President by the [Rockefeller] Commission on CIA Activities within the United States. New York: Manor Books, 1975.

Reynolds, David. "Beyond Bipolarity in Space and Time," in *End of the Cold War*, ed. Hogan.

Richell, Matthew. "Trends in Contemporary American Spy Fiction During and After the Cold War." M.Sc. diss., Edinburgh University, 1995.

Richelson, Jeffrey T. "The Wizards of Langley: The CIA's Directorate of Science and Technology," in *Eternal Vigilance?*, ed. Jeffreys-Jones and Andrew.

Roosevelt, Kermit. *Countercoup*. New York: McGraw-Hill, 1979.

——. *War Report of the OSS*. New York: Walker, 1976 (1947).

Roper, John. "Intelligence and International Agencies: Discussion," in *Agents for Change*, ed. Shuckman.

Rose, P. K. "The Civil War: Black American Contributions to Union Intelligence." *Studies in Intelligence* (Winter 1998–1999): 73–80.

Rout, Leslie B., and John F. Bratzell, Jr. *The Shadow War: German Espionage and United States Counterespionage in Latin America during World War II*. Frederick, Md.: University Publications of America, 1986.

Rowan, Richard W. *The Story of Secret Service*. London: John Miles, 1938.

Rubin, Barry. *Istanbul Intrigues: A True-Life Casablanca*. New York: McGraw-Hill, 1989.

Rudgers, David F. *Creating the Secret State: The Origins of the Central Intelligence Agency, 1943–1947* (Lawrence: University Press of Kansas, 2000).

Ruffner, Kevin C., ed. *Corona: America's First Satellite Program*. Washington, D.C.: CIA, 1995.

Rusbridger, James, and Eric Nave. *Betrayal at Pearl Harbor: How Churchill Lured Roosevelt into World War II*. New York: Summit Books, 1991.

Saunders, Frances Stonor. *Who Paid the Piper? The CIA and the Cultural Cold War*. London: Granta, 1999.

Schlesinger, Arthur M., Jr. *A Thousand Days: John F. Kennedy in the White House*. Boston: Houghton Mifflin, 1965.

Schlesinger, Stephen, and Stephen Kinzer. *Bitter Fruit: The Untold Story of the American Coup in Guatemala*. New York: Doubleday, 1982.

Schorr, Daniel. *Clearing the Air*. Boston: Houghton Mifflin, 1977.

Schweizer, Peter. *Victory: The Reagan Administration's Secret Strategy that Hastened the Collapse of the Soviet Union*. New York: Atlantic Monthly Press, 1994.

Shuckman, Harold, ed. *Agents for Change: Intelligence Services in the 21st Century*. London: St. Ermin's Press, 2000.

Sick, Gary. *All Fall Down: America's Fateful Encounter with Iran*. London: I.B. Tauris, 1985.

Slotkin, Richard. *Gunfighter Nation: The Myth of the Frontier in Twentieth-Century America*. Norman: University of Oklahoma Press, 1998.

Smist, Frank J., Jr. *Congress Oversees the United States Intelligence Community, 1947–1989*. Knoxville: University of Tennessee Press, 1990.

——. "Congress Oversees the United States Intelligence Community, 1947–1984." Ph.D. diss., University of Oklahoma, 1988.

Smith, Bradley F. "Admiral Godfrey's Mission to America, June/July 1941." *Intelligence and National Security* 1 (September 1986): 441–50.

——. "The American Road to Central Intelligence," in *Eternal Vigilance?*, ed. Jeffreys-Jones and Andrew.

——. *The Shadow Warriors: OSS and the Origins of the CIA.* New York: Basic, 1983.

——. *The Ultra-Magic Deals and the Most Secret Special Relationship, 1940–1946.* Novato, Calif.: Presidio, 1993.

Smith, Gerard. *Doubletalk: The Story of the First Strategic Arms Limitations Talks.* New York: Doubleday, 1980.

Smith, R. Harris. *OSS: The Secret History of America's First Central Intelligence Agency.* New York: Delta, 1973.

Smith, Russell Jack. *The Unknown CIA: My Three Decades with the Agency.* Washington, D.C.: Pergamon-Brassey's, 1989.

Smith, Stanley H., comp. *Investigations of the Attack on Pearl Harbor: Index to Government Hearings.* New York: Greenwood, 1990.

Snider, L. Britt. "Unlucky Shamrock: Recollections from the Church Committee's Investigation of NSA." *Studies in Intelligence* (Winter 1999–2000): 43–51.

Sorensen, Theodore C. *Kennedy.* London: Hodder and Stoughton, 1965.

Stafford, David. *Roosevelt and Churchill: Men of Secrets.* London: Little, Brown, 1999.

——. *The Silent Game: The Real World of Imaginary Spies.* Athens: University of Georgia Press, 1991.

Stafford, David, and Rhodri Jeffreys-Jones, eds., *American-British-Canadian Intelligence Relations 1939–2000.* London: Frank Cass, 2000.

Stimson, Henry L., and McGeorge Bundy. *On Active Service in Peace and War.* New York: Harper, 1947.

Stinnett, Robert B. *Day of Deceit: The Truth about Pearl Harbor.* New York: Free Press, 2000.

Summers, Anthony. *Official and Confidential: The Secret Life of J. Edgar Hoover.* New York: G.P. Putnam, 1993.

Tansill, Charles C. *Back Door to War: The Roosevelt Foreign Policy, 1933–1941.* Chicago: Regnery, 1952.

Theoharis, Athan G., ed. *A Culture of Secrecy: The Government versus the People's Right to Know.* Lawrence: University Press of Kansas, 1998.

——, ed. *The FBI: A Comprehensive Reference Guide.* Phoenix, Ariz.: Oryx Press, 1999.

——. *J. Edgar Hoover, Sex, and Crime: An Historical Antidote.* Chicago: Ivan R. Dee, 1995.

Theoharis, Athan G., and John Stuart Cox. *The Boss: J. Edgar Hoover and the Great American Inquisition.* Philadelphia: Temple University Press, 1988.

Thomas, Evan. *The Very Best Men: Four Who Dared: The Early Years of the CIA.* New York: Simon & Schuster, 1995.

Thorne, C. Thomas, Jr., and David S. Patterson, eds. *Foreign Relations of the United States, 1945–1950: Emergence of the Intelligence Establishment.* Washington, D.C.: GPO, 1996.

Tidwell, William A. with James O. Hall and David W. Caddy, *Come Retribution: The Confederate Secret Service and the Assassination of Lincoln*. Jackson: University Press of Mississippi, 1988.

Torres, Donald A. *Handbook of Federal Police and Investigative Agencies*. Westport, Conn.: Greenwood, 1985.

Tower Commission Report. New York: Bantam, 1987.

Treverton, Gregory F. *Covert Action: The CIA and the Limits of American Intervention in the Postwar World*. London: I.B. Taurus, 1987.

——. "Intelligence Since Cold War's End," in *In From the Cold*.

——. *Reshaping National Intelligence for an Age of Information*. Cambridge: Cambridge University Press, 2001.

Troy, Thomas F. *Donovan and the CIA: A History of the Central Intelligence Agency*. Frederick, Md.: Aletheia/University Publications of America, 1981.

——. *Wild Bill and Intrepid: Donovan, Stephenson, and the Origin of the CIA*. New Haven: Yale University Press, 1996.

Tuchman, Barbara W. *The Zimmermann Telegram*. New York: Ballantine, 1986 (1958).

Turner, Stansfield. *Secrecy and Democracy: The CIA in Transition*. Boston: Houghton Mifflin, 1985.

Tye, Larry. *The Father of Spin: Edward L. Bernays and the Birth of Public Relations*. New York: Crown, 1998.

Usofsky, Peter S. "John F. Kennedy and the Central Intelligence Agency: Policy and Intelligence." Ph.D. Diss., George Washington University, 1987.

Valladsen, Ole R. "Prospects for a European Common Intelligence Policy," *Studies in Intelligence* 9 (Summer 2000): 81–94.

Vaughan, Stephen. "Spies, National Security, and the 'Inertia Projector': The Secret Service Films of Ronald Reagan." *American Quarterly* 39 (Fall 1987): 355–80.

Walker, David. "Democracy Goes to War: Politics, Intelligence, and Decision-Making in the United States in 1942," in *North American Spies,* ed. Jeffreys-Jones and Lownie.

Walker, Martin. *The President We Deserve: Bill Clinton: His Rise, Falls, and Comebacks*. New York: Crown, 1996.

Walker III, William O. "Drug Control and the Issue of Culture in American Foreign Relations." *Diplomatic History* 12 (Fall 1988): 362–82.

Waller, George M., ed. *Pearl Harbor and the Coming of the War,* rev. ed. Boston: D.C. Heath, 1965.

Walsh, Lawrence E. *Iran-Contra: The Final Report*. New York: Times Books/ Random House, 1994.

Wark, Wesley K. *The Ultimate Enemy: British Intelligence and Nazi Germany, 1933–1939*. Oxford: Oxford University Press, 1986.

Warner, Roger. *Back Fire: The CIA's Secret War in Laos and Its Link to the War in Vietnam*. New York: Simon & Schuster, 1995.

Weinstein, Allen, and Alexander Vassiliev. *The Haunted Wood: Soviet Espionage in America, the Stalin Era*. New York: Random House, 1999.

Welch, D. Don. "Secrecy, Democracy and Responsibility: The Central Intelligence Agency and the Congress." Ph.D. diss., Vanderbilt University, 1976.

Welch, Richard E., Jr. *Response to Revolution: The United States and the Cuban*

Revolution, 1959–1961. Chapel Hill: University of North Carolina Press, 1985.

Wells, Samuel F., Jr. "Nuclear Weapons and European Security During the Cold War," in *End of Cold War*, ed. Hogan.

West, Nigel, ed. *British Security Coordination: The Secret History of British Intelligence in the Americas, 1940–45*. London: St. Ermin's Press, 1998.

Westerfield, H. Bradford, ed. *Inside CIA's Private World: Declassified Articles from the Agency's Internal Journal, 1955–1992*. New Haven: Yale University Press, 1995.

Whitaker, Reg. "Cold War Alchemy: How America, Britain and Canada Transformed Espionage into Subversion," in Stafford and Jeffreys-Jones, eds., *American-British-Canadian Intelligence Relations 1939–2000*.

White, Mark J. *Missiles in Cuba: Kennedy, Khrushchev, Castro and the 1962 Crisis*. Chicago: Ivan R. Dee, 1997.

Wilkie, Donald W. *American Secret Service Agent*. New York: Frederick A. Stokes Co., 1934.

Wilkie, John E. "The Secret Service in the War," in *The American-Spanish War: A History by the War Leaders*. Norwich, Conn.: Chas. C. Haskell, 1899.

Williams, David J. "'Without Understanding': The FBI and Political Surveillance, 1908–1941," Ph.D. diss., University of New Hampshire, 1981.

Williams, Grover S., ed. *Legislative History of the Central Intelligence Agency as Documented in Published Congressional Sources*. Washington, D.C.: Congressional Research Service, Library of Congress, 1975.

Wills, Garry. *Reagan's America*. New York: Penguin, 1988.

Winks, Robin W. *Cloak and Gown: Scholars in the Secret War, 1939–1961*. New York: William Morrow, 1987.

Winterhalt, Todd M. "The Debate on the Future of the CIA, 1989–1995, with Particular Reference to the Press." M.Sc. diss., Edinburgh University, 1995.

Wirtz, James J. "Intelligence to Please? The Order of Battle Controversy during the Vietnam War." *Political Science Quarterly* 106 (1991): 239–63.

———. "Organizing for Crisis Intelligence: Lessons from the Cuban Missile Crisis," in *Intelligence and the Cuban Missile Crisis*, ed. Blight and Welch.

———. *The Tet Offensive*. Ithaca, N.Y.: Cornell University Press, 1991.

Wise, David. *Nightmover: How Aldrich Ames Sold the CIA to the KGB for $4.6 Million*. New York: HarperCollins, 1995.

Witcover, Jules. *Sabotage at Black Tom: Imperial Germany's Secret War in America, 1914–1917*. Algonquin: Chapel Hill, N.C., 1989.

Wohlstetter, Albert. "Is There a Strategic Arms Race?" *Foreign Policy* 15 (Summer 1974): 3–20; 16 (Fall 1974): 48–81.

Wohlstetter, Roberta. *Pearl Harbor: Warning and Decision*. Stanford, Calif.: Stanford University Press, 1962.

Woodiwiss, Michael. *Crime, Crusades and Corruption: Prohibitions in the United States, 1900–1987*. London: Pinter, 1988.

———. *Organized Crime, USA: Changing Perceptions from Prohibition to the Present Day*. Brighton: British Association for American Studies, 1990.

Woodward, Bob. *Veil: The Secret Wars of the CIA, 1981–1987*. London: Simon & Schuster, 1987.

Worth, Roland H., Jr., ed. *Pearl Harbor: Selected Testimonies, Fully Indexed, from the Congressional Hearings (1945–1946) and Prior Investigations of the Events Leading up to the Attack*. Jefferson, N.C.: McFarland, 1993.

Wriston, Henry M. *Executive Agents in American Foreign Relations*. Baltimore: Johns Hopkins Press, 1929.

Wyden, Peter. *Bay of Pigs: The Untold Story*. New York: Simon & Schuster, 1979.

Yakovlev, Nikolai. *CIA Target: The USSR*. Moscow: Progress Publishers, 1982.

Yardley, Herbert O. *The American Black Chamber*. London: Faber and Faber, 1931.

——. *The Education of a Poker Player*. London: Sphere, 1970 (1957).

Yu, Maochun. *OSS in China: Prelude to Cold War*. New Haven: Yale University Press, 1996.

Zacharius, Ellis M. *Secret Missions: The Story of an Intelligence Officer*. New York: G.P. Putnam, 1946.

Zelikow, Philip. "American Economic Intelligence: Past Practice and Future Principles," in *Eternal Vigilance?*, ed. Jeffreys-Jones and Andrew.

——. "American Intelligence and the World Economy," in *In From the Cold*.

Index